THE LOGIC OF THE SPIRIT

THE LOGIC OF THE SPIRIT

Human Development in Theological Perspective

James E. Loder

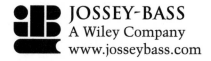

JOSSEY-BASS
A Wiley Company
www.josseybass.com

Published by

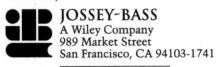

JOSSEY-BASS
A Wiley Company
989 Market Street
San Francisco, CA 94103-1741

www.josseybass.com

Jossey-Bass books and products are available through most bookstores. To contact Jossey-Bass directly, call (888) 378-2537, fax to (800) 605-2665, or visit our website at www.josseybass.com.

Substantial discounts on bulk quantities of Jossey-Bass books are available to corporations, professional associations, and other organizations. For details and discount information, contact the special sales department at Jossey-Bass.

Library of Congress Cataloging-in-Publication Data

Loder, James E. (James Edwin).
    The logic of the spirit : human development in theological
perspective / James E. Loder.
      p. cm.
    Includes bibliographical references and index.
    ISBN 0-7879-0919-X
    1. Christianity—Psychology.   2. Developmental psychology—
Religious aspects—Christianity. I. Title.
    BR110.L615   1998
    261.5'15—dc21   98-29681

FIRST EDITION

PB Printing   10 9 8 7 6 5

CONTENTS

Preface   ix

The Author   xv

PART ONE
The Cry of the Spirit

1. What Is a Lifetime, and Why Do I Live It?   3
2. Examining the Relationality Between the Human Spirit
   and the Divine   17
3. Human Development Reenvisioned: The Case of Helen   46

PART TWO
The Triumph of Negation

4. Infancy in Psychological Perspective: The Emerging Ego   81
5. Infancy in Theological Perspective: The Spirit's
   Confrontation with Nothingness   109

PART THREE
The Struggle of the Spirit

6. The Toddler: Conformity and the Root of Human
   Freedom   129
7. The Oedipal Child: Sex, Death, and the
   Origin of Worship   149
8. The School-Age Child: Work and the Ambiguity
   of Achievement   173

PART FOUR
The Release of the Spirit

9. Adolescence in Psychological Perspective:
   Five Axes of Youth Identity   203
10. Adolescence in Theological Perspective:
    Coming into the Presence of God   231
11. Young Adulthood: Risking Identity in the Service of Love   251
12. The Middle Years: Ego Transitions and Transfigurations
    of the Soul   281
13. Beyond 65: Dreaming Dreams and Talking with God   316
    Conclusion   339

Index   343

PREFACE

These pages, first formulated for the ear as lectures, have been reconceived and rewritten for the eye as a book. In the course of doing the lectures as an introduction to human development for seminary students, the theme of the human spirit surfaced repeatedly in both its power and its perversities. This spirit seemed to have a logic of its own that could be called into focus and given definition by theological understandings, which in turn redefined the meaning and purpose of human development.

The overall structure of the argument owes an initial debt of gratitude to Søren Kierkegaard. Many persons have tried to bring Kierkegaard's concept of the stages along life's way into some coherence with the stages that typify theories of human development. In this book I argue that Kierkegaard's stages—the Aesthetic, Ethical, Religiousness A, and Religiousness B—are aspects of a more fundamental argument embracing the whole of human existence. It is similar in its aim and incisiveness to Pascal's famous wager. Forced by our finitude to bet our life on the existence or nonexistence of God, the odds favor God's existence. That is, if one wagers one's life on God's existence, all may be gained and nothing lost, even if it is the wrong bet. This is Pascal's apologetic argument addressed to any potential gambler.

Kierkegaard places human existence between two absurds: the negative absurd, which points to the tragic futility and ultimate meaningless of existence, which he terms "despair"; and the positive absurd, that human nature is redeemed by God who enters his own creation as fully divine and fully human, Kierkegaard's "God-man" of faith. In the final analysis, we must choose which absurd to live by. Of course, a choice not to choose—to "play it cool," to be "purely rational," to "wait and see"—is automatically a choice for the negative absurd, since death, when all bets are off, decisively terminates choice.

In contemporary cosmological terms, if the whole fifteen billion years of the history of the universe were one year, the existence of human life would appear only in the last minute of the last day. This means that anyone's given lifetime set against cosmic history is scarcely long enough to be called a predeath experience. In itself, it is a "striving after wind," "a mere breath," "signifying nothing"—the negative absurd.

A choice for the positive absurd puts death in the context of the Creator of the universe, who, by entering redemptively into the midst of human history, established the ultimate meaning of all creation, including the death that pervades it. The Spirit of this God transforms human existence for the appropriation of eternal life through faith in Jesus Christ. This set of alternatives is not merely an abstract theological choice for believers and unbelievers to mull over; rather, it is a critical and constructive way to look at the stuff and substance of the whole life span and its place in creation.

We live in a rapidly expanding universe that manifests itself in a far more complex culture than Kierkegaard ever experienced. Thus, our language and our interpretations of nature, persons, society, and culture will be very different from his, yet the fundamental questions facing human existence have not changed. For this book, the fundamental questions, which in different terms lie behind Kierkegaard's authorship, are: "What is a lifetime?" and "Why do I live it?" In response to the first, we will lean toward the human sciences and, in the second, lean toward a theology of human existence. Nevertheless, in the final analysis, the two questions are inseparable.

From the standpoint of the human sciences, the Kierkegaardian structure of the argument of this book may seem like an imperialistic approach to the human situation generally and to human development in particular. It may seem to know the purpose and meaning of human development before giving it a chance to speak for itself. However, the methodology for preserving the integrity of the human sciences in their relation to theology is carefully worked out in the following chapters. A theological basis for the interpretation of anthropological and developmental findings must preserve the integrity of those findings to preserve its own integrity as theological anthropology. However, theological anthropology, as theological, can call forth, illuminate, and interpret aspects of development that are not within the presumed purview of the human sciences.

To take a page from the history of science, consider the case of James Clerk-Maxwell. T. F. Torrance has convincingly argued that Maxwell's discovery and formulation of the electromagnetic field, which awakened the scientific world from its Newtonian slumber and laid the foundation for Einstein's theory of relativity, was rooted in his devout, biblical theology as it came to him through the Scottish and Reformed tradition.[1] It appears that through Maxwell, a theology of creation enabled a great scientist to reenvision the natural order in unexpectedly significant ways. In

Maxwell's own time, Lord Kelvin claimed that he, Maxwell, had "lapsed into mysticism," because his view of creation and science departed from the mechanical model of Newtonian physics in favor of a relational model. Nevertheless, Richard Feynman, in our own time, claimed that, from a long view of the history of humankind, Maxwell's eventual discovery was the most significant event of the nineteenth century, exceeding even the American Civil War.

The position I take in this book is that a Christian theological interpretation must be allowed to influence our studies of human development. It should be recognized that the functionalism, structuralism, and empiricism toward which the human sciences are inclined keep them in a dualistic Newtonian world, where the person of the investigator is bracketed for the sake of objectifying the findings and meeting the canons of an empirical test. However, in contemporary physics, the hardest of sciences, it is recognized that the observer is an irreducible part of what must be accounted for in any scientific investigation. In Niels Bohr's understanding of subatomic phenomena and in Heisenberg's (a student of Bohr) uncertainty principle, to mention only two, it is evident that all observations at this level are observer conditioned.

Bohr was once asked, after he had watched a B-grade western movie, what he thought of it. He said he could accept that the heroine fled to the edge of a cliff and threw herself off to escape the outlaws; he could even accept that the hero was waiting at the bottom to catch her; but he could not accept that a camera was waiting there all the time to catch the action.[2] The action without the observer was acceptable for the sake of illusion and pretense, but if one gets real about it at any level, the eye of the observer or any observing mechanism had to be taken into account.

Like it or not, theological issues permeate both the student and the study of human nature. It should be accepted that all persons have ultimate longings, conjectures, and questions about the meaning and purpose of human existence. These cannot be ignored in the study of human nature, even if the scope of the study is narrowed to an empirical level of inquiry. The issues of purpose and meaning are so central to human nature they cannot be bracketed, even in empirically designed studies. Indeed, their impact is prevalent on the investigators as well as on the subjects being studied, and their influence is often tacit and unexamined, as has often been demonstrated (in, for example, *Personal Knowledge* by Michael Polanyi and *Religious Thought and the Modern Psychologies* by Don Browning). Michael Polanyi has shown that all knowledge, even in the physical sciences, is personal knowledge,[3] so it is doubly ironic when the subject under investigation is a person or persons and the subject must be depersonalized and objectified as a way to get at some "truth" about them and their behavior. However, such studies are not irrelevant, nor are generalizations about human behavior useless or inherently false because of their depersonalizing methodology. Rather, such studies and observations need to be brought into a larger frame of reference to serve understandings of human nature that are grounded in the uniqueness, purposiveness, and meaningfulness of human existence.

The temptation on the part of the ardent empiricist is to bring ultimate purpose, meaning, and the uniqueness of persons under the canons of the empirical method. To distort the object of inquiry to fit the method is surely poor science; each object of scientific study should be permitted to say how it is to be known. Even if this is not conceded by the investigating scientist, the reality of the situation will eventually prove the results of such a distortion to be false. To illustrate this, let us return to Maxwell, theology, and the history of science.

Newton's uncritical and mechanistic assumptions about Euclidean space and clock time controlled and restricted what he could conceive about God and the universe. Thus, his objectivist, Arian view of God essentially sacralized an erroneous, dualistic view of the natural order and its relation to that God. Maxwell, on the other hand, started not with the natural order but with a theological position. He claimed that God created things in a nondualistic, realistic, irreducibly relational way. Theology shaped his mind, his view of reality, and his science. Maxwell's idea of objectivity was not depersonalized empiricism, but the objective reality of the transcendent God. Thus, his famous formulation of the electromagnetic field must be seen as a physical expression of the relational reality evident in all creation and supremely in God's triune being and God's relation to the contingent being of the natural order.[4]

Einstein, following Maxwell, further exposed the limits of the mechanistic Newtonian view and brought about a transformation of Newton's universe through special and general relativity. Theology, concerned as it is with relational reality and the redemption of all creation, has, in Maxwell's case, moved our understandings of the physical universe closer to how it is, even in terms that secular science has come to acknowledge.

What has been true of the physical sciences should also be true of the human sciences, first because the latter operates within a Newtonian frame of reference, and second, because meaning, purpose, and personal uniqueness are at the very core of the human subject being studied. Based on Christian theology in the Reformed tradition and, in part, on the concept of spirit in Kierkegaard, I argue here that the human spirit is the uninvited guest in every study conducted in the human sciences. It is inherently relational, transformational, self-transcending, and the dynamic basis of choice; it is the dynamism that drives human development forward. Yet it is regularly ignored in favor of more empirical considerations. To be sure, it is always within the matrix of the physical, natural, and material order where the human spirit can and must be understood. But if we ask which way is "forward" in the course of human development, then we must have a theological frame of reference that grounds and guides the human spirit without reducing its dynamism to simplistic notions of adaptation.

Such a grounding must in itself be Spirit and transcend the rationalistic issues surrounding foundationalism and move toward a post-Newtonian, scientifically postmodern view of reality, which has always been the character and prerogative of the Holy Spirit in Christian theology. When the self that is "spirit" is "transparently grounded in the power that posits it," to use Kierkegaard's language, then the basis for an unlimited openness to the world and to God is established with a wisdom that includes but transforms the contributions to understanding that come from a scientifically shaped postmodern mentality. In a word, approaching the study of human nature through an understanding of the human spirit in the context of a Christian theology of the Holy Spirit promises to move current understandings available through the human sciences toward a postmodern world. Einstein's thought did *not* make everything relative; it made some things relative that we thought were absolute, but the speed of light remained the determinative invariant. Metaphorically, this book might be conceived of as a search for the speed of light equivalent in the open-ended, multivariant relationship between theology and the human sciences.

I do not propose a Maxwellian revolution, but I do propose to take theology, particularly the theology of the spirit, seriously as a way to assess and interpret scientific findings about human nature. My expectation is that theology, human science, and human development can benefit significantly from such an inquiry. However, the larger aim of my inquiry is to demonstrate the overall context that a Christian theology of the Spirit provides for the study of human nature, and especially for issues of purpose and meaning implicit in and often insufficiently articulated through the facts and theories of human development.

Acknowledgments

Acknowledgments to those who have put much work and time into this book are beyond any listing I could give. Let these few be sufficient. First,

I am deeply indebted to T. F. Torrance for his writings and personal encouragement in my dealing with the theology-science dialogue. My hope is that my references to his work are consistent with his vision of the relationship between theology and science, even though this area of study is not one that he has engaged. Second, I am most indebted to the late W. Jim Neidhardt, physicist at New Jersey Institute of Technology and remarkable personal friend, who gave me ongoing tutorial instruction in physics during our joint authorship of *The Knight's Move*. The references to science here come largely from him and from Professor Torrance. I am indebted to my secretary, Kay Vogen, who labored extra hours to bring my scribbled notes into readable form. I have been very fortunate to have a patient and discerning editor, Sara Polster. I am also indebted to two of my doctoral students, Lisa Hess and Russell Haitch. Finally, I am grateful to Princeton Seminary for a year-long sabbatical, which enabled me to finish the text in one time frame.

The final resolution to the dilemma posed at the beginning of this book is the lived reality of the one person I know who manages to drive love to its extremities, whose hours of prayer and passionate devotion are simply the natural course of the day, and whose critical reading of this text repeatedly issued in, "What are you trying to say?" This person, my wife, Arlene, is to be most commended for her patience and her deep-down encouragement of me and of this project. It could not have been written without her love.

Princeton, New Jersey   JAMES E. LODER
July 1998

NOTES

1. T. F. Torrance, *Transformation and Convergence in the Frame of Knowledge* (Belfast: Christian Journals Limited, 1984), chap. 6.

2. Stefen Rozental, *Niels Bohr* (New York: Wiley, 1967), p. 112.

3. Michael Polanyi, *Personal Knowledge* (New York: Routledge, 1959).

4. Torrance, *Transformation and Convergence*, p. 235.

THE AUTHOR

JAMES E. LODER is the Mary D. Synnott Professor of the Philosophy of Christian Education at Princeton Theological Seminary. He received his M.Div. degree from Princeton Theological Seminary and his Ph.D. degree from Harvard University. As a Danforth Fellow he studied theology and psychiatric theory at the Menninger Foundation. He has done post-doctoral study at the University of Geneva and Oxford University. He is the author of *The Transforming Moment* (second edition, 1989) and joint author (with physicist W. Jim Neidhardt) of *The Knight's Move* (1992), a study of the logic of the spirit in theology and science. He is an ordained Presbyterian minister, has two daughters, and lives with his wife in Princeton, New Jersey.

This book is dedicated to my mother,
Frances Elizabeth Goodhue Loder,
a woman of strong and resilient spirit.

THE LOGIC OF THE SPIRIT

PART ONE

THE CRY OF THE SPIRIT

WHAT IS A LIFETIME, AND WHY DO I LIVE IT?

For the Spirit searches everything, even the depths of God.
For what human being knows what is truly human except the
human spirit that is within? So also no one comprehends
what is truly God's except the Spirit of God. Now we have
received not the spirit of the world, but the Spirit that is
from God . . . [so] we have the mind of Christ.

—I Corinthians 2:10–16

WHEN THEY TURNED UP the sound on the monitor, I could hear her tiny heart like the galloping of a stallion: "I *will* be born," "I *will* be born," "I *will* be born." Between her valiant, heartfelt determination to be thrust into this world and the eventual cry of shock and distress on arrival would come the mother's excruciating pain, her struggle to keep pushing, the wrong drug to relieve pain, near loss of the mother's pulse, "Emergency!" then the recovery, and finally the quivering, squalling, wrinkled, red-blotched voyager had arrived. Through pain, blood, shock, and near death, Julie had come. But come where? To do what? And why?

If my daughter had died giving birth, we would all ask "Why?" but she lived and gave birth to a beautiful little girl, so we do not ask why; we are all much too grateful to God that it came out right. However, behind the whys of both the sudden loss of life and the stunning arrival of new life lies the persistent question: Why do we live? Why do we cherish life with such passion? Why, when there is every reason to despair, do we continue to affirm life; and what happens when that affirmation goes sour and the passion to die becomes unstoppable? These questions all have to do with the human spirit and the fundamental two-part question behind this book: "What is a lifetime?" and "Why do I live it?" Camus asked the question in a surly and sardonic manner: "Does life deserve to be lived?" implying that death makes it absurd. In his moral protest against political oppression and the meaninglessness of life, he struggles for freedom and meaning without the benefit of the Christian God. For just that reason, his protest is an outcry of the human spirit, a poignant but groundless protest against death.

Miguel de Unamuno, the great Spanish philosopher, said that what distinguishes human beings from other creatures is that humans have a unique practice of burying their dead.[1] We speak our words over the dead body. We will not let death have the last word. This is a mark of the human spirit that something in us knows we can overcome this thing. Death stops the heartbeat but does not quench the human spirit; its inherent logic tells us that there is a way to transcend and transform death. Even when the spirit itself chooses death, whether in suicide or in baptism, it is in hope of a better life. Even in the pathetic cry of the abused child, "If I die, then will you love me?" there is transcendence that wants to make use of death to achieve another higher end. What is a lifetime, and why do I live it? This cry arises out of the human spirit, sometimes in anguish, sometimes in awe-struck silence, but always a call to someone or some place beyond the self.

What is at stake in this study is the integrity, the hidden wisdom, and the frequent genius of the human spirit alongside its groundlessness, contaminations, and frequent perversities. To understand the human spirit is to gain entrée to the central driving force in human development that separates humanity from the rest of nature. Many studies of human development are preoccupied with demonstrating how human beings are the same as or similar to other creatures and aspects of nature, but it is vitally important to study human uniqueness; otherwise the act of studying itself, a uniquely human enterprise, would not make sense. This quest for human uniqueness leads us into a study of the human spirit.

To give some account of the human spirit, we will first approach it from below, from the standpoint of science and experience. Then we will approach it from above, from the standpoint of God's self-revelation in Jesus Christ in whom it is disclosed what God means by humanity in relationship to what God means by God. Finally, we will bring the two views together to provide a preliminary sketch of the methodology for studying human development in this book.

The View from Below

Most commonly it is thought that the human spirit expresses itself in the arts, music, literature, sculpture, painting, drama, dance, and the like. This common assumption points to the expansiveness, transcendence, inclusiveness, and inspiration that inhere in the human spirit in every dimension of human existence. It is this more inclusive notion of the human spirit that we want to understand, but first we will concentrate on the spirit in the less likely context of the sciences, including artistic expressions of the spirit, where they may be illuminative of the spirit in itself and in human nature more generally.

First I must attempt to supply some provisional perspectives on the human spirit. Although a great deal more will be said in subsequent chapters about the nature and dynamic of the human spirit, two vignettes will help to give definition to the discussion. Wolfhart Pannenberg, in his discussion of the uniqueness of humanity in nature, cites favorably Max Scheler's work, *Man's Place in Nature*.[2] Scheler argues for human uniqueness as "openness to the world" and speaks of the person as "the spiritual being . . . no longer subject to its drives and its environment" but "free from the environment." That is, instinctual impulses can be inhibited by the person, so "voluntary inhibition" transcends what we call life in the most general sense. Spirit is the principle that may be opposed to a naturalistic view of life and contravenes in evolution. Human openness to the world and self-transcendence is what Pannenberg calls "exocentricity," and in this one word he designates the human spirit.

The second vignette refers to the studies of Wilder Penfield, a neurologist whose research included highly sensitive electrical probes of the brains of epileptic patients during open skull surgery, while the patients remain conscious under a local anesthetic.[3] The probes proved to be groundbreaking for locating the specific functions of certain structures in the brain. Music, speech, motor activity, memory, and, if Julian Jaynes (an interpreter of Penfield) is to be believed, even the ancient voices of the gods can be specifically located at various points in the neuronal structure of the brain.[4]

For our purposes, the discovery of so-called tapes in the brain is secondary to a more striking observation. When Penfield touched a portion of the cortex and a patient moved his arm or heard music, he would say to Penfield, "*You* did that. *I* didn't." No matter how Penfield probed the various centers of the brain, he could not locate the "I" who said, "I didn't." Penfield concludes that if one were simply to take the evidence available, one would have to posit two essences: one would be the brain, its structures, and programmed patterns of behavior; the other would be the "I" who had the capacity to enter into the program and "blaze new trails through the neuronal structure," create new programs, and redirect previously programmed behavior. This is the source of choice, meaning, and belief.

What Penfield discovered was not evidence for a Cartesian dualism. Rather, he found in tangible, neurological, and experiential terms the "strange loops in the brain" that we call self-relatedness. Self-relatedness is a strange loop because the statement of the patient is invariably made in his own language and formulated as a clear idea, recognizable to all who speak his language. That is, it is within a preprogrammed system of language and thought that the transcendence of the "I" appears, and yet it expresses itself as being in some other respect outside that system of language and thought. This meaningful combination of continuity and contradiction makes this a strange loop, which resides at the very core of what we take to be distinctively human: our powers of self-transcendence and self-relatedness in choice, meaning, and belief. Against current tendencies toward neurological reductionism, Roger Sperry, John Eccles, and Karl Popper fundamentally agree with Penfield's findings.

What Scheler, via Pannenberg, described as spirit in human nature, "openness to the world," and "transcendence over life" is a philosophical description of what Penfield described neurologically. These characterizations of the human spirit will be further elaborated to include transformation and the image of God. For this first chapter, though, it must suffice to stress self-transcendence and its implicitly unlimited openness to ultimacy.

If we turn to the sciences, it will be evident that the human spirit reaches into the depths and unto the outer limits of the universe and beyond. The final results of such explorations remain beyond our grasp, but there are important analogies between the exocentric dynamics of the human spirit and the expanding universe it seeks to comprehend and transcend. In effect, to study the human spirit, not in the abstract but within the matrices of human development, is not only to take our physical existence seriously; it is also implicitly to study certain aspects of the physical universe and what lies beyond it.

To give such a statement a context and make it more plausible, consider the placing of the human person in the universe. You may have seen the film *Powers of Ten*. The camera begins with a man and a woman dozing in the sun after a picnic in a Chicago park. Then it takes the viewer by powers of ten out into the big infinity, where persons, park, and Chicago disappear into a pale blue dot, and then the blue dot itself disappears into the universe. The camera eventually descends again to our planet, to Chicago, to the couple lying in the park basking in the sun. But this is only half the story. Now, beginning with a close-up of the man's hand, the camera descends by the powers of ten down into the little infinity, into the subatomic, quantum world, before returning again to the park, the picnic, and the daily life of Chicago.

This is a stunning perspective that reaches all the way from the big infinity to the little infinity in about half an hour. The awesome grandeur of the universe with human nature about midway (somewhat closer to the little infinity) between the two infinities is so astonishing that one fails to notice what lies beyond it, the most staggering aspect of all: the transcending human spirit generating and inspiring human intelligence. The intelligent human mind that can begin to grasp the immense scope of this reality, knows that it grasps it, and is able, at least in part, to make it intelligible, transcends all that it knows, including the multiple powers of ten "in all directions." As Einstein said, "The most incomprehensible thing about the universe is that it is comprehensible."[5] The ongoing recognition and articulation of the mystery of our human comprehension of the universe suggests to T. F. Torrance a mirror relationship between certain structures of the human mind and the universe. The development and elaboration on those structures is a manifestation of human uniqueness, an expression of the inspiration, transcendence, and illuminative power of the human spirit.[6]

The mirror relationship between intelligence and the intelligible universe suggests important analogies between the study of human development and the study of the universe, of which we are a part and which is a part of us. I will mention a few thematically; the richness of these analogies will be developed in the following chapters. First is the emergence of order in the universe and of congruent orders of mind in human development. The rational order that we say makes something intelligible is not just in our heads; it is able to disclose order hidden in the universe. Thus, the developing capacity to make things intelligible is a move into an order shared by the mind and the universe. Indeed, the order implicit in knowing anything has both congruence with the external world and an a priori value since order must be presupposed even by any effort to refute it. Second is the analogical connection between entropy and death. Order on both the personal and universal scale is open-ended, giving rise to apparent chaos, disintegration, and entropy. Hidden in the orders of both persons and the physical universe is a powerful degenerative force that drives toward the reduction of all order to a state of void and nothingness. Third is transformation and new order. Under certain circumstances, in open systems, chaos may give rise to a genuinely new order not imagined before or apparently predictable from its precursors. This emergence of a new order appears in the universe as new structures of energy emerge out of dissipating systems; it appears in human development as new stages emerge out of developmental disequilibrium. Indeed, when the whole of human development anticipates its ultimate dissipation in death, even then new orders emerge, which theologians speak of as regeneration and resurrection. Order out of chaos on a universal scale was brought to public attention when Ilya Prigogine won a Nobel Prize in 1977 for his mathematical demonstration of just such an emergence. Fourth is relationality as ontologically prior to rationality.[7] As one enters the subatomic world, it becomes decisively clear that relationality stands under and in many respects determines the limits and explanatory power of rationality. In human development, especially in Jean Piaget's paradigm of cognitive development, rationality is profoundly dependent on a relational context so as to emerge with its fullest potential. This priority of relationality over rationality, in both developmental sequence and quality of being, is deeply embedded in human experience. This makes it possible for us to envision and take seriously the probability that, viewed through the window of "quantum weirdness," the whole of the universe is everywhere and in all its aspects deeply interconnected.[8]

Alain Aspect and, recently, Nicholas Gisin have confirmed experimentally the quantum prediction set forth by John Bell that there is instantaneous connection between quantum events (such as two electrons split off from the same atom), even though they may in principle be at opposite ends of the universe. This continuity Einstein called "spooky action at a distance"; it suggests a relational unity that subtends the universe. Russell Stanard, a British physicist, makes the claim that this phenomenon points to the ultimate unity of all truths about the physical universe. Relationality stands under and makes rationality possible, even by rationality's own canons of proof.

These four analogical connections are intended to point to the likelihood that what we know and understand about the universe is in some respect already a part of how we have developed. This is not an isomorphism or a strict cause-and-effect argument, but it does say that because we have developed in the way we have, certain understandings of the universe are more plausible than others. The universe we have got our heads into is in some respects already in our heads to begin with.

On the other hand, we have to stand outside the universe to know that. In scriptural terms, we are made of the dust of the earth—in scientific terms, dust created by gigantic cosmic events and dust from disintegrating stars. So by our physical nature, we are intimately tied to the history of the universe. But we are also and definitively the breath of God by which we become spiritual beings, and as spirit we are uniquely set apart from that history so we may transcend and comprehend it.

Intriguing as it might be to discover correlations between developing human nature and the expanding universe, the analogies and material connections mentioned so far do not make the larger point at stake for the human spirit. The larger issue is linked to a theological version of what is called in cosmology the "anthropic principle." In its strong form, this cosmological principle states that in the earliest split second of the history of the universe, there had to be an immensely complex balance of forces (for example, a balance between explosive expansion and gravitational contraction) so that the universe could bring forth human intelligence. The slightest fraction of a tilt in one direction or the other, and human life could not have appeared. The chances of this balance happening by accident are so remote as to make the suggestion almost absurd. The congruence between human intelligence and the intelligible universe is way beyond chance.

The astonishing improbability that the history of the universe should bring forth a mirror of itself in the human mind not only defies any explanation by chance but also points far beyond the universe itself. Human nature and the universe do mirror each other, but as theologian T. F. Torrance notices, this realization is rarely carried to its proper conclusion. They mirror one another not only in respect of what they are in themselves (which is why mathematics works) but also in their openness to what is altogether beyond them (which is why human development and the universe must be studied theologically). The human mind is adapted to the rational structures and laws of the universe, and the universe is so coordinated with the developing mind of persons that, via the anthropic principle, we must recognize that we are caught up in an unbounded range of relational intelligibility. Thus, as Torrance puts it, "Not only is the universe the home of humankind, but the personal nature of humankind belongs to the nature of nature, and we are thereby called to recognize that the universe owes its existence, nature and structure to a personal Author infinitely greater than we can ever conceive—to God the Creator."[9]

This is not to establish once and for all the existence of God; only God can do that. But it is to demonstrate that, according to the logic of the spirit, by which an intelligible comprehension of this inherently relational universe is constructed and human personality itself develops, there is an ultimate ground for the human spirit; it is not an accident doomed to wander aimlessly in the universe, endlessly crying out "Why?" in the still darkness of empty space. Its inner logic, its creative drive to construct coherence and remain open to ultimacy, its irrepressible self-transcendance and transformational potential, its revulsion at confusion and its discovery of order in chaos: all of these characteristics working to disclose the structures, patterns, and power hidden in the universe and in human nature point toward God the Creator.

The logic of the human spirit will always point beyond itself, but by itself it has no ultimate ground for itself as spirit without reducing spirit to one of its products, a work of art or a scientific advancement. The spirit qua spirit has no way to be nourished, deepened, healed, or given purpose; the danger is that the human spirit will be reduced to what it can produce and become consumed by its results. So, what is called for is One who is infinitely conscious, intelligent, and intentionally creative, whose very presence brings order out of chaos and continually restores the spirit to itself as spirit. That is what is needed.

The View from Above

We must now turn this discussion on its head and examine it from the standpoint of the Author of creation as self-revealed in Jesus Christ and brought to life in the work of the Creator Spirit. When we let the Author of creation speak, it becomes evident that we are dealing with both a "divine and contingent order," as Torrance has put it. Human development and its reciprocity with the unfolding of the universe through time is the created and therefore contingent order. It has its own life and inherent lawfulness, but it is contingent on the undergirding, intervening, recreative, and redemptive order of God's action in creation. God's supreme singular act is entering God's own creation and, without ceasing to be God, becoming a particular human being at a particular point in history so as to bring about, for us and for all the rest of creation, the transformation of the created and contingent order for the sake of an agreement and ultimate harmony with the divine order.

The great human difficulty is that the human spirit has been separated from its ultimate ground in the Spirit of God. It has a measure of constructive power, but without its proper ground, it becomes a loose cannon of creativity. In its bewildered, blundering brilliance, it cries out for wisdom to an "unknown God." But it is the personal Author of the universe whose Spirit alone can set the human spirit free *from* its proclivity to self-inflation, self-doubt, self-absorption, and self-destruction, and free *for* its "magnificent obsession" to participate in the Spirit of God and to know the mind of God. As the scriptural heading of this chapter says, the human spirit searches the human mind, and so the human mind comes to know itself through its spirit. Analogically, the Spirit of God searches the mind of God, so when we have received the Spirit of God, Spirit-to-spirit, we may participate in the self-knowledge of God. This is to have the mind of Christ: the disclosure by God of the mind of God Spirit-to-spirit. Apart from the Spirit-to-spirit communication of the mind of God, the attempt of the human mind to know itself, to say nothing of knowing the mind of God, is utter foolishness, says Scripture.[10]

Physicist Stephen Hawking wanted to "know the mind of God," but he did not understand that if such knowledge occurs, it will be through a radical transformation of the human mind; the human is stripped of its eros and arrogance so as to behold in awe a magnificence in God that only God can bestow.

Although this is something Hawking did not understand, his colleague at Cambridge, thermodynamacist A. B. Pippard, did understand it when he wrote an article on the invincible ignorance of science.[11] Where matters of human self-consciousness and divine reality are concerned, he saw clearly the upheaval that is inflicted on human intelligence when it attempts to contain the mind of God. He wrote, "What is surely impossible is that a theoretical physicist, given unlimited computing powers, should deduce from the laws of physics that a certain complex structure is aware of its own existence."

In self-awareness, human reason is up against "something it cannot think," as Kierkegaard put it: the self-transcendent, transformational reality of the human spirit out of which reason itself is generated. In reading Pippard's article, one is reminded of Roger Penrose's opening and concluding parable in his book, *The Emperor's New Mind*.[12] The parable is about the great master computer that becomes dysfunctional when it attempts to answer a child's question: "What does it feel like to be a computer?"

The paradox presented here is the same one presented by Kurt Gödel's famous incompleteness theorem. In 1931 Gödel showed that Bertrand Russell and A. N. Whitehead's *Principia Mathematica* contained no proof of its own argument. As Douglas Hofstadter puts it, Gödel showed that "all consistent axiomatic formulations of number theory include undecidable propositions." More specific to *Principia Mathematica*, "This statement of number theory does not have any proof in the system of *Principia Mathematica*."[13] In effect, when any mathematical theory is made "introspective," as Hofstadter put it, it is clear that the truth will always exceed the proof.[14]

What Pippard understood so well is that the irreducible self-transcendence of the human spirit, even in its refined expression as mathematical intelligence, has no ground in itself. Thus, Gödel's incompleteness theory discloses indirectly through mathematics the inherent incompleteness of the human spirit. It must be grounded beyond itself if it is to become intelligible even to itself. Since the only adequate ground of the human spirit is the Spirit of God, the logic of the spirit makes it clear that to "comprehend the mind of God," as Hawking spoke of it, is an intrinsic contradiction of how the human mind works; the human mind is utterly dependent on the human spirit. Similarly, to understand the mind of God, one must have the Spirit of God. Apart from God's Spirit, such a comprehension (albeit partial) would be humanly impossible. Only if the one comprehending the mind of God is in fact God could Hawking's understanding pertain.

The human spirit makes all acts of human intelligence self-transcendent and self-relational. When God acts, Spirit-to-spirit, then human intelligence is transformed into a "faith seeking understanding" of God's self-revelation— that is, the disclosure of God's mind in the Face of God in Jesus Christ. This is a disclosure that far exceeds "the grandeur of the universe," as Pippard puts it.[15]

In this book, the study of human development is fundamentally the study of the human spirit, embedded as it is in the visible, tangible, and experiential stuff of a human lifetime. Yet as Hawking's statement makes plain, the human spirit is continually creating without knowing why, discovering without any enduring purpose, consuming vast reams of knowledge without meaning, and thrives principally on the excitement of the action entailed in its being spirited. Finally, it sinks all too soon into oblivion, usually before it ever gets an adequate answer to, "Why create?" "Why bother with purpose?" "Why must there be meaning?" "Why do I live?" When there is no answer forthcoming to meet these questions, the result is "a spiritless generation," as Kierkegaard put it.

My argument, then, is not primarily one for the existence of God; it is for the human spirit itself: for its reality, its legitimacy, its remarkable genius, its genuine but blind longing for the Spirit of God—and its tragic end when that longing is not satisfied. We need to find in our theological understanding of what it means to be human the divine response to the outcry of the human spirit.

Because the abyss between the human and the divine is humanly unfathomable, it must be crossed by the act of God; but the argument from above is that this has already been done in the paradox of God's becoming fully human while remaining fully God in Jesus Christ. What remains for us is the awakening to this reality and to all that it implies for the conviction, illumination, and sanctification of the development of persons. This, which takes place centrally Spirit-to-spirit, is the larger purpose to which this book seeks to contribute.

Above and Below: A Relational Unity

The view from below and the view from above are not actually separate perspectives but, like the two edges of a Möbius band, the apparent distinction is at the same time a unity, a paradox that baffles perception. A Möbius band is a topological phenomenon that can be created by taking a strip of paper and, through a 180-degree twist, connecting the two ends of the strip. The result is a phenomenon that has only one edge and one side, but two sides and two edges are evident in any cross-sectional view (see Figure 1.1). The Möbius band is a visual image of the form of understanding that lies at the core of the methodology of this book. However, conceptually it should be clear that, contrary to what first appears, the duality is a unity. What the metaphor of the Möbius band should convey is that to speak of a unity is not a retreat into "substance" or "being," but the unity is precisely the relationality between the two apparently opposed or contradictory polarities or viewpoints.

Such a bipolar relational unity, although paradoxical, is not unfamiliar in experience or a strange form of explanation. It appears in epistemology as the inevitable duality of the I-me relationship, which is always experienced as a unity of the self. In physics, it appears in quantum theory as the concept of complementarity constructed by Niels Bohr to

Figure 1.1. Möbius Band.

Top

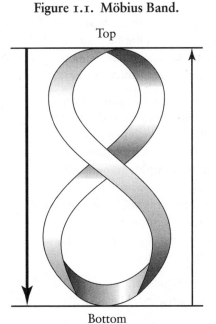

Bottom

explain the bipolar relationality between wave and particle in the nature of light. It appears definitively in the church's definition of the person of Jesus Christ formulated at the ecumenical council of Chalcedon in 451 A.D. The Chalcedonian definition of Jesus Christ states that he is fully God and fully human—one person, two natures.

It should also be clear that the duality is not a relationality among equals. It is, rather, the case that the asymmetry in the duality gives consistent ontological priority to one side over the other within the dynamic of the relationality. Thus, in the I-me relationality, the "I" maintains priority over the "me." In complementarity, priority is given to wave over particle because the wave exists in mathematical space. In the Chalcedonian formulation, the divine maintains priority over the human.

A Concluding Caveat

Given the finite, irreducibly self-transcendent and self-relational character of the human spirit, the answer to "What is a lifetime?" and "Why do I live it?" must finally be bestowed by the Creator Spirit. But it can only be grasped humanly as a total, existential response to the way in which the Creator Spirit takes up and transforms the negation, the nothingness, the frightening abyss that pervades and haunts human development as a whole. No answer to the two-sided question of this book is adequate unless and until it has definitively overcome the incipient serpentine nihilism that uncoils throughout every lifetime from the moment of birth, and at the end deceitfully claims to have spoken the final word. Without an answer of such adequacy, Macbeth's famous lines remain the classic and most spiritually profound response to the dark underside of human existence as it climaxes in death, making every unredeemed life essentially tragic:

> Tomorrow, and tomorrow, and tomorrow,
> Creeps in this petty pace from day to day
> To the last syllable of recorded time,
> And all our yesterdays have lighted fools
> The way to dusty death. Out, out, brief candle!
> Life's but a walking shadow, a poor player
> That struts and frets his hour upon the stage
> And then is heard no more; it is a tale
> Told by an idiot, full of sound and fury,
> Signifying nothing.[16]

When the ambitious, guilt-ridden queen, Lady Macbeth, finally dies, ending the torture in her own mind, Macbeth, about to confront his own death, recites this famous eulogy of despair over the meaninglessness of all human life. The fatalism behind Macbeth's tragic end personifies and dramatizes the larger theological picture, probably not lost on King James I for whom the play was written, which is the inevitable self-destruction of evil. As it takes possession of Macbeth and gradually erodes his once courageous human spirit, the evil portrayed in him is too close to the way the dark side of human development can gradually and quietly undercut the whole meaning of life—too close for us not to see it. Macbeth is forced by the violent extremities of his actions and his circumstances to recognize and describe what most of us in polite society do not permit ourselves to see or to speak of; but given a moment of truth, we will recognize that Macbeth has spoken in some respect for all of us. Why else are these lines so famous among persons who have known nothing of Macbeth's extremity? We all in some respect recognize ourselves in this speech because it captures the full measure of our potential despair, whether we articulate it or not.

Of course, the expanding vastness of the universe of which we are an integral part was unknown in Shakespeare's world. Somewhat surprisingly, that vastness suggests not deeper despair but an answer to Macbeth's tragic view of life. A young woman was sitting in the audience as the lecturer laid out the endless range of galaxies, the infinite depth of black holes, the mystery of dark matter, and the comparative insignificance of that pale blue dot—planet earth. Suddenly she exclaimed, "That frightens me!" When Professor Torrance heard this exclamation, his response was, "Don't be afraid. That's how much God loves you!"

It takes a universe and more to create a child, and it takes a "love that surpasses knowledge" (Eph. 3:19) to cast out the fear that reverberates between the internal emptiness of persons and the vast emptiness of outer space. To see that this silent resonance of emptiness is the obverse side of a love so great it can be comprehended only from the inside out as human emptiness is filled with all the fullness of God, is to have been grasped by the Spirit of God in total transformation. It is to have experienced from the ground up a transformation of one's lifetime so complete that all proximate transformations are themselves transformed into subparts of the whole.

NOTES

1. Miguel de Unamuno, cited by Sharon Parks, *Critical Years: The Young Adult Search for a Faith to Live By* (San Francisco: Harper San Francisco, 1986), p. 107.

2. Wolfhart Pannenberg, *Anthropology in Theological Perspective* (Philadelphia: Westminster Press, 1985), pp. 35–36.

3. Wilder Penfield, *The Mystery of the Mind* (Princeton, N.J.: Princeton University Press, 1975). See also James E. Loder and W. Jim Neidhardt, *The Knight's Move* (Colorado Springs: Helmers & Howard, 1992), pp. 43–44.

4. Julian Jaynes, *The Origin of Consciousness in the Breakdown of the Bicameral Mind* (Boston: Houghton Mifflin, 1977).

5. See Albert Einstein, *Out of My Later Years* (New York: Bonanza Books, 1956), p. 61.

6. In his recent book, *The Whole Shebang: A State-of-the-Universe(s) Report* (New York: Simon & Schuster, 1997), Timothy Ferris provides a highly readable report on the vastness of the universe or universes toward which the creativity of the human spirit reaches. Of course, this only amplifies the import of Einstein's statement.

7. "Relationality" is similar to, but not synonymous with, "relationship." A connection that is maintained by two polarities is a relationship; when that relationship takes on a life of its own, defining and sustaining the polarities—not the other way around—then we will speak of a relationality.

8. Ferris's *The Whole Shebang* and Loder and Neihardt's *The Knight's Move* make the same point from scientific as well as other contexts.

9. T. F. Torrance, "The Transcendental Role of Wisdom in Science" (lecture delivered at Princeton Theological Seminary, March 1990).

10. I Cor. 2:10–16, *The Holy Bible*, NRSV (Oxford: Oxford University Press 1989), pp. 174–175.

11. A. B. Pippard, "The Invincible Ignorance of Science," *Contemporary Physics* 29, no. 4 (1988): 405.

12. Roger Penrose, *The Emperor's New Mind* (Oxford: Oxford University Press, 1989).

13. Douglas R. Hofstadter, *Gödel, Escher, Bach: An Eternal Golden Braid* (New York: Vintage Books, 1980).

14. See also Loder and Neihardt, *The Knight's Move*, pp. 38–40.

15. Pippard, "Invincible Ignorance," p. 405.

16. William Shakespeare, *The Complete Works of Shakespeare* (New York: Ginn Press, 1936), Act V, scene 5.

2

EXAMINING THE RELATIONALITY BETWEEN THE HUMAN SPIRIT AND THE DIVINE

THE RELATIONSHIP between theology and human development may yield up fresh insights for addressing the questions, "What is a lifetime?" and "Why do I live it?" The psychological aspect of this book adopts a relational or interactionist perspective on human development. The emphasis on the kinetics of development is consistent with relational grounds of reason and the process of transformation where order emerges from chaos and where we will find common grounds of central significance for both theology and human development. Theologically, this emphasis on the relational and transformational kinetics of human development is most appropriately envisioned from within the language of the Divine Spirit, especially as it is understood transformationally in the Reformed tradition as *Spiritus Creator*. By looking at development theologically, through the lenses of the Creator Spirit, we will eventually see that the dynamics of development, down to the particulars of language, thought, patterns of affect, and moral judgment, as well as the more global moves from stage to stage in ego development, are compelled forward according to a transformational pattern that reflects on a human level the same pattern as that which characterizes the Creator Spirit. Although distinctly different in origin, destiny, and magnitude, the human spirit and the Divine Spirit are made for each other, according to a relationality ultimately designed to replicate the relationality of the divine and the human in the person of Jesus Christ.

Psychological Approach

Normal human development is an emergent reality, a resultant of the interaction between a personality and its environment. That interaction gives the developmental potential of the personality particular and varied shape over the course of a lifetime. We infer from a variety of behavioral manifestations that development takes place in stages, and those stages tend to advance according to the principle that they manage increasing complexity with greater simplicity and efficiency in the use of energy. Most studies of human development focus on defining and mapping stages, but I will focus on the dynamics of development within and beyond the context of stages. This shift in focus will tend to turn our attention away from stages (even though they are easier to think about) to the dynamics that create and move beyond them.

An example of interactionist development generally can be given in a brief note on the development of language. Children raised outside a linguistic environment do not learn to speak. Feral children or abused children kept in an attic and fed food through a hole, not spoken to, and deprived of all social interaction, do not learn to speak. It takes a linguistic environment to bring forth language, though the developmental potential is there with the infant's earliest babbling sounds. Unless a child is provided a linguistic environment, he will no more learn a language than a wild chimp would. And, of course, the particular language learned reflects the environment: Chinese children speak Chinese, and Danish children speak Danish. The development of language is an open-ended relational gestalt linking the developmental potential of the child with the social and cultural environment, so each is creative and formative of the other over time.

Language apparently emerges in stages. Babbling becomes holophrastic speech, whereby single words stand for whole ranges of action. "Ma" may mean "Feed me!" "Aren't I cute!" "Smile at me!" "Pick me up!" and so forth. This stage is followed by patterned speech, in which the child links words in ways that simulate language, linking nouns, verbs, and adjectives in segments. Then at about age four, grammar, which the child has been constructing more or less under the surface, emerges, and the competence this creates means that many new words can be managed by an underlying structure from which an almost infinite variety of meaningful sentences can be generated. The typical four or five year old generates speech in a great outpouring of verbiage on any topic. And what is true of language is generally true of other registers of behavior, intelligence, judgment, and ego formation.

Alternative Theories

By selecting the relational, interactionist position, locating development relationally between the person and the environment, and speaking of certain innate structural potentials (such as grammar), I have automatically excluded certain other theoretical options, among them preformationism, predeterminism, and environmentalism.

Preformationism is a naive seventeenth-century notion of Anton van Leeuwenhoek, inventor of the microscope. Studying sperm under his microscope, he believed he saw miniature human figures who simply had to expand, in balloon fashion, to produce human beings. Naive as that may seem, it has been a prevalent covert assumption in child rearing, even to the latter part of the nineteenth century, or at any other period when a child is thought of as a little adult ("Remember you are a young lady." "Act like a little man."). Preformationism identifies a common and once widespread illusion about human development: that it is fundamentally a matter of balloon-like growth. This is excluded by the interactionist premise.

G. Stanley Hall, sometimes said to be the founder of child psychology in America, propounded a developmental Darwinism sometimes called predeterminism; "ontogeny recapitulates phylogeny" was applied to psychological development.[1] Here developmental forms emerged, but their emergence was preprogrammed. Each individual, it was assumed, recapitulates the developmental history of the species. Such a position fails to take account of human uniqueness. In this error, phylogenetic history becomes not a contributor to our understanding of human development (which it most certainly is), but an exhaustive account of human development. We are, in fact, born much less adequately programmed for our environment than any other creature, but we have a large mass of cerebral cortex, which is designed to enable us to create and compose our own environment, especially culture. Hence, again, the emphasis on interaction is a correction to this hypothesis of predeterminism.

A third view discredited by our basic premise is environmentalism. This view of the early behaviorist, J. B. Watson, and more recently B. F. Skinner, makes an apotheosis of the environment, saying that by controlled training, any newborn child can be molded into any type of adult.[2] This makes the same mistake as predeterminism, only now from the outside in rather than from the phylogenetic inside out. It assumes that persons can be shaped in all registers of behavior by the same techniques that form the behavior of laboratory rats and pigeons.

Although Skinner is a good learning theorist, he is not a developmentalist, and his study of verbal behavior, that uniquely human capacity to construct the world symbolically, has been thoroughly discredited by Noam Chomsky and others.[3]

Each of these approaches or hypotheses about development has some contribution to make to our understanding, but we will not be working explicitly with them. We will, rather, work with development as an emergent resultant of the interaction between the person and her environment, with that interaction giving rise and shape to structural potentials within the personality. If you are familiar with this discussion in terms of a nature-nurture controversy, the issue here is not "Which?" or "How much?" but simply "How?" How do environments and persons interact to give rise to the personality?

Key Interactionists

The key psychological theorists discussed in the following chapters emphasize three major psychological domains: the personal unconscious and ego development (Sigmund Freud, Anna Freud, Erik Erikson, and the psychoanalytic tradition), the conscious mind and cognitive development (Jean Piaget, Lawrence Kohlberg, Carol Gilligan, and the structuralist tradition), and the collective unconscious (Carl G. Jung, Ann Ulanov, and the analytical tradition). They are listed here according to the order of their importance in explaining successive phases of the life span from infancy. Each of these views will contribute to our understanding of the human spirit, since each in different ways acknowledges and tacitly builds on the primacy of that spirit, which both transcends and implements the life of the psyche. The implicit presence of that spirit (and its ultimate insufficiency) will first be evident in the pervasive concern that each foundational theorist had for religion, particularly the religious life of the individual.

These are not the key figures because they have the final word, but because they set forth the positions with respect to which almost all research in this field, including cross-cultural and feminist studies, is conducted.[4] They have asked the most fundamental questions about human development with which we continue to wrestle and for which we still seek sufficient answers.

The first figure is Sigmund Freud (originally "Sigismund," a name he changed to Sigmund when he was twenty-two). Psychoanalyst Marie Jahoda once remarked that after forty years of research on Freud's model, "Freud would still not go away." Now, after a century of debate, this is still the case. He raised many of the developmental issues we still engage in countless variations.

Freud was born May 6, 1856, and died September 23, 1939.[5] He was, first, a physician and neurologist who worked with severely regressed patients, and his notion of human development came from working backward from manifestations of a pathology to its origins. Since the conscious life of his patients was distorted, he concentrated on the unconscious life. Dream analysis and free association techniques were, for him and modern psychoanalysis, "the royal road to the unconscious life." What Freud eventually found in the unconscious was "a dual drive theory of motivation": a life instinct and a death instinct, respectively, libido and destrudo. These two drives, which comprise the id, are inseparable. As a person matures, these motivational drives relate to the environment through what he called erogenous or erotogenic zones: especially sensitive and potentially pleasurable ways or bodily apertures through which we interact with the environment. He viewed the course of development through stages he called oral, anal, phallic, latency (when nothing sexual was happening), and genital (in which one is able to *lieben* and *arbeiten*, love and work).

Explanation for Freud was more than psychological. It was also biological, cultural, and religious. His earliest attempt was bioneurological, *The Project of 1895*. However, this approach proved to be unhelpful in dealing with the phenomena that confronted him in his clinical experiences. His subsequent explanations were cultural, symbolic, and mythic. As to the religious, Freud thought of himself as having a distinctly Jewish mind. Other notable religious influences include the claim by several biographers that Freud had a Roman Catholic nanny who may have had him baptized, but most certainly in his book, *Freud and the Jewish Mystical Tradition*,[6] David Bakan pointed out that Freud read and devoured the Jewish mystics. He thought of himself as "Joseph," able to interpret dreams and so arrive at the truth of human nature in relation to "God." Viewing the whole of the Freudian psyche in theological perspective will bring out the theological significance of often-neglected aspects of Freud's view, such as the death instinct and its role in the act of creation, a manifestation of spirit out of which Freud's own constructive thought emerged.

Freud had three basic models of the human psyche: the topographic, laying out the territories within the psyche; the economic, discussing the distribution of energy among these territories; and the dynamic, indicating the ways in which these territories, with their quantum of energy, were able to adapt or not adapt, control or fail to control, their relationship to the environment. In a synthetic model of the psyche (see Figure 2.1), we can see that there are three realities: the intrapsychic, the extrapsychic public reality, and the reality principle by which intrapsychic life is

Figure 2.1. Topographic Model Indicating Dynamics.

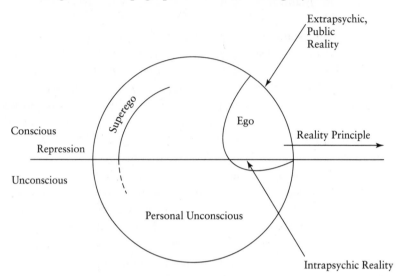

balanced against external reality, and so provides the rule of the ego. The ego is the intrapsychic agency that emerges as the governor of the inter-action between the person and her environment, and the rule of the ego, the reality principle, is designed to maximize satisfaction and ensure survival. However, Freud concentrated more on the unconscious than on the ego per se. This is the point where his followers have taken up his work and developed it. The neo-Freudians concentrate on ego development. I will also refer to self-theorists and object-relations theorists. All of these positions elaborate on different aspects of the psyche, but all are within the psychoanalytic tradition, building on the generative power of Freud's original position.

Our second major source for the interactionist approach is Erik Erikson.[7] He should be classified with Anna Freud (Freud's daughter), Helene Deutsche, Ernst Kris, Heinz Hartmann, David Rapaport, and others who, though dependent on Freud, focused on the development of the concept of the ego. Erikson was born in 1902 in Denmark and died in 1994. His birth, it turned out, was the result of his Lutheran mother's extramarital affair. He apparently never knew his Danish father. He was raised as Erik Homburger, the surname of his stepfather, a German Jew who was also his pediatrician. He was perceived, therefore, as a blond, Nordic Jew. Before he migrated to the United States, he changed his surname to Erikson, becoming, in effect, "Erik, Son of Erik," thus giving birth to his own identity.

As a young man, he was an artist often taking children as his subjects. Eventually he found his way to Freud's Vienna, studied the Montessori method, and was analyzed by Anna Freud. Unlike most other analysts, he did not have a medical background and worked more out of a sheer intuitive genius and a conscientious and careful study of cases. Some are historical; most are clinical. Given his personal history, it is perhaps not surprising that most of his early cases were children. His writings were greatly facilitated by his wife, who taught English and English literature in Vienna, and she enhanced the literary quality of his work. As with Freud, part of the power of his theory is the felicity of his theoretical expositions.

Rather than concentrate on the dynamics of the unconscious and the pathological twists and turns of libidinal energy, Erikson concentrated more on the ego as having a structural and developmental potential of its own. This was implicit in Freud and also more fully developed by the object-relations school. The result of Erikson's work was a view of so-called normal development that covered the whole life span (not just children up through adolescence, as it had been with Freud). His view was sociocultural as well as personal, and it included religion as part of normal development. He also put psychological development into the study of history.

He mapped out eight stages, which emerge on schedule according to an epigenetic view of development. There is a developmental clock in the organism and, according to Erikson, in the psyche. Epigenesis means, then, that under the surface, development of a particular stage has been in process from birth, but it emerges only at a certain time with certain clear-cut consequences. As in the example of language, epigenesis gives rise to full-blown grammatical speech only at a particular time after underground preparation has taken place, and, as a result, certain consequences such as meaningful, interpersonal conversation can take place. But if one aspect develops out of phase, failing to appear at the right time, it can cause disequilibrium throughout the whole organism.

One of Erikson's most challenging notions is that of historical figures (*homo religiosus*) who rise up and show directions that later generations find to be paradigmatic. This concept of the paradigmatic figure who takes in the problems of a period in history and points the way to the future lies behind Erikson's landmark studies of Luther and Gandhi.[8]

The key figure regarding the cognitive side of development, especially the structure and dynamics of intelligence as it emerges throughout a lifetime, is Jean Piaget (1896–1980), but derivatives from his position include Lawrence Kohlberg, Carol Gilligan, Robert Kegan, and James Fowler.[9] He was a Swiss psychologist who taught at the University of Geneva and did research at the Institut Jean Jacques Rousseau and the Center for Genetic Epistemology. As a child, he was a prodigy in biology, roaming around the lakes of Neuchatel, observing mollusks floating in the lakes and the behavior of birds in the local parks. He was such a careful observer that he had published his first scientific paper at the age of eleven, a study of a partly albino sparrow he had observed in a public park. He published some twenty papers before he was twenty-one, and while he was still in secondary school, he was offered the curatorship of the mollusk collection at the Geneva Museum. They did not hire him when they found out how young he was.

Piaget studied for a short time with Freud and also studied and taught philosophy at the Sorbonne. When in Paris, he studied with Simon of the Simon-Binet intelligence tests. He found he was more interested in why children got wrong answers than in how to standardize right-answer tests for children with respect to their chronological age. He left Paris and began his observations on his own children. After that time, he wrote and worked prodigiously and almost continually until his death. There are over twelve hundred separate publications listed in his bibliography.

Piaget wanted to be thought of as an epistemologist, not a psychologist, but his impact on modern psychology is probably equaled only by Freud.[10] As an epistemologist, he is self-classified as a structuralist. He wanted to comprehend the structure of mind. More specifically, he believed that out of interaction with the environment, the innate structural potential of the psyche produced intelligence, language, moral judgment, and imagery, to mention a few registers of behavior. For Piaget, the structures of intelligence are formally congruent or isomorphic with respect to the structures of the universe, and so there is a parallel between the unfolding of intelligence child-to-adult and the unfolding of the history of science. Ultimately love and logic reach a kind of empirical version of a Spinozian unity.

Although he was never able to demonstrate all this, he had, in keeping with the French intellectual tradition, a passionate drive to understand the human mind. From his early studies with Freud, he developed a profound distrust of "the tricks of the unconscious"; he preferred to focus on the development of the cognitive competencies of the conscious ego. His view of metaphysics was that it was wisdom without knowledge; his studies, he claimed, would supply knowledge in the way that only science can supply it. However, as we will see, his intense focus on the cognitive side of development was overly determined, to his detriment.

In the spring of 1994, Fernando Vidal published his dissertation, a study of Piaget's early life up to 1918.[11] What is little known or appreciated is that Piaget was an avid Christian in his youth. He was active in his church, underwent a conversion, and was a moving force in his university Christian fellowship. From 1914 to 1918, he was reading philosophy and theology with the intention of becoming a philosopher or a theologian. (Some of his early writings include an essay advocating the new birth of Christianity out of the ashes of World War I ("The Mission of the Idea"), and another in which he attempted to work out the interdisciplinary relationship between science, philosophy, and faith (*"Recherche"*). In another instance he intended to demonstrate the analogical relationship between the philosophy of Henri Bergson and the theology of the spirit in the works of Auguste Sabatier, the nineteenth-century dean of the University of Paris.[12]

The ambivalent motivating factor in this was that his mother was a neurotically driven French Calvinist, who was at once the interpersonal source of Piaget's faith and his reason for rejecting it. His father, a medieval scholar and professor of language and literature, was an agnostic but did not exert a counterforce to the mother and faded very much into the background. Eventually Piaget had to opt for the religion of immanence, but the power of Bergson's *élan vital,* in combination with the theological understanding of the spirit in Sabatier, implicitly gives his work profound spiritual significance, although that has remained tacit and undeveloped so far. Nevertheless, it does explain some anomalies in Piaget's thought, such as why he believes transformation is a more powerful force in development than structure, even though Piaget says he is a structuralist.

This background for Piaget's thought is important not only for reading his work but also for a discussion of intelligence generally. Other researchers in this field, such as Howard Gardner, do not talk about theological intelligence in any way that relates a frame of mind to that unique way of thinking that fills millions of volumes of reflection on God worldwide. Gardner does suggest in *Creating Minds* that religious commitments (such as Einstein's commitment to Christianity) in adolescence may foster creativity by its enhancing a sense of ultimacy, expressing spiritual needs and reinforcing the learner's capacity to stand against conventional wisdom. However, one might get the impression from such studies of intelligence that theological intelligence, reflection by a believer on God, is something to be outgrown. Most of the world, including many developmentalists, realize that theological intelligence may more likely be expressive of a higher form of maturity. Is this not the form of intelligence by which to address for oneself the prior question of why be intelligent, whichever the frame of mind in question?

In Piaget's case, the approach he took to intelligence is more closely linked to theological thinking than many other more "spiritual" intelligences (such as artistic, musical, or interpersonal) precisely because of its roots in philosophy, theology, and Piaget's early personal commitment to Christianity. This potentially spiritual quality of Piaget's work can be documented by reference to Wolfhart Pannenberg's *Anthropology in Theological Perspective.*[13] Piaget's reliance on transformation, the human spirit, totality, relationality, and the quest for universality in his later work carry his view of intelligence into an understanding of religious immanence and far beyond the cognitive stereotypes often attributed to him. His last book, *Psychogenesis and the History of Science,* showed a clear move in his thought toward the preeminence of transformation, a move well beyond his earlier, more rigid structuralist position.[14]

The Piaget who concerns us in this book will not take anything away from the Piaget who is a rigorous researcher and creative scientist, but it does seek to appreciate his work and its meaning as including but far greater than the textbook Piaget of the American psychological establishment. For Piaget, intelligence derived its significance from a comprehensive sense of the order of all that is, including the sensory motor behavior of the knower, the moral order of human existence, and the ultimate comprehensibility of the universe. In this respect, his vision complements the theological vision of intelligibility and ultimate order described by T. F. Torrance in Chapter One.

The fourth key psychological figure is Carl Jung (1875–1961).[15] Jung too is an interactionist, but the emerging substructure in his position has archetypical proportions. The archetypes emerge to structure the wholeness of the psyche, leading toward the individuation of the self during the middle years of life. Archetypes (a phylogenetic inheritance) emerge from a psychic level (the objective psyche or collective unconscious) deeper than the personal unconscious (Freud and Erikson), and present themselves through powerful images that have mythic and religious force for the formation of persons. Thus, religious solutions to the struggles and potential deformities of human development are at the very center of Jungian thought (see Chapter Twelve).

Theological Approach

Everything in the psychological approach may be seen as the work of the human spirit in its effort to understand and interpret itself. But for all of the analytical power of such theories, their preoccupation with adaptation (important as that may be) prevents them from self-criticism in relation to the more profound issues of human existence. That is, even after we have carefully examined human development from the various standpoints, including criticisms and revisions of the theories, we will not have explicitly said anything of theological significance. We always must ask, "What is theological about human development?" and allow theology to call the tune if the scope of the inquiry is to be sufficient. Theological consideration must be explicitly brought to bear on these understandings of human development if these understandings are to yield up their theological potential, and if theology is to articulate from within the matrix of human development the meaning and purpose of a lifetime. To look at development theologically will call for different ways of viewing development by anyone's standards. The analogy from the physical sciences is James Clerk-Maxwell's revolutionary discovery of the electromagnetic field.

In the broad spectrum of Christian theological perspectives, this book is placed under the heading of theological anthropology, the study of human nature as revealed in the Word of God. To bring some focus to this wide-ranging topic, I will present four fundamental theological arguments, which will place anthropology in the context of theology generally and formulate the basic theological approach of this book. These four arguments center on Wolfhart Pannenberg, Karl Barth, T. F. Torrance, and George Hendry. The way in which their positions interconnect and critique each other on the questions of theological anthropology generally, and on the human spirit in particular, will lead us into the theological premises of the following chapters.[16]

Pannenberg's landmark study, *Anthropology in Theological Perspective,* is easily the most comprehensive study of theology and the human sciences in this field. Pannenberg sets up his approach to theological anthropology by first establishing the centrality of the anthropological question for contemporary theological thinking by citing three influences. First is the historical movement in philosophy away from anything resembling the "God hypothesis" of the patristic or medieval period through the Reformation to the modern period, where human beings seemed to understand themselves better philosophically if they concentrated on the human person as the subject of all experience and of philosophical reflection. Second is the Reformation tendency to be preoccupied with salvation as over against issues of God's creation and his future eschatological kingdom, which has come down to the present in existentialism, represented supremely in such figures as Kierkegaard, Bultmann, and Tillich. The third influence is the privatization and segmentation of religion in modern and contemporary society—that is, the tendency to restrict religion to the private sphere and to institutions and cults that support this. The tendency has been to argue for the universal human validity of religious interiority, and thus reinforce the theological tendency to state and validate the claims of the Christian faith in anthropological terms. This convergence of philosophical, theological, and sociohistorical influences has drawn Christian theology into an anthropological emphasis. Thus, Pannenberg argues that Christian theology in the modern age must provide itself with a foundation in general anthropological studies.

He proposes to do a "fundamental-theological" anthropology in which he turns his attention directly to human nature as investigated by the human sciences. He proposes to examine these disciplines with an eye to implications that may be relevant for religion and theology. The aim is a critical theological appropriation of the human phenomenon as described by the anthropological disciplines. Thus, the secular description of human nature is accepted as a provisional version of the objective reality, one that needs to be expanded and deepened by showing that the anthropological data themselves contain a theologically relevant dimension. Looking from the standpoint of dogmatic anthropology, Pannenberg marks out the terrain for the discussion. He argues that there are two major themes to be accounted for in anthropological terms: the image of God in human beings and human sin. Interpreting these themes, he claims that to speak of the image of God in human beings is to speak of their closeness to the divine reality, a closeness that also determines their uniqueness in the natural order of creation. To speak of sin, on the other hand, is to speak of the de facto separation from God of human beings whose true destiny is union with God.

To speak of *imago dei* in anthropological terms is to talk about the uniqueness of the human person in relation to the rest of the natural order. Pannenberg finds the generation of this uniqueness in the natural human endowment for ecstasis—the standing outside oneself in "exocentric centeredness," his naturalistic synonym for spirit. This translates into the built-in human proclivity toward a self-transcendence that is simultaneously self-formative. It is a potentially infinite movement from the person outward that simultaneously feeds back into one's selfhood, yielding internal formation and personal transcendence with respect to the issue at stake.

Helen Keller's famous discovery of the sign for water is exemplary of this aspect of the human spirit. She did not merely learn a sign; she discovered the power of signing, and implicitly of language as a whole. In this, she transcended the single sensation and the sign, and simultaneously she gained an inner sense of confidence that she could transcend and name whatever came next. The liberation of her spirit was simultaneously exocentric and self-confirming. Pannenberg provides a generic account of the "spirit" in human nature whose most obvious major achievement, short of the knowledge of God, is the creation of selfhood, societies, and culture in the unfolding course of history.

Sin is to be understood as the perversion or turning inward of the human spirit, producing internal conflict, anxiety, and self-destructive behavior. The failure of persons to create and compose lived and livable worlds may be studied in the human sciences as adaptational failures—disintegration of groups, societies, and culture. However, for Pannenberg, such failures are the result not of a prehistoric Fall but of the incompleteness of history, which has not yet reached its culmination as promised in the resurrected Christ. For Pannenberg, the end of history is proleptically given in the midst of history in the resurrection of Jesus Christ. This position clearly makes an effort to accept contemporary scientific cosmology when it recognizes the irreversibility of the arrow of time in an expanding universe. It also recognizes the scientific importance of a final demonstration to establish the truth of historical events leading up to the end of history. That is, Jesus is the only one who can give us the meaning of life because he alone has overcome its end point; he alone has satisfied the drive of the human spirit to claim the last word in the face of death. Thus, Pannenberg claims only provisional or anticipatory validity for his Christian interpretation of human history as delineated by the anthropological sciences. Validation remains in the hands of eschatology.

Pannenberg's effort to make a claim for a Christian interpretation of anthropology through this sort of fundamental theology works a corrective on subjectivism. It sets the human sciences over against pietistic individualism or existentialist self-absorption. At the same time, Pannenberg wants to avoid the potential humanistic reductionism implicit in the human sciences taken at face value. The integrity of theology must be preserved, even in the context of its efforts to take its anthropological tendencies seriously.

Pannenberg credits Karl Barth with the recognition that the tendency toward anthropocentrism in theology must be radically counteracted.[17] The danger is that in an interdisciplinary discussion between theology and the human sciences, theology will be bracketed, and "The Godness of God" will be lost to the self-interests of the theologian. For Pannenberg, the answer to this is not the strong theological objectivism of Barth's dialectical theology; Barth's refusal to take any position on the anthropological terrain and begin with "God himself" is, in Pannenberg's view, the most extreme form of theological subjectivism. Thus, Pannenberg argues that Barth's position is defenseless against the suspicion that his theology and the faith behind it is something arbitrarily legislated by human beings.

Rather than take Barth's approach, Pannenberg seeks to counter subjectivism, existentialism, and reductionism by directly addressing the anthropological issue first in its own terms and thereby to demonstrate the nature of the irreducible religious thematic in human nature (that is, Pannenberg's understanding of *spirit*) and its inherent need for a theological interpretation. Thus, the apologetic force of Pannenberg's position is simultaneously to purge theology of any anthropological distortion and to inform and transform the human sciences where they themselves are in need of self-understanding. Once informed and transformed, the relevant human sciences can then further the theological task where an understanding of human nature is concerned.

My argument in this book shares many aspects of Pannenberg's approach to theological anthropology, but does not reject the contribution Barth makes to this discussion. Instead I will make his Christological position pivotal as God's revelation of what God means by "human" and at the same time what God means by "God."

When Pannenberg first did theological anthropology, he did it primarily from the bottom up, holding his systematic theology apart and in the background. Later in his three-volume *Systematic Theology,* he explicitly turned his approach around and worked from God's self-revelation, that is, from the top down. Both approaches are necessary but, for Pannenberg, the two approaches complement each other as "method" and "material" in the quest for truth as measured by ultimate coherence. The "fundamental theology" (as he called it) that he did in *Anthropology in Theological Perspective* is only methodologically fundamental. Materially, only God or his self-revelation in Jesus Christ is fundamental. "No other foundation can anyone lay than that which is laid, which is Jesus Christ" (I Cor. 3:11).[18]

This is an important distinction for this book, as at this juncture we are focusing on method and so, if we follow Pannenberg, we are attending primarily to the "fundamental theology" that characterizes his *Anthropology* and only secondarily to the material substance of God's self-revelation. As distinct from Pannenberg, what I am claiming here is that the material supplies the method. This is possibly implicit in Pannenberg's position, but Pannenberg's emphasis on philosophical coherence and historical reason in the development of his methodology and theology detracts from the Christological center, which both Karl Barth and T. F. Torrance insist must be primary for our understanding human nature from any perspective.

This is not really a matter of theological preference. Pannenberg's approach lacks sufficient dialectical force to deal with the power of life against death, which lies at the core of human existence. If the theological understanding of human nature is kept in firm tension with anthropological findings, then it will push anthropological claims further into their own resources and deeper into the human phenomenon than many current empirical methods permit. Pannenberg's approach is not intense enough on either side. Moreover, he tends to let human science do most of the pushing. For example, he too quickly accepts basic trust, as Erik Erikson discusses it, as the human ground for faith. For Pannenberg, this experience of basic trust beginning at eighteen months of life is an expression of a religious thematic that expands infinitely toward an ultimately and universally trustworthy reality, namely God. In this claim, theology has not transformed the behavioral science observation but simply accommodated its own terms to suit and to extend the behavioral science given. The irony is that his claim is not consistent with what Erikson says nor does it satisfy the theological conditions for faith.

That is, for Erikson trust is inseparable from mistrust, so to say it expands infinitely toward a universal reality that may be called God is not taking the scientific data or its claims seriously. This reflects a deeper problem in Pannenberg's method, which tends consistently to suppress the negative side of the anthropological reality in question and to move from the human to the divine by a like-to-like analogy. This bypasses the rule of difference implied in any sound analogy, and it ignores the existential negations that accompany all of life.

On the other side, faith is not fundamentally a developmental phenomenon. If faith is a human response to God's grace, it must be rooted in God and be grounded deeper in psychic bedrock than the developing ego's foundation in a favorable balance of trust over mistrust, all of which is primarily dependent on interaction with a human environment. A theology of faith needs to push the human sciences deeper than Erikson's view of trust without departing from human givens.

The two sides of this example show how an interdisciplinary approach, even if it is working both from the bottom up and from the top down, may only serve to water down claims on both sides and end up saying less than what each side said separately.

In order to intensify the interdisciplinary exchanges and thereby push further theologically into anthropological realities, I will turn to Karl Barth, T. F. Torrance, and their Christological emphases. It is here that I expect to find that the material substance of theology also supplies the methodological approach by which we can more adequately disclose what it means to be human in a way that is accountable to both sides of the theology–human sciences dialogue.

Barth is rightly criticized by Pannenberg when he refuses to acknowledge the humanistic assumptions at work in his theology, but this, I believe, is a truncated reading of Barth. In fact, a different reading of Barth, T. F. Torrance's, will make Barth's Christological position the keystone in the methodological argument of this book.[19]

The fundamental question for our purposes is not whether to deal with Barth, but how to understand Barth's theological method for this particular interdisciplinary discussion. The noted Scottish theologian T. F. Torrance, in his seminal essay, "The Natural Theology of Karl Barth," effectively overcomes the dualism apparent in Barth's great "*Nein*" to natural theology and all dialogue with the physical and human sciences. By his report, Torrance had Barth's firm approval for his argument as it was drawn from the history of the physical sciences.

Torrance argued that in the relation between Barth's theology and the sciences of the natural order, there is an unrecognized analogy to the relation between geometry and contemporary physics. That is, in the Newtonian world, all physics took place within three-dimensional Euclidean space; this meant that space could be understood independent of physics as the uncriticized presupposition of all physical phenomena. But in the Einsteinian universe, based on Clerk-Maxwell's equations describing the nature of light, and the move to multidimensional geometries, space is incorporated into the physical universe and so into physics; no longer absolute, it was made relative to the speed of light, a universal constant. Geometry, then, is transformed by being moved from an unexamined presupposition about where physics took place into being a subscience of the inner rational structure of physics and so becomes an essential part of the empirical and theoretical interpretation of nature in physics as a whole.

Torrance then argues that natural theology, the study of the natural order as a way to understand God independent of the positive theology of revelation in Jesus Christ, is like pre-Einsteinian understandings of geometry in relation to physics. The natural order, which extends to infinity in all directions, including the culture and society within which it is understood, must be transformed by the more comprehensive and dynamic revelation of the Creator God in Jesus Christ and by his Spirit. The natural order is not the context in which to understand God, but the natural order itself must be understood in the context of what God has revealed. By this theological paradigm shift, the sciences of the natural order, including the human sciences, must undergo a transformation by which they enter into an indissoluble, contingent relation to revealed theology, functioning as subsciences of its inner intelligibility and as an essential part of the empirical and theoretical claims of its interpretation of God's action in the world. By Torrance's account, Barth said, "I must have been a blind hen not to have seen that analogy before."[20]

I will accept Torrance's reinterpretation of Barth and argue in Barthian fashion that the relationship between the divine and the human as delineated in the Chalcedonian formula can provide the optimal way to relate theology and the human sciences. In Barth's language, the Chalcedonian pattern says that between the divine and the human in the person of Jesus Christ, there is an "indissoluble differentiation," "inseparable unity," and "indestructible order."[21] This constitutes a form of relationality that appears in a variety of other contexts[22] and works well as a way of overcoming the numerous problems raised by interdisciplinary studies involving Christian theology.

Before continuing, it should be clear by now that the implications of the discussion so far have begun to shape the theological stance of this book. First, I agree with Pannenberg's solution to the threat posed by the advancing influence of secular studies on theological anthropology; we need to face the issue and bring theology to bear on the threat as posed. However, I disagree with his method and some of its conclusions. Thus, I accept the Chalcedonian model as a way of working (both methodologically and materially) from below and above at the same time, allowing the objectivity of the revelation to deal transformatively with the objectivity of the sciences.

Second, the human sciences may inform theology as subsciences of its inner intelligibility, but the theological perspective must transform human science understandings in ways that strive to preserve the integrity of both sides of the interaction and thereby enhance our understanding of human nature generally.

Third, I agree that Pannenberg's locating the human spirit in the exocentric centeredness of persons is correct, but he has not understood the intensity of its underlying drive toward reciprocity and continuity in the context of contradiction. As a result, his notion of exocentricity seems too reflexive, too much like an automatic reaction; the human spirit is instead a powerful drive, endowed with energy and determination in the face of persistent obstacles to its expansion. A stronger way to say it is that the expansive self-transcending power of the human spirit drives toward the transformation of every obstacle in its path, making the obstacle into a vehicle for attaining a wider or higher horizon. In the Helen Keller illustration, the human spirit is not only the exocentricity and transcendence in her discovery of language. It is also the enduring transformational drive within her to recover the rudiments of signing she lost at nineteen months of age, and to move from there to create a unique kind of linguistic world.

The paradox at the core of the human spirit is that such a self-transcending outward move is simultaneously an inward move, reinforcing one's sense of self. It is a contribution of Barthian thought as further developed by Torrance to recognize that in the human sphere, as well as within the divine life, relationality constitutes the reality at stake. Exocentric centeredness can be conceived of as spirit not merely because it "transcends transformationally," but because it is inherently and irreducibly relational. Just as the Holy Spirit is spoken of as the "go-between God," the human spirit can be spoken of as the go-between image of God in us.

Fourth, in both Pannenberg and Barth, there is a tendency to depreciate, if not extinguish, the distinctive significance of the human spirit. Pannenberg tends to absorb the human spirit into an all-encompassing view of the Divine Spirit; Barth gives no weight to it, consigning it to the realm of the unredeemed, the target of his famous "*Nein.*" However, there are important biblical and theological reasons that a differentiated unity between the Holy Spirit and human spirit should be kept in place. Since this last point is particularly vital to theological anthropology, it must be spelled out further.

At this point, we must turn to the Reformed theologian George Hendry. In his important little book, *The Holy Spirit in Christian Theology,* he argued that the Reformed tradition has done a disservice in minimizing the significance of the human spirit.[23] In brief, his often-cited argument is that the Reformers, in stressing *sola gratia* (saved by grace alone), have led us to a misunderstanding of grace. In a word, grace is the meaning of the incarnation, but there are two aspects to grace as expressed there. Augustine, from whom the Reformers got their primary understanding of grace, stressed the first element, which is *condescension*. In this aspect, grace means that the Almighty God who dwells in "the high and holy place" (Isa. 57:15) as a light no human can approach (I Tim. 6:16) has condescended to establish a relation between God's self and human beings. Condescension is clearly indispensable to the realization of God's purposes.

Augustine, however, made the mistake of equating indispensable with irresistible, because he did not take account of the second element of grace present in the incarnation, the element of *accommodation*: "The only begotten Son of God . . . came down from heaven . . . and he was made man" (Nicene Creed) and the eternal Word of God who was God "became flesh and dwelt among us" (John 1:1–14). For Hendry, the humanity to whom God accommodates is humanity as endowed with a created spirit, the hallmark of which is human freedom. To be in relation with God is to be related Spirit-to-spirit, or Freedom-to-freedom. God does not dehumanize humanity or "un-man" humanity, to use Hendry's words, in order to relate to humans. Irresistible grace, so called, needs to be reinterpreted as a grace whose keynote is nonresistance; God does not overrule human freedom but engages it in order that the I-Thou of the God-human relationship not be reduced to the I-it order. By choosing to become human, God affirms humanity, but the humanity affirmed is essentially spirit. It is not correct to say that humanity has lost the image of God; it would be better to say that humanity has lost its original of which it is the image. Moreover, there is no way the human spirit by itself as human spirit can reverse the loss; the created spirit is ontologically incapable of choosing the Creator as a possibility. Thus, when grace enters the situation, the disoriented human spirit is not destroyed by grace; it is transformed so that it may choose freely to testify with God's Spirit that we are the children of God (Rom. 8:16). Thus, the impact of grace on the human spirit is to awaken it to a true sense of its freedom to be itself as image restored to its original.

The preservation of a differentiated relationality of human spirit to Holy Spirit can be defended biblically and from within the Reformed tradition. However, it will be necessary to describe the human spirit somewhat more broadly, including, but not being exhausted by, freedom, if we are to take the human sciences seriously as efforts of the human spirit to understand itself. In this respect, I will draw on much of what Pannenberg has described regarding the spirit in human nature, but all the contributions of the human sciences will be understood according to the Chalcedonian model. In this, I will argue that the human spirit is to humanity what the Holy Spirit is to God (I Cor. 2:10), so these two are interrelated according to the bipolar relationality.

This leads to the fifth aspect of the theological position of the book: the *analogia spiritus*, the analogy between the human spirit and the Holy Spirit. The similarity lies in the transformational pattern that characterizes the dynamics of each spirit as it operates through time. Transformation is defined as follows: when within any given frame of reference hidden orders of meaning and coherence arise to call the axioms of that frame into question and reorder its elements accordingly, transformation has occurred. This similarity can be briefly noted in that the human spirit is inherently creative, and the Holy Spirit works in human history as *Spiritus Creator*, where creativity is understood transformationally. The dissimilarity in the analogy lies in the fact that the human spirit is rooted and grounded in the human psyche, but the Holy Spirit is rooted and grounded in God.

When the human spirit operates as an image separated from its original, it works as ungrounded transformation, a kind of loose canon of creativity giving rise to a random sense of freedom. When it testifies with the Holy Spirit, its transformations are themselves transformed so that all of its creativity in its many variations throughout the whole field of human action points toward the same origin and destiny as the Holy Spirit: God became human in Jesus Christ. Although operative throughout Scripture, the most explicit text is I Corinthians 2:10–12, cited at the beginning of Chapter One. Also, Romans 8:16 refers to a bipolar relational unity between the two spirits, as do all other biblical references to a dialectical identity. One of the most interesting is Philippians 2:12–13. All of these texts point to the pervasive theme of an appropriate analogy of the Spirit, which calls the human spirit out of its futility and perversity into the light of the Divine Spirit, where, and only where, it can be true to itself without losing its distinctive nature as *human* spirit and human *spirit*.

Sixth, and finally, the analogy of the Spirit that ultimately calls for a transformation of the human spirit makes it clear that beyond *imago dei* and sin as basic anthropological categories, a third category must be added: the new creation in Christ. Although this might seem to be a subcategory under *imago dei,* the image restored, from an anthropological standpoint, significant changes in the structure of human nature occur that need to be accounted for both theologically and psychologically. Whether one speaks of justification and sanctification, conversion and walking in the Spirit, or new being and the life in Christ, a category in which nearness to God and distance from God are combined in a dialectical identity, such as "I-not I-but Christ" or "I-not I-but the Father," must be laid out and discussed. Indeed, it is only from this standpoint that we can finally, freely, and adequately address the issue of the "I" in the dominant question of this book, "Why do I live it?"

Interdisciplinary Methodology

The interactionist theories of human development and the theological understanding of the human as spirit may work together to preserve the integrity of both disciplines, yield up new insight for both sides, and disclose new dimensions of the human phenomena in question. In setting up this methodology, there is a wide spectrum of possible approaches. The method I propose and use here is to combine the view from above with the view from below. In working from the human sciences into theology in the order of this chapter, that same method has been at work. It is the method stated by T. F. Torrance when he describes the natural sciences as becoming subsciences under the "science of the theology."

Three points need to be made about this methodology. First, the natural or human science involved must undergo a transformation whereby its limitations and implicit rejection of theological concerns must be negated in order that its positive findings can be appropriated by cognate theological themes in the bipolar unity that is the essential shape of this method. Second, this bipolar unity is definitively set forth in the Chalcedonian formulation of the person of Jesus Christ. As one person who is both fully divine and fully human, he provides the living reality by which and from which this method derives its structure, historicity, universality, and ultimate credibility. Third, the essential character of this bipolar relational unity is described by Karl Barth as an "indissoluble differentiation," "inseparable unity," and "indestructible order." The last of these three essential characteristics of the Chalcedonian understanding refers to the asymmetry that pertains between the divine and the human in Christ, with the divine exercising logical and ontological priority over the human.

Some may see this entire approach as a Christological imperialism. It is, rather, a Christological answer to the question other interdisciplinary methodologies fail to address, and so they unwittingly introduce the very dualism that Barth, via Torrance, has managed to overcome. To relate theology and human sciences by existentialism and correlation via a philosophy of culture (Paul Tillich), a phenomenological method (Edward Farley), an anthropological and linguistic method (George Lindbeck), a structuralist method (James Fowler), a philosophy of being (Thomas Groome), or a process philosophy (Don Browning) is begging the question. These otherwise important and far-reaching positions tacitly introduce a third theme by which theology and nontheological disciplines are held together and interrelated. Obviously, in these approaches, the ruling principle and consequent outcome are neither theology nor human science, but precisely the *tertium quid*.

In Torrance's analogy between natural theology and the history of modern science, this lapse into a *tertium quid* reductionism is like revisiting pre-Einsteinian geometry; it enters into the wholeness and integrity of revealed theological understandings to divide the reality that is held together by Christ into fragments held together by nothing more than the speculative preference of the interpreter. Culture and existence, being, structures, language, phenomenology, and general philosophical understandings are all held together in him; he is not held together by them or with anything else. I hope the following chapters will make good on the claim that integrity on both sides of the theology-science dialogue can be maintained and that illumination may work both ways between theology and the study of human development when this Christomorphic methodology is employed in the context of the universal human experience of development through time.

From this position, we can recognize that "He [Christ] himself is the whole."[24] Although Jesus Christ is "single, unitary, consistent and free from contradiction, yet for all his singularity and unity his form is inexhaustibly rich." Thus, it is not merely legitimate but mandatory that "faith should continually see and understand the forms of Christ in new lights and aspects."[25] "He does not present himself in one form but in many—indeed, he is not in himself uniform but multiform. How can it be otherwise when he is . . . eternally rich."[26] Thus, as manifest in Christ, the fundamental relationality with which we have to do is infinitely varied and rich, but always marked by the "indissoluble differentiation," "inseparable unity," and "indestructible (asymmetrical) order" that is evident in his person.[27] In this understanding, the person of Christ replaces all metaphysics of being or becoming. To paraphrase Kierkegaard, Jesus Christ is the rock on which metaphysics suffers shipwreck.[28] By implication, then, the interplay between theology and the human sciences properly reflects his person when the Chalcedonian characteristics of their relationality[29] are determinative.

Illustrations of the Methodology

In her illuminating work on Karl Barth in pastoral counseling, Deborah van Deusen Hunsinger provides this concise illustration.[30] In Jesus' healing of the paralytic, Jesus first says, "My son, your sins are forgiven" (Mark 2:5), but on seeing the Scribes' reaction, he says, "Why do you question in your hearts? Which is easier, to say to the paralytic, 'Your sins are forgiven' or to say 'Rise, take up your pallet and walk'?" Then Jesus demonstrates that he has the power to forgive sins, by healing the paralytic.

Barth's interpretation of this text, as Hunsinger shows, is in keeping with the Chalcedonian model of relationality. Healing and forgiveness are seen to occur in a differentiated unity. They occur together (unity), but each remains distinct (differentiation), and the divine power to forgive sins is understood as logically and ontologically prior to and independent of the act of healing (asymmetrical order). The two notions of healing and forgiveness are so ordered that forgiveness is free and unconditioned, but healing is seen as existing in the service of Jesus' power to forgive sins.

If we stress the paradoxical unity of his person as constituted by the relationships just mentioned, then another important point can be made. The ultimate determinative reality of all that is, is present in his person, and what Jesus does reflects accurately who he is. Thus, it follows that in the text, his very presence—and his presence alone—is sufficient to redefine the entire situation. In turn, this powerful event of forgiveness and healing occurs according to the fundamental bipolarity of his all-embracing person and presence.

The far-reaching methodological implications of this approach centers on the relational unity itself. If we recall the *analogia spiritus,* then it is evident that in the interdisciplinary relationship between theology and the human sciences, we are seeking the present and manifest unity of Christ's Person in whatever issue may be at stake.

The human sciences are the human spirit attempting to understand itself, but by itself it is a loose canon of creativity, accordingly, the human sciences are a baseless search for the ground of the human spirit. This search is doomed to repeat in its outcome the same essential shortcomings and limitations that drove the human spirit to begin the search. Thus, the results are disappointing and cut down to the measure of what the human spirit in its disjunctive relation to God can grasp.

To illustrate this, I take a page from John Milbank's challenging study, *Theology and Social Theory.*[31] Milbank recognizes that current leaders in the field of the sociology of religion (Clifford Geertz, Peter Berger, Thomas Luckmann, Robert Bellah, and Niklas Luhmann) are fundamentally followers of Talcott Parson's grand theory of social action, which is in the final analysis a tension-reduction pattern maintenance system. Milbank insists that this connection pertains even when it is denied. Such a sociologist may say (albeit in a more complex manner), "The function of the Eucharist is to bind together the disparate elements of the Christian community." But since this explains a phenomenon in terms of what it is and does, it not only verges on tautology, but it reduces an essentially theological reality to a universalizing abstraction doing violence to the intrinsic significance of the event.

My approach to such a reductionistic account is different from Milbank's, and it is in keeping with the Chalcedonian model of bipolar relational unity, as evident in the *analogia spiritus.* The negation of theological reality implicit in the social science interpretation of the Eucharist must itself be negated as a misunderstanding of the event, its purpose, and its meaning. Once negated, functionalist understandings contributed by social theorists may then be transformed into subsciences of theological understanding. As transformed, they can disclose human longings, needs, and patterns of behavior, but in an appropriate self-critical stance, they must recognize that they cannot grasp the purpose and meaning of what is at stake in such phenomena as the Eucharistic event from within the event itself. The essence of the event and why it is so vital to the Christian community cannot be made into an object of scientific inquiry, given the Newtonian or Enlightenment mentality and the underlying violence and depersonalization implicit in social science theory and method (Milbank).

An accurate understanding of the Eucharist depends on the Christomorphic relationality between God and humanity. The capacity of that relationality to influence the human spirit through faith and bring it under the direction and mercy of the Creator Spirit makes Christ's Person present in that sacred and transforming event. The presupposition of the gracious spiritual presence of Christ at the Eucharistic table does not eliminate the relevance and value of analysis and interpretation by the human sciences, but it alters the primary direction of such understandings (toward God, not humanity) and the way in which persons themselves are valued.

Thus, the social theory of the Eucharist gets transformed, and the integrative reality is not simply a Durkheimian communalism designed to intensify preestablished beliefs; rather, the Spiritual Presence of Christ emerges, transforming socialization and sociology into a new kind of communion, the koinonia: the communion-creating presence of Jesus Christ. Koinonia is thoroughly social, but not able to be socialized; persons are present to each other in ways not able to be fully grasped by functional categories because the fullness of the communion is the premise, not the outcome, of relationships in the koinonia. Nevertheless, human science categories are useful for analyzing and breaking down false understandings of the spirit and spiritual life, and for supplying basic categories that enable theology to deepen its own self-understanding. Thereby, koinonia may become more self-aware and self-critical lest it degenerate into role play or simply another liminal experience.

Conclusions

The methodology used in this book is constructed in a fashion consistent with the interactionist views of human development and the focus in theological anthropology on the human spirit as the lost image of God in human nature. As such, it has the following characteristics:

1. It will be Christocentric, after the pattern of Chalcedon. As the richness of this pattern is transposed into various nontheological or

paratheological contexts, we will speak of the pattern in more formal terms as Christomorphic.

2. It will be focused on the human spirit in its relation or disrelation to *Spiritus Creator.* The proper relation between these two is Christomorphic.

3. It will understand the dynamics of both the human spirit and the Creator Spirit as transformational. As all creation lies under the burden of the lost image of God in persons and the brokenness of all contingent orders of creation, transformation into conformity with Christ as the restored image of God and mediator of the redemption of all creation characterizes the mission of the Creator Spirit.

4. It understands that the human sciences are to become subsciences of this Christomorphic approach through a transformation. This transformation will be under the agency of the Creator Spirit, who will negate any presuppositional negation of theological reality and reappropriate human science findings for the concretization, illumination, or application of theological categories as they come to bear on human experience.

5. Consistent with the Christomorphic character of this methodology, theology and the human sciences will enter into a relationality that assumes that theological categories have ontological priority over those in the human sciences. However, it is the relationality, the dynamism of the exchange between these fields of inquiry, that is the reality to be prized. In human science, this is to stress the critical and constructive development of the human spirit. As it joins with the Creator Spirit, there is a bipolar witness to the redemption and consummation of creation in Jesus Christ. Taken together, human spirit and Creator Spirit constitute the relational wholeness of Jesus Christ present to us and effective for us in the immediacy of experience.

6. Finally is an implication drawn from these implications. Employing the Chalcedonian model has important significance for the distinct views of time operative in developmental perspectives, on the one hand, and in theological perspectives, on the other. Chalcedon predicts that these two views of time are paradoxically unified.

In regard to this last conclusion, note that in his intriguing novel, *Einstein's Dreams,* Alan Lightman inquires imaginatively into Einstein's ruminations in the last few months before he finished his special theory of relativity in 1905. Each chapter is a fable that conjures up a different view of time. In one, time is circular, so the people in this realm must repeat their life's events over and over again. In another, time is split into three dimensions, all dimensions taking place side by side simultaneously, and persons must decide how to live in a multidimensional time.

To put human development in a theological context is to introduce a relationality between two dimensions of time that are not easily reconciled. One transcends and embraces the full amplitude of chronological time, and the other is bound to repeat certain stages in chronological sequence. To live in two-dimensional time, understood this way, is to live always between continuity and surprise; both have human and divine implications. Thus, transformational time, combining coherence and insight, characterizes both human spirit and the Creator Spirit and describes the paradoxical unity of the otherwise disparate temporal dimensions.

Living in the relationality between the two dimensions is to understand that any event will be multiplied by two: human development in time and the action of the eternal God that embraces all time, and that duality inevitably has transformational potential. For example, in the argument for infant baptism, it is said that what God does in the act of baptism represents a once-for-all-time event. Yet as development unfolds for the baptized infant, he will confirm in chronological time and in a way suitable to development what has been established in baptism. This is a witness to the transforming work of God's Spirit in the life of the young believer. There is no way to bridge these two views of time unless the Spirit of God, the "go-between God," makes the connection between time and eternity according to the bipolarity of Chalcedon.

The paradigmatic instance of baptism, in which the child receives his identity in Christ by the power of his Spirit, reveals an ongoing paradoxical relationality between developmental time and God's eternity.

The basic implication for the study of human development is that, from a theological standpoint, it is possible to see two events separated in developmental time, say, one at age five and another in young adulthood, as making essentially the same theological point. For instance, when the young child and the young adult affirm their faith in Jesus Christ against the opinions of their peers who are well known to be opposed to their faith, it will mean something different developmentally in each case, but it embodies the same theological truth. Analogous to baptism, what God has put into the person is definitive; each one of these persons knows without a doubt that the significance of Christ in his life is more important and more significant for who he is than anything his peers can do to him, for him, or against him. Again, appropriating that truth will vary from stage to stage, but from the standpoint of the revelation of God in Christ, human reality is transformed and redefined by the faithful witness at any age.

NOTES

1. G. Stanley Hall, *Adolescence: Its Psychology and Its Relations to Physiology, Anthropology, Sociology, Sex, Crime, Religion, and Education* (New York: Appleton Publishers, 1908).

2. J. B. Watson, *Behaviorism* (London: Kegan, Paul, 1925); B. F. Skinner, *Science and Human Behavior* (New York: Macmillan, 1953).

3. Noam Chomsky, in J. Fodor and J. Katz, *The Structure of Language* (Upper Saddle River, N.J.: Prentice Hall, 1964), chap. 21.

4. An important example of this can be found in Robert Kegan's discussion of Nancy Chodorow's *The Reproduction of Mothering* and a reworking of the Oedipus complex for postmodern thinking. See *In Over Our Heads: The Mental Demands of Modern Life* (Cambridge, Mass.: Harvard University Press, 1994).

5. Ernest Jones, *The Life and Work of Sigmund Freud*, 3 vols. (New York: Basic Books, 1953–1957).

6. David Bakan, *Sigmund Freud and the Jewish Mystical Tradition* (London: Free Association Books, 1990).

7. See Robert Coles, *Erik H. Erikson: The Growth of His Work* (Boston: Little, Brown, 1970).

8. Erik H. Erikson, *Gandhi's Truth on the Origins of Militant Nonviolence* (New York: Norton, 1969), and *Young Man Luther: A Study in Psychoanalysis and History* (New York: Norton, 1958).

9. To focus on Piaget is not to ignore the many criticisms and debates that have surrounded Piaget's work, even in its most sophisticated form (see *Language and Learning: The Debate Between Jean Piaget and Noam Chomsky*, ed. Massimo Piattelli-Palmarini [Cambridge, Mass.: Harvard University Press, 1980]). However, as with other key figures in this book, Piaget has set the issues in the study of intelligence, and most often his opponents get their own stance by defining their position relative to his. For our purpose, it is the development of mathematical, scientific, and linguistic intelligence that seems least likely to yield up the universal understanding of the human spirit we are seeking. Therefore it is precisely the most important place to look if we want a test case that has both rigor and richness.

10. According to Harvard psychologists Roger Brown, *Social Psychiatry* (New York: Free Press, 1965), p. 197, and Jerome Bruner, *Toward a Theory of Instruction* (Cambridge, Mass.: Harvard University Press, 1966), pp. 6–7.

11. Fernando Vidal, *Piaget Before Piaget* (Cambridge, Mass.: Harvard University Press, 1994).

12. Howard E. Grueber and J. Jacques Vonesche, eds., *The Essential Piaget* (New York: Basic Books, 1977).

13. Wolfhart Pannenberg, *Anthropology in Theological Perspective,* trans. Matthew J. O'Connell (Philadelphia, Pa.: Westminster Press, 1985), chap. 7.

14. Jean Piaget and Rolando Garcia, *Psychogenesis and the History of Science,* trans. Helga Feider (New York: Columbia University Press, 1989).

15. For further information than is presented here, see Carl G. Jung, *Memories, Dreams, and Reflections* (New York: Pantheon Books, 1973).

16. A more complete understanding of the concept of spirit, as it is used in this book, has been developed with coauthor W. Jim Neidhardt in *The Knight's Move* (Colorado Springs: Helmers and Howard, 1993). Here the logic of the spirit is given expression in the larger contexts of history and the physical sciences.

17. Wolfhart Pannenberg, *Anthropology in Theological Perspective,* p. 15.

18. Wolfhard Pannenberg, *Systematic Theology,* vol. 1, trans. Geoffrey W. Bromiley (Grand Rapids, Mich.: 1991), p. 6.

19. T. F. Torrance, *Transformation and Convergence in the Frame of Knowledge* (Grand Rapids, Mich.: Eerdmans, 1984), p. 294.

20. T. F. Torrance, *Space, Time, and Resurrection* (Grand Rapids, Mich.: Eerdmans, 1976).

21. Karl Barth, *Church Dogmatics,* ed. T. F. Torrance and G. W. Bromiley, III/2 (Edinburgh: T & T Clark, 1975), p. 437.

22. See Loder and Neidhardt, *The Knight's Move.*

23. George Hendry, *The Holy Spirit in Christian Theology* (Philadelphia: Westminster Press, 1976), pp. 96–117.

24. Barth, *Church Dogmatics,* IV/1, p. 20.

25. Ibid., IV/1, p. 763. The references here are to Barth's *Church Dogmatics,* but the basically Barthian position developed in this chapter is appropriated through T. F. Torrance, particularly in his seminal article, "The Natural Theology of Karl Barth," in *Transformation and Convergence,* chap. 9.

26. Ibid., p. 763.

27. Ibid., III/2, p. 437.

28. Søren A. Kierkegaard, *Philosophical Fragments,* trans. David F. Swenson (Princeton, N.J.: Princeton University Press, 1962).

29. In his recent work on the postmodern mentality, Robert Kegan, *In Over Our Heads: The Mental Demands of Modern Life* (Cambridge, Mass.: Harvard University Press, 1994), sec. 4, describes the move from modern to postmodern as recognizing relationality as definitive of polarity, rather than stressing fixed polarities, which then generate a relationship between them. This corresponds to the Christian theological understanding of life in the Spirit and the Spiritual Presence of Christ by whom all ultimate bipolar dichotomies are held in an asymmetrical differentiated unity.

30. Deborah van Deusen Hunsinger, *Theology and Pastoral Counseling* (Grand Rapids, Mich.: Eerdmans, 1995), pp. 65–69.

31. John Milbank, *Theology and Social Theory* (Oxford: Blackwell, 1994), esp. pp. 104ff.

3

HUMAN DEVELOPMENT REENVISIONED

THE CASE OF HELEN

BEFORE ME SAT a tall, lanky woman with straw blond hair, dressed in overalls, sneakers, and a slept-in t-shirt. She was crouched in her chair, knotted with tension like a cornered animal, her face swollen with thinly suppressed rage. In subsequent sessions, she would assume the same posture and dig blood out of her arms with an open paper clip, growling under her breath, as she did now, that she was going to "kill him!" Who was she going to kill? A male graduate student in her Ph.D. program, who always managed to put her down and make her look stupid in seminars.

The Struggle of Her Spirit

There was a positive side of this potentially violent first interview. Helen had been reluctantly willing to come for counseling on a referral from her academic adviser. Her explanation for coming was guarded, suffused with resentment and suspicion. But unexpectedly, and to my surprise, something I said genuinely amused her. Like a sudden glimpse of buried sunlight, there came a truly engaging smile, the very antithesis of her dark determination to kill. This sudden shift in affect did not have the schizoid qualities one might expect; the smile was a brief disclosure of an underground stream of light, which was to me an invitation to keep going and to look deeper.

In the counseling that I do, the contract includes the usual accounting of procedures, expected times of meeting, the assurance of confidentiality, and safety for self-disclosure.[1] In addition, I say that the counseling goes on in the presence and under the guidance of the Holy Spirit. I then told Helen that this can include prayer, since we may want to talk to the One who is doing the healing.

Before I could say another word, she lunged out of her chair, shouted in my face, "Prayer! Oh, for God's sake!" raged out of the office, and slammed the door. I let her go without responding. Her reaction was too strong even for someone already fuming. Fortunately, we had already set the date for the next session. When the time came, she was there. I knew she had heard me well, and her return was her response.

I said nothing about the previous session, nor did I raise the issue of prayer. Instead, I listened, and she began to tell me her story. She was twenty-six years old, the oldest of three children in a working-class family. She was born and lived in a small town in Kansas, where everybody knew everybody else. Helen had been conceived as a "substitute child," after her mother had lost a little boy who was stillborn, about ten months before Helen's birth. The problem was that Helen was the wrong sex, and maternal resentment against Helen was there from the outset.

The compensating factor was that Helen was the apple of her father's eye. He delighted in his little blond-haired girl with the striking smile. He liked to see her dressed in pink because it set her off to the best advantage, and he even had her room painted pink. Eventually there were other children, but Helen, the oldest, was by far the brightest and the most assertive.

When she was ten years old, she went with her father to her girlfriend's house, where it was assumed that she would play with her friend outside while her father talked with her friend's mother. But Helen grew tired of playing in the backyard and wandered into the house in search of her father. She found him and her friend's mother undressed in the mother's bedroom. They told Helen they were doing exercises, but Helen was not persuaded.

When Helen told her mother, her family collapsed; humiliated, the father left town, deserting Helen's mother and the children. This forced Helen's mother to take additional work scrubbing floors in the local theater to keep food on the table. Helen remembered walking downtown with her mother, carrying the cleaning equipment past their neighbor's house, whose undisguised scorn for this tainted family made Helen cringe inside. At school it was worse; the children taunted her, "Nyah, nyah. Where's your father? Where's your father? Hee, hee, hee!"

Helen sought every way possible to avoid the other children on the way to school. She would go early and hide behind the building while the other children played in front. Her revenge was to be smarter and more tough-minded than any of the other children. However, what she gained in intellectual respect did not compensate for what she had lost in self-esteem.

The loss turned into anger, aggression, drugs, wild behavior, and attacks against other members of her family, schoolmates, and teachers. She was eventually relocated in another family, another town, another school, and so she began her brilliant climb up the academic ladder, eventually to college and graduate school in history.

She was taken in by a Baptist pastor and his wife. This turned out to be a highly manipulative situation in which Helen managed to get her way through intimacy with the pastor at the expense of his marriage relationship. She got a solid dose of Baptist theology, but it was laced with hypocrisy, so it generated deep cynicism. Seeing the faith practiced with distorted intention and empty assurances made the spiritual life a sham and mockery. It is no wonder she railed against prayer; it had been part of the problem. But, irony of ironies, she had learned more than she realized, and this eventually became the key to the solution.

Our sessions unfolded in an uncertain set of moves on Helen's part to manipulate the relationship so she could gain control over what happened in our interactions. Finally, after several months of struggling with manipulative behavior and gradually building trust, she said, "Why were you so eager to pray at the beginning, and now you don't want to pray anymore?"! The question came forth as a mixture of aggression, blame, and a plea for help. She seemed a bit embarrassed to ask for what she had so violently rejected at the beginning, but she was also blaming me for not helping her on her own terms, even though she knew her terms are what got her into trouble. So we prayed.

At first she wanted to confess her sins, which by now had exceeded her father's, and I was to give her absolution. This I did, and she seemed finally to be glad to surrender some of the control to the One who heard us and gave absolution. But there was no significant change in her outward behavior. When she left the office, she did not walk, she marched. She had a case of bruxism, but the teeth grinding in her sleep did not stop, and it seemed to me that the motivation to kill had not significantly abated.

The Awakening

One night the telephone rang, and Helen was on the other end. "Dr. Loder! Dr. Loder! I've got to see you right now!" It was her usual slightly husky, take-command tone of voice, but it had a different sound. She said she could not tell me about it; she had to see me. Part of me was afraid she had killed the graduate student and was going to show me the body, but the other part, aided by my drowsiness, decided to hold the boundaries we had agreed on. "Not now. In the morning." Over her protests, we set the time.

When we met the next morning, she asked, in her familiar officious manner, "Dr. Loder, have you ever been thrown to your knees?" When I asked what she meant, she gave me the following account.

In desperation the previous night, she had about decided to kill herself. "Why do people go away?" was the question she had turned over and over in her mind and repeated in almost every session. Given her history, the superficial meaning of the question was clear enough, but the answer was not to be found there. When her father left, she knew it was her fault that the family collapsed. She hated her smile because he had loved it so much, but when he left, she vowed never to smile or cry again. She hid under the porch and put toothpicks in her cheeks to inhibit both her smile and her tears. She would grit her teeth and fight through it all, but it had only come to this degrading conclusion. No form of expiation, from toothpicks to prayer, had worked. That night the intensity of the emotional pain reached its climax when she took all her academic recommendations, spread them out on the bed, and demanded that they speak to her. But, of course, they just lay there and silently recounted in each case what a brilliant, competent student she was: academic honors, top of the class, with a great career ahead of her.

In a rage, she started to jerk books out of her bookcase, hurling them against the walls and the door. She was building up to some way of destroying herself. Fortunately she did not really have a plan, but she certainly did have the motivation. Finally, as the book-banging rage mounted, she came suddenly to a Bible that had been given to her as a parting gift of friendship by some friends she had met in Germany. They were returning to Poland, and they had given Helen this Bible as a parting gift of friendship. When she saw the Bible with the marker in it, it stopped her. She couldn't throw that against the wall; she had to know what text the marker designated. When she opened the Bible, it was John 16, and she started to read at verse 12, "I still have many things to say to you, but you cannot bear them now. When the Spirit of truth comes . . ."— and she was thrown to her knees. The Spirit came upon her with an intensity that far exceeded her rage as the heavens exceeded the ceiling of her room, so now prayer was everything!

In our subsequent sessions, we would talk briefly, but before I could say much, she would interrupt, "All right! Are we gonna pray or not?!" Three-fourths of every session thereafter was devoted to prayer.

But didn't she already *have* the answer? Why did we have to go on after the rage was broken and prayer became so real to her? It is not hard to see that the Holy Spirit had come upon her in an extraordinary way, testifying to Jesus Christ, even as Jesus was testifying to the Spirit according to John's account. The text had become the Word of God to her just like it was supposed to, but she still marched! And she still ground her teeth in the night. In effect, the Holy Spirit had acted decisively, but the work of healing was not done. The human spirit had yet to be unbound from its perversity, fears, and desperation. Although God had acted, she had yet to receive inwardly and to appropriate spirit-to-Spirit what had been accomplished. She read some charismatic literature and prayed in the Spirit for more of the Holy Spirit, so the focus of her life had changed dramatically.

The Purgation

Now that Helen had been released from her bondage to the past, we could go back into it and get it healed. We began in the intensity of prayer to talk together. Confident of the Spiritual Presence of Christ, we talked almost as three persons, rather than using more familiar forms of prayer. Although we began in conventional terms and language, there nearly always came a time when we ceased praying and found the initiative behind the prayer shifted from us to God, and we were "being prayed." The intensity of these times is hard to overstate, but in that time of transition, openness to the Spiritual Presence of Christ seemed completely accessible, and Helen asked to be taken back into the past and be shown how Christ (the One who had thrown her to her knees) *was* there and what he would have done to set it right had he been invited into the situation then as he was now. Would he now do this in the events as they still lived in her mind? What needs to be healed now? Take us there, take us there now.

Although we seemed led into this process, we apparently needed more confidence in it. The first episode was on the surface trivial, but it seemed to have almost unfathomable implications, a foretaste of the healing to come. Helen said, "He's taking me back to the time after my father left, and it was Easter, but no one gave my little sister an Easter basket. So I got one for her with candy eggs in it. But some of the neighborhood boys came and stole her basket, candy eggs and all. She was crushed and crying. I knew it was my fault that this had happened."

Now Jesus is invited into the scene; he knelt beside the child, comforted her, and said, "I will be your Easter basket for you."

The multidimensional impact of this imagery in prayer was stunning. He was not only bringing comfort through his Spiritual Presence made visible to Helen, but implicitly undoing the guilt that Helen felt because her mother said there was no money to celebrate Easter; the father had left, and it was Helen's fault. But the real point is much larger: the redemptive power of Easter was a historical and ontological event, precisely to the end that all our sins may be forgiven. Helen was confirmed in her act of concern for her sister, so the event occurs in a relationship of care. Much more is implied, but the central point for our process was that you can count on these images to lead you into the truth; the particular will embody the universal because in it the Spirit of truth is at work.

Our counseling relationship extended over three years, so there were several other such images that appeared in the deep prayer situation. Three others, in particular, including the climatic episode, make major points about the healing of the human spirit through the Holy Spirit's formation of our prayers.

The second episode occurred in the school yard. Helen is hiding behind the schoolhouse, waiting for the bell to ring so she can run into class without having to face the taunts of her schoolmates. Again, in deep prayer, Helen says, "I am hiding behind the school. I am scrunched down in a corner of the building because it is cold. I can hear the other children playing out in front, but I am afraid of them—I am afraid they might come and find me.

"I look out from my hiding place, and he is coming toward me. He kneels down beside me. He takes out my heart. It is hard, cold, like a stone. Then he takes out his heart and he puts it into me. Now I begin to feel warm all over. He takes me by the hand and leads me out in front. He confronts the other children, saying, 'This is Helen. She is a friend of mine!'"

The desperate fear of being shamed and made an object of ridicule is silenced, shut down, and replaced by an empowered warmth that protects and heals at the same time. It is as if the harmony of the universe embodied in that moment put shame to shame, and the uncompromising, unqualified affirmation of real friendship with God suddenly put all other friendships in their right place, making them compelling, truly, and profoundly heart warming.

But still Helen marched and ground her teeth when she walked across the campus where my office was located.

The third episode was, so far, the most difficult of all for Helen, since she was taken back to that dreaded bedroom where she is standing outside the closed door. She had recounted the scene before, but now she is there in prayer, and Jesus is standing before the door. She says, "I can see him standing there. I know he is going in there, and he wants me to come in with him. But I am not going! But he goes in anyway. I know he wants me to follow him, but I am not going!"

At this point Helen leaped out of her chair and headed for the office door, but I grabbed her arm and, after a brief struggle, brought her back into the room and set her down on the sofa. We tried again: "I know I am supposed to go in there, but I don't think I can. I put my hand on the doorknob, and the door opens. . . . Oh, it's all light in here! My father and that woman are fully dressed, standing with Jesus. I go in and take my father by the hand, and we kneel by the bed. We ask forgiveness of God, and we forgive each other."

The memory does not live in her with the dark, terrifying significance it had before. She had let it come up, walked back into it, and did what she could never have done in her own strength. Forgiving her father, and implicitly the woman, she was also receiving forgiveness from Jesus as the specific tangible manifestation of the Spirit who filled that place.

But still Helen marched and ground her teeth.

The Illumination

One day as we entered prayer, she said, "I know God wants me to go back to my birth." Helen's relationship with her mother had never been as close as with her father before the breakup, and afterward the relationship deteriorated even further. Helen came downstairs the morning she was thirteen years old. "Good morning, Mother. It's my birthday; I'm thirteen years old!" And her mother wheeled around and slapped her across the face. Now it was time to reenter the most powerful relationship of her life, but on new and different terms. So we did: "I can see the hospital room, the beige walls, the white steel bed. I can smell the room, all medicinal, clean and spotless. But I am strapped down on a little table. I am shaking and screaming, and my mother is just staring at me. Something is wrong! Something is wrong! I can't stand her eyes. She just keeps staring at me. I'm still screaming! (A long silence.) I'm still screaming."

Sometimes in deep prayer, the resolving image comes to the other one. In this case it came to me. I said, "That's not you. That's Jesus. He's taken your place; he's become a child; he's suffering for you."

Suddenly Helen let go with a huge sigh and then, with exhilaration and excitement, she said, "He's holding me! He's holding me! We're dancing around the room together!" This was the ultimate triumph. Under the power of her mother's eye, she was terrified, and even in our prayer she could not get out from under those eyes. She could not even think of Jesus' presence in the room. Her spirit was paralyzed; something was irrevocably wrong. Helen, conceived as a replacement for her stillborn brother, was the wrong sex. She had been fundamentally and irreversibly wrong from the beginning. The Spirit had come and the image had told the truth; the source of fear, guilt, and corrosive resentment had not come upon her for the reasons she thought. The cry went up from the infant who in innocence knew with paralyzing fear that the primary source of her life was also the source of her agony. The more important truth is that the potential for evil apparent here is taken up in the innocence of Christ; in perfect innocence, he comes in and then takes up Helen, as if in the joy of the resurrection. She is not her mother's child; she is *his* child, and he delights in her as she delights in him.

The next time I saw Helen, she was dressed in a pink suit, wearing high heels, and she said, "I thank God for the woman he made me to be." It was always perfectly clear to us that this is not a general formula for how women are supposed to dress, but for Helen this was the most accurate set of symbols by which she could incorporate the full, cumulative impact of almost three years of regularly walking into deep prayer in the Spiritual Presence of Jesus Christ.

Toward Unification

The following spring, Helen completed her qualifying examinations and took a job teaching in a college that had never before in its over hundred-year history hired a woman on its faculty. When Helen and I parted, she said in reference to our three years of work together, "This belongs to the church."

The epilogue is quite compelling. When Helen left to take her teaching post, I gave her a picture of a little girl that hung in my office. The child is standing just on the threshold of an open door, as if she were about to come home from being outside. The picture was something we had often talked about in relation to Helen's coming "home" from being on the outside for so long. Her identification with the little girl was one way we would begin to talk and pray.

It had been several years since she had seen or talked to her mother or her father. She had heard indirectly that her father had returned, and he and her mother were reunited. So after getting started in her teaching position, she wrote to her parents and invited them to visit her. Somewhat to her surprise, they agreed to come. The picture of the little girl hung just at the threshold of her apartment door, so it was impossible to miss it on entering. When Helen's mother walked into the apartment, almost the first thing she did was point to the picture and say, "What a beautiful little girl!" It was a bit late, but it was absolutely correct.

Reflecting on Helen's Case

Reflecting on Helen's case within the Chalcedonian frame of reference is an attempt to understand the overall transformation of her spirit through the cumulative impact and mediatorial significance of a series of Christ-centered images. What she could see, and we could experience in prayer together, was her spirit being gradually unknotted, remolded, and liberated by the Spirit of Jesus Christ. Her spirit, turned inward by primal rejection, blame, guilt, and family violence, was tangibly called out of hiding by the Spiritual Presence of Christ, who was represented to her not only through an image but as the image of the very One who had thrown her to her knees. As the Divine and the human are paradoxically unified in the one person of Jesus Christ, so her spirit was drawn into unity with the Divine Spirit through him who mediates relational unity Spirit-to-spirit, without mixing or confusing the two spirits, holding the divine above the human, but eliminating neither one in favor of the other.

The fundamental drive behind the heterogeneous continuity of Helen's images is coherence.[2] Not only is the Christ of John 16 the Christ of the images, but the Spirit who drove her to her knees is the one empowering the Christ of the images to heal those emotionally crippling memories. The Spirit to which the Christ of John 16 pointed is the Spirit of truth about Helen, even as he is the One who makes it possible for Helen to recognize and appropriate the ultimate reality of him who in his very being is the truth. He is the truth because in the paradoxical unity of his person, humanity and divinity are in their definitive relationality. Jesus is what God means by true humanity, and the God revealed in Jesus is what God means by God. The continuity between the paradoxical unity of Christ's person and the paradoxical unity of the Spirit-to-spirit relationality that comes into being through Helen's transforming images is the key to recognizing her case as a Christomorphic transformation that thrusts her back into the world as God's new creation.

Helen's case points in the direction of my original hypothesis that the human spirit, for all its creative energy, will wander aimlessly through time without any sense of its true center of gravity unless it is seized by the Spirit of God. Then it may beg on its knees to be transformed and thereby be conformed to what God is doing in the world to make persons human the way Jesus was human. This is not to put faith in works, but this is the very work of faith to bring forth a Christomorphic bipolarity in the spiritual life of the believer.

When the so-called normal course of ego development is disturbed from the beginning, as it was in Helen's case, it is especially clear that the transformational power of the human spirit must be seen as transcending the constraints of any stage-development sequence or any distortions that may occur therein. This transcendence is why the human spirit is not only able to create and recreate the order that such stages introduce, but to generate different, even seemingly delinquent and potentially dangerous, new orders, so as to bring about in persons higher forms of psychophysical coherence and openness to the world and the universe. As subsequent chapters will show, "normal" will need to be redefined beyond ego-structured reality in terms of the coherence and openness that occurs when the ego is transformed by the Christomorphic relationality of human spirit and Holy Spirit.

Three Analytical Approaches

Certain analytical tools and methods of interpretation will help to establish the depth, power, and plausibility of what has been described so far. The three approaches follow roughly the familiar anthropological categories of body, soul, and spirit, but it is the whole of the person with which we are primarily concerned.

BODY (SOMA) The body is created out of the dust of the earth—the dust of disintegrating stars carrying precious carbon and other chemicals essential to life to the crust of the cooling earth. From the beginning of this book, I have argued that one's developmental history is rooted in the history of the universe. Thus, the power of integrative insights that create a coherence that transcends experience and, indeed, anything that has been previously learned or observed reflects the order of the universe. That which is radically and decisively new is recognizably important and powerful primarily because it has the power to give coherence to disjunctive fragments and place the knower in a surprisingly meaningful position in the world. Within the microcosm of human experience, the macrocosmic drive toward disintegration and death is undone; entropy is reversed, and new being appears, as in the birth of a child so also in the rebirth of human wholeness.

Helen's capacity to construct coherence out of the warring fragments of her life is the creative work of her spirit under the guidance, wisdom, and power of Christ's Spirit. What does this have to do with the human body? Isn't this all just psyche and spirit? Not if the hypothesis that we are physical beings first and only later, by the breath of God, become psyche and spirit. The whole psychophysical unity of the person, not merely certain of its parts, is at stake here. Indeed, this wholeness is essential to each of its parts as are the parts to the whole, so we must ask how Helen's experience is a physical event.

My hypothesis is that out of the structure of the universe and in response to its Author come the structures of the human brain. Helen as a psychoneurological being is created by the Author for such transforming experiences just as surely as she is created for language, mathematics, or the study of history. That is, what happened in Helen's case was already potentially present in her as a physical being; but that potentiality could not be actualized apart from the Author of all creation, the creation of Helen in particular.

Visions that emerge spontaneously to give new and unexpected order to persons and societies are not so unusual. Consider Anthony Wallace's studies of revitalization in disintegrating societies.[3] He cites nativistic and revivalistic movements, cargo cults, millenarian movements and describes the emergence of new order through a prophetic vision. That is, a prophet will arise in anomic societies. He will go into a trance, have a vision given to him from a divine being, and know from that vision how to revitalize that society. Such visions not only work to revive and heal the society, but the prophets are themselves healed of any infirmity they had prior to the vision.

When psychoneurologists investigated what happens in the prophet's brain, they came up with a model of intensification.[4] This is a model of what happens when the transformational dynamic of the human spirit, endemic to human development, discovery, and creativity, was totally immersed in resolving the dilemma of how to reconstruct life in a disintegrating social order. Such intensive immersion meant that ordinary constraints in maintaining ego control were abandoned, and the prophet fell into an altered state of consciousness where visions became accessible. The striking thing is the continuity between the visions and a workable social and political order that had yet to come into being. The visions tapped into a more profound order of creation that was inclusive of the prophet and his society. This is not magic; this is the discovery of the created order within a particular context of need.

The neurologists said that what is happening in the brain can be described as the interaction between two distinguishable neurological systems. The first system puts the person on guard, prepares for intentional action, and thrusts him into the world in a state of intense alertness to counter threats and achieve goals. This is an energy-generating, work-producing system. Called the ergotropic system (ET), it combines the left hemisphere, which is analytical, linguistic, and linear, with the sympathetic nervous system and the central nervous system. The second system puts the person at ease and performs housekeeping tasks of relaxing, eating, sleeping, and maintaining vegetative functions in the organism. This system, called trophotropic (TT), combines the right hemisphere, which is holistic, analogical, and spatial, with the parasympathetic and central nervous systems. Ordinarily the two systems interact and maintain a balance such that if a person is hard at work on a manuscript (ET), the smell of dinner (TT) may turn it off, and the person goes to eat and relax. Or if one is about to go to sleep and then hears a hand on the doorknob, immediately TT shuts off and ET takes over. This reciprocity describes in neurological terms the ordinary psychological behavior of a balanced ego seeking adaptation to its environment. However, the interaction between the two systems varies, and under conditions of intensifying disequilibrium, it gives rise to visions, myths, and images of transforming potential.

When Helen came to talk, the ET system was already outrunning the capacity of the opposite system (TT) to establish equilibrium on any steady basis so the interaction was already spinning into a new phase. What the neurologists determined was that there are four phases through which a person might go in order to restore equilibration through a transformation of the person and his or her world.

First was equilibrium, as already described. The second was passion and reversed reaction. This phase occurs when one's behavior has been so long governed by one system over against the other that any attempt to bring balance only intensifies the power of the first system. For example, any attempt to pacify or calm passionate anger (ET) may well intensify the anger. Helen's violent reaction to my suggestion of prayer in our first meeting can partly be explained in this way. On the other side, sometimes there are "women who love too much" (Norwood),[5] so even when they receive rejection, they intensify their determination to give love and do acts of kindness to the rejecting lover in the face of rejection.

Passion or intense involvement in an issue or conflict is crucial to releasing the power of the spirit into the situation, and the spirit, in turn, creates visions. However, passion is a two-edged sword; misdirected, it can drive one to self-destruction. Helen's original passion was to achieve, to overcome all rejection and abuse by her hard work, her angry drive to excel, and so to prove her worth beyond any shadow of a doubt. But her passionate anger yielded up a false vision because no vision of the all-powerful achiever putting down all challenges could get her out of her

deep personal dilemmas. The antithesis to this overly determined ET system had to be more powerful than the false passion and the false vision if
anything were to change.

The third phase in the intensification model is new vision. Neurologically this occurs when one system is firing intensely for a prolonged period
of time unabated. The result of this overload on one system is that both
systems begin firing at once, and here is where a trancelike state may occur.
Helen was "thrown to her knees," collapsed into prayer, and overcome by
the power of her spirit in communion with Christ's Spirit. Neurologically,
passion is crucial because it is through passion that both systems can fire
together. That is, the analytical, critical, linear left hemisphere that differ-
entiates life and death, God and human, good and evil, particular and universal, is suddenly combined with the unifying, analogical sense of the
whole that comes from the right hemisphere. Ordinarily, the right hemisphere cannot communicate a sense of wholeness or totality to the left.
This is the case because although the two hemispheres are in continual
communication through the corpus callosum, the large band of fibers that
hold the two hemispheres together, the holistic messages from the right are
continually chopped up and seriated as they move into the left hemisphere.
However, when the holistic message is communicated with passion it
comes through the limbic system, which is in charge of the regulation and
distribution of emotion; then it combines with the left hemisphere, and one
senses a differentiated whole with surprising suddenness. Consider how
one may be unexpectedly moved by a line of poetry, and think how visions
are all the more powerful than poetry. Passion crosses the gap between the
two hemispheres, combining right and left in visions that are differentiated
and holistic at the same time. They are all-consuming, as the passion must
be if the vision is to appear with transforming force.

Helen was stunned by her sense of the spiritual presence of Christ
throwing her to her knees. His presence was a differentiated unity; he was
all in all for her at the moment, yet his identity was perfectly clear: it was
the spiritual presence of the One who was fully God and fully human. The
Author of the universe could fall upon her with the full force of his love
because he had made her from the dust of the earth for just such a love.

There is a fourth phase, as remarkable neurologically as it is spiritually.
This is the numinous, imageless passage into the absolute unity of all
things. Here no-thingness is experienced as more real than the ordinary
state of ego balance because it conveys the ultimate sense of unity in
which all being and nothing are the same. This can be attained only by a
kind of *via negativa* and is implicit in the visions of God in St. Augustine,
Hildegaard, Teresa of Avila, Meister Eckhart, and others. Helen did not

glimpse this until she uttered her great sigh of relief in the final vision. At the moment in which one enters absolutely into the Divine Presence, there can be no image at all; the actual reality of the Divine Presence cannot be made into an object of our perceptual imagination. For that moment *we* are the objects composed into *his* presence by his initiative. But then the images rush in to fill the otherwise incomprehensible moment of such a pure and transparent awareness. When these images come, they are designed to help us comprehend the incomprehensible. Even here, neurology is not limited to the restorative images; it has its own way to convey the absolute.

The neurological foundation of this experience is the profoundly significant capacity of the brain to present to consciousness not only an ordered content but the very way in which that content is itself presented: the order itself, which in religious consciousness is a totality, a nonrepresentational cognition of the whole. Five observations on this neurological perspective as it pertains to Helen's experience are as follows:

First, although this might seem to be a reductive analysis of Helen's transformation, it is actually just the opposite. It says that we are all constituted, as was Helen, so as to sustain and give expression to these powerful transforming experiences. We are made for these events just as surely as we are made for language, mathematics, and physics, but the experiences of intensification require more concentration and passion than the usual practices of academic disciplines. Arguably, however, discovery in mathematics or creativity in literature requires the same order of intensity. This is not a reduction of Helen's experience, but a cosmological enlargement of it.

Second, the move in Helen's nighttime trauma from violence to grace is a move we subsequently replicated in prayer. As we entered prayer intensely and engaged the portions of the violence done to her, the vision of Christ appeared again and again to perform acts of healing. The drive in Helen was to make the connection between the universal and the particular—the connection between the Spirit of Truth who overwhelmed her and the hard particularities of her life's struggle. Her drive toward continuity, shutting down false passions and dispelling false visions, is the expression of her spirit in full agreement and cooperation with the Divine Spirit. This was not merely an act of will; her whole being, including her psychoneurological constitution, drove toward coherence as if it were a stolen birthright—for indeed it was. She had been created by God for the continuity toward which she strove in her spirit.

Third, in the movement back and forth from the vision, or the sense of absolute unity, to the particularities of ego-oriented life, Helen was experiencing the axis of spiritual development. The transformation that takes place on the divine-human axis is fundamentally different from the transformations that inhere in ego development. The former transforms the achievements of the latter, refocusing the purpose and meaning of all ego functions upon God.

Fourth, note that the coherent relationality between the sense of absolute unity and the particularity of human existence is Christomorphic. This formal pattern is substantive and personally powerful only when the vision is of the One who defines divine-human, life-death, true-false, and particularity-universality in his own person. Other images may point to this consummate vision in which the formal pattern becomes embodied, but when Jesus Christ himself is the vision, then the full power of the spiritual axis is released and all creation is implicated therein.

Finally, the consequence of practicing this pattern of spirituality is the deepening sense of a dialectical identity in which one continually senses the Divine Presence as the fundamental basis for declaring one's identity. I-not I-but Christ becomes the way one thinks of oneself. Thus, Helen declares, "This belongs to the church."

SOUL (PSYCHE) A second method of analysis will approach the fundamental unity of human nature using a psychological model. If we adopt a psychoanalytically and developmentally informed approach to Helen's case, we can begin with the recognition that she was twenty-six years old when she came to my office the first time. Developmentally, a young person at this age is in Erikson's view principally concerned with the issue of intimacy versus isolation.[6] Although these terms have fairly definite meaning in relation to each other in Erikson's thought, which we will discuss later in this book, their meaning in wider usage can serve to enrich his particular definitions. *Intimacy* derives from the Latin *intimus,* and refers to the innermost place in oneself at the core of one's identity. Here one may say correctly, "You may know what it is like to be me, but you will never know what is for *me* to be me." In an intimate relationship, what it is "for me to be me" is disclosed as openly as possible, each one to the other. When each side receives the other with accurate empathy, then a synergy is generated that can make such a relationship feel almost like an interpersonal trance. Whether identity is wrought primarily out of intimacy or is its precursor is an important debate, but in Helen's case, it is clear that her true identity emerges from the intimacy of prayer.

Isolation as a basic ego posture represents the chronic absence of intimacy and is constructed by the ego in response to repeated betrayal of "intimacies" risked in past relationships. The sensitive recoil into isolation from a wounded or betrayed intimacy recalls the etymological similarity between intimacy and intimidate, as in, "Why am I afraid to let you know me?" The pain of betrayed intimacy thrusts the ego back into the sense of void and nothingness, so isolation becomes increasingly a fortress against future betrayal. This fortress is built on the assumption that betrayal always haunts interpersonal relationships. Thus, ironically, it builds into its defense system what it would prefer to be rid of.

This developmental crisis runs deeper in Helen's psyche than in most others because the interpersonal attempts at intimacy in her personal history had been severely contaminated or betrayed. So when it comes to this developmental period, decisive for the intimacy question, her buried wounds come forth with redoubled force reminiscent of Freud's "return of the repressed."[7] Once the precipitating episodes occurred in her doctoral seminar, the conflict between intimacy and isolation hit her with the accrued power of a long-repressed rage. This reaction intensified the fearful prospect of an irreversible isolation and her never finding the longed-for intimacy; all of this lay behind the question that echoed through all our conversations: "Why do people go away?"

As she perceived it, her mother had rejected her without ever knowing her because Helen was not a male child, so she could not replace her stillborn brother. The measure of intimacy implied in the acceptance and genuine appreciation she received from her father had also betrayed her. He had left her to pick up the pieces and take the blame. This would have rendered her entirely powerless and potentially self-destructive were it not for her keen intelligence and remarkable memory. She fought her way back to credibility with her mind, but now this viciously competitive male graduate student had taken that power away. She had been disarmed at her one great point of strength, once again by a male who eroded her self-confidence. As a consequence, she had to come face to face with the inner turmoil she had fought off for so long by the aggressive use of her academic competence. When all this underground material hit her, it threatened to force her back into the terrifying shame and humiliation she experienced in her community and with her childhood peers, and back into her guilt for destroying the family from which she had so aggressively sought to extricate herself. It appeared at the outset that she was desperately afraid that her defenses, designed to protect her isolation from others and from herself, would be crushed in the traumatic collision between outside and inside, between humiliation continually coming from outside through her seminar and the concomitant shame and rage rushing up from the past, threatening to explode from within. Rather than be killed psychically, she would kill him first.

But what about that momentary but arresting smile? Maybe it was a covert invitation for me to become the lost father, but I inadvertently but effectively canceled that by suggesting prayer as a part of the process. At first, it felt to her more like rejection than an invitation to a more profound intimacy than she had ever known, so she stormed out and slammed the door.

Why did she come back? Hadn't she had enough rejection? I suspect it was because she had made an agreement to come at a certain time, and she could not tolerate any further guilt-engendering action on her own part. She did not want to be blamed anymore, even in her own head, and certainly not by God. However, there are, I think, deeper reasons, more tied into the implications of prayer as tacitly promising the deepest possible intimacy, but these comments must wait for the next section.

She did come back, and told me her story, a story that contained an obvious answer to her perennial question, "Why do people go away?" But surprisingly, any connection to her father's behavior or her own did not satisfy her. It was obviously not a situational question; it had the urgent force of an existential or theological issue. Along with this question, the thinly disguised rage continued to coexist with that spontaneous smile. But I could now see the smile was the ten-year-old child whose development was traumatically arrested at the time of her father's flight from the home. Making connections, disclosing associations, and my bearing with a lot of testing and manipulation enabled the process to become reassuring to the ten year old, and she began expressing herself more freely. Then *she* turned the whole process back to prayer, and I became not the potentially betraying father but the father confessor.

This psychodynamic line of thinking and interpretation can be helpful for the therapeutic redevelopment of the ego. One is reminded of Freud's stated goal of therapy: "to enable the patient to choose for or against the neurosis."[8] It was this procedure that Helen and I followed during the beginning weeks of our contract. However, as her spirit began to be liberated from the double-binds and traumatic shocks of her past, she sensed the limits of this approach and chose to return to prayer. Strictly speaking, the psychodynamic approach cannot accept the reality of prayer as part of the process. It is understood as the practice of an illusion, manifestation of a guilt neurosis, and valuable only so far as it enables the ego to adapt more adequately to its environment.

It is only in this sense that ego-oriented psychology can accept what might seem to be, on the surface, bizarre images as potentially healing. In Freud's famous case of Little Hans, where he first demonstrated the significance of childhood sexuality, it was precisely a bizarre oedipal fantasy lived out by Hans that brought healing to this five-year-old boy.[9] Thus, it might be possible in a similar frame of reference that Helen's bizarre images could be accepted: illusion constructed in the service of the ego. Is this what is happening in Helen's case? If not, why not?

Elsewhere I have argued that Little Hans's fantasies and similar healing images and visions are the creation of the human spirit.[10] The image or vision works in these cases as it works in Wallace's prophets, not because it is merely conflict resolving and tension reducing, as if adaptation were the only goal of human existence. After all, what is the source of coherence, the intelligibility, and workability of what has never before been conceived? Rather, the vision works because the transforming potential in the human spirit constructs what is radically new out of the physical and psychic resources of the person. Moreover, these resources implicitly extend beyond the history of the individual, beyond the human race, into the history of the universe, of which we are heirs. Here, given the appropriate conditions, the constructive power of the human spirit can draw from a profoundly ordered universe that has a personal Author.

The human spirit, whose origin is in the Author of the universe, can make remarkable leaps in the disclosure of hidden orders in the universe, which is why mathematics works. Thus, Nobel laureate Eugene Wigner wrote of "the unreasonable effectiveness of mathematics," and Einstein called it a "miracle."[11] It is said, recalling our relation to the history of the universe, that neurologically we are wired for mathematics, but it appears that we are just as surely wired for visions of new order regarding the proper place of humanity in the universe. To be sure, the human spirit generates images that resolve conflicts and help us get on with life, but to say that images take the form they do because of the shape of the adaptational conflict foreshortens understanding. The intervening issue is where these images come from such that they bring unprecedented order, heal minds, bodies, and even societies, and reveal hitherto unimagined coherence and intelligibility to consciousness. To follow the psychoanalytically oriented approach alone and by itself is to truncate the human spirit and trim its contributions to the size and shape of the human ego. The human spirit cannot be so constrained.

It was, I believe, some such realization as this that led Helen to want to pray. Her question necessarily involved redevelopment and resocialization at the level of ego function, but her spirit drove her issues deeper than resocialization could ever go. "Why do people go away?" had its roots in abandonment, powerlessness, and the potential sense of nonbeing that human beings can know only at the ground level of their existence, where they can ask with existential force: "Why do I live?" Helen was not pleading for an answer to her question as such. She was asking for—indeed, her spirit was pleading for—a reason to live.

Psychoanalytic thinking cannot touch that question because the ego is constructed to protect us from having to face that question directly. However, prayer runs deeper than the ego and its struggles to adapt and survive. Guided by the logic of her spirit, she sensed that she might come up with all kinds of insights that would illumine her past and help her ego to adjust and adapt, but she still would not have an answer to her most important question, the question raised for her by her very existence.

At the threshold of puberty, when this question erupts in some form for all adolescents, this devastated ten year old seized on that question and would not let go until she had an answer that would give her a reason to live. Only then could she cry and smile again without fear of betrayal. Now, in the context of this question, the developmental situation has itself become decisively theological.

SPIRIT (PNEUMA) In turning to this third approach to an interpretation of Helen, the emphasis shifts away from determinative influences of the past, analytical categories, cause-and-effect connections, and empirical proof. This occurs because the entire context of explanation has shifted from pragmatic human concerns to what God is doing in human lives and human history. The importance of the past, analysis, causality, and proof are not ignored, but now they are subordinated and transformed according to the meanings and purposes of God's Spirit as that Spirit brings Jesus Christ out of the remoteness of history into the immediate situation at hand.

We will be able to see that the four phases of spiritual development represent a transformation of the four levels of intensification, and passage through the phases represents a transformation of continuity, the backbone of intensification. Further, the intimacy that Helen sought, given her stage in human development, clearly had to go deeper than anything the psychology of the ego could grasp. Intimacy had also been transformed from a physical, emotional, and psychological reality to intimacy in relation to the Spiritual Presence of God, in whom intimacy is ultimately understood as unification. This is not to discount the previous two approaches since they enable this discussion of spirituality to avoid a reductionism upward, consuming of Helen's situation into global categories that may verge on spiritualism or gnosticism. The reality of Helen's case lives and breathes in the relationality between the concreteness of her psychophysical being and her transcending and transforming spirit, all in the power of God's Spirit.

What follows takes its direction from certain aspects of the classical tradition of spiritual development that are indicated in the subdivisions of the opening section of this chapter: awakening, purgation, illumination, and unification.

Awakening When Helen had her night of violence, she was suddenly awakened to the reality of the power of God; intuitively she knew that her questions were far deeper than psychological understandings could ever comprehend. Awakening in this spiritual sense is not within the purview and grasp of the human ego. Awakening in the Spirit is the outcry of the whole person who recognizes the vast abyss between herself and God, and simultaneously knows this is recognizable only because "the kingdom of God is at hand." That is, only the nearness and reign of the Holy God can make the awareness of such an abyss possible.

Helen's almost blind passion that night made it possible for the Spirit to shatter false visions of herself as hopelessly betrayed, victimized, and abandoned, unable to be loved, sold out to a game of academic achievement that could never answer her deepest questions and give her a reason to live. These false visions could be shattered that night partly because for months they were being gradually unearthed and disclosed in our sessions; now they could come out because she had come to hate them all with a vengeance. The danger lay in the fact that she was identified with them, so she hated herself. But what counseling could never do was transform that passionate hatred into a radical submission to God. In the logic of the Spirit, intensity is the key to new vision, so the response of the Spirit cannot be like that of the ego, which would be to shut down the passion and bring things under control. Rather, in keeping with the logic of the human spirit, the Creator Spirit will drive the dichotomy of her separation as deep as possible, then disclose, expose, and meet the infant panic curled up beneath the angry passion and false self-images. Such a convicting act drives the love of God so deep into her that the rage is uprooted, and the passionate vengeance against all that was false takes the form of passionate commitment to the truth: Helen is a beloved child begotten by God. The way to take vengeance on falsity is to commit everything to its opposite, so the Scripture she read announced just moments ahead of time that the Spirit of Truth would come. And it did, and she was awakened.

In the language of intensification, she was awakened to the disastrous incoherence in her relation to her self, to her society, to her culture, and above all to God. Although supremely competent in many ways, she absolutely did not fit anywhere with anyone or into any kind of future.

The abyss cut all the way through every aspect of her existence, so any effort she might make to rectify her situation was already contaminated because the agent herself was "all wrong." Her own efforts to fix it would only make it worse.

More profoundly, she was awakened to the reality of the Divine Presence, who makes the first aspect of her awakening possible and presents himself as its solution. In theological terms, this is the joy and satisfaction of being convicted of sin; were it not that the Kingdom of God is at hand, sin, as distance from God, would be too terrible to be recognized. Even if it were recognized, it could not be borne; to be convicted of separation from God is mortifying. However, the reign of the God who convicts is at hand to enable the mortifying conviction of sin to be borne, to be forgiven, and so to be passionately transformed into the fullest possible measure of gratitude.

Thus, Helen is first awakened to the abyss underlying her existence and then to an authentic spiritual life. Spiritual development is different from the ordinary life span, where the immediate aim is always the creation of adaptational worlds without any clarity about purpose or ultimate meaning. Now purpose and the ultimate meaning of the human spirit have become immediately and powerfully available because both its origin and its destiny are already given in the Spiritual Presence of Christ. The creativity of the human spirit now knows that its origin and destiny are in God, but all the former patterns of behavior, adaptational constructs, and assumptions remain as grist for the mill of reconstruction after the human spirit has come out from under the weight of the ego's defenses and, in Helen's case, its futile preoccupation with vengeance and thus its hidden pact with its own death. Awakening is to the sphere of the Spirit, where now at last the human spirit is grounded in its origin and destiny and a new being is born out of the dark womb of nothingness that occupies the abyss of ordinary life.

Purgation The second phase in the classical pattern of spiritual development, purgation, begins with the eager realization and passion to move deeper into the life of God, whose presence has redefined everything and calls the awakened spirit into the full range and richness of the sphere of the Divine Spirit. Purgation is the work of the human spirit, still at a distance from God, to appropriate the paradox that less is more: less of self is more of God; to die to self is to have more of the life of God. Conversely, to have more of the life of God is to receive as a gift the liberation of the human spirit so earnestly and blindly sought before one's own great awakening.

The sphere of the Spirit is like another universe, hidden in and behind the orders of this one. In one's awakening, the sphere of the spirit dawns upon the believer, and in purgation it draws the human spirit through its entanglements and residual remains of shattered falsehoods toward the purifying embrace of the person of Christ. The sphere of the spirit is the embrace of his love.

The difficulty is that, in spite of the breakthrough, the deep heart of his pure love still seems far off; the embrace is beyond fathoming, so there is passionate effort in this phase to immerse oneself in Scripture, as when Augustine decided he would simply and unqualifyingly trust the Scripture.[12] If there are contradictions in the text, they are to be borne, since contradictions in Scripture have more truth than any effort to resolve them by the exercise of human reason. For trivial truths, contradictions may pertain, but for every truly great truth, its opposite may also be true. Augustine's passionate study and search persuaded him that everything depended on the primacy of the love of God and his returning that love with all the passion with which he had once resisted it. Purgation in his case meant that he made the passionate effort. But it ended, as purgation by itself always does, in despair. Augustine realized he could never do what was required to move decisively and without regression into the heart of that pure love that held him and beckoned him to draw nearer.

In Helen's case, purgation began with the intense, prayerful reengagement with her sometimes violent memories. Time and time again we sought the face of Christ in memory after memory, but always he took us deeper. Still Helen's bruxism continued, and she marched like a man everywhere she went. She read spiritual literature and immersed herself in Scripture, but nothing really did it until the final episode. Up to that time, purgation was taking place, but nothing gave assurance that we were approaching a decisive conclusion, and despair was a persistent threat.

In Augustine's case, he determined even in his despair that he would nevertheless push on toward the love of God, even though he knew he could never get to the heart of it.[13] In Latin, this phrase is called *fortitudo*. He determined to keep after what he knew he could never attain. This increases passion, yet nothing else was more important, so he exerted every effort he could to keep on in the quest to which he had been awakened and for which he knew he had been recreated.

Illumination Augustine was finally met from the other side in the phase of illumination, which he called "the counsel of mercies."[14] In Helen's case, it was only after all the other barriers coming out of her past had been mediated by the Spiritual Presence of Christ that she could confront the most bewitching memory of all. In confrontation with the despising eyes of her mother, she, as an innocent victim, was able to recognize that Christ in *his* innocence had taken her place. She was finally being met from the other side; she now belonged to him and to no other—least of all to those eyes that had rejected her from the beginning and cursed her self-understanding for years thereafter. The illumination had dawned on her in her vision of his joyful embrace.

The passionate search for the heart of Christ's love is not a work that produces faith; rather, it is the work of faith that takes place in response to the grace of God bestowed by the Spirit of Christ. All that takes place in the sphere of the Spirit is his Spirit at work in the human spirit, enabling faith to work out salvation "with fear and trembling" (Phil. 3:16).

In Teresa of Avila's *Interior Castle,* this passage from purgation to illumination lies between the third and the fourth mansion.[15] In her image, the Source of her spiritual nourishment was at first far distant, and metaphorically she had to receive living water through a complicated irrigation system. But now, in the fourth mansion, the place of illumination, the spiritual learner is exactly at the Source.

Like the beloved disciple John, Helen can lay her head on the heart of Christ and feel his embrace as he dances around the room with her. Now secure in the sphere of the Spirit, she can heave a great sigh of relief and become the woman he had made her to be. Coherence had been accomplished as it stretched from her original vision of the One who threw her to her knees through the accumulated visions of Christ's deliverance of her from a tormented past and forward into the lived world. In this unique continuity, she had strength and integrity she had not ever known before, but it was as if she had only worked out through time what was already implicit and eternally present in that first night of her great awakening.

As when lightning flashes across the night sky and for an instant the whole landscape is bright as day before the darkness descends again, so Helen walked step by step through a space she had already glimpsed in her first encounter with the Spirit of Truth. The sphere of the Spirit had already embraced the whole of those days of deliverance and restoration. She had been given an experience of intimacy that could never be undone because it did not depend on chronological time, yet it made all the difference for her within the time of her life.

Toward Unification The spiritual union that Christ establishes with his beloved ones is well beyond where Helen had been taken in her appropriation of what the Spirit of truth had originally showed her. She had yet to experience deeper losses in the realm of the spirit, dark nights of the soul and of the spirit without the lightning flash to guide her before such a union could take place. Yet there was now no other way for her to find the sense of completeness for which she longed, even more than she had longed for a reason to live. To live eternally in spiritual union with Christ is the ultimate longing, and without at least the promise of such a union is the ultimate loneliness.

But what about human intimacy, closeness with flesh and blood, hands-on hugging and holding, trusted and beloved persons? Here it may be worth recalling Teresa's ecstatic visions of penetrating arrows and her being turned inside out with painful pleasure. Those who see in Teresa's ultimate vision of union in marriage to Christ nothing more than a sublimated sexuality, which in some circles explains "what is *really* going on," have missed the point. Anyone who knows the intensity of the spiritual life knows, as one of my colleagues put it, that "spiritual heat is hotter than sexual heat." To reduce Teresa's visions of union with Christ to sublimated sexuality is to strain at a gnat and swallow a camel. The larger, more profound, and eternal reality that is at stake here is the reality that also provides the ultimate definition of the relationality that pertains between human intimacy and union with the Divine Presence. This bipolarity is defined by the person of Christ in whom all human intimacy is transfigured by the ontological priority of the divine and our spiritual union and communion in him.

The stronger and more complete is Helen's appropriation of the illumination given her from Christ's heart of love, the more fully she can participate in both the eternal and temporal aspects of his person. To look toward the final marriage supper of the lamb at the end of time from the proximate union with Christ in this life is to be thrust further into the body of Christ in the present time. Thus, the import of his two natures in one person is that her making lasting intimate human connections can issue only from a spiritual communion in which all are dwelling in the sphere of the spirit. Only his embrace of love keeps human love alive; only this quality of human love concretizes that spiritual embrace.

Thus, the way toward unification with Christ begins for Helen when she seeks to restore her relation to her parents, to redeem the time that can only be accomplished from a place outside time and in him who unites in his person both time and eternity. Beyond this move, which issued from her emerging union with Christ, toward reunion with her family, I cannot say what became of human intimacy in her case. However, when Helen and I parted and she left to take up her teaching responsibilities, it seemed evident that she had found, and had been embraced by, the only quality of intimacy that could make personal intimacy between and among human beings possible. It was the quality of intimacy that would endure through betrayal and resiliently recreate communion among even estranged members of the body of Christ, the church, to which Helen claimed her entire account belonged.

In all four phases of spiritual development, continuity in intensification is transformed from the human dynamic that needs to hold things together or to tie back from the present to the past for the sake of a consummatory future. It is transformed into an all-embracing coherence in which the end is given from the beginning, and the passage from phase to phase is an increasingly comprehensive appropriation of the intuition of the whole. Thus, with each phase, the whole is more fully illuminated, and one is more fully a part of the whole that is being appropriated.

Helen's case provides an image of the totality of the life span in transformational perspective. The mediator is Jesus Christ in whom birth, death, and the intervening struggles of the human spirit are taken up and returned to the world in an inexhaustible love and forgiveness that is redemptive, not only for persons directly involved but for their neighbors, not only for this time but for eternity, not only for the benefit of humankind but for the glory of God. Helen's case is a dramatic demonstration of the power of the Holy Spirit to reach at any time from one end of the life span to the other, and so to bring the human spirit into line with what God is doing in the world to bring persons into conformity to the humanity of Jesus Christ.

Why Begin with Miracle

The German physicist Gunter Höwe, who, with C. F. von Weiszächer, initiated the theology-science dialogue in postwar Europe in 1945, once said he expected theologians would "begin with miracle and think out the consequences accordingly." In some respects, this is what we are doing with the case of Helen.

However, miracle cannot be construed in the modernist sense of defiance of natural law in a basically deterministic universe. That would be to begin with a view of natural science that no longer pertains and to develop a dualistic theology on false premises. Miracle needs to be seen not as a momentary disruption but as a partial disclosure of the dynamic order that underlies the creation and redemption of the entire universe: the logic of the spirit that brings order out of chaos and transforms human lives into the human likeness of Christ. Instances of transformation like

Helen's point not to a breakdown of natural law as rationalistically conceived, but to the relentless dynamic order of creation and redemption in the Creator Spirit. This is not to forget that by this very Spirit every intelligible order in the universe, including intelligibility itself, has come into being. Thus, when that creative order erupts redemptively in specific cases, as it did with Helen, then it becomes evident that attempts to make such events conform to rational models of interpretation, as we have undertaken in the neurological and psychological discussions above, are certainly called for, but they are derivative. However, they are not derivative from some ultimate scientific explanation, but from the Creator Spirit by whom the inner logic of transformation moves all things toward conformity to Christ; in him the *logos,* the ultimate wisdom through which all things were created, became manifest. It is this realization that dawns with ever greater depth upon spiritual awareness, as in the third discussion above. This is not to denigrate the effort to construct a rational account of things but, rather, to place rationality and its systems in the larger context of its origins and destiny theologically understood. If such a context is not given, then rational constructs of order, epitomized in science and technology, subtly begin to claim a self-sufficiency and ultimacy they cannot sustain. As A. B. Pippard, above-noted Cambridge thermodynamicist, said, the grandeur of God must exceed the grandeur of the universe so as to transcend "the invincible ignorance of science" where matters of human consciousness and the Divine are concerned.[16]

As the following chapters unfold, it may be possible to see that "miracle," in the modern deterministic sense, issues not only from a deficient understanding of postmodern science, but from the tendency of the human ego to fit God into Newton's world. In such a context, of course, "miracles" are seen as an exception to order because the rationalistic human ego cannot grasp, much less contain by itself, creation and transformation. It cannot grasp the fashion in which God has placed *his* order into the structure of a redeemed human nature so that, through us, the universe may become conscious of itself, its origins and its destiny, and so disclose that it and we ourselves are the work of an intensely personal, infinitely intelligent, and redemptive Creator.

What we see in Helen's case is a radical reordering of a human life in accordance with that ultimate order, which is grasped only by faith in the power of God's Spirit who transforms the ego and brings that more profound order to bear on individual lives. To begin with miracle is not to begin with the exception, but to grasp at the outset what can be glimpsed of that profound order by which all creation has come, and continues to come, into being.

This is not to denigrate the remarkable capacities of the human ego for language and reason, but it is to liberate the ego from tasks it cannot possibly grasp, much less perform. For instance, on the negative side it cannot maintain its position as the center of the personality against aging, because its very structure is built on its capacity to screen out the underlying nothingness in human existence toward which aging inevitably takes us all. On the positive side, it cannot comprehend its own potential transformation because its boundaries are carefully preserved to protect it against any overpowering intrusions from outside forces, including the Spirit of God. In this interplay between the divine and the contingent orders of creation is where all human development unfolds, but Helen's "miracle" makes it clear that the divine order, the logic inherent in the Creator Spirit, will predominate wherever faith prevails.

Conclusions and Hypotheses

Let us consider as hypotheses some of the conclusions that can be tentatively drawn from Helen's case.

First, it seems clear that *human development studied as the development of the human ego is not destiny.* Individuality is not able to be preprogrammed, even by genetic manipulation and cloning, because of the open-endedness of the human spirit. More significant, the spiritual action of God makes it plain that even the physical aspects of human nature are subject to change and transformation in keeping with God's presence and God's order.

Second, it seems evident that the *development of the ego* and all its various competencies (for example, language, intelligence, moral judgment) *unfolds along a different axis from that of spiritual development.* The two axes of development may intersect and complement each other, but they diverge preeminently as to primary aim. The ego's aim is adaptation to its physical, social, and cultural environment so as to maximize satisfaction and ensure survival.

The human spirit both is in the service of the ego and transcends it. True to its transformative character, it implies that with every new insight, constructive act of imagination, and formation of new stages, a higher aim is beckoning, and that human nature belongs to a higher but hidden order. When the human spirit finds its ground in the Divine Spirit, then its aim is disclosed as harmony between the divine and contingent orders, specifically personal union with the presence and purposes of God. Subsequently the human spirit, in agreement with divine order, will seek to bring all ego competencies into line with those purposes, even if it means counteradaptive behavior and suffering in place of satisfaction and survival. Human development needs to be studied in terms of both the divergence and the convergence of these two axes, recognizing that ultimately they converge only according to the higher, divine order, but never strictly within the purview of ego function.

Third, the spiritual axis is not otherworldly. In fact, there is a psychoneurological basis for experiences of a distinctly spiritual nature. Agreement between the human spirit and the Divine Spirit, as in inspired visions or master gestalts, can be seen as based in a model of intensification, suggesting that *human nature is as wired for spiritual insight as it is for mathematics.* The pattern of discipline required in both is neurophysically rooted, but no more important in one than in the other.

Fourth, the negative side of development is a threat to the emerging ego, and so the ego attempts to construct a conflict-free existence. Correlatively, studies of ego development tend to construct theories and understandings that encourage the denial of death. This is ironic since the organic model so fundamental to developmentalist thinking necessarily entails death as one absolutely invariant feature of all organisms. *The study of development from a spiritual and theological perspective necessarily includes the negative side.* Recognizing that human beings begin to die the moment they are born, the higher order of reality revealed in the life, death, and resurrection of Jesus Christ includes the ego's development, but only in the light of its incipient death and potentiality for new being in him. Thus, the spiritual axis not only exposes the suppression of death, which is so prevalent in studies of ego development, but also makes death a dominant theme as the human spirit seeks union with God and God's purpose.

Fifth, the continuity between neuropsychological foundations and Divine Presence in moments of profound spiritual insight establishes a basis for personal integrity that bypasses the adaptive preoccupation of the ego. As such, *this continuity establishes an essential backbone for the faith that has personally appropriated the union of the divine and the human in Jesus Christ.* This "Christ in me" becomes definitive for one's entire existence, transforming ego functions into its service and supplanting the superego-making conscience a matter of "inward integrity of heart," as Calvin put it.[17]

Sixth, derivative from this reality of "Christ in me," *one can overcome the defensive, protective patterns of ego functions,* enabling forgiveness, returning good for evil, loving the enemy, and, in the face of persecution, rejoicing. These and other counteradaptive moves do not eliminate the ego and its functions; they bring these functions into the service of one's conscience in Christ.

Seventh, *the "Christ in me" is the reciprocal of its larger context "I am in Christ."* Specifically, this refers to the church, but this reciprocity resonates throughout all creation, uniting the convicted person (in this case, Helen) with all others who have known with convictional force the same reconstruction of their existence around the spiritual axis of Christ. The wide-ranging significance of this reciprocity is captured in the Barthian dialectical couplet: the covenant is the internal basis of creation, and creation is the external basis of the covenant. Thus, when Helen said, "This belongs to the church," it was implicitly a statement of cosmological proportions.

Eighth, these hypotheses all suggest that *the whole configuration of human development needs to be reconceptualized.* A lifetime ought not to be thought of in a linear manner, an ascending upward gradient, or a kind of bell-shaped curve in which persons develop from one stage of helplessness as an infant through a lifetime to a final stage of helplessness in old age. If the above hypotheses pertain, then so-called "normal development" should be conceived as a wandering in cosmic emptiness or, at best, a circumambulation of the human spirit around the center, who is the One triune God. In this God resides the ultimate coherence from whom each passion for understanding, each new insight, new stage, new vision of the universe, derives its ultimate intelligibility and toward which all such phenomena point. To be sure, there are false passions, false visions, and misleading paradigms, but the drive toward inner integrity of heart is restless until it finds its rest in that One God. The One God, the source and center of all things, related to all contingent orders of creation through Christ, makes integrity of heart a personal and existential reflection of the paradoxical unity of the divine and the human in Jesus Christ. Preserving his integrity as one person, two natures, in the context of one's own existence by the power of his Spirit is the reality by which one tests the spirits (John 4:1).

It is a truism that diagrams help only the sort of persons who are helped by diagrams, but for these readers, at least, the diagram of this approach in Figure 3.1 may be helpful. This diagram is designed to draw together the first three chapters of this book. The larger context of creation in which this study of human development was originally set forth in Chapter One is to be understood as contingent on the continuing grace and redemptive purpose of the Creator. "The One triune God" is both at the center (the little infinity) and beyond the outer limit of all contingent orders in all directions (the big infinity), and, consequently, it both permeates and transcends the whole picture, from center to periphery. As such, the coherent unity of the triune God and the internal, differentiated

Figure 3.1. Human Development Reconfigured.

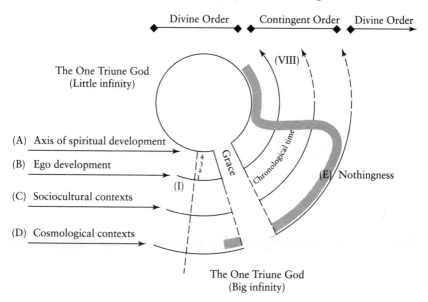

relationality of the trinity that constitutes that unity become the ultimate ground for unity-in-relationality and relationality-in-unity for all subordinate, contingent orders of creation.

The entry designated B is the line of so-called normal human development. A person may move through the life span within his or her sociocultural milieu (C) and within the cosmic order (D) and never engage issues of ultimate significance. One may circumambulate from stage to stage and never engage the ultimate center or the outer boundaries of one's existence, but grace and redemption continue to uphold and preserve that lifetime within the limits of its biological, psychological, social, cultural, and cosmic contexts, all of which will become increasingly important as one matures. However, the questions, "What is a lifetime?" and "Why do I live it?" necessarily and inevitably arise; yet they can be dismissed or repressed because the threats of nonbeing, nothingness, and annihilation (E), which are implicit in discovering one's contingency on grace and redemption, may be overwhelming. This threat is suggested by the shadowed areas on the diagram.

Nevertheless, if one engages these existential questions with some passion, then one begins to move on a different axis (A), which departs from the meaningless circularity of an indecisive existence and begins to enact the Christomorphic character of existence. Here the lines that run approximately vertically from the center outward and back again begin to describe the spiritual axis of human development. This axis is called spiritual because it connects in depth and universality the human and the divine. The numbers from 1 to 4 on this axis designate the phases of intensification, which correspond to the four classic phases of spiritual maturation.

Finally, the diagram graphically depicts my claim that there are at least two views of time implicit in the theological study of human development. We tend to think chronologically about development, assuming that the sequence of stages depicted in the outer rings is the obvious way to view a lifetime as a whole. However, that is a developmental egocentrism. The view from the center, which is simultaneously the view from beyond, is different because it stands in a position to see the whole sequence all at once from both the little and the big infinity. This view is provided by the theological perspective.

Theology takes chronological and historical time seriously, but not definitively; it does not determine the meaning of time in linear terms. As developmental studies show, children do not learn to tell time until they are about eight years of age. However, prior to that, duration and event time are very real. Moreover, as Piaget, in conversation with Einstein, has shown, the view of space and time before the age of eight is closer to how relativity understands these elementary aspects of our experience than the clock-time perspective, which is more Newtonian.[18] Chronological time is not absolute, and it must be put in the perspective of a larger and qualitatively different frame of reference, even within a strictly physical context of explanation, as Einstein's theory showed.

The still larger, relevant, and qualitatively different frame of reference for studying development is theological. What the invariant speed of light as a universal constant does to relativize space and time in Einstein's theory, the theological perspective must do to the study of human development. From the theological perspective, the revealed center around which lived-time moves and the stages in the chronological sequence of a lifetime must be seen as continually in a relational interplay with each other. They affect each other both within and beyond the structures of the stages, but always predominantly according to the One who sees it all, all at once. Nevertheless, in this perspective, chronology and history are taken seriously in their own right, but only relative to the center as revealed in Christ. The Chalcedonian relationality between God and humanity plays out into the relationality between eternity and time, and so ontological priority is given to the eternal without denying, separating, or confusing the two views. But there is an inevitable asymmetry as captured in the verse, "All your years are as a single day when they are past."

The Christomorphic relationality between eternity and time will appear again and again as we work through the following chapters. The discussion will move back and forth on the developmental ring around the center in the light of the theological perspective that revelation gives us. It was out of the theological center that the Spiritual Presence of God in Christ was able to make the chronology of Helen's life reversible and so reconstruct the past. To be sure, finite time in all its facets, including clock time, was restored to her, but now it was to be understood from the standpoint of the theological center.

NOTES

1. Throughout this case, I was in consultation with a clinical psychologist who also saw Helen briefly and advised me along the way. I am here working partly from his notes as well as my own.

2. Continuity in human change and development may be homogeneous, as in eye color, or heterogeneous, as in negative aggression that gets displaced or sublimated but retains its character as destructive. In this case, the motivation is positive and creative.

3. Anthony Wallace, "Revitalization Movements," in William Armand Lessa and Evon Zartman Vogt, *A Reader in Comparative Religion: An Anthropological Approach* (New York: HarperCollins, 1979), pp. 503–512.

4. This model is preferable to those that focus only on hemisphericity and do not engage the wider neurological dimensions that are involved in the passion of intensity such as Polanyi describes as "fiduciary passion" and Wallace's prophets experience. It stems primarily from the work of E. Gellhorn and his associates. See E. Gellhorn, *Principles of Autonomic-Somatic Integration* (Minneapolis: University of Minnesota Press, 1967); E. Gellhorn and W. F. Kiely, "Mystical States of Consciousness: Neurophysiological and Clinical Aspects," *Journal of Nervous and Mental Diseases* 154 (1972): 399–405; Barbara Lex, "Neurological Bases of Revitalization Movement," *Zygon* 13, no. 1 (December 1978): 276–314; Victor Turner, "Body, Brain and Culture," *Zygon* 18, no. 3 (September 1983); Charles D. Laughlin, John McManus, and Eugene d'Quili, *Brain, Symbol and Experience* (Boston: New Science Library, 1990), esp. chap. 11. See further the discussion of the model in James E. Loder and W. J. Neidhardt, *The Knight's Move* (Colorado Springs: Helmers and Howard, 1995).

5. Robin Norwood, *Women Who Love Too Much* (New York: Pocket Books, 1986).

6. Erik H. Erikson, *Childhood and Society,* 2d ed. (New York: Norton, 1963).

7. Sigmund Freud, *Moses and Monotheism* (London: Hogarth Press and the Institute of Psychoanalysis, 1939).

8. Sigmund Freud, *Ego and the Id* (New York: Norton, 1962).

9. See Chapter 7. If Carl Jung were brought into this discussion, such images could be multiplied at great length. But that requires positing an "objective psyche," racially inherited archetypes, and the work of active imagination. We will discuss all this in subsequent chapters, but here I am taking the minimal case, which is the most direct challenge to the spiritual integrity of Helen's healing by psychoanalytic thinking.

10. See James E. Loder, *The Transforming Moment*, 2d ed. (Colorado Springs: Helmers and Howard, 1989), and Chapter Five in this book.

11. See also Loder and Neidhardt, *The Knight's Move*, p. 232.

12. Augustine, *Christian Doctrine*, Bk. II, Ch. 7, in *A Select Library of the Nicene and Post-Nicene Fathers of the Christian Church*, vol. II, p. 537f.

13. Ibid.

14. Ibid.

15. Teresa of Avila, *The Interior Castle*, trans. Kieran Kavanaugh and Otilio Rodriguez (New York: Paulist Press, 1979), pp. 55–84.

16. A. B. Pippard, "The Invincible Ignorance of Science," *Contemporary Physics* 29, no. 4 (1988): 393–405.

17. "Conscience is referred to God; thus a good conscience is nothing other than inward integrity of heart." John Calvin, *Institutes of the Christian Religion*, trans. Allen (Philadelphia: Westminster Press, 1936), Bk. III, chap. 19.16.

18. See John Hurley Flavell, *The Developmental Psychology of Jean Piaget* (Princeton, N.J.: Van Nostrand, 1964).

PART TWO

THE TRIUMPH OF NEGATION

4

INFANCY IN PSYCHOLOGICAL PERSPECTIVE

THE EMERGING EGO

BIRTH, THE FIRST GREAT transition of life, is a masterpiece of physiological coherence and efficiency in the face of a life-against-death encounter. In normal birth, the child is prepared biochemically and posturally for a period of overpowering stimulation and stress in which its body will be pounded and painfully subjected to the bombardment of environmental stimuli. This is a survival act like nothing else the child will ever undergo again (short of a life-after-life experience).

There is a remarkable, complex economy of factors operative in the normal act of birth. In a majority of births, the child leads with the head. Typically the head serves as a battering ram; the toes are pointed, arms are at the side and fists clenched, back is arched, and the child is thrust into the world by the painful process of the mother's labor.

This posture is interesting to note, since a number of autistic children lock themselves into this position, as do some of us when we must undergo an ordeal in which our survival is threatened. Psychoanalyst Phyllis Greenacre thought that the way we dealt with anxiety at birth was preparatory for how we faced anxiety later on.[1] Psychoanalyst Arthur Janov connects neurotic behavior or forms of anxiety to the birth experience.[2] When someone says, "I just can't get going," it may reflect an arrested birth process due to drugs or some other irregularity. This kind of direct cause-and-effect connection is certainly questionable, but it does suggest the magnitude of the birth experience and its possible impact on the child.

The primary physical or survival reason for the head to lead is to get the nose and mouth into the air as soon as possible, since in the process of birth, the child comes close to suffocation. As the child is born, the umbilical cord is squeezed shut, and the supply of oxygen is greatly reduced. In the resulting chemical imbalance, there is too much carbon dioxide in the blood and the breathing reflex is triggered, so the child will take air into the lungs through the mouth and nose for the first time . . . if there is air to breath.

Greenacre thought the rhythm of labor gave the body a stimulating inducement to respond to the new environment. The cerebral massage experienced in labor facilitates healthy neurological development later on. In the ordinary economy of birth, the child is biochemically and environmentally prepared for the most totally engrossing learning experience it will ever undertake. However, not all births are normal; cesarean section is the most common exception. In these cases, the physiological needs are met in other ways. Stroking and affection, holding, and other methods accomplish the same end as the ordinary birth process. This illustrates a basic developmental principle that the human organism, for all its complexity, is very flexible and adaptable, able to achieve the same goals by alternative means. We know this to be true later on in life; otherwise psychoanalysis would not be able to redirect a life when development had been arrested.

A Parisian physician, Frederick Leboyer, has taken the learning process of birth seriously and dramatized its inherent coherence. For him, the medical approach treats the birth process too much like a disease. The mother is put in a hospital, treated like a victim of an affliction, and the child enters the world with deep sobs of grief.[3] He felt the process was debasing and violent. Consequently, he left his Parisian practice. When he returned from India three years later, he brought a new approach with him. He produced literature and a film, *Blissful Birth*. The essence of his approach is to reduce the stress of birth as much as possible: turn down the lights because it is dark in the womb, lower the voices because all sounds are hushed, and recognize that breathing hurts the lungs, so do not cut the umbilical cord immediately. Do not jerk the child upside down to induce breathing, but put the child on the mother's stomach and do not wrap it in blankets; a warm bath soon after birth will bring forth full awakening on the child's part and smiles instead of sobs of grief. The transition from the known to the unknown needs to be as smooth as possible.

The long-term significance of treating birth as a learning experience that shapes subsequent life patterns is not yet clear, although there are several types of responses to this possibility. Harvard's Gordon Allport, a well-known nonclinical personality theorist who did a classical work on intrinsic and extrinsic religion, questioned how much cortical activity is actually taking place prior to birth and in the early period.[4] He thought very little could be remembered. But this objection has long since been discarded. There is clear evidence of a great deal of cortical activity, as can be observed in the womb through modern technology. The human organism does not wait for birth to get started with higher orders of development. Janov developed intensive psychoanalytic techniques for inducing a recovery of the original birth trauma as a basis for starting over again. René Spitz found little evidence for a great trauma during this period, but saw a generalized sense of loss that was laid down across the whole of the child's brain and recorded in the hypothalamus.[5] This led him to assume that a pervasive psychological sense of negation accompanies the act of birth. As we will see, negation is a major theme in development, yet most major theorists largely ignore it. Carl Jung, Julian Jaynes, and others see that in the act of birth the archetype of the birth pattern, which appears in so many different cultures, is awakened.[6] They want to go back further and say that we can inherit the attitudes of our primal ancestors. One of these attitudes is to affirm the power of the birth process as an archetype for shaping future experiences. Scripture, of course, reaches further back, before time, claiming that the child existed first in the mind of God.

Nevertheless, the tendency of psychologists to believe that developmental history determines one's destiny actually runs contrary to some of the most important findings in the study of human development. Suffice it to say here that human development is inherently open-ended. This is why the theme of negation intrinsic to the experience of birth can lead to primitive disintegration and hopelessness; it is also why therapy works and the transformation of developmental histories is possible. Perhaps the best example is the case of Helen, discussed in Chapter Three. Keep in mind the irreducible open-ended character of development as we turn to the theories of certain interactionists and their discussions of the first year of life with particular attention to instinct and bonding.

Freud

The cornerstone of Freud's position on development was *Three Contributions to a Theory of Sex*.[7] Here he initiates his hypothesis concerning psychosexual development and his famous connections between libidinal energy and bodily zones: oral, anal, phallic, latency, and genital. However, these far-reaching hypotheses were originally based in a more analytical and empirical frame of reference. Freud, at first a neurologist, sought to trace all forms of mental illness to neurological conditions and understandings of the brain. He eventually abandoned this approach because he had to deal with the rich complexities of real people, and his reductive analysis was not and could not be sufficiently complex. He realized what contemporary neurologists are realizing: they must learn to work from the whole to the parts, never assuming that adding the parts will give the whole. Freud, who worked with severely regressed patients in a clinical setting, induced from their pathology the origins of their illness in human development. He used dreams, free associations, and several models—biological, mechanical, topographical, and religious—to work backward from the pathology to the developmental origins of the illness.

One major aspect of his theory that continued to have an influence, even when he shifted from neurology to clinical studies, was the notion of energy, which in his early neurological material he called the Q factor. His idea about energy was not originally sexual but an electrical quantum.[8] This energy would move through the neurons, build up tension, and then fire across the synapses. This became the libido hypothesis in which it was assumed that a generalized sexual energy is moving within the organism and causing certain aspects of the body to be particularly sensitive and receptive to the outside world. There was a buildup of energy around these openings at the skin boundary to the outside world. These apertures at the skin boundary become highly invested with libidinal energy and so shape the person's response to the environment, especially the personal and interpersonal environment. This is the neurological root of Freud's famous stages of development.

In his view, the earliest zone is the mouth. This period lasts from birth to eighteen months or two years. Through this first period, the child takes in life through the mouth and so organizes life orally. For some people, this continues to be a dominant mode of conduct throughout life. Hence Erich Fromm, a neo-Freudian, talked about the oral personality as one who tends to be easily awed, easily hypnotized, inclined toward religious experience, and will earn a living through the mouth, if possible.

Fixation at this early period suggests a negative side of the birth experience. Alongside the drive to live and to get born, there is also a desire to return to a less stressful context, even to die. This is the death instinct that accompanies the life instinct from the moment of birth. This is sometimes called destrudo (in opposition to the libido) and sometimes thanatos (in opposition to eros). From this perspective, the minute we are born, we are beginning to die. Although many contemporary developmentalists want to discount Freud's instinct theory, it is important to remember that every life-affirming act has an aggressive or counteractive component. All organisms die, and the dying process is continuous with life. Indeed, it wins out over life in every case.

Arguably suicide, startlingly prevalent in teenagers but even in young children, is a collapse of the drive to live into the ever-present undercurrent of the regressive wish to die. Regression in the service of the conduct of life, as in sleep, is universal, but regression as an act of violence against the self is an ever-present possibility. It may come forth as an ultimate regression designed not only as a way out but as an act of rejection of and an attack on the presumed life givers and caretakers, and perhaps the hope of a better birth.

The negative side of human development is prevalent from birth and may, in fact, in later life under traumatic conditions as engrossing as birth itself, induce an attack on life through the life giver. As psychoanalyst David Bakan suggested, on the instinctual level suicide is an attack on the caretaker and an effort to undo the birth process.[9]

However, the human spirit is immanent in the birth process, and it can be reappropriated at later periods in life as the "new birth," a spiritual transformation that restores life in the face of death. Thus, the transforming power of the human spirit is not something added on later; it is intrinsic to the birth instinct and bonding. Consequently, empowered by the Holy Spirit, it has the power to alter instincts and dramatically change what one "wants" or "must have."

A striking illustration of this in relation to a potential suicide is the case of Lucy. Lucy was a thirty-year-old Taiwanese woman, studying in the United States, whose betrayal by her lover and her rejection by her parents, particularly her mother in her homeland, brought her to the edge of suicide. She had it all planned; she had the pills and expected simply to go to sleep forever. But, curiously, she did not want anyone to find her body in a messy room, so she cleaned and straightened her room in preparation for her death. As she went through her things, she came upon an icon, a stone carving of the head and shoulders of Christ with a small tray in front for burning incense. She decided to pray one last prayer for forgiveness. As she knelt before the icon with the wisps of smoke rising before the face of Christ, she was struck by an unexpected surge of joy and hope that turned her prayer for forgiveness into a prayer of praise and thanksgiving. To her surprise, she rose up with a renewed desire to live.

Note that the new life does not simply cancel the drive toward death. In fact, it transforms Lucy's aggression into a constructive act of joy, overcoming death to herself and to the death-dealing people in her world. As the resurrection of Christ gives death to death, so the spiritual life that poured into her brought forth the aggressive side of grace, which will not allow death to have the final word. Her human spirit, beaten down by the rejection of those she had wanted to love, was awakened to itself by Christ's Spirit. She could now get off her knees and recompose her world. An accomplished artist, she returned to her studio in New York and eventually revisited her homeland and her family. The Spirit of Christ did not take her out of the world but put her, now reborn, back into the world with a fresh determination to recompose it in her own terms. Death had "lost its sting" (I Cor. 15).

This case shows that the life of the Spirit runs deeper than instinct and works to transform instinctual life even in its rawest and most primitive form; it works to preserve and empower the open-endedness of the human spirit.

Neo-Freudians

Post-Freudian theorists, including Erikson, shifted gradually away from the unconscious to the conscious life and the formation of the ego. There is a Freudian dictum that states that the ego is "the shape of the body."[10] That is, the personality is formatively influenced by the way the body is treated by its interpersonal environment. To make the transition to post-Freudian thought and ego formation, let us shift from the neurological to the activity and postural model of the body. Especially important for both Freud's and Erikson's affirmation of life is something called primary narcissism. The libidinization of the body and the spontaneous engagement of it and its satisfactions is what is intended. Here the child lives in a kind of "psychic egg," as Margaret Mahler calls it.[11] The child gets much sleep, is awakened by "needs" (surplus energy), and then falls back to sleep again. There is a great deal of cortical activity in sleep, so presumably the unconscious or half-waking life of the child is organizing and connecting things during sleep.

But the child is not all passivity. The experience of birth is an alarm that puts a variety of reflexes in motion all at once—grasping and sucking, for example. Touch the lips and the child will suck; put your finger in the hand of the child, and the child will grip it. There are many other such reflexes; for example, in the Moro reflex, the child's arms suddenly reach out sideways as if to embrace or to fly. These and other such reflexes suggest an evolutionary history of the physical organism as given with birth. However, reflexive interaction with the environment must be processed and stored in an organism that likes itself and its world. Hence, primary narcissism is crucial; it may be manipulated or, in its chronic absence, the child might not even want to live. Primary narcissism at a physical level is the key to the bond between the mother and the child. The physical level prepares the way for the child's receiving the all-important "look in the mother's eye" that communicates, "You're just great!" The child needs this affirmation at an interpersonal level on top of and in addition to the physical stroking that induces primary narcissism.

This, then, is a crucial period for bonding, that is, establishing the attachment between mother and child, which can form the foundation for the future organization of life. Joseph Pearce, in his book *The Magical Child*, reports a number of studies that focus the issue well.[12] The Ugandan Zhun and Twasi mothers carry their children in a sling in front of them; the child can nurse at any time and is never diapered or swaddled, yet none of the mothers were soiled. When asked about this, one mother said, "When he needs to go, I just take him into the bush and he goes." "How do you know?" "Well," she said, "how would you know?" The bond initially is so close that the internal psychophysical needs are communicated between the mother and the child. My older daughter, Kim, when her baby Julie was very small, said she knew ahead of time when Julie was about to wake up and would want to nurse. Every child needs this primary connection during the first year of life; otherwise the negative side associated with separation and the pain of birth begins to surface.

Although bonding is universal, it is managed in different ways in different cultures.[13] Sometimes it is used as a way of controlling the eventual socialization of the child. In Uganda, according to Pearce, the bond is maintained for about four years, when the child is suddenly and totally abandoned by the mother. The child then becomes desperate and clings to the tribe and its culture as a surrogate solution to the sudden breaking of the bonding relationship with the mother.

The effect of bonding has long-term consequences and is potentially crucial for the rest of life. In one study, the researchers passed a message before the eyes of their schizophrenic patients through a tachistoscope, which meant that the message passed before them in four milliseconds. The idea was to bypass consciousness and reach an unconscious level with the message, "Mommy and I are one." The striking results were that significant improvement in the schizophrenic behavior was achieved.[14] The same process was shown to be effective in enabling persons to break the most addictive habit of all, smoking.

The Fundamental Shape of the Human Spirit

In Western culture, the usual human situation, assuming what is called "good-enough mothering,"[15] the developmental work of this period, in Erikson's terms, focuses on the effort of the child to construct a favorable balance between trust and mistrust in relationship to the environment. By the time the child is eighteen months to two years old, he will have come to some conclusions about whether the environmental relationship is predominantly trustworthy and to what degree and in what direction the balance is tipped.

Remember that the child has to construct this out of the interaction with the environment. Being born adaptationally open-ended, and thus more unstable than other creatures, the human child has unique cortical capacities for creating the environment. The child must construct, compose, and construe the world in a predominantly trustworthy or untrustworthy manner.

What is most often overlooked or not sufficiently thematized by developmentalists is the pervasive dynamic patterns by which this and all other stages come into being. The process of constructing a trustworthy relation to the environment begins in the chaos of forces unleashed at birth. The child then pulls together many resources from the environment, from within her own body and from her own burgeoning psyche, and then a new order begins to emerge. Following the conflictual totalism of birth, there is a scanning period in which the child is reaching, grasping, sucking, and taking in objects from the world, and implicitly forming the order of the universe. She uses all her resources to come up with a resolution, hopefully a predominance of trust over mistrust. Out of this temporarily stable resolution, the child will invest new energy and conduct subsequent interactions in and with the environment. Once the relationship to the environment proves to be predominantly trustworthy, the child will transcend this level of balance and thrust herself into the world. She will engage new levels of complexity, and the same process, following essentially the same steps, will be repeated in the construction of the next stage through a transformation of the first or previous stages.

I am pointing to a stage transition dynamic that begins in conflict and moves through scanning to the construction of an insight about one's place in the world, or the construction of a new way of construing personal world order out of chaos, followed by the release of tension bound up within the original conflict. Now new energy is available to be redistributed, and thus development proves out and moves ahead, building on this newly constructed sense of order.[16]

This pattern, built into the earliest period of the child's life, works to make the difference between life and death. Partly because of the sheer survival power of this pattern, but also because of its uncanny capacity to construct the world, the child creates a future that is indebted to but not controlled by the past. Indeed, the past is totally reworked and recomposed as new forms of relating self and environment emerge. For these and other reasons, this pattern of transformation typifies the work of the human spirit in the creation of the human ego and all its adaptational functions.[17]

This pattern represents the fundamental form of the human spirit in five basic phases (conflict, interlude, insight, release of energy/appropriation, and proving out). However, these are not steps to be followed or stages in the usual developmental sense. They are turning points in a linear gestalt, like turning points in a plot, or the buildup and release that, according to Susanne Langer, characterize the dynamic essence of music.[18] Literary critic Frank Kermode talks about plot in terms of "the sense of an ending" and uses the image of "tic-toc"; if, in the context of clocks, one says "tic" the sense of an ending calls for "toc."[19] The human spirit is a linear gestalt that presses through time toward completion and closure, which discloses new levels of openness to the future. Whether one enters the pattern consciously at the point of conflict, insight, or any other of the turning points, the internal drive is to cover all points as if to spell out the whole—to complete the plot or finish the song, so a new story or song can begin. In this respect, early development discloses the hidden potential of the lifetime that is yet to come.

This transformational pattern was operative in Helen's and Lucy's accounts of what happened. Their emerging insight and reconstruction of reality transformed the self-world relationality with existential force. This makes the important point that the creative range and power of the human spirit, which begins to surface in the first year and a half of life, will eventually be transposed to every arena of human action (from organic to personal, to social and cultural worlds). This is because it constitutes the dynamic core of what it means to become a person. At this period, the spirit of the child is only beginning to be aware of self and the power implicit in its capacity to construct a lived and livable world.

The Creative Work of the First Eighteen Months

What happens, step by step, in this first year and a half of life, such that the construct of a trustworthy self-environment relationship can be created? This construct is the keystone of subsequent ego development.

Spitz describes four basic phases in the creation of the foundation of the ego in this eighteen-month period.[20] These steps focus on what he calls the primary organizer of the personality, that is, the primary way a developing person relates to the interpersonal environment. Up to three months of age, the primary organizer is the mouth. This is the primal reflex mode for taking in the world and construing the environment. It involves touch, taste, smell, and the deep sensitivity of swallowing. But, of course, the elementary motive is organic survival and satisfaction. Thus, the mouth begins to do in a primitive way what the ego will eventually do in a much more complex and sophisticated way: serve the drive for survival and satisfaction.

Until she was about eighteen months old, my little granddaughter Julie put all things in her mouth, from quarters to marbles to feathers, and swallowed them. This was not because she was hungry, this was her way of trying to take in the world; she was trying to ingest the external environment in order to make it a part of herself and herself a part of it. Thus, parents have to be very careful with children during these first months that they do not put something destructive into their mouths.

At the age of three to six months, a remarkable shift occurs from organic survival to interpersonal realization and reality. At three months, if one holds just the configuration of a face on a stick beside the crib and moves it up and down, the child will smile. If it is a real face, of course, real faces tend to smile back at the infant. So important and regular is this phenomenon that it is like imprinting on what it is to be human, this mirror relationship between the adult face and the child's face, the smiling child and the return of that smile from the adult. Imprinting is well known; little ducks have to imprint on mama duck at a precise time in their infancy to know they are ducks. If, during that period, they imprint on a dog or upon Konrad Lorenz, the ethologist who studied such things, it will confuse their mating patterns later on.[21]

Erikson and others who have no particular theological axe to grind agree that this has religious significance, so it is consistent with such developmental perspectives to say that this smiling response to the face or the consistent nurturing presence of another is a cosmic ordering, self-confirming presence of a loving other. That is, to be human is implicitly to be religious.

The prototype of this posture toward the face may come physically from the child's being held by the nurturing person, embraced and supported from the outside, and satisfied down inside by the mother's warm milk, and all the time the eye-to-eye contact communicates recognition and affirmation, saying, "You're wonderful." Of course, the child does not reflect on this situation. For her, the embrace *is* the cosmic order; the outside world has not yet been recognized as "out there." *This* is *it,* and it is confirming of oneself, inside and out; the presence of the mother is her face, especially her eyes.

It is fortuitous that both the Greek and Hebrew words for *face* (*prosopon* and *panîm*) are also the words for "presence," so what is at work is not merely a literal face, but the human presence, something that may be experienced without being literally seen. Moreover, the face phenomenon is not strictly something that comes only from the environment; it is also a construct created by the child and developed out of the child's inherent resources and deep-seated longing. Children seem uniquely endowed with a potential capacity to sum up all the complexity of the nurturing presence in the figure of the face. However, even if the nurturing is not regularly given or even mostly absent, the child is nevertheless endowed with an enduring latent potential that, like language, needs an appropriate environment in which to flourish. In the case of language, if that environment is not there, the linguistic potential remains dormant but can be reawakened if it is provided before adolescence. A similar pattern may be applicable to all that is implied in the face phenomenon, since in adolescence these early resolutions to regular developmental conflicts all get reworked and are given a new setting for the second decade of life.

The face is the primal prototype of the religious experience in which one is placed with recognition and affirmation in the context of the cosmic order. Universality and particularity, individuality and belonging, deep subjective satisfaction and a sense of the ultimate objective order: all combine in a single living, harmonious presence. One need only imagine the transfiguration of such a prototypical presence to see why the imprint on the face is implicitly religious and an incipient sense of the presence of God.

Another way to make this point would be to use Jungian categories. Jungians such as Jolanda Jacobi, citing Justin Martyr, see the archetype of the cross in the basic structure of the face; the oval shape of the face is divided by the horizontal line of the eyes crossing the vertical line of the nose.[22] Thus, the mandala, the sacred circle with a cross in the middle, where the God appears in ancient religions, seems to make the face at least potentially an archetype of the Jungian self. This, says Jung, is where we experience the presence of God. For several reasons, Jung's overall position is fundamentally misleading, although his insights are helpful on this point.

All is well and good for the child until six months, when the child begins to realize that the face as organizer of the world and the self does go away at times. Moreover, not just any face will do. Sometimes the wrong face shows up at cribside, and then, "Whaaa!" Moreover, at this time, the child is learning to respond to "no" imposed from the external environment, so from six to fourteen months, the interpersonal organizer of the personality is anxiety, and anxiety of traumatic proportions.

Think of a traumatic situation as one in which the external world actually makes happen the very thing you most desperately fear inwardly will

come upon you. It is a time when you are trapped between two overwhelming negative forces, and there is no alternative. For example, if you
stand at a street corner and a car comes along, jumps the curb, knocks
you down, and sends you to the hospital, you go back to that corner only
with some trepidation. If a second time a car jumps that curb, knocks you
down, and sends you to the hospital, you will go back with even greater
trepidation. If it happens a third time, no one could drag you back to that
corner, because you will be traumatized. The inner fear of the thing happening, converging with its external actuality, is traumatic.

What this means for development is that the six-month-old child is
learning to understand and anticipate the parental "no." Simultaneously,
the child is beginning to distinguish among faces and anticipate the departure of the most important face. This builds up as an internal sense of
absence. When the face that organized the personality with potentially
religious proportions seems to go away, it is a matter of existential significance. At the same time, the external environment is recognizably and
forcefully saying "no." Parents and other important persons have said
"no" in several ways before, but now the child hears clearly what the
word means. Thus, for the small child's psyche, compounding the sense
of loss and negation, and the existential impact of these converging forces
of negation, leaves no space for the developing child's emerging sense of
self. The primary organizer of the personality at this period, according to
Spitz, is anxiety.[23]

By fourteen months, the child has made an ingenious developmental
move, something that later on we would call a reaction formation. Reaction formation is a defense mechanism in which you do just the opposite
of what you really want to do with all the energy you wanted to do the
first thing. For example, if I come home late at night weary and frustrated, and a cat runs in front of me as I approach the back door, almost
knocking me down and making me stumble into the screen door, then I
want to kick the cat into the next yard. But if I do a reaction formation,
then I will lean over, pick up the kitty, and be so-o-o tender and so-o-o
kind. With all the energy I wanted to kick the cat into the next yard, I
will kneel down, feed the cat, and smother it with affection. This is a
reaction formation.

By the age of fourteen months, the child does the equivalent of a reaction formation on the traumatic situation: that is, she inflicts "no" on the
environment *before* the environment can inflict "no" on the child, and
with considerable determination and energy. By the dawning of the terrible twos, so called, the child is using "no" as a basis for controlling personal and interpersonal relationships. The interpersonal organizer at

fourteen months is "no." All parents have experiences of this. We say to the child, "Do you want to eat more cereal?" "No." "All right, I'll take it away." "Whaaaaa, I want my cereal!" The point has nothing to do with the cereal; it has to do with controlling the external environment. Freud's paper "On Negation"[24] describes the implications of this very well, and it is further developed by René Spitz's treatment of the same theme.

How does the child come up with such an ingenious solution? Why doesn't she fall crushed or simply regress to earlier bonding? These less effective moves do occur in childhood autism or depression, but in the more common situations, when the spirit of the child is not crushed, it will invent this solution. The child does not merely imitate parental "no"; rather, she spontaneously *uses* "no," and takes initiative with "no," making it a basis for organizing her relationships to everything and everyone. Using various forms of negation, she creates boundaries, delineates space, and draws on the buried memories of negation that extend back to the birth process,[25] now making what had previously hurt her ward off threat and protect her.

This transformation of negation is a spiritual move of existential proportions, establishing the line of repression between conscious and unconscious, inside and outside. This is a magnificent move defensively, since it establishes the basis for primary repression. It establishes "my world" as against "your world," my inner space against unwanted intrusions from both outside and inside. By means of negation, we construct the nonself, objective world over against and distinct from our human subjective sense of self. No-saying and reactions to no-saying, by translating into the psychic function of primary repression, lay the foundation for subsequent ego development. This is where we begin to learn how to keep inside inside and outside outside, and so begin the creation of culture and the objective world.

An example may clarify how repression becomes the intrapsychic functional translation of "no." In psychoanalysis, the aim will often be to work through repression to hidden sources of pathological behavior. What frequently occurs in the undoing of repression is the reverse of how repression first occurred. Millie, a twenty-seven-year-old woman, unable to understand her erratic emotional behavior, was haunted by a guilt-engendering presence of her deceased mother. The issue came to focus on the fact that she felt that she had let her mother die when she might have intervened to save her. This all came to the light through a dream in which she felt herself trapped in a weird old house at night. Then, she said, "I heard footsteps and saw just the corner of a petticoat whip by my door. *It was not my mother.*" The undoing of the repression through negation, that is, allowing confession to take place by denying it, now began to make redevelopment possible. The developmental move from negation to repression, repeated again and again in negating circumstances later in life, can be thus reversed. In that case, repression begins to break open with the negation of the repressed content.

Ingenious as the developmental transformation of negation into repression may be, we must note these pervasively unfortunate consequences. First, all subsequent so-called normal development is ego development, so it takes place on the basis of repression, that is, on the basis of "no." Negation as separation is the basis for grasping the objective world objectively, for objectifying oneself in self-understanding and maintaining interpersonal distance. It is ironic that the great achievements we so highly prize in the child are built on negation transformed into repression, the fundamentally defensive origins of ego formation.

A second major consequence is that although this is a magnificent move defensively, it means that the power and significance of the face as the imprint on what it means to be human is buried under the repression. The consequence is an emerging ego that is increasingly competent in ensuring survival and maintaining satisfaction, but underlying the ego's development and surrounding all its achievements is a profound sense of cosmic loneliness.

As we say clinically, "the secret secretes." Even primal repression never works perfectly. Thus, there is thereafter a deep longing for a face that will do for the adult person what the mother's face did for the child, a longing for a face that will not go away. This cosmic loneliness, set down at this early stage of ego development, will erupt again with greater force in adolescence, the middle years, and the final years of life. But already it is primal evidence that there is something theologically abnormal about so-called normal ego development.

In spite of the emergence of the small child's impressive adaptational competencies (language, intelligence, moral judgment), it seems clear that under the surface, existentially speaking, negation has triumphed. The human spirit has been forced by the sense of dread, "the anxiety of nonbeing,"[26] to contradict itself and lose touch with its original creation, the face phenomenon, and its power to shape human destiny in the direction of the divine. This powerful hidden longing continues to influence the ego from under the surface as the human spirit continues to scan for ways to overcome this deep fault in the bedrock of human development.

Thus, the much-lauded achievement of human development in the first year and a half of life ultimately is ironic. According to Erikson, ego formation involves both affirmation and negation; it is both trust and mistrust. If Erikson has his way, the child will come up with a predominance of trust over mistrust and lay the foundation for the virtue or the ego strength of hope, which gets institutionalized in formalized religion.

Erikson's trust versus mistrust organization of the ego is a defensive, functional solution to an existential and irreducibly theological crisis. Consequently, human existence throughout the rest of the life span, especially through the great eruptions of adolescence, the middle years, and later life, urges persons toward a more adequate solution that will nullify the existentially formative power of negation, transform the ego and its defenses, and put the totality of human existence into a relationship with the One who is the cosmic ordering, self-confirming presence—the Face of God who does not go away

The Human Spirit in the Creation of Intelligence

The struggle of the human spirit during this period focuses as well on the emerging functions of the ego—its linguistic, intellectual, and ethical expressions, which feed back into and partially shape the ego itself. Often played down or ignored in the study of developing ego functions is the formative power of the child's physical activity, the sensorimotor action and interaction with her environment. Focus here will lead us into the cognitive domain and its roots in the infant's negotiation of physical objects, especially those of touch, sight, and sound. What follows is the beginning development of language and intelligence as the human spirit of the child strives to overcome the sense of internalized separation, void, and nothingness, and so bridge the actual chasm between the ego and ultimate reality. These remarkable ego functions, built on the internalized negation at the base of the ego, are designed to search out, find, and describe the equivalent of the Face in the outside world extending beyond the entire universe. The primal drive behind the cognitive construction of the world is the ego's search beyond itself for the self-definition it has repressed within.

Sylvan Tomkins, a former research psychologist at Princeton University, once thought the search for universality began as a search for the face as repressed.[27] Now, from under the ego's repression, the secret longing is secreting, shaping the ultimate direction of the cognitive domain. What was lost inwardly secretes outwardly, first in our sense of awe and majesty when we survey the grandeur of the universe, and then in our quest to make it all comprehensible and so tell us who we are in what is otherwise the vast emptiness of expanding space. The self-transcending dynamic of the human spirit compels development forward in this quest for ultimacy, and language and intelligence are the means for this exploration. If we have lost the Face and its intimations of the Divine Presence, then perhaps through the ego's functions, we can come to know, at least indirectly, the mind of God—or so cognitive development seems to suggest.

Piaget: Basic Themes

In Piaget's terms, sensorimotor activity is the psychophysiological basis for the development of the highest orders of intelligence.[28]

Piaget is primarily an epistemologist, rather than a psychologist or a cognitive theorist, but his studies of intelligence are to be understood in the largest context possible. His developmental theories focus on the theme of adaptation, but it is by intelligence that we adapt to the entire universe. It is because human nature develops relationally within the ordered structures of the total universe that intelligence can reach to the biological, physical, and mathematical limits of the natural order. Piaget sees cognitive development as underlying the history of science, and even recapitulating that history. Thus, the developing structures of intelligence are not innate; they are, however, the resultant of an innate human potential for adapting to the structures of the universe.

Piaget's understanding of cognitive development from birth through the first eighteen months of life stems from his basic organic model and what he calls its functional invariants. By speaking of functional invariants, he presupposes an organized, ultimately intelligible totality of nature in which organism-environmental interactions occur. In any organism, from a simple unicellular organism, such as an amoeba, to the most complex organism, such as human nature, there are certain behaviors of the organism in its drive to survive that do not vary from one level of complexity to the next or from one context to the next. The key to survival is adaptation to the situation. These invariant behaviors or functions constitute a pattern of interaction by which a level of relational equilibrium or adaptation can consistently be achieved.

This overall pattern has two basic subparts: assimilation, which emphasizes the organism's side, and accommodation, which emphasizes the environmental side. These two are never separate behaviors, but they are analytically separable aspects of any organism-environment interaction. Any organism, however complex, will seek a balance between these two aspects, which is the basis for adaptation. Adaptation to extremely complex environments achieved through abstract signs and symbols is intelligence as we ordinarily think of it. Regardless of the level of organic complexity or environmental difficulty, the pattern or interaction among the invariant functions does not change.

For example, at a very concrete level, if a hungry child takes a piece of apple and eats it, the accommodation aspect requires that the child accommodate arm, hand, mouth, and digestion to the apple's position, contour, consistency, and all other physical properties. This modification in the organism is balanced by what the organism does to the apple to assimilate it. It will remove it, chew and devour it, and decompose and digest it, making it part of the organism. The original organic need or disequilibrium will now come to rest in an equilibrated balance between organism and environment, so an adaptational act has occurred. Eating the apple was the intelligent thing for the hungry child to do.

Suppose this same pattern were transposed to the more abstract realm of symbols and ideas. Then one would accommodate, if possible, to the idea being expressed. For Piaget, accommodation at more advanced levels of development is imitation; one will try to imitate in one's imagination how the idea works, imagine thinking with it as its author might suggest. But at the same time, one will be assimilating it to known frames of reference. For Piaget, assimilation becomes play at higher levels of interaction. That is, one will take the idea out of its original context, put it in different contexts of one's own contrivance, making it do things the original author or context did not necessarily suggest. The interaction between imitation and play gradually reaches equilibrium and makes the idea intelligible.

When Hercule Poirot, Agatha Christie's famous fictional detective, confronts a disturbing criminal case, he is drawn outside himself into a decidedly disequilibrated environment in which at least one murder has occurred. He enters imaginatively into its several facets, imitating in his own mind the presumed behavior of the characters. At the same time, drawing from his own knowledge and experience, he is playing with certain hypotheses as to how the crime was committed and who did it. Then, through a remarkable leap of insight, the variables come together—sometimes piece by piece, sometimes all at once. Equilibration is achieved, and everything leading up to the resolution becomes intelligible as the case is solved. Of course, the reader is going through the same process trying to second-guess Christie and solve the crime, before Poirot does, if possible.

By definition, assimilation refers to the organism or person's bringing some external object (food or ideas) into conformity with a given frame of reference (the organic need or the mind-set) already present in the organism or person. Accommodation refers to the organism or person's altering some aspect of its own frame of reference (organic need or mindset) in order to take account of the object in the environment. The dominance of assimilation is expressed in play, and the dominance of accommodation is expressed in imitation. A relatively stable equilibrium established between these two aspects of any interaction between the organism and its environment is adaptation, that is, intelligence.

In human development, repeatedly successful adaptational achievements build on one another as the ego becomes increasingly intelligent about the complexity of its environment. Thus, levels or stages in the expanding competence of any given ego function (in this case, intelligence) become evident. That is, adaptational levels of intelligence increase in their capacity to objectify and manage ever wider ranges of complexity with greater efficiency over the course of the first sixteen or seventeen years of life.

What is going on here is the simultaneous expanding and consolidating work of the human spirit in the behavioral register of intelligence. Assimilation tends to be more conservative, bringing the demands or conditions of the unknown environment into the known contexts of the organism or the person. Accommodation bends the given reference frames into new and unexpected shapes, so that the original frames have to be expanded or increased in complexity in order that the environment can be made intelligible.

Physicist George Gamow wrote a very popular book explaining the new science of relativity and quantum phenomenon entitled *One, Two, Three . . . Infinity*. This might have been the title of Piaget's account of the four stages in the development of intelligence as the spirit of the mind reaches toward the outer boundaries of the universe. The progression in these four stages is the exocentric movement of the spirit out of egocentrism toward greater and greater complexity, until the fourth stage, the capacity to do scientific thinking about infinity in all directions, is reached.

Briefly, the stages are as follows:

1. *Sensorimotor intelligence (from birth to two years)*. Adaptation is almost entirely through the body's motor and sensory activity, issuing initially from inborn instinctual activities. Grasping, sucking, crying, and sleeping are all ways the child is able to achieve an adaptational equilibrium with the new environment of people, objects, and the physical universe it enters at the moment of birth.

2. *Intuitive or preoperational intelligence (ages two to six years)*. The toddler's adaptational strategies begin to include symbolic represen-

tations (the "semiotic function" emerges at eighteen months) of his environment and language, which emerges with grammatical adequacy at about the age of four. However, the intelligence of the child, insofar as it is dependent on logical operations (inductive and deductive thinking), has not yet fully appeared.

3. *Concrete operations (ages seven to eleven)*. The six- to seven-year-old maturing child is able to think in terms of logical classifications (concept identity, inclusion and exclusion, particular and universal, and so forth) to perform inductive and deductive operations and, indeed, to do all the basic mathematical operations as well. During this period, thinking about numbers, time, causality, and all the objects of one's world develops with increasing capacity to continue to master more complexity with greater efficiency.

4. *Formal operations (age eleven onward)*. This stage emerges when the early adolescent begins to take her own thinking as an object of thought; thinking about thinking leads the development of intelligence to its highest level of structural competence. Intelligence can now perform the basic steps in scientific procedure. It can formulate a problem propositionally, construct and explore hypotheses, try them out mentally, select the most likely one, and devise a test for its validity.

These four stages represent an invariant sequence and, even if they unfold in a chronologically prodigious manner as they did in Piaget's own case, they must still appear in order. It is not only not possible to skip a stage, but each successive stage picks up what went before it and transforms its basic structure to create the next new stage. Notably, language is a necessary but insufficient factor in the emergence of the highest stage of intelligence and, as studies have shown,[29] the complexity of the language learned may be a factor in facilitating the development of the upper competencies of intelligence. The net result for the competencies of the developing ego is a capacity to view oneself from outside and to make rational, accurate judgments about the most complex issues of nature and human existence, including judgments about that capacity itself. This stage-by-stage movement out of egocentrism is the fundamental direction and goal in the maturation of intelligence. The overview may be summarily sketched as shown in Figure 4.1.

Egocentrism, and the developmental movement out of it, is a central theme in Piaget's thought and in all those positions based on it. Egocentrism in Piaget's thought is a developmental category, not an ethical one.

Figure 4.1. Overview of the Development of Intelligence.

Assimilation			(1) Sensorimotor
———————	— → Adaptation (equilibrium)	— → Intelligence	(2) Intuitive (preoperational)
Accommodation			(3) Concrete Operational
			(4) Formal Operational

Selfishness is a different issue. Piaget's structural egocentrism is the cognitive frame of mind in which the knower sees reality from only his own point of view, without knowledge of any other perspectives and without awareness that he is captive of his own. Unlike a defensive authoritarian or other rigid prejudicial position, egocentrism is a developmental given; under the influence of the human spirit, it is open to the external world and moving exocentrically through new encounters with the environment.

Although considerably elaborated through several registers of behavior (such as language and moral judgment), clinical studies, and illustrations, this account of structures and stages is the basic fashion in which Piaget has been understood in most American, European, and British academic circles. However, this perspective on his immense productivity can be fundamentally misleading, as Piaget himself said.[30] It tends to emphasize structures, stages, and a kind of parochial rigidity that misses the true genius of Piaget's descriptions. This is hidden in his admission that transformation is stronger than structure, and a tacit affirmation of the spirit of the developing person. This we will see and identify as we look more closely at the first eighteen months of life.

The First Stage of the Development of Intelligence

The first stage in the development of intelligence, sensorimotor intelligence, pertains to the first eighteen months of life and corresponds directly to the first phase of ego development. The unfolding subparts of this stage illustrate the exocentric movement toward the objective world and reciprocal strengthening of the ego, which I am arguing is the work of the human spirit implicit in Piaget's thought.

BIRTH TO ONE MONTH OF AGE In the first month, the principal relationship between the child and the environment is through the mouth and reflex management of the environment; that is, for Piaget, the action of the child within the total organic relationship of the child to the environment is definitive. There are reflexes that are triggered, such as grasping and sucking, which are then modified during the first month of life. For example, sucking is modified so that the child minimizes rooting and focuses in more quickly on the nipple. Bruno Bettelheim thought that it was important for strengthening the intentionality of the child to facilitate this zeroing in and refinement of the sucking reflex.[31] Even at this level, far-reaching cognitive concerns may be at stake.

ONE TO FOUR MONTHS OF AGE From one to four months of age, reflex activities undergo further modification toward objectifying reality, and acquired patterns are now repeated. Piaget refers to this sometimes as primary circular reactions, in which the infant repeats chance adaptations. One of Piaget's children, Laurent, at the age of two months, was scratching and grasping, holding and letting go of the sheet, or holding and letting go of the shirt on the shoulder that was holding him. Repeated activities are eventually followed by a gradual loss of interest as they become acquired patterns of action.

It is part of Piaget's observational genius that he recognized repetition as a foundation in sensorimotor terms for the subsequent development of cognitive constructs of objectivity. The construction of the object over against the subjective self requires that the thought of the child repeat its experience of a perceived object (later he will "turn it over in the mind") so that the object becomes a constant in its own right.

A second type of behavior refining the objective world is that certain basic schemas are combined. The child will learn to combine ear and eye reactions, eye and hand reactions, mouth and hand reactions. While this may take place by chance at first, it becomes increasingly intentional. Schemata, or elementary patterns of action, are gradually established in the mind and brain of the child. Sensations associated with patterns of action in the child are still very much within her subjective world; primal egocentrism continues to dominate thought. Stimulus from the external environment is felt internally, and satisfactions are internal. This means that at this early period, the child's construction of the world exhibits a predominance of assimilation over accommodation, even though the object world is beginning to take on a life of its own beyond that of the child.

FOUR TO EIGHT MONTHS OF AGE Now there is something called secondary circular reactions. The child gradually turns her attention to the environmental consequences of the act. She begins to see the object as object, and it gradually establishes permanence. The object appears and disappears, but out of sight is no longer out of mind; the child can retain the sense of the object in its own right and find it in its hiding place. There is an establishment of the continuity or the permanence of the object during this period. What is especially worth noting here is the strengthening of object-as-a-goal, or intentionality, the backbone of consciousness. Intentionality is so important because it is a major factor in intelligence, and at this stage it is partly measured by the number of intervening acts that a child will go through to obtain an object that has been removed from sight or become temporarily inaccessible.

This period includes the crucial six-month period of ego formation according to the psychoanalytical model. The timing is important since the child is learning to construct the objective world as objective during the same period when she is experiencing interpersonal and existential loss. Thus, in the economy of development, constructs of the objective world provide a partial solution to the loss of the Face, along with its implicit ordering of the child's environment; as ego competencies emerge, personal and primal orders are further submerged. Such emerging functional competencies may be seen as a counteracting response of the child's spirit generating new resources for ordering the world; but they are built on "no." That is, as a response to anxiety at the loss of the order implicit in the face-to-face interaction, the child begins to construct the objective, external world in her own terms. The loss of presence and its implicit order actually calls forth and facilitates objectivity. The generative power of the child's spirit is here driving intelligence toward adaptation at ever higher levels of objective complexity and reciprocally strengthening the self-awareness of the ego.

EIGHT TO TWELVE MONTHS OF AGE Piaget called this stage the coordination of secondary schemas. This amounts to the clear-cut use of tools on the part of the developing child. For example, one of Piaget's children reaches for the mother's hand to make her repeat a movement by which she was making some cloth wag up and down. He put her hand on the cloth to make her do it again. This is a beginning of tool using; the child is using intervening factors to achieve a goal that he determines.

This period also includes the ten-month creeping period in which the body itself is being used as a tool to get to points of interest and acquire desired objects. Note that the child is gradually shifting in relationship to his body; it is less "I am a body" and more "I have a body." The child is moving from being a body to having a body and using it as a tool, without, of course, ceasing to be a body. Thus, the child is deriving the distinction between ends and means and how to put them together.

One of the other most prominent tools to appear during this period is sound and the formation of words. The child enters into holophrastic speech, where single words encompass a whole classification of activities.

The child will say "ball," and that will mean any number of different things, all contained in the classification "ball"—for example, "I can say the word!" "Get the ball!" "Let's play!"

The striking point is not just that the child uses single words with multiple associated meanings. Also, the child, exhibiting uniquely human characteristics, will play with an object, get your attention, then give you the object and point to it. The child wants you to *say* something—"Thank you," or name the object, or anything else. The purpose seems to be to bridge the gap between where the child feels he is and where you are. This is reaching across a void that the child is feeling, because this is during the period of time when the sense of emptiness and anxiety is setting in from the standpoint of ego formation, and the repeated pointing is a forerunner of culture, as we try to find our way and make connections in an otherwise interpersonally empty universe.

TWELVE TO EIGHTEEN MONTHS OF AGE Now, at the period of tertiary circular reactions, the spirit of the child operative throughout the creation of her linguistic world becomes most evident. She is not just using means to acquire desired ends, but is actually inventing new means, discovering new ways of getting to desired objects. Most prominent in this is that the child learns to use "no" and uses it in a way to accomplish such goals as preserving personal possessions, achieving personal autonomy, and getting her way under coercive circumstances. This is one example of the invention of new means; of course there are many others.

We may sum up this eighteen-month sequence by watching as the child first plays with her hands in cereal. As she begins to throw cereal out of the bowl, then on to the floor, she will notice the effect of the cereal, splashing on the floor and walls. Then she will try new ways of throwing cereal on the floor—with her spoon, with the whole dish—all to invent a new ends-means connection. The patient Piagetian parent will recognize this experimentation as an advancement in intelligence and an expansion of the human spirit.

End of the First Period

The end of this period, at twelve to eighteen months of age, comes with what Piaget called the dawn of the semiotic function. The child can now intentionally use one thing to signify or represent another, and so construct the world symbolically in a reliable way. Piaget observed an early form of the semiotic function in the activity of his daughter who exhibited deferred imitation. Jacqueline threw a tantrum that was an exact imitation of a tantrum that she had seen a neighbor boy throw the day before. Piaget had witnessed the first tantrum and then saw the imitation. He noticed the exact replication after a day's delay, and recognized this as the dawn of the semiotic function through deferred imitation.

In other words, the child could take a concrete situation, convert it into symbolic forms, transpose it to another context, and reenact it, knowing that she was reenacting it symbolically. This means that now the child can make mental combinations and begin to do genuine reflective work at the level of what we call intelligence. Thus, by the end of eighteen months, semiotic competence has emerged for constructing the world "out there," and here is where we begin to fill in the cosmic loneliness with symbolic constructions of the world and of the universe.

Such expansive implications are intrinsic to Piaget's thought. His early studies noted well the sense of totality that accompanies each new intellectual achievement; to grasp some new object consciously or attain some new level of competence is automatically to have transcended it. Development gives rise at each stage to a kind of excitement that, having understood this or that word pattern or idea, a totality of related knowledge has become available. When Helen Keller first grasped the sign for water, she was so excited, not merely because she grasped the sign, but because it meant to her that the whole range of symbolic function, the linguistic world, was suddenly thrown open to her. The sense of totality that reaches out before the child at each level of attainment is a manifestation of the intrinsically transcendent spirit of the child that reaches outward, to encompass eventually the whole of the cosmic order and so, if possible, to recover the lost universe of infancy. What is implicit in the totality response and what emerges with ever greater clarity are not merely compensation for what was lost but a constructive and purposive potential that is gradually coming into its own.

It is clear that there are significant correlations between ego development and cognitive development and that these two perspectives overlay, complement, and critique each other. The common feature of both is the transformational dynamic, which relentlessly expands the horizons of both personal and cognitive competencies. Thus, the human spirit is the "Yes" that repeatedly drives out of egocentrism and beyond adaptation toward higher levels of meaning and purpose. Yet in itself as spirit, it has no meaning, no answer to the question, Why create? This suggests that the underlying sense of nothingness, the No, which is the basis of the ego and all of its cognitive achievements, has effectively separated the human spirit from its ground and from its capacity to situate itself in the universe as the creation of a personal Author.

Focusing the Psychological Perspective

In anticipation of the theological perspective, explored in the next chapter, four themes cutting across the psychoanalytic and the cognitive perspectives can be focused.

First, the five-step transformational pattern (conflict, scanning, insight, release of energy, proving out) is operative across the board as it makes the transitions between stages. This is the case from birth to trust through the dynamics of the face and its negation in ego formation, and from sensorimotor intelligence to intuitive and symbolic intelligence. This is on the linear, person-environment axis of development, which drives toward adaptation and rational order without regard to issues of meaning and purpose.

Second, understanding the transformational pattern as key to the dynamics of the spirit, it is possible to recognize in its pattern and coherence the tacit presence of a higher order that promises to give meaning and purpose to linear forms of adaptation. This might be called the vertical axis of development, where new orders of meaning and being intervene through the insight. At the point of insight, the human spirit is called back to its origin in the "one triune God." Through such intervening inventions, the whole of the ego-environment relationship is repeatedly reconstructed. Strictly speaking, such new orders do not come from either the person or the environment; instead, they are created by the spirit of the developing person out of the person-environment interaction. To be sure, psychoneurological foundations are evident, but what ultimately guides the act of creation? Why is the act of creation in development not strictly personal but recognizably universal in its capacity to yield up understandings of persons and the universe? Toward what ultimate goal is this repeated intervening act of creation directed? These questions clearly have theological implications.

Third, the underlying negation of human existence has many manifestations, such as loneliness, dread, or mistrust. However, most pervasively as primary repression, it constitutes the foundation of the ego and its functions. Thus, negation haunts the development of intelligence. By preserving the object-forming capacity of intelligence, it thereby nullifies any cognitive grasp of the existential truth of human nature. Since human existence as a whole (including its cognitive aspects) defies objectification, it can be comprehended only from a position beyond itself. This raises the question of the theological ground of human existence and its potential nonexistence or void.

And fourth, the interplay between centeredness and openness appears in the development of both the ego and intelligence. This paradoxical reciprocity, typical of the human spirit, works simultaneously to consoli-date and to open—that is, to consolidate both the sense of the self and its object world, and at the same time to open both to the quest for the Author of their creation. Again, the tacit but pressing issue is theological.

The patterns and themes that emerge as early as the first eighteen months of life implicitly raise fundamental questions that only theology is prepared to address. It is evident that human development is not the answer to anything of ultimate significance. Every answer it does provide only pushes the issue deeper, back to the ultimate question, "What is a lifetime?" and "Why do I live it?"

NOTES

1. Phyllis Greenacre, "The Economy of Birth," in *The Psychoanalytic Study of the Child,* vol. 1.

2. Arthur Janov, *Imprints* (New York: Coward-McCann, 1983), p. 47.

3. Frederik Leboyer, *Blissful Birth* (film). The potential for contamination in this "warm water birth" has been a major medical objection to Leboyer's method. This is an objection LeBoyer denies. See Caterine Milinaire, *Birth: Facts and Legends* (New York: Crown, 1979), pp. 205–209. It is cited here for its insightful sensitivity to several aspects of the birth process. Some have argued that this method produces potentially more balanced children (Janov, *Imprints*) but such outcomes are not proven.

4. Gordon Allport, *The Individual and His Religion: A Psychological Inter-pretation* (New York: Macmillan, 1950).

5. René Spitz, *The First Year of Life: A Psychoanalytic Study of Normal and Deviant Development of Object* (New York: International Universities Press, 1965).

6. Bruno Bettelheim, *Symbolic Wounds, Puberty Rites, and the Envious Male* (New York: Collier, 1962), and others, such as Joseph Campbell, C. G. Jung, and Julian Jaynes.

7. Sigmund Freud, *Three Contributions to a Theory of Sex* (New York: Dut-ton, 1962).

8. You can see how he developed this in Sigmund Freud, "Project for a Scien-tific Psychology," in *The Origins of Psychoanalysis* (New York: Basic Books, 1954) p. 347.

9. David Bakan, *The Duality of Human Existence: An Essay on Psychology and Religion* (Chicago: Rand McNally, 1966), and *On Method* (San Fran-cisco: Jossey-Bass, 1968), chap. 10.

10. Sigmund Freud, *Ego and the Id,* trans. James Strachey (New York: Norton, 1960).

11. Margaret S. Mahler, Fred Pine, and Anni Bergman, *The Psychological Birth of the Human Infant: Symbiosis and Individuation* (New York: Basic Books, 1975).

12. Joseph Pearce, *The Magical Child* (New York: Dutton, 1977).

13. H. C. Triantlis and Alastair Heron (eds.), *Handbook of Cross-Cultural Psychology,* vol. 4, *Developmental Psychology* (Needham Heights, Mass.: Allyn & Bacon, 1981).

14. Lloyd Silverman, Frank Lackmann, and Robert Milich, *The Search for Oneness* (New York: International Universities Press, 1982).

15 See D. W. Winnicott, *Family and Individual Development* (London: Social Science Paperbacks in association with Tavistock, 1968), and *Through Pediatrics to Psychoanalysis* (New York: Basic Books, 1975).

16. This process is reminiscent of the pattern of the spontaneous emergence of order out of apparent randomness that is attributed to Ilya Prigogine, Nobel laureate, 1977, a forerunner of chaos theory.

17. George Thomas, founder of the religion department at Princeton University, has suggested that in Western culture, the human spirit has been characterized by reason, universality, freedom, personality, love, and creativity. I have taken creativity as the most fundamental and generative of these themes, arguing that the other options all presuppose and depend on a transformational creativity as the central dynamic behind their operations. This claim will be spelled out as we continue. George Thomas, *Spirit and Its Freedom* (Chapel Hill: University of North Carolina Press, 1939).

18. Susanne Langer, *Philosophy in a New Key* (Cambridge, Mass.: Harvard University Press, 1979).

19. Frank Kermode, *The Sense of an Ending* (Oxford: Oxford University Press, 1967).

20. Spitz, *First Year of Life,* Ch. Vff.

21. See especially Konrad Lorenz, *Studies in Animal and Human Behavior* (Cambridge, Mass.: Harvard University Press, 1970).

22. Jolande Szekacs Jacobi, *The Psychology of Jung* (New Haven, Conn.: Yale University Press, 1943).

23. Spitz, *First Year of Life*, Ch. VIII.

24. Sigmund Freud, "Negation," in *Collective Papers* (London: Hogarth Press, 1950), vol. 5.

25. René Spitz, *Yes and No* (New York: International Universities Press, 1957). Recall Spitz's view that birth laid down a generalized sense of loss across the brain and it was recorded in the hypothalamus.

26. Søren Kierkegaard, *The Concept of Dread,* trans. Walter Lowrie (Princeton, N.J.: Princeton University Press, 1946), and Paul Tillich, "Anxiety," in *The Meaning of Health* (Chicago: Exploration Press, 1984), chap. 22.

27. Silvan Tomkins, *Affect, Imagery, Consciousness* (New York: Springer, 1962).

28. It might be objected that other figures such as Howard Gardner should be the source, but the form of intelligence he uses to study intelligence is Piagetian. See his *Frames of Mind* (New York: Basic Books, 1983), *The Mind's New Science* (New York: Basic Books, 1987), and *Leading Minds: An Anatomy of Leadership* (New York: Basic Books, 1995). This in no way denigrates other forms of intelligence, but the Piagetian approach alone appears to make intelligence of all sorts intelligible.

29. Jerome Bruner, *Studies in Cognitive Growth* (New York: Wiley, 1966).

30. Jean Piaget, personal conversation, 1968.

31. Bruno Bettelheim, *Symbolic Wounds, Puberty Rites, and the Envious Male* (New York: Collier, 1962).

5

INFANCY IN THEOLOGICAL PERSPECTIVE

THE SPIRIT'S CONFRONTATION

WITH NOTHINGNESS

THE TWO CLASSICAL doctrines central to any discussion of theological anthropology are the image of God, or human likeness to God, and original sin, or human distance from God. These are not topics for just one phase, but for the whole life span; each stage of development influences and illuminates the human meaning of the doctrines even as the doctrines provide theological dimension to the stages, separately and as a whole. Bringing these doctrines and developmental theory to bear on each other, following the Chalcedonian methodology described in Chapter Two, will shed fresh light on the issues involved.

Three patterns fundamental to the whole life span are already evident in the first eighteen months of life. The first two are primarily concerned with the human side of the image of God; the third focuses on the human side of the doctrine of sin. The three patterns, taken together with their corresponding theological theme, are the experience of the analogy between the human spirit and Creator Spirit, the experience of the analogy between the human face and Jesus Christ as the Face of God, and the experience of the analogy between developmental negation and original sin. The major emphasis here will be on the *analogia spiritus*, that analogy between the human spirit and the Creator Spirit, since other themes are derivative from this generative formulation.

The Analogy Between Human Spirit and Creator Spirit

The human spirit viewed as the image of God is like a mirror image separated from its original and unable to identify itself with anything real. But for all its wonders, beauty, and creativity, the human spirit is a self-contradictory dynamic without ground, meaning, or purpose in itself. It is like a troubled genius whose works astonish us, but whose torment ends in self-destruction. The Creator Spirit of God, whose dynamic of transformation establishes the likeness of the human spirit to itself in the *analogia spiritus,* transforms even the transforming power of the human spirit, nullifying its self-destructive qualities and liberating it for groundedness in and agreement with the Creator Spirit. This groundedness establishes the "glorious liberty of the children of God" and is what was experienced in the final phase of the cases of Helen and Lucy.

If there is a notable analogy between the human spirit and the troubled genius, then the human spirit, transformed through the mediation of Christ and embedded in his Spirit, becomes apostolic (that is, one taken up in Christ and sent into the world). However, between the genius and the apostle is a chasm of eternity, proclaimed Kierkegaard to the intellectual elite of Copenhagen.[1] The genius transforms his medium—art, philosophy, or science—but the apostle is himself transformed by the Creator of all things. The genius creates for the present age, but the apostle is himself recreated for all eternity. The point here is not ultimately negative; it is to show that the ingenious transformational pattern of the human spirit, though set at an eternal distance from God, is nevertheless the prototypical pattern for establishing similarity to or likeness between the human spirit and the Creator Spirit. Even in its twisted patterns of perversity and radical unlikeness to the Creator Spirit, the human spirit is a harbinger of its own transformation.[2]

In creating the world up to eighteen months of life, the human spirit continually brings personal order and intelligibility to the child. However, in its creation of the face phenomenon, followed by the creation of the ego, the spirit, having been separated from its ground, has generated two internally contradictory forces: the face whose primal force is an underlying "yes," and the ego whose underlying force is "no." Although the ego that emerges at this time is clearly dominant in consciousness throughout the ordinary life span, the secret secretes and the "yes" claims of the buried face subtly but persistently work under the surface to negate the negations of the ego and redirect its objectivating tendencies toward ultimate meaning and the transformation of the ego itself.

Could such a spirit be the image of God in us? When one considers the way in which the primal "yes" of the human spirit resists any form of oppression, from social and political domination to rigid paradigms of thought, even to the determination to overcome death, it is not hard to see the human spirit as the image of God. However, the image is broken off from its original, and in that respect essentially it is lost. It retains a transformational character and longs for the Face of God. Yet transformation ungrounded in the Spirit of Christ can issue in violent revolution and new forms of oppression, and the God it seeks may be of its own making. Yet even in its ignorance of God, in the emptiness, confusion, and ultimate darkness of its separation from God's Spirit, it longs for the liberty that only the Creator Spirit can provide.

The Human Spirit as *Imago Dei*

In his book *The Holy Spirit in Christian Theology,* George Hendry makes the case that biblically and theologically, it is in the human spirit that we find the one true, original image of God. In support of Hendry, it is not hard to see that in the two creation narratives in Genesis, God is characterized preeminently as Creator and as self-relational Spirit doing the creating. This observation, together with Jesus's statement that "God is Spirit" (John 4:24), form the first general premise of this case.[3] Thus, to be made in the image of God is to be made, in a similar sense, spirit. More definitively, the descent of the Spirit and the creation of the church in Acts 2 make it clear that God's continuing action in the world is by God's Spirit. To have that image restored to its original is to be immersed in God's Spirit such that the human spirit reflects the nature and work of God's Spirit in the world.

In this connection, note that the Greek word *breathe* (*emfusao*) is used only once in the entire New Testament, when Jesus breathes on the disciples saying, "Receive the Holy Spirit" (John 20:22–23). However, its occurrence in Genesis 2:7 in the Septuagint makes the important connection between the human reception of the Spirit of God in the creation of persons and in the creation of the church. Other places where this is used in the Septuagint are I Kings 17:21, Ezekiel 37:9 ("Breathe on these dead ones"), and Wisdom 15:11 ("He breathed a living spirit into them").

As Cullen Story notes, this anointing of John (20:22–23) is a harbinger of Pentecost.[4] What was bestowed on a few must be received by many (Acts 1:15). The gift received privately, personally, and in particular must be manifest publicly and universally. What could indicate the dawn of the new era of the Spirit of Christ in more graphic fashion than the use of the same verb form in John 20:22 as the one that appears in the Septuagint version of the creation of Adam? The giving and the anointing of the Spirit is both personal and universal. The celestial signs surrounding the Savior's birth (Luke 2:8–14) anticipate other celestial phenomena that mark the birth of his church (Acts 2:1–4).

Thus, the new era of the Spirit is inaugurated cosmologically, universally, and personally, but the new era calls for a human response. Just as Adam, formed and "in-breathed" with the breath of life (Gen. 2:7), was given a task to perform (Gen. 2:18), so, according to John 20, disciples are "in-breathed" and given a mission to accomplish comparable to the mission of Jesus. In other words, once the human spirit is awakened to its origin and true ground, it must exercise the freedom inherent in being spirit and choose to respond and conform to the in-breathing of the life of God. Both gift and task are crucial; they are not to be separated, confused, or reduced one side to the other. In their relationality, they may be seen as the behavioral manifestation of the restored image of God, Spirit-to-spirit.

In his exegetical argument, Hendry discusses the connection between the two creation narratives in Genesis.[5] The in-breathing of the divine breath or Spirit (Gen. 2:7, the J document) directly corresponds to the creation of human nature in the divine image (Gen. 1:27, the P document). As cosmological dust, human existence, like all the rest of creation, is dependent on God. But by the in-breathing of the Spirit of God, human existence takes on a life of its own. It makes the relationship spirit-to-Spirit with God essential to an accurate and adequate understanding of human nature in its truest form.

By making the assumption that the human spirit is the broken-off image of God and by interpreting what has been said about the human spirit, now, through the eyes of faith, we can recognize the *analogia spiritus* and understand its Chalcedonian call for an ultimate transformation of all the proximate transformations that appear in the natural course of a life time.

Analogia Spiritus

The exocentric centeredness that Pannenberg described is understood as a paradoxical relationality, moving outward and inward at the same time. However, the transcending exocentricity of the spirit is not a reflexive but a transformational dynamic. Thus, every obstacle in the way of its working out of its paradoxical relationality gets transformed in the spirit's relentless drive both to center and to transcend the individual and his or her circumstances.

The transformational dynamic begins in *conflict*, moves through a *scanning* phase, comes up with an *insight* that resolves the conflict, and *releases the energy* bound up with it in a "Eureka!" *repatterning* of the self-world relationality and *proving* out the adequacy of the resolution. This dynamic combines continuity and discontinuity in what Michael Polanyi calls the most fundamental form of knowing: the act of discovery in the sciences, the act of creation in the arts—both powerful expressions of the human spirit.[6]

The logic of transformation helps to specify the core dynamic of the human spirit as it includes the exocentricity that Pannenberg helpfully stresses. Moreover, it corrects from within the human context some misappropriations of the developmental material by theologians, specifically Pannenberg and Hans Kung. When Pannenberg grounds Christian faith developmentally in Erikson's view of basic trust, he neglects the pervasive negative force that prevails in development.[7] This force is explicit in Erikson's concern for both trust and mistrust to be included in the child's resolution to this first year and a half of life. Basic trust has to take account of its opposition and its limits; otherwise it is naive and unsustainable. Pannenberg's view is that the expanding horizons of awareness, derivative from basic trust, are implicitly infinite, "without limitation." For Pannenberg, this expansion of the theme of basic trust is directed beyond the nurturing maternal context to God. However, this claim cannot be grounded in Erikson's view of the first year of life the way Pannenberg wants it to be. Mistrust cancels infinity; infinite expansion as *imago dei* is not developmentally sound.

A similar issue pertains to Hans Kung's argument in *Does God Exist? An Answer for Today.*[8] As Pannenberg himself points out, Kung attempts to make basic trust into a new justification for the idea of God in opposition to atheism and nihilism. According to Kung, only an act of "decision" moves one from the simple idea of God as a "hypothesis" to the acceptance of God as real. But this shifts the human side of faith in God from its rootedness in the bedrock of human development to a level of detachment in which alternatives are assessed and dismissed. The existential wholeness of belief in God is thereby diminished rather than substantiated by this appeal to decide for a radical basic trust.

In fact, neither theologian makes accurate or effective use of Erikson's observations. However, it may be that Erikson himself has not got it quite right when he talks about basic trust-mistrust being primarily dependent on the nurturing environment. Surely in adaptational terms the environment is immensely important, as studies of attachment have shown.[9] Nevertheless, it is the creative capacity of the child to construct and compose the self-environment relationship—not the environment itself—that must become the foundation for the child's sense of basic trust. The environment will change or may outwardly appear to be untrustworthy, but the key factor is whether the spirit of the child can create a livable world out of whatever is there to work with.

Moreover, this spiritual capacity of the child will continue to be exercised as she moves into subsequent stages of human development. Every register of behavior has to be recreated again and again as transformational logic works to bring forth new and wider forms of world order for the child. Trust must reside essentially in the spirit of the child. When this is the case, the negative as well as the positive side of development is dealt with according to the logic of transformation.

Even if it is clear that the dynamics of the human spirit run deeper than the trust created by them, for all of its transformational potential and ingenious capacity to construct and expand human horizons of meaning, the human spirit is by itself without ground and without meaning for itself *as spirit*. By allowing the human spirit to reflect on itself as spirit, we arrive at the intrinsic cry of the human spirit for ground, meaning, and purpose. In itself, it has no answer to the question of why it should create an environment of trust, why it should go on creating the structures of development, or why it should exist at all. This is a cry of the image for reunion with its original.

If we turn to the theological doctrine of the Creator Spirit, we can see how the theological tradition anticipates the needs and longings of the human spirit, and calls for the restoration of the human spirit as image of God. The human spirit and the Creator Spirit belong together in a communion in which it is possible to recognize the analogy that pertains between them. It is an *analogia spiritus* in which the dominant characteristics of the human spirit are stripped of their anxieties and perversities, and are transformed into the likeness of the Creator Spirit. In this analogical communion, the human spirit can recognize itself as the mirror image of the Creator Spirit and find its original, its ground, its reason for being.

Two aspects of the analogy are especially notable when we look at the tradition through Regin Prenter's treatment of Luther in *Spiritus Creator*: the transformational pattern and the covariant action of the spirit as simultaneously exocentric and centering.[10] Two distinct aspects in the work of the Creator Spirit mark it as transformational: *mortificatio* and *illuminatio*. The Creator Spirit comes to mortify, to convict of sin before

God. Thus, like the human spirit, it begins in conflict and works through transformation into a new creation.

Mortification—to convict of sin—sounds dark and oppressive, but as an act of the Creator Spirit, it is intended to be just the opposite. It is, of course, sin itself that is dark and oppressive, *not* the convicting act of the Spirit. To come under conviction before God is not a matter addressed to a person's superego or a socially constructed conscience. It is addressed to the fault lines in the bedrock of the human psyche, most evident in the double-bind structure of the human ego.

Developmentally, this condition of human existence is the inversion of the human spirit in its confrontation with abandonment and nothingness. The original existential loss or negation implicit in birth, revisited as the emptiness of the abyss that separates us from the face, is incorporated into the human ego, the central agency of human action. To be convicted is not a matter of conscience; it is to be stripped of one's defenses and led back into this abyss, recognizing the inevitable downfall of the ego in its efforts to incorporate and conceal the abyss from awareness.

Of course, the ego inevitably will lose this lifelong battle against nothingness. Death takes all, so under conviction, the ego may be seen as a kind of tragic hero whose fatal flaw was the negation it incorporated in order to begin the journey of human development in the first place. This developmental phenomenon may even be a hidden source of Athenian drama in which the fatal ironies implicit in the ego's heralded competencies are personified and played out on stage for the cathartic relief of those who can recognize in these dramas a reenactment of the tragic side of human development.

In *Young Man Luther*, Erikson describes something called ego chill in which a young child is shocked suddenly into the realization that there was a time when he did not exist.[11] If ego chill is the sudden awareness of one's own nonbeing, then conviction is ego chill before the presence of the Holy God. If one realizes the stunning significance of the holy, then in this respect, conviction is more stunning than ego chill. But precisely because of that Holy Presence, conviction is not violent; it is not designed to crush the ego.[12] No less radical than the concept of ego chill, conviction is the awareness that one's being or nonbeing resides utterly in the hands of the living God, and nowhere else.

But the Creator Spirit, creating *ex nihilo* as from the beginning, brings the illumination of the Gospel. To say "repent," one must simultaneously say, "The kingdom of God is at hand." This should come as a proclamation of freedom to an ego that has continuously run from its own annihilation, fought down the darkness, and finally incorporated it, only to realize that what it has incorporated is devouring the ego from within itself. "Repent, for the kingdom of God is at hand" means you can lay aside the defenses; you can undergo a paradigm shift of existential proportions because an utterly different choice is immediately at hand. This is not just good advice; it is creative power addressed to the foundation of human existence.

Thus, to be convicted of sin should be met with something like an "Aha! So that's what's wrong! Praise God, there is an alternative!" It is thoroughly gracious to realize that the basic issue is not your bad behavior, your immoral acts, your treatment by parents, siblings, or circumstantial loss of a future. To be convicted of sin is to be led to see at first that it is much worse than you thought it was. In fact, to be conscience stricken can be very painful, but this is preferable to the existential realization that even the criterion of a socially constructed conscience is deeply faulted; even the good we thought we did was as flawed as the evil we thought we were opposing.[13] This would be unbearable, totally offensive, even unrecognizable if it were not that such a realization is preceded by the grace that makes such a realization not only bearable but profoundly generative of a new being. The Creator Spirit must create *ex nihilo* in individuals as it created in the beginning of the whole of creation. Thus, mortification precedes the illumination in our accounting of it, but in the sphere of the spirit, the illumination precedes and anticipates the mortification.

To put this in developmental terms, the ego can release its defensive patterns, lay aside its self-imposed boundaries, and allow the "ego-alien righteousness" of Christ to bestow the Gospel, and to establish for the person a higher order of meaning and purpose for which ego functions and patterns of defense may or may not be well suited. Now the choosing ego can take or leave its functions and defenses because the alien righteousness of Christ, evident only in the sphere of the Spirit, constitutes the center and maintains the order of human existence. Death is given to the death incorporated in the ego, and the human spirit is now grounded in the Creator Spirit without ceasing to be the human spirit and without ceasing to use the ego and its competencies. Purpose and meaning are established for the human spirit in its bipolar unity with the Creator Spirit, its source and ground. Thus, the human spirit works out its salvation "with fear and trembling" because it is "God who is at work" in the convicted person (Phil. 2:16).

Now we must ask, What is illuminated? The answer, for the believer in the sphere of the Spirit, is essentially "the alien righteousness of Christ." The "alien" is ego alien in the sense that one does not identify with Jesus, one does not etch the face of Jesus into one's own, as Erikson suggested in his psychohistorical analysis of Luther. The "alien" also means that the "experience" of the Spirit cannot be identified with any particular psychological manifestation, such as an altered state of consciousness, a sensation of warmth, or a tingling in the hands. "Experience of the Spirit" is distinctly apart from any particular pietistic or spiritualistic manifestation, yet the Spirit *is* experienced. Physical manifestations may accompany the action of the Spirit, as in Luther's famous tower experience when the Spirit revealed to him that the just God does not condemn but the just God justifies (Rom. 5:1ff.). This realization came, he said, while he was on the privy in the tower, and it came as a great relief to him. On the more gracious side, Luther does not deny such manifestations as spiritual healing, but in the sphere of the Spirit, the only physical manifestations are the Word of God and the sacraments.

The point of "alien" is to protect the sovereign freedom of God's Spirit, but it is not to eliminate tangible responses to the Spirit's transformative action. The righteousness of Christ is to preserve for Christ alone the whole matter of justification and salvation, and to make him, and him alone, the one for whom and in whom the transformation (from mortification to illumination) by the Spirit takes place.

A second aspect of the *analogia spiritus* needs to be spelled out: the paradoxical relationality between exocentricity and centeredness. The most obvious way to talk about the *analogia spiritus* is to show similarity and difference around the concept of transformation, as I have already done. Another important aspect of the analogy lies in the paradox as the covariant reciprocity between centeredness and transcendent exocentricity.

This phenomenon has been observed by psychologists and theologians alike. It is at the core of Piaget's understanding of how the child centers on the creation of objects as objects in reciprocity with a transcending sense of totality. The example already noted concerned Helen Keller's discovery of the whole field of language as she centered on the one word, *water*. In effect, the child moves out of egocentricism by the progressive practice of this reciprocity, but in the cognitive domain, there is no transcendence without object formation, just as object formation always initiates transcendence. This is a tacit concession to the spirit of the child in Piaget's thought.

What Piaget describes with respect to the cognitive domain applies also to ego development. Pannenberg describes the formation of ego identity by virtue of the spirit, "exocentric centeredness," in a similar manner. The covariant reciprocity between the centrifugal movement of the human spirit toward infinity and its reciprocal centripetal movement toward the consolidation of ego identity is, in Pannenberg's description, a "religious thematic" built into human nature.[14] Notably, there is a similar bipolar movement in Paul Tillich's understanding of the core of human freedom. When he asks, "What is basic to human nature?" he answers by describing a covariant relationship between the "integrated self" and "what drives beyond it."[15] These two moves form one structure, the structure of freedom, which he says constitutes the core of human nature. This bipolar reciprocity is an important way to conceive of the human spirit; as it moves outward transformationally, it simultaneously feeds back into the formation of the core of one's person.

However, both psychologists and theologians are here describing the human spirit, and neither suggests or develops the analogical connection to the person of Christ and the expansion of his Spirit into the world. *Spiritus Creator* repeatedly creates *ex nihilo* by powerful transformations that bring life out of death, but for every new act of creation that expands the horizon of the reign of Christ's Spirit, there is a reciprocal testimony to and glorification of the specific historical man, Jesus as the Christ. Similarly, for every new-found faith in Jesus Christ, there is an outward movement of his Spirit into the world as a Pentecostal outpouring emanating from Jesus Christ as the center. That outpouring reciprocally testifies to who he is. This theological reciprocity was at the center of Helen's night of violence. In her text for that night, Jesus foretold of the Spirit, and in the Spirit, through prayer, we returned again and again to images of Jesus Christ, until Helen's spirit was liberated for reunion with his Spirit, as the image restored to its original, for the sake of the church, his body. This pattern had the power to turn Helen's psyche inside out and reverse the developmental time of her life because it was rooted in her from birth. But until the awakening of her spirit, there could be nothing but deep despair and no reason to live. Again, the fragmented, sheeplike wandering of the natural child longs for an ultimate groundedness that rescues the human spirit from despair, but it is only a theological perspective that can recognize the longing for what is and can set forth an account of the alternative.

The Face of God

When Lucy knelt before the icon of Jesus to ask forgiveness for what she was about to do, everything was at stake. Her suicide was a settled matter; the plan was all laid out, and she had only to say her final prayers. Her bitter anger and utter helplessness had been with her day and night. What was first grief had become deep depression and now despair. In this way, she could be done with the pain and punish those who had hurt her forever. But it was not merely a situational reaction; it was the loss of any reason to go on living. The icon placed her before the image of Jesus, and she had to look through the slow smoke that rose from the incense into "the Face of God," and ask forgiveness. It was not the guilt that stopped her, or fear or ambivalence. It was a sense of joy that welled up within her. The spiritual power of the Divine Presence lifted her off her knees and held her in an affirmation of life that made her want to live again, create a new life, and eventually reach out and be restored to her family. The Spirit of God runs deeper than instinct, deeper than vengeance and the wish to die. It is no vague mist, but the reality of his presence evident in Jesus, the Face of God.

To say that Jesus Christ is the Face of God is to make reference to the long tradition and many-faceted metaphorical uses of "the face" in Scripture to designate the personal presence of the holy God. In both Greek (*prosopon*) and Hebrew (*panîm*) the word for *face* also means "presence." However, the Face of God ceases to be a metaphor and becomes historically and empirically concrete in the person of Jesus Christ. In him, the relation between God and humanity is full, complete, and actualized in the same spatiotemporal and historical context in which we also exist.

However, the human source of the scriptural metaphor and the human basis for its appropriation in faith lie more deeply embedded in human nature than the literary power of metaphor and the claims of historical actuality can fathom. This is what the developmental exposition of the significance of the face phenomenon spells out. It makes it clear that when we are speaking of the Face of God, we are speaking humanly and existentially to the longing in persons for a cosmic ordering, self-confirming presence of a loving other, a longing for that which defines what it means to be human and makes us over in its image. This is in no way to diminish the value of metaphor and history in giving an account of Jesus Christ as the Face of God; indeed, they are necessary but not existentially sufficient. It should also be restated that human nature is so constituted that built into its ego structure and implicit in its greatest achievements is a cosmic loneliness that longs for a Face that will do all that the mother's face did for the child, but now a Face that will transfigure human existence, inspire worship, and not go away, even in and through the ultimate separation of death.

The discussion of development has laid the groundwork for understanding how human nature is made for appropriating the claim that Jesus Christ is the Face of God. Such a discussion helps to concretize and account for the existential power of the metaphor, but it does not explain how Jesus is the Face of God or what it means to speak of Jesus as the restoration of the image of God, when the image of God is understood as spirit and restoration is accomplished in the spirit-to-Spirit relationship.

Jesus becomes the Face of God for us only through faith and by the power of his Spirit; to bring Jesus Christ out of the past by the power of his Spirit does *not* mean merely that the understandings we have of his nature and his teachings have considerable relevance for today; this Jesus is not simply a relevant figure for reflecting on contemporary culture. Rather, for Jesus to become our contemporary means that the very form of his bipolar person becomes the structure of our own identity. In spiritual language, the relationality between the Divine Spirit and the human spirit in us has to become Christomorphic. He remains captive of history, culture, or the religious imagination until he comes into us Spirit-to-spirit. For him to come out of history into the fullness of the present time means that our spirits and all their creations are transformed, so we want this dynamic Christomorphism to define us, and in our humanity we want to become like him in his humanity—not as a role model, ethical paradigm, or beautiful feeling. He must dwell in us by virtue of the spirit-to-Spirit dialectic that replicates in us and beyond us the Chalcedonian bipolar relational unity that characterizes two natures in one person. This issues for us in a dialectical identity in which we say "I-not I-but Christ." This expresses a bipolar unity in which Christ exercises ontological priority. From this identity, we live out the *analogia spiritus*. This means that in our humanity we are transformed again and again as we behold in him the One to whom we are meant to be conformed.

Consider the biblical texts II Corinthians 3:13–18 and 4:5–6:

> We . . . are not like Moses, who put a veil over his face to keep the people of Israel from gazing at the end of glory that was being set aside. But their minds were hardened. Indeed, to this very day, when they hear the reading of the old covenant, that same veil is still there. . . . Indeed, to this very day whenever Moses is read a veil lies over their minds, but when one turns to the Lord, the veil is removed. Now the Lord is the Spirit, and where the Spirit of the Lord is, there is freedom. And all of us with unveiled faces, seeing the glory of the Lord as though reflected in a mirror, are being transformed into the same image from one degree of glory to another; for this comes from the Lord who is the Spirit. . . . For we do not proclaim ourselves; we proclaim Jesus Christ as Lord and ourselves as your slaves for Jesus' sake. For it is the God who said, "Let light shine out of darkness,"

who has shone in our hearts to give the light of the knowledge of the glory of God in the face of Christ.

On a psychological level, appropriation of the Spiritual Presence of Christ is like imprinting on a human face in order to know with your whole nature what species you belong to; but in human beings, imprinting refers to the specific, material contours of a human face. In theological terms, imprinting is transformed into beholding or "seeing" Christ's presence. This is similar to but profoundly different from being gripped by the presence of a charismatic figure.

In the Corinthian passage, the comparison Paul makes between Moses and Jesus dramatizes the difference between a luminous human presence (Moses), whose charismatic impact passes away, and Jesus, whose illuminating presence appears with the force of another reality, the source of its own light, redefining human existence from within our hearts. As we behold his presence in this way, we ourselves are transformed into his likeness. Taking the notion of figure quite literally, this is a transfiguration of imprinting from something natural to something irreducibly spiritual, but the result is similar: in this relation to his presence, we know what "species" we belong to. The result is the dialectical identity. In this, one's psychological identity, created and empowered by the human spirit, is in a dialectical relation with the Spiritual Presence of Christ (the Face of God alive in us), which is made powerful and rich for us by the Creator Spirit. The Creator Spirit is to our human spirit what God is to man in the person of Jesus, and the joint activity of the two spirits becomes a dynamic version of Chalcedon—"Chalcedon on wheels," as someone said.

Thus, the restoration of the human spirit to its ground and origin in the Creator Spirit is the restoration of the image of God in three important respects:

1. *Substantive.* The image of God in Jesus Christ is made contemporary and personally powerful for us by the presence of his Spirit in us and in relation to our human spirit. This addresses definitively the issue of presence as it appears in contemporary philosophy and psychology as well as in theology.

2. *Formal.* The relationality between God's Spirit and the human spirit is analogous to the Chalcedonian understanding of Jesus as two natures, one person. Thus, the very form of our existence in the Spirit is Christomorphic.

3. *Consistency.* The fundamental consistency between the Spiritual Presence of Christ and the historical reality of Jesus is attested by

the scriptural claim that just as Jesus witnessed to the coming and present reality of the Spirit, so the Spirit witnesses always to Jesus. Thus, to say that Jesus is the Face of God is the prerogative of the inner witness of the Spirit; but the inner witness of the Spirit is possible for us to appropriate only as the broken image of God is restored to its original.

The coherence of these three aspects of the restoration of the image is important not merely for the sake of the argument but also for the satisfaction of the developmental longing. It is only in a deeply personal and cosmic ordering reality, understood together with and in love, that the developmental longing is satisfied. All three constituents as a whole are required; if one constituent is missing, the longing remains. We cannot be satisfied until we have put a loving Face on the Author of Creation.

The Origin of Sin

To mature in Christ is to behold who we are in Jesus Christ as the Face of God, and so be held there while his Spirit transforms our spirits in conformity to his person. This is the one and only situation in which perfect conformity amounts to perfect liberty. Thus, as one intensifies one's participation along the spiritual axis of development, liberty at the level of one's developing psychological selfhood is increasingly enhanced and empowered for the risks of loving the world and one's neighbor. This pattern deepens our participation in the created order, as the cases of Helen and Lucy illustrated.

This is not a simple, straightforward matter. From the moment of birth, there are forces at work antithetical to the paradoxical exocentricity of the human spirit. In fact, these forces will eventually prevail against our human efforts to sustain life in the Spirit. I have already introduced the theme of original sin implicitly in discussions of the Spirit and the image of God, and like these themes, it will continue throughout development to its end, since the ultimate aim of original sin is death. However, it must now be introduced directly to prepare future discussion.

Pannenberg's discussion of sin makes it clear that our tendency is to say what the original sin was (pride, concupiscence, egoism) in terms of its consequences, but the consequences of original sin cannot explain its origins. For his own position, Pannenberg transposes original sin into "unfinished" or "incomplete" conformation to the Christ, who in his resurrection revealed the end and ultimate meaning of history.[16] The doctrine as it has usually been discussed is an attack on the integrity of human identity, an example in itself of sin as Pannenberg has redefined it.

Once again this seems to beg the question, shifting the issue of origins to the issue of destiny. Thus, a reexamination of the collapse of innocence into guilt as an inveterate quality of human nature may be called for. The fundamental point is that the psychological pattern of development in the genesis of a lifetime, viewed from the Genesis of all creation, deepens meaning in both directions. This is Kierkegaard's project in *The Concept of Anxiety*.[17] Pannenberg criticizes Kierkegaard's analysis, claiming that he imports egoism into the Adamic situation, making a consequence into a cause. However, this does not reckon with Kierkegaard's distinction between qualitative and quantitative anxiety. Qualitative anxiety refers to the way in which we are like Adam, bringing self-destruction on ourselves, individually and corporately. The pattern here bears a close relation to ego development. It is especially interesting that in J's account of "the Fall" in Genesis, there is a movement from Face-to-face interaction with God, to anxiety (the woman is already anxious because she puts words into God's mouth; God did not say not to "touch" it, only not to "eat" of it), to a denial or no-saying rejection of God's commandment to them, hiding behind fig leaves (not a bad symbol of repression), and ultimate expulsion from the Garden to wandering on the face of the earth in search of the restored union with God to overcome the consequent cosmic loneliness.

The parallel to the formation of the ego in the first eighteen months of life is important not only because the steps are there, but because the overall movement from the Face-to-face to the negation and cosmic loneliness is a general pattern for alienation in a number of other contexts that appear regularly in the course of a lifetime. This may be called a developmental version of Kierkegaard's qualitative anxiety. We each repeatedly experience the inevitable self-alienation of Adam in our own psychic life.

Kierkegaard, in his notion of quantitative anxiety, argues that consequent manifestations of qualitative anxiety increase and intensify the probability of self-destruction that follows on qualitative anxiety. The first is a condition of brokenness; the second refers to the accumulation of manifestations of brokenness, which make it more likely that brokenness will increase and become intensified. Egoism is obviously a part of quantitative anxiety, but it could not be part of the original precipitating event because, as Kierkegaard realizes, anxiety precedes the formation of the ego. In fact, Pannenberg himself returns to a restatement of Kierkegaard's position on qualitative anxiety when he tries to describe developmentally how we enter into our unfinished condition. In our discussion of human brokenness, we must take account of both the condition and the consequences, and we will use Kierkegaard's discussion repeatedly to show how this brokenness is inevitable, but not necessary.

The description of the first eighteen months of life in Chapter Four sets forth an account of the struggle of the human spirit and the inevitable collapse of the psyche into an ego based on "no." This buries the face, resulting in a cosmic loneliness that the human spirit strives to reconstruct through the functions of the ego as in the quest for universals and the mind of God. This, of course, is a futile venture; wanderings in the universe result in all sorts of aggravation of the original brokenness, since the ego is in its very structure a double-bind, which cannot correct its negation-based existence without making it worse, burying the face ever deeper.

The first eighteen months of life may have enormous consequences for the rest of life. From this perspective alone, life is inevitably tragic, but nothing has been said here about good or bad, guilt or shame. Pannenberg seems correct in taking the moral issue out of "original sin" and making it descriptive of a condition, but the condition is closer to our origins than he seems to think. Original brokenness becomes "original sin" only when this brokenness, which Kierkegaard called "despair," is brought before God. The Spiritual Presence of God exposes the condition and simultaneously offers a real alternative to the brokenness.

This brings us to a new level of human development, which begins to appear in the next phase of ego formation. This developmental perspective suggests that the doctrine of original sin is in fact something one grows into as much as one falls into. The distinction that Kierkegaard makes between quantitative and qualitative anxiety is implied here, but developmental studies can specify that the doctrine becomes intelligible only for a person who has reached adolescence. This is not because adolescence is a difficult time, but because it is the first time anyone can grasp the relentless sense of nonbeing or nothingness, which, as Sartre said, haunts human existence.[18] This, of course, returns us to the primary questions of this book, and adolescence is the first time anyone can ask it with some awareness of what is at stake, "What is a lifetime?" and "Why do I live it?"

NOTES

1. Søren Kierkegaard, "The Genius and the Apostle," in *The Present Age* (New York: HarperCollins, 1962).

2. This is essentially the way in which Kierkegaard describes how movement through "stages on life's way" actually intensifies one's awareness of the absolute distance between the existing individual and God. At the same time, the stages are constructive, even necessary, for one to get into a position to recognize "the God-man" for who he is. However, in his own case, Kierkegaard got to the end at the beginning in a vision of "inexpressible joy." Thus, in transformational time, he leaped over the sequence of any stages, and from that standpoint he could recognize that any notion of progress by stages was at best a truth-producing error, not a condition for salvation, but decisive for appropriation.

3. Full-scale development of this argument that the human spirit is the most adequate way to discuss the *imago dei* is to be found in James E. Loder and W. Jim Neidhardt, *The Knight's Move* (Colorado Springs: Helmers and Howard, 1993), chap. 1 and sec. 1, pp. 1–125. Discussion of this position in relation to Pannenberg and others may be found on pp. 48–49.

4. Cullen I. K. Story, *The Fourth Gospel* (Shippensburg, Pa.: Ragged Edge Press, 1997), p. 444.

5. George Hendry, *The Holy Spirit in Christian Theology* (Philadelphia: Westminster Press, 1976), pp. 106–107.

6. Michael Polanyi, *Personal Knowledge* (New York: HarperCollins, 1964), pp. 49ff.

7. Wolfhart Pannenberg, *Anthropology in Theological Perspective* (Philadelphia: Westminster Press, 1985).

8. Hans Küng, *Does God Exist? An Answer for Today* (New York: Doubleday, 1980).

9. See Margaret Mahler, *The Psychological Birth of the Human Infant* (New York: Basic Books, 1975).

10. Regin Prenter, *Spiritus Creator* (Philadelphia: Muhlenberg Press, 1953).

11. Erik H. Erikson, *Young Man Luther* (New York: Norton, 1962).

12. Even in one of the most violent conversions recorded in Scripture, Paul's being struck down on the Damascus road, Jesus addresses him with a question to elicit a response, to awaken choice, not to annihilate the ego but, in the light of its potential nonbeing, to give it a chance for new being.

13. The social criticism implied in this is intentional for biblical reasons. Much further discussion would be necessary to clarify the point fully, but this is to suggest that those who crucified Christ did it in "good conscience." This is arguably a thing we continue to do.

14. Pannenberg, *Anthropology in Theological Perspective*, chap. 1.

15. Paul Tillich, *The Meaning of Health* (Chicago: Exploration Press, 1984), chap. 22.

16. Pannenberg, *Anthology in Theological Perspective,* p. 523; *Jesus, God and Man* (Philadelphia: Westminster, 1977), chap. 3; and *Systematic Theology,* vol. 1, pp. 319 ff.

17. Søren Kierkegaard, *The Concept of Anxiety,* ed. and trans. Reidar Thomte and Albert B. Anderson (Princeton, N.J.: Princeton University Press, 1980).

18. Jean Paul Sartre, *Being and Nothingness* (London: Methuen, 1957).

PART THREE

THE STRUGGLE OF THE SPIRIT

6

THE TODDLER

CONFORMITY AND THE ROOT OF HUMAN FREEDOM

PROPHETS, REVOLUTIONARIES, master criminals, and great poets all, though in different ways, stand against the mainstream of life and make radical claims for their own vision of the world. Conformity is an anathema because it stifles awareness; the rest of the world "just doesn't get it." Or if they do, they lack the drive, passion, or spirit to enact the vision that is in them. Sherlock Holmes and Professor Moriarty, Einstein and Bohr, and Madame Curie and Mother Teresa are dramatically set apart from any conventional ways in which they practice their respective arts. Whether fictional or mythically enlarged historical figures, their uniqueness is something we believe in. We set them apart and protect their differences since their unlikeness is important to us. They challenge the imagination and lure it into a world of genius, unfettered by common expectations. Regardless of the ethical implications, such figures belong to a world of meanings the rest of us can enter only through our imaginations. But if they belong to a world beyond our understanding and so set apart from where most of us think and act, why do we want to get into their worlds at all?

We all have a root of nonconformity, an urge to break away from the common practice of our everyday world. This root is deeper than an unfinished adolescence or a midlife crisis; it reaches into the very earliest years of our lives when we first discover we can act with autonomy in an otherwise ambiguous world. This root is the residual remains of a battle for a confident sense of one's own freedom to act in the face of a controlling environment—an environment that seems determined to stifle one's gathering sense of personal selfhood in the name of "goodness," "safety,"

"propriety," "consideration of others," and seemingly arbitrary interdictions. In the early years, "they" are the big people, so we give in and begin to doubt ourselves, and the look in their eyes makes us feel ashamed if we do not meet those expectations. But that longing for autonomy—"my own way," "my own voice," "my world"—never quite dies. It goes underground and resurfaces again and again, maybe in adolescence or middlescence, or in our shared images of Holmes, Moriarity, and other larger-than-life individuals.

The theological issue at stake here is that even if one developmentally wins the fight for a generic sense of self in an otherwise controlling context, even this healthy sense of autonomy will eventually come to the light as a magnificent illusion. There is no such thing as complete autonomy because every so-called version of it is deeply embedded in genetics, psychodynamics, and patterned interactions of the sociocultural milieu in which it originated. But the freedom that gives rise to just such a realization is itself an expression of the irrepressible human spirit as it seeks to transcend those powerful conditioning matrices and find the ground and purpose of itself as spirit. The theological telos for the spirit at this period, when a personal sense of freedom is being born, is the one ultimate and decisive choice in which the individual surrenders all freedom to the only One who, beyond conditioning, can give it back day by day. Only in this conformity is autonomy secure. Once this choice is made and a transformed sense of freedom is daily received, then the developing person may, like the One who defines true humanity, "despise the shame" and appropriate his version of a transforming nonconformity spirit-to-Spirit.

This chapter seeks out the developmental roots of human freedom as generated by the human spirit, discusses the hazards and hidden reefs on which development gets shipwrecked, and points toward the transformation of that freedom into the larger context of God's action in the world. Since only God's action is truly free, only our conformity to God's action is true freedom for us. This is "the glorious liberty of the children of God," the developmental roots of which are as deep as the spirit's creation of "autonomy" before we reach the age of two.

Developmental Perspective on the Toddler Period

The period from eighteen months to three years, what some people call the toddler period, is a phenomenological or behavioral description in which many developmental strands are woven together in the unfolding fabric of the child's personality. Although each child is unique, some regularities can be noted.

In terms of interpersonal dynamics and ego development, the issue is described by Erikson as autonomy versus shame. If we think epigenetically, we look to the underground sources of the emergence of autonomy as against shame. Neurologically, the child is processing more information more rapidly than any adult caretaker. As interaction with the environment ensues, some cell-to-cell connections are being reinforced and even physically strengthened, but in other aspects, normal cell death is occurring to enable neural pathways to be refined and streamlined in terms of usage. This interaction, which sculpts the brain and forms the ego, has two aspects: positive, the affirmation of the child's autonomy, and negative, separation from the sources of affirmation, which will, in the negative outcome, issue in self-doubt and shame.

Positive Side of the Toddler Period

On the positive side, there is the growth of bodily movement. By ten months, the child is at least crawling rapidly, and by ten to fifteen months is up investigating the world. Cognitively, according to Piaget, putting ends and means together is a key to this period and to the child's initial constructions of space, time, and objective reality. By eighteen months the child is beginning to run with the herd. Bodily movement is both awkward and graceful, but the child has acquired more mobility and cognitive competence than sound judgment. Hence, the child has to be constantly watched; any long silence from the other room warrants immediate investigation.

This developmental situation introduces a major theme in the child's struggle to create her own world during this period: control. And not just external control over the child, but the child's spirit is also building up competencies that bring about self-control. Working out this reciprocity between external and internal control has potential long-term consequences.

Increased use of symbols, images, and language are the psychic correlate of the body during this period. The child can now embody the world in patterned speech. Words are used over and over again as the child struggles toward grammar. Furthermore, as the child uses words, a sense of power to control her own world begins to emerge.

In interpersonal interactions with the child's peers, play is, in Piaget's terms, parallel play rather than any real interaction or cooperation. Here we have collective monologue, in which children seem to be playing or talking together, but there is no genuine exchange of information or of objects, except when there are sudden outbursts over possession of territory or outright frustration when words do not get what the child believes she has the right to acquire.

By the age of two, there is usually the capacity to say "I" and "me" spontaneously and correctly, so some self-consciousness is emerging with the activity of the body and linguistic autonomy. As these personal pronouns are used correctly, some sense of self-initiated mastery is taking place. The primal interplay between the use of language and self-confidence has its roots here; it will play out later in the power of having one's own voice as a basis for self-confidence.

At the level of developing moral judgment, the child's capacity remains egocentric and heteronomous. That is, the moral judgment of the child depends on external authorities and how that authority impinges on "me." The force of right or wrong depends not on quality of behavior but on the observed quantity of damage or the observed parental reaction, extreme or modified. Thus, it is far worse to smash the mother's favorite dishes by accident than to steal a cookie from the forbidden jar of goodies. The law stands outside oneself, and all moral judgment—any sense of right and wrong—is governed by external standards and the consequences of obedience or disobedience. This returns us to the major theme of this period: control imposed by others in reciprocity with emerging powers of freedom and self-control.

Transitional Dynamics

To return to Erikson's framework, the spirit struggles to create a predominance of autonomy over shame and self-doubt by the same process that created the predominance of trust over mistrust earlier. So let us look again at the transformational pattern of the stage transition process. Here the fundamental conflict centers on control in a context of trust issues in the child's continuous testing of boundaries, scanning for limits and how to transcend them or incorporate them. Thus, two-year-old Julie scrambles up on the kitchen table, all the time repeating to herself her mother's interdictions, "Don't climb on the table, Julie." By repeating her mother's restraining words, Julie juxtaposes her nonconforming activity with her mother's directive and scans for a way to mediate between two opposites. Her affect indicates she is not in rebellion; rather, she is testing an intuitive judgment that she can make a decision that will both please her mother and satisfy her own desires.

This striking juxtaposition is the human spirit at work in her to create eventually the capacity for self-control, a capacity that honors both self and control. In this capacity, outer interdictions become a basis for acts of genuinely free self-expression. This capacity will derive from a bisociation between the impulse to freedom and outer restraint, in which outer restraint is transformed into guidelines, and impulse is transformed into self-transcendent choice in the context of what the guidelines indicate. Too much restraint shrinks and may crush the realm of free choice, and too much gratification of impulse reduces free choice to loss of direction and reactionary behavior. By taking charge of the command, Julie gains control over it and so takes away its power to inhibit her activity. Eventually reinforcement of the limit will presumably prevail, but not, we hope, at the expense of her emerging sense of freedom and autonomy eventually to *choose* for the interdiction as a genuine form of *self-expression*. This capacity represents a *bisociation*[1] between inner and outer control—a creative construct of existential proportions that opens the future and *releases new energy* for asserting autonomy and *proving it out* in the developmental tasks that lie ahead.

This five-step pattern of stage transition takes on specific and different forms of expression from stage to stage, but remains constant as a pattern throughout the life span; that is, every stage transition will call forth this dynamic, so the pattern of the human spirit is repeatedly reinforced from stage to stage.

By eighteen months of age, symbols have attained some adaptational value. Thus, the mediating and adaptational power of transitional objects (such as a blanket, a teddy bear, or a favorite doll) comes into play. In terms of the transformational pattern, transitional objects function like a mediating insight that supplies an image of the solution even before the problem has been fully grasped. The pervasive significance of transitional objects is made evident in Robert Kegan's description of the stage transition pattern.[2] In the first period of life, the child makes the move from being in a dual unity with the mother to disembedding herself from the maternal matrix and reembedding in the family as one of its members. Now she is not in a dual unity with the mother; rather, she *has* a mother and is *in* the family. The achievement of this transformational transition is based on Piaget's basic premise that development is a transformational move out of egocentrism. The child's self-awareness, which goes from being in to having of, thereby undergoes the basic transformation that allows the spirit of the child simultaneously to confirm the self and to construct a wider, other-centered world.

The dynamics by which this transition is accomplished follows the basic transformational pattern, with the added crucial importance of the transitional object. Transitional objects have an almost "sacred quality."[3] They are rarely washed, so they have a familiar and comfortable odor, they are soft and portable, and they have power to bestow security and peace when nothing else will. In their absence, the child's whole world may seem to collapse, and sleep becomes impossible.

Developmentalists point out that these transitional objects have such power because they are symbols of the space to be traversed. They reach across the abyss of separation; they are warm, comforting, and familiar, like the mother's presence, but they are also detachable and portable, so they can go with the child while he is becoming autonomous. They are the creations of the human spirit, symbolically combining the known and the unknown, the familiar present state of being and the emerging new state. They therefore deal symbolically with the primal sense of emptiness echoing back to birth that now surrounds the first intentional move away from mother toward a new state of being.

Kegan argues that we continue to need and use transitional objects throughout life. Later, it is "the imaginary playmate," then the "chum," and then "going away to college" or "seminary." Transitional objects may be progressive advances in what it means to develop toward a full maturity. They are not regressive unless one is using one's baby blanket when it is time to go to college.

In the theological area, we also need a concrete image to enable us to make the ultimate transition from this life through death into a resurrected life. That is, what we need is One whose very existence takes both sides seriously and unites in His person the space we must traverse. The creative advance of the spirit often occurs through mediators who supply the solution even before we have fully faced the problem, even on the most advanced human level. This piece of human wisdom gets a transformed and ultimate expression in Jesus' resurrection appearances, whose coming and going concretizes the transition we all must make.

Negative Side of the Toddler Period

The developmental history of negation begins with the potentially traumatic sense of loss and utter negation in birth. The child, threatened by the traumatic return of this negation, turns it around, inflicting "no" on the world before the world can inflict "no" on the child. This defensive maneuver becomes the basis of repression, keeping one's insides inside and outside "out there," thus establishing distance and space in which to be oneself. This is the ego sphere, which takes considerable energy to keep it in place. That is why if we go seventy-two hours without sleep, we begin to dream while we are still awake; while hallucinating, we lose the distinction between subject and object, inside and outside.

Repression is not all that occurs. There is a cosmic sense of loneliness that persists because the ego is a functional solution to an existential problem. The underlying loneliness repeatedly and indirectly signals to the conscious ego that it is built on negation and nothing—hence our longing for a face that will not go away, for a face that will do for the maturing ego what it did for the child at three months. It is important to remember that the ego as defense system works mightily to maximize survival and satisfaction, and it tries not to allow the sense of negation and abyss to break into awareness.

Yet the "secret secretes," and so we have the developmental foundation for the existentialist philosophical assertion supremely expressed by Jean Paul Sartre in his statement that human existence is a "hole" in being. "Nothingness haunts" the ego and eventually wins out in the death of the person; thus, the ego is a kind of tragic hero who appears to slay the dragon of nothingness, but must eventually succumb because fundamentally its victory is based on incorporating the nothingness it is trying to overcome. The ongoing developmental history of negation will undergo many permutations in the brief drama of a lifetime, but it always signals the implicit futility of the ego's best and most gallant efforts. In this stage, the incorporation of negation will take the form of shame and self-doubt.

The general struggle of the toddler's ego in this period has to do with autonomy versus shame. In interpersonal terms, the issue is control: mastery of self in relation to the demands of others. Psychoanalytically, this comes to focus classically and paradigmatically, but not definitively, on toilet training, which our culture expects may be done by the end of the second year but no later than the end of the third year. Keep in mind that this paradigm is more descriptive of the Victorian era in which it arose than of our more liberal culture, but it applies to any repressive authoritarian family or parental context. In any case, the poignancy of this period is that this is the child's first conscious engagement with the pervasive developmental theme of separateness versus belonging, a theme that Kegan has claimed dominates the whole of the life span in any era. This is the first period in which the child herself must struggle with whether she wants to "do it our way" and belong, or do it her way and be separated from us. Usually the separation is not actual, but nevertheless is deeply felt by the child.

In classic psychoanalytic theory, the libido gradually shifts from the oral zone to the anal zone. This means that the way in which the body relates to the environment, personal and impersonal, has to do less with taking in nurture and more with the expulsion of poisons from the body. This is an internal, biological, autonomic shift from upper to lower, from face forward to bottom backward. It is a bodily metaphor for the shift from yes to no, from agreement in bonding to difference and potential separation.

The working out of this alimentary shift gets focused on the specific task of where and when to go to the bathroom. For the child, it is necessary for survival to expel these poisons and wastes from the body, but the child does not always see the feces as repulsive. In fact, they may be seen as a gift: "See what I made for you. This is an extension of my body." What makes toilet training difficult is that for the first time in the child's life, a survival mechanism consistently and consciously comes up against social restriction. Before this, the society of the child, especially the mother, is on the side of comfort, nurture, and survival. Now the child no longer feels this without ambivalence. The critical issue is whether society (in the person of the training parents) can bring the child to introduce choice between the cue and the response, to bring about self-control, along with the emergence of the mobile and autonomous self—or whether shame and self-doubt will prevail.

Ordinarily this may be the least agreeable time developmentally to do this, since "no" has emerged as the active organizer of the personality. This may be a period of maximum resistance because the child is old enough to make self-conscious decisions to comply, resist, or manipulate. This is a reason to keep respect for the individuality of the child ahead of cultural codes and norms, though both are of crucial importance.

This is the classical psychoanalytic paradigm, but, as Erikson points out in his study of the Yurok people, the issues at stake here may concern food as much as elimination.[4] Here the dynamics focus not necessarily on any particular object, feces or food, but on internalized contamination and the social demands concerning felt biological necessity. For the child, it is a fundamental conflict between survival and social control. There is some connection to the perception on the part of anorexic and bulimic women that food is "contaminating"; it makes one ugly in self-perception and more deeply ties the young woman back into the maternal matrix from which she must eventually extricate herself. Too small and too weak to fight back, the woman who refuses to eat is refusing to be contaminated by a negative maternal influence. Psychodynamically, on the outward and more aggressive side, this is a variation on psychic matricide; death to herself, then, is implicitly death to the contaminating mother.

As eating disorders suggest, if the struggle between survival and social control in any mode becomes an all-consuming issue, it soon communicates to the child that "there is something bad in you; if you don't get rid of it, your very survival is wrong. You are bad." This is dramatized in the mind-set of anorexic or bulimic young woman. In her discussion of this,

Peggy Claude-Pierre has stressed the entrenched conviction in these women that they are bad and do not deserve to live; they should punish themselves and suffer pain.[5] The healing, therapeutic alternative to this illness also exemplifies the appropriate attitude of the parent during this period. Unconditional love, positive reinforcement, easing blame, and objectivity training should be not therapy alone, but also basic parental behavior toward the two-year-old child.

Once sufficiently affirmed by parents on this matter, the child will soon come to the realization that it is more rewarding to be able to say, "I did it myself," than to insist on her own way. One young fellow emerged from the toilet flexing his little muscle, saying, "I am terrific!" Success should generate much more attention than mistakes. Here Skinner's learning theory, which says rewarded behavior will be repeated, is on the mark.[6]

When this training process is disturbed by blame, shame, or self-doubt brought into the situation by the parents, or for any other reason a cause for trauma between parent and children, the implicit message to the child is, "You have some poisons in you that need to be deposited somewhere, but these poisons in you make you socially unacceptable and are a cause for blame."

"Shame on you!" can come to mean that you are essentially and existentially wrong; there is something intrinsically antisocial or shameful about the very way you are made. In the hands of very imaginative Freudian historians such as Norman O. Brown (*Life Against Death*)[7] the whole study of anality and scatology is one of the intrinsic and developmental foundations for sin, when taken inwardly, and for the devil or the demonic, when projected outward.

This situation in fact has a demonic quality about it because it introduces an existential double bind: if one is "good" by social standards, one must end up sometime in painful self-denial that at first may feel somewhat like self-destruction. On the other hand, if one is "bad" and avoids self-destruction and goes when and where one feels like it, then one is attacked and punished by the social environment. Since this is an unavoidable and inevitable condition, this double bind has some demonic qualities about it. Thus, it is reasonable that this psychosocial and physical situation provides a kind of metaphor for a much deeper approach to the meaning and reality of evil. The developmental history of negation moves increasingly toward a construction of the reality of evil; it moves from the earliest sense of separation to the construction of an existential double-bind relationship with the very ones the developing child has come to trust. As in later adult life and in biblical history, betrayal into the hands of evil begins in trust.

What is at stake developmentally at this stage is not so much a matter of the demonic as it is one of human freedom, rooted as it is in the human spirit. From the standpoint of the human spirit's creation of free choice, the issue becomes whether the spirit can create a way for the child to choose for the self (autonomy) and at the same time do what society (parents) tell him to do or whether the spirit is so constricted that the child feels shamed into conformity and self-doubt. (Notice in the two terms, *shame* and *self-doubt,* a division between outside and inside is implied. Originally shame is felt from the outside in, as when you just want to sink through the floor to avoid the eyes of others; self-doubt is felt from the inside out, even when others look on you approvingly.)

How the child resolves the focal issue of this period will depend in part on, first, the personal history of the child, that is, whether the child has a backlog of basic trust to draw on. How confident has the child's spirit become in its ability to create and claim its world? The second point is the personal history of the parents, whose own measure of trust and autonomy or mistrust and shame comes to bear on this situation. The reality, remember, lies not so much in the separate units but in how parent and child interrelate spirit-to-spirit. Finally, the sociocultural context has bearing. Contrary to the Freudian emphasis on anality, Erikson cites the Yurok children who work out much of the freedom and shame issue around food and feeding.

In an essay on eating disorders as social prophecy, Carol Lakey Hess makes the case that the culture that imposes a stereotypical ideology about what it means to be a woman is a major cause for such disorders so prevalent among women in American society.[8] Certainly matricide would not be sufficient to explain the relatively recent appearance of the prevalence of such disorders. Sociocultural and historical causes, perhaps related to the rise of feminism, the bombardment of society with media images, and rapid mobility, come to bear on the developmental situation. That is, the culture may or may not legitimate a constructive resolution. If it does not, then resolution at a psychic level may be overtaken by rejection, protest, or buried resentment fostered by the sociocultural milieu.

Going Deeper

Anyone observing children of this age cannot help but be amazed at their achievements and their outgoing and giving attitude. However, at the same time one is impressed with the emergence of aggressive behavior that is more overt, unreasonable, demanding, and seemingly incorrigible. How we understand aggression makes a big difference in how we deal with the child's behavior and how the spirit of the child matures during this crucial time.

Ad-gredior, the Latin root of *aggression,* does not have any negative affective component. It is a neutral notion that simply means "moving toward"; so in this respect, moving toward someone to love the person is as much an act of aggression as moving to harm that same person. In theological terms, "going the second mile" or "turning the other cheek" is an act of aggression; it has positive meaning but, in effect, it takes charge of the situation and moves it in a direction of one's own choosing. Positive aggression is future oriented, hopeful, and life giving. Understood this way, the human spirit at all ages is aggressive in its drive to create and compose the world, and especially when it encounters obstacles that need to be transformed. In the *analogia spiritus,* the Creator Spirit is most profoundly aggressive when it mortifies, illumines, and vivifies, but this is life giving, bringing life out of death.

Negative aggression, then, is essentially and ultimately the reverse: to bring life under the power of death and, if possible, destroy it. This is the ultimate aim of evil: not merely to destroy human life and all other creation, but, if possible, to destroy God, the very source of life itself. Evil is not directed primarily at the creation but at the Creator through destroying the creation, which God said was "good." This ultimate perspective that theology provides makes it clear that theories of aggression based on social influence;[9] frustration, aggression, and displacement;[10] or aggression as instinct[11] do not go deep enough. Even aggression as instinct does not go far enough to explain what the aim of the instinct is; death has more to say about aggression, if only because it is an ever-present threat and the inevitable outcome of all behavior and all of life. Arguably it is both the origin and the aim of negative aggression.

Thus, death, which is present from the beginning of life, partly as wish and partly as threat, becomes more threatening as development unfolds and as the affirmation of life becomes more exciting and fulfilling. The consequent repression of death and anything that suggests it is the very foundation of the ego, but this is ignored, denied, or forgotten in every way possible by the age of eighteen months or two years. As a result, whatever serves to recall the intimations of death and void turns the incorporated sense of death outward, to inflict it on the person or situation that does not let the psyche forget its inevitable and ultimately undeniable destiny.

This line of argument, which essentially describes negative aggression as incorporated death turned outward, finds its first conscious and intentional expression in the terrible twos. It says that the death threat, present from birth, intensified in "no," now imposes itself again through social restriction against life-sustaining functions (eating or defecating). It is too much! When one is small, unable to communicate effectively in words, and physically helpless to fight back, the child explodes. When hitting the big people does not prevail, then the child will attack himself, throw himself on the floor, bang his head on the wall, and so forth.

In response, the general principle derived from the biblical context is to return positive aggression for negative aggression. For instance, it was Erikson's genius with children that prompted him to play with little anal regressive Anne, one of his cases.[12] When he first met her, he kneeled down and played with her rather than talking to her. If he had talked, it would have accentuated his adult power over her, but he said nothing, stooped down to her level, and became life affirming for her. That is, he played. Remember that in Piagetian terms, play is the dominance of assimilation over accommodation, taking life in—and so, for a brief moment, Anne could convert her fear and anger into play and tell him symbolically what was on her mind.

This is not a bad idea generally, to see play as positive aggression and as an antidote to negative aggression. Often in less explosive situations, play can be the key to discipline—for example, "Time to get in your bath, please." "No, No!" "Okay, here's what we'll do. I'll put my hands over my eyes and count to ten, and when I open my eyes I don't want *anyone* in that bath tub." Child: (Splash.) (Hopefully.) The double negation of prescribing the symptom is playful, life affirming in the face of the negative. The point here is that play is a form of positive aggression and may be a life-affirming way to redirect negative aggression and set boundaries that liberates rather than limits the human spirit.[13] Theologically, the implications of this understanding are more far-reaching, so we will turn to them at the end of this chapter.

More Serious Disorders

If the negative side continues to get reinforced by negative parenting without a corrective, then character disorders and more serious pathologies emerge.

Clinically it is familiar to see certain pathological behavior associated with constipation, dramatizing anal control of other persons and fantasized mastery of the external situation, sometimes even the world. Such are the cases of Anne and Peter, which Erikson describes.[14] Short of these more serious cases, two character disorders may emerge from disturbance of development at this period. One is the anal expressive. Here one may become an artist who loves to live in a mess. When there is a fixation at this stage, it may develop this kind of character disorder. The famous case of the deeply troubled artist, Van Gogh, may be an example. This illustration makes another important point: because there is a character disorder does not necessarily mean that the person is socially or culturally counterproductive. Indeed, something that puts one on the margin may well make one more creative.

The other character disorder type is anal retentive: very tense, excessively neat, attentive to detail, very slow but very thorough and perseverant. These persons feel others are always trying to get something from them; they are usually very concerned about money, and either chronically tardy in paying bills or obsessively on time. In one case, the wife confided that her husband was very neat outwardly but his drawers were a mess.[15] I think she was unaware of the implicit Freudian significance of her comment, but the point is that he kept things inside himself as secret, usually assuming that if his true feelings were known, he would be rejected. In both character types, these persons hide hostilities and aggression, and they are built up out of early self-doubt and shame instilled probably first during this period.

Third, it is possible that entire cultures may manifest and encourage a kind of character disorder. Generally, the United States encourages as normal an achievement-oriented addiction. Another sort of disorder related to this period might be something one could see in the Swiss culture. If one were to look at it from the standpoint of the old city of Geneva, holding its own against modernization, the disorders described here might be culturally induced. Think of all those clocks, the chocolate, the money, the mountains. Old Geneva is a tight little town, and this might say something about why the Genevois, until at least the seventies, used to raise their children with top-sheets that form-fit the child from the waist up, holding the waist and legs down under the sheet tightly drawn over the mattress. The kind of control represented here is consistent with an anal character type, played out in broad cultural proportions.

Returning to individual disorders, clinical paranoia is characteristically associated with this period. Not as serious a regression as some schizophrenic types, the paranoic assumes that there is always a danger of "an attack from behind." Conversely, constipation is often extreme, since the paranoic patient may have fantasies of destroying the world through defecation, getting them before they get you in the back. There is an exaggerated fear of death being inflicted (for example, "people are poisoning me," or "they're trying to get something out of me"). Modified forms of this are manifest in authoritarianism.

The most common pathology in this period is that of choice, the crippling of freedom evident in obsessive compulsive behavior. This form of pathology is classically represented by Lady MacBeth's obsessive hand-washing rituals. One senses that one is not clean inside. To feel that some antisocial inclination lurks inwardly is to be constantly in self-doubt about one's choices, about the future, about how one will be outwardly regarded, and how one will be able to maintain one's life. Consequently, there are ritualistic efforts to cover up what is perceived to be incipient antisocial behavior. This traps freedom and the capacity to create a future in enervating repetitions of defense against a dreaded and unwanted past. This is obviously a negative condition, but the pattern also applies when the thing being concealed, however good it may be in itself, is perceived to be socially unacceptable.

Here I want to mention something I call a convictional neurosis that pervades many mainline churches throughout the Western world. Individuals who have powerful religious experiences may not allow the insight that comes from these experiences to be known because they have not found receptivity on the part of the church or their religious peers. These experiences often represent embarrassing moments when the person himself was not in control of his life. Therefore, they repress the experiences; they live off of them inwardly, but outwardly say nothing, practicing the socially acceptable rituals of the church, perhaps with greater investment of energy than otherwise. The richness, vitality, and theological potential of these experiences are lost to the Christian community because the church does not know how to respond to them, given the theological limitations of the Christian enculturation of the ego. Convictional neurosis represents a sociocultural imprisonment of the spiritual life.

Constructive Alternatives

Development is not destiny. Under the power of the transforming work of the Spirit, a serious characterological difficulty or an obsessive compulsive pattern of behavior can become the basis for certain virtues, such as perseverance, thoroughness in work, ability to save, and scholarly intensity. Thus, there are potentially positive transformations of the negative dynamics that may be generated at this early developmental period. Such transformations may occur within the psychological arena, but most obviously they do so under the impact of a spiritual awakening and conversion.

In terms of ego development, a normal resolution to this period is the predominance of autonomy over shame, but note that susceptibility to shame is the norm. This is based on the accurate recognition that the emerging ego is fundamentally a false face. This creates the tenuous situation: will the social system accept it? If not, shame follows. In terms of the underlying structure of the ego, shame is not so much loss of face as it is loss of defenses against an exposure of one's deep emptiness, cosmic loneliness, and the evidence that one has not found centeredness in the Face of God. The deep fear of shame is expressive of loss of face, but it is the Face of God, not a human persona, that has been lost.

This is illuminating for the text in Hebrews[16] where it is said that Jesus "despised the shame" and went to the cross, the most shameful form of execution, disregarding the shame because there was a deeper ground in and for his existence. In the ordinary course of things, one has to put on a false face, a defensive ego posture, which is the ego's capacity to adapt to demands and expectations of the social system. Jesus does not conduct his life according to the ordinary course of things since all that is based on "no." It is the underlying and everlasting "yes" by which he acts, exposing shame as a sham where the affirmation of God's purposes are concerned. But how does the sham work?

Erikson has argued that shame is insufficiently studied in our society because we are preoccupied with guilt. In that connection, it is important to note that to be guiltless is to be good, but to be shameless is to be bad.[17] Why is this? Shame is wanting "to sink out of sight," to get away from the eyes of others. The eyes of others, or "the gaze," as Jean Paul Sartre put it, represents incipient exposure of one's hidden emptiness, dirtiness, or hypocrisy, so we look away "in shame."[18] Social roles, which are socialized extensions of the ego, protect us somewhat; they hold us together—and apart at a proper distance—because of our fear of shame. The reason it is wrong to be shameless is that shame is social glue, and anyone who is shameless threatens the fabric of social system. Prophets who stand unabashedly before the presence of God and declare what God is saying do not fit into the social fabric. Blessed are you when persons persecute you for Christ's sake; you are not stuck in the social glue.

Erikson's description of the normal resolution sets out a balanced opposition or tension between freedom to be oneself (autonomy) and shame or self-doubt. One can exercise freedom within the shame boundaries set by the social code of one's society and culture. However, this is once again the ego's effort to center the personality in a way that cannot endure.

Let's turn to Erikson's understanding of the virtue or ego strength that is based in this period and its social and cultural expressions. For Erikson, will is the virtue or positive strength of character that eventually comes out of this period. This virtue is parallel to hope for the first period. Will is the unbroken determination to exercise free choice as well as self-restraint in spite of the unavoidable experience of shame and doubt in both infancy and later social situations. The favorable balance of autonomy over shame here makes later virtue possible, but there is now built into the person's self-awareness a sense of having a good and a bad side, a lovable side and a hateful or hating side. The same is true of the parent; the parent now is forever an ambivalent figure who is both loved and hated. Will is the virtue or strength that allows one, in the face of the inevitable presence of the negative aspect of the self or the parent, to assert the freedom of choice that one's separate, autonomous existence permits. The social modality or institutional reality that guarantees and rewards good will, but punishes bad will, is "the law." "Law and order" is the social cry for the restoration of control in the midst of chaos; it represents the will of society.

The phrase "law and order" may have some negative connotations, partly from social and political history and partly from the New Testament's claim that the law has been transformed for the faithful by the gospel. The authoritarian abuse of this social institution, whether it is a totalitarian abuse of political power or a pharisaical insistence on the Mosaic law, is developmentally linked to an early fixation in this developmental period. In church contexts, it helps to see authoritarianism as based in fear, particularly fear of being shamed, or shown to be dirty, even fear of one's own destructive impulses. It is, above all, the fear of being shown to be weak. The authoritarian cannot be attentive to ambivalences, cannot be attentive to what is going on inside the personality, in himself or in others. Authoritarianism is laden with denial and a monolithic vision of right and wrong.

Is someone who exercises authority, such as St. Paul, an authoritarian? This question compels us to make an important distinction between having authority and using it appropriately with sensitivity and awareness of ambivalences, on the one hand, and being authoritarian and inflicting authority in a unilateral and nonreciprocal manner, on the other. By these standards, the post-Damascus Paul exercises authority, but by his faith and by the grace of God, his pharasaical authoritarianism was transformed into the unique bisociation between authority and compassion, which only God's Spirit can bestow and which lies at the core of human freedom. Thus, Paul's declaration to the Galatians, "for freedom, Christ has set us free."

Theological Significance

The essential theological issue at the core of this developmental period is not the origins of evil but the foundations of human freedom. What is being established within the developing person at this early period is the foundation for a psychological sense of "I." That is the "I" that is eventually transformed by the face-to-face encounter with Christ into an "I-not I-but Christ." Such a dialectical identity means that the sense of "I" is affirmed, not primarily on the basis of repression and being good, but on the basis of grace, the eternal "yes" of God, that brings a cosmic ordering, loving presence of God, to bear on human life and, in that, confirms the self at a level that is deeper than guilt or shame, deeper than good or evil.

The sense of autonomy emerging here is predicated on negation (repression) and on being good according to socialization standards. This means it is indeed a creative act of the human spirit, but it is defensive. When it is transformed by the Creator Spirit, previous transformations are themselves transformed and autonomy is given back as gift; the "I" is predicated not on defense and social virtue but on grace. Thus, "I" will eventually be able to stand over against society—not as retaliatory, but as an irrepressible expression of grace.

Here again we may look at the disembedding phenomenon. Transformation effected by the Creator Spirit disembeds the ego from its bondage to shame, so the "I" is claimed not on the basis of virtue but on the basis of God's action. That is why the "I" is followed by "not I," that is, not the "I" of the ego but the transformed "I" bestowed by God. Thus, revelation through the prophets, through Jesus, and through St. Paul has always been given in the shape of a dialectical identity. The prophet says, "I, not I, but Yahweh." Jesus says, "I, not I, but the Father." Paul says, "I, not I, but Christ." As Ricoeur puts it, "This is the Voice behind the voice" and is paradigmatic for every revelation in every genre of Scripture.[19] In every figure whose witness is a revelation of God in Christ, there is "a Voice behind a voice," a dialectical identity.

This is a reversible structure. It is also important to be able to say, "Christ, yet not Christ, but I." This is not pride but intentional appropriation of the autonomy that grace itself preserves in the divine-human relationship, lest the "I" be absorbed into the Godhead, as in certain mystical and meditation practices, or lest the Godhead be absorbed into the "I" as in certain ego-inflated cultic leaders who call for suicide as a way to manifest faith in the forthcoming future.[20] In the dialectical identity, negation is now confronted, nullified, and transformed by the only One who can negate the negation, give death to death, and set the individual free for the freedom that grace alone can provide.

The human spirit's generating autonomy over shame is of primary developmental importance, but there is also the importance of recognizing that nothing theological has happened until that "I" is transformed into a dialectical identity that runs deeper than shame or mistrust, and the human spirit can then testify with the Holy Spirit that we are not natural children, but children of God, heirs of the kingdom of God.

Finally, this is the foundation for human freedom. That is, there is ultimately only one truly free choice a person can make: to surrender the ego's power to choose to the only One who can give it back shamelessly. All other choices are choices to serve a shame-enslaved ego and its extensions into social structure.

This is not merely a theory but a description of the nature of healthy identity whose ground is in the spiritual presence of Christ. This is an identity that, when it is called for, can exercise autonomy even in the face of negative aggression and redefine reality in his own terms because he has given death to death.

Consider my friend Paul who works with gangs and street kids in San Francisco. He and his wife have a storefront, drop-in church in the heart of gangland. The young people who come in the church know Paul from the little business he has selling pencils on the street and from his witnessing to them as they come by to talk.

One day Paul was walking down the street and saw one of his kids down an alley drawing on the walls with spray paint. As he recounted it, "The Spirit told me not to go down there. But I went anyway to remind this tagger that painting the walls was illegal and not in line with the faith."

But he had scarcely begun to talk to him when he discovered why he was not supposed to go down there. Another kid, high on some drugs, came swaggering down the alley, waving a pistol. He walked directly up to Paul, put the pistol against Paul's forehead, right between his eyes, and said, "I'm gonna waste you!"

To his surprise, Paul suddenly became very calm; a deep peace came into him, so with perfect confidence he looked the boy in the eye and, in the full strength of the Spirit coming up within him, he said, "God's going to make *you* a whole new man!" The boy was baffled; he had not scared Paul. Instead, Paul had redefined the whole situation with a prophetic utterance. But he was not stopped yet: "I've got six bullets here and I'm gonna go kill six people." Paul responded in the same redoubtable power and conviction, "God doesn't want *anyone* to die!"

Undone, the young boy turned his gun on the tagger, who cringed and begged to be spared. Now, satisfied that he had the power to terrify, the young gunman swaggered off.

The power of positive aggression to redefine the situation is surely a gift of the Divine Spirit, but the roots of one's capacity to appropriate that power, to stand against one's environment—whether it threatens shame or even death—lie in the capacity to exercise autonomy and not be afraid of negative aggression, but rather transform it in the re-creation of the entire situation through the power of the Spirit to transform all things.

Some of the many permutations of freedom and nonconformity appear beginning in the very earliest years of human development. It is humanly impossible to reach any enduring resolution to the inevitable impasse between autonomy and belonging. But this period may initiate the resolution that can be completed by the Spirit of Christ. When conformity to his nature transforms nonconformity and freedom, then these gifts are established not with reference to any human group but with reference to what God is doing in the world. From this perspective, it is evident that when Jesus Christ is viewed as a scathing prophet, a countercultural revolutionary, a crucified criminal, and so radically inspiring in his rhetoric that he has generated the greatest literature of the Western world, we see in him the epitome of God's version of creative nonconformity to the world. The seeds of our appropriation of such creative nonconformity are planted and generated by the human spirit before and during the tumultuous age of two. To reach their true fulfillment in the earth-shaking, transforming impact of Jesus Christ on all contemporary civilizations is their implicit aim and purpose. Many traps, snares, pitfalls, and tragedies will intervene to crush, if possible, the spirit of the child and abort any transformation of nonconformity and Christomorphic fulfillment toward which the Divine Spirit nevertheless relentlessly urges each individual and the whole human enterprise.

NOTES

1. The definition of this term is: "The basic key to insight when at least two hitherto unrelated frames of reference converge to create an original and meaningful unity."

2. Robert Kegan, *The Evolving Self* (Cambridge, Mass.: Harvard University Press, 1982).

3. Ibid.

4. Erik H. Erikson, *Childhood and Society* (New York: Norton, 1963), 2d ed., chap. 4.

5. Peggy Claude-Pierre, *The Secret Language of Eating Disorders* (New York: Random House, 1997), especially chap. 2.

6. B. F. Skinner, *Science and Human Behavior* (New York: Macmillan, 1953).

7. Norman O. Brown, *Life Against Death: The Psychoanalytic Meaning of History* (Middletown, Conn.: Wesleyan University Press, 1970).

8. Carol Lakey Hess, *Caretakers of Our Common House* (Nashville: Abingdon, 1997).

9. Albert Bandura and S. A. Ross, "Imitation of Film-Mediated Aggressive Models," *Journal of Abnormal and Social Psychology* 66 (1963): 3–11. This was a seminal study behind the current plethora of studies that currently link violent behavior to television.

10. John Dollard, Leonard W. Doob, Neal Miller, O. Hobart Mower, and Robert R. Sears, *Frustration and Aggression* (New Haven, Conn.: Yale University Press, 1939). This was the primary formulation of an interpretation of aggression that has now reached the level of common wisdom.

11. Konrad Lorenz, *On Aggression* (New York: Harcourt, 1966). The fundamental research that claims aggression is an instinct.

12. Erikson, *Childhood and Society.*

13. G. Kenneth West, *Parenting Without Guilt* (Springfield, Ill.: Charles C. Thomas, 1986).

14. Erikson, *Childhood and Society.*

15. Theodore Lidz, *The Person* (New York: Basic Books, 1968).

16. Hebrews ch.12: 1–2.

17. This may be due to the fact that shame is ambiguous. It is both painful and an essential part of the socialization process. The legal system makes a very clear-cut distinction between guilty or not guilty.

18. Jean Paul Sartre, *Being and Nothingness* (London: Methuen, 1957).

19. Paul Ricoeur, "Toward a Hermeneutic of the Idea of Revelation," *Harvard Theological Review* 70 (January–April 1977).

20. Jonestown to New Age cultic practice, as in Marshall Applewhite's tragic "Heavens Gate."

7

THE OEDIPAL CHILD

SEX, DEATH, AND THE ORIGIN OF WORSHIP

IN C. S. LEWIS's *The Great Divorce,* the clergyman does not want to enter heaven because he must get back to a meeting of his theological society.[1] He is presenting a paper on the question of how Jesus might have outgrown some of his earlier views if he had lived out the complete life span. "What a different Christianity we might have had if only the Founder had reached his full stature!" Thus, theological speculation may foster self-deception and obscure the truth it seeks to explain. In this case, it would be hard to find a more deeply ironic refutation of the power of developmental understandings to subvert theological truths about a lifetime.

Developmental understandings are in grave danger of consuming what is of greatest spiritual and theological significance. Not only is this the period in which Freud located the origin of childhood sexuality, but it is also where he thought he had discovered the psychological origins of religion. The discussion in this chapter does argue that the origins of mature spirituality may be found in the forefront of this stage, but they are not what Freud thought they were. They are not primarily sexual and not neurotic. Rather, they are more powerful, pervasive, and enduring than the oedipal concept as Freud interpreted it.

Freud's interpretation of Sophocles' classic drama *Oedipus Rex* has long since stolen any impact the latter part of the play might have had for contemporary culture. However, the drama concludes in Oedipus's blind wanderings and finally his death. The god Apollo promised that the place of his death would remain sacred and bring great benefit to the city of Athens. The larger context of the drama might say that our understandings of sexuality should be kept in the context of death and spirituality, both of which endure longer than sexuality. Many popular discussions of sexuality would be deepened if it were recalled that the bottom line is that sex is simply nature's answer to death. In itself sex has no other meaning. It is the human spirit that gives sex its meaning according to the relative purity or perversity of the spirit. But in no case can sexuality be adequately understood apart from death. Sex, death, and spirituality are deeply intertwined.

From the standpoint of the human spirit, a focus on *initiative* (which Erikson says characterizes this period of ego development) is more adequate than a focus on sexuality. Although not divorced from sexuality, initiative takes up the remarkable imaginative powers of the child and issues in play and symbolic games. Here we find the developmental origin of culture and worship. In games, children move to being-outside-themselves in the way in which adults move outside themselves in the creation of culture and beyond culture into worship. The great move ahead at this period is the partial liberation of the human spirit, which moves human consciousness beyond itself and thus begins the awareness of God.

Both sexuality and culture are naturalistic alternatives to the sense of void and nothingness at the base of the ego. Their surfacing at this stage reflects the attainment of some sense of self-control and autonomy, on the one hand, and, on the other, a concomitant, tacit realization that ego competencies will never overcome negation and death.

The child during this period (age three to five) is able to create meaningful imaginative worlds consciously and intentionally, so the creative and transformative capacity of the human spirit is gradually able to be transposed from its place as the intrinsic drive of human development to intentional transformational acts. It may now become a process that is intentionally invoked by the child or by therapy, where healing amounts not only to redevelopment but to an intentional appropriation of the transformational dynamic of the spirit for dealing with psychological disorders. As we will see, spiritual dynamics run deeper than the sexual preoccupations of this period, putting sexual disorders in their larger context of meaning and purpose.

Bodily Development

This period extends approximately from ages three to five years. By the age of three to four, the child's brain uses about two times as much energy as an adult brain, much of this activity taking place in the cerebral cortex, where higher brain functions are coordinated. The cerebral cortex of the brain is largely unprogrammed at birth, so during this period, we are beginning to create our own environment more intentionally in our own terms. Overall, the child is more active and energetic, and wakes up in the morning full of plans for the day.

Sexual development is an evidence of overall bodily growth. New awareness of sexual feelings makes the ages of three to five a critical period, when gender identity gets its first setting. Sexual identity development is biphasic, so whatever happens at this stage will be reworked again in adolescence. This period represents the culmination of the underlying eroticization of the child by the caretaker, usually the mother. Epigenetically, diffuse sexual feelings have been developing under the surface; now sexual feelings come to direct expression in the genital area. Usually socialization conforms to primary sex characteristics, but confusion of sexual identity can begin at this period of time.

Cognition and Language

Constructive capacities of conceptualization are at work very early in the mental life of the child. The conceptual competence of the child may take the lead over sensation and experience, employing symbolic adaptations. A clear example of the early dominance of the conceptual side is that children do not draw what they see; they draw what they know or what they can construct out of what they have seen. They draw the sky up at the top of the page and the grass down below because that is how they conceive it; it is not how they perceive it.

Language, that remarkable vehicle of the human spirit, now begins to develop in a full-blown grammatical way. It is quite clear that children do not learn the structure of language primarily by imitating adults; rather, they construct their own grammatical rules out of what they hear, and thereby develop their own approach to speech within their cultural environment. A child may say, "Look at the sheeps," even though he has never heard it that way because he has constructed the rule that adds "s" for plural.

In Roger Brown's research, by age two and a half, the child can produce complete sentences that are indistinguishable from those of the adult—for example, "I put them in the refrigeration to freeze" or "I go get a pencil and write."[2] In the construction of these complete sentences, it is evident that children are building up a grammar out of their understanding, rather than learning it directly from the environment. One of the more common mistakes that children make in English is to overgeneralize the regular ending for the past tense. Here is a common sort of exchange:

CHILD: My teacher holded the baby rabbits and we petted them.

MOTHER: Did you say your teacher held the baby rabbits?

CHILD: Yes.

MOTHER: What did you say she did?

CHILD: She holded the baby rabbits and we petted them.

MOTHER: Did you say she held them tightly?

CHILD: No, she holded them loosely.

Children often stick to their own notions of language, disregarding anyone who tries to correct them, persisting in their peculiar usages until they are ready to adopt new ones. Another example is that of the child who said, "Nobody don't like me." His mother tried to correct him: "Nobody likes me." They repeated this exchange no fewer than eight times until it dawned on the boy that he had been making a mistake. "Oh!" he said at last. "Nobody don't likes me." The point is that the child is constructing the grammatical world according to and guided by an internal logic, a form of abstraction, that is his own.

The child also talks to himself a lot, carrying on a monologue while developing what is called synpractic speech or inner speech.[3] Here residual forms of simpler speech remain in the inner speech arena. Inner speech is thought that is verbalized but not vocalized.[4] Since the speaker is the sole auditor, no new information needs to be codified for another. Typically this form of speech omits the subjects of sentences; it is speech of predicates only. When two people are of the same mind, as with two lovers, then communication can be in the form of inner speech. This is also like the way we encourage ourselves—"Get going!"—or blame ourselves—"Stupid!"—but it is also related to the way we pray silently. The words are there and they are effective as expressions, but they need not get vocalized since the one praying is of one mind with the Listener. It was such a one-mindedness that allowed the climactic image in the case of Helen to come to me in our prayer together. Lev S. Vygotsky hypothesized that this intimate language stays within us throughout life, and it is often the way we talk to ourselves, intimate friends, or lovers.

"Collective monologue" continues and expands; the child is, however, becoming more of a companion. As inner speech becomes more private, public speech becomes more social and grammatical.

This stage is notable for the considerable symbolic progress that is occurring. In the previous stage, marked at its end by deferred imitation, the child began to differentiate the signifier from the thing signified. Thus, Jacqueline is intentionally imitating the neighbor boy's tantrum. However, the child did not yet differentiate symbols and signs from each other. This comes later, but for Piaget, symbols mean those signifiers that in some way resemble what they are saying, such as pictures; and signs are arbitrary designations assigned by social custom, such as words. Jacqueline's imitation is symbolic; Piaget's designation of it as deferred imitation is signatory.

As symbol and sign are distinguished intuitively for the child, they together aid in the child's construction of the lived world as a differentiated unity of inner and outer. The inner world tends toward the self-involving and symbolic, and the outer world toward the arbitrary and signatory. This begins the intentional formation of the arena of self-consciousness. An account of one of my former professors, provided me by his mother, went like this: At the age of three, this little boy said to his mother, "You don't know what I'm thinking, do you?" And she replied, "No," at which point he curled up and laughed seditiously and deliciously to himself. He was intentionally constructing an inner world as differentiated from outer culture, which, by comparison, seems psychologically distant and arbitrary.

Constructing Inner and Outer Worlds

Just as ego development in the previous period focused on autonomy, in which the child developed an inner world of choice and freedom, so now the inner world is imaginatively elaborated. Another way to put it is that the child now intentionally constructs and elaborates an autonomous inner world of images and imagined activities out of the raw material of previous experience. What was previously enacted behaviorally and generated primarily out of social interaction gets internally elaborated and becomes generative for new activities in highly imaginative events. Thus, in this period, the positive symbolic and signatory effort to construct one's world inwardly and outwardly, to put things together and express them in a new way and especially in one's own way, is a paramount task of the human spirit.

Erikson and Piaget both speak of this as a play period. If imitation was a prevalent force in the earlier years, play dominates during this period. The child still imitates, but in a new way. Whereas the earlier imitation was to get into the adult world so as to be oneself but avoid shame and self-doubt, imitation now attempts to bring various forms of adult life into the child's own frames of reference—to make them her own as a basis for eventually entering adult society on her own terms. Thus, the predominance of assimilation over accommodation, which is Piaget's definition for play, marks the whole range of adaptational efforts of the child at this time in her development.

The Power of Imagination

Partly because of the maturation of the differentiation of signifiers from the things signified and partly because of the freedom implicit in the construction of one's own inner world, imagination is freed for full expression. This is the time when imagination is accelerated and empowered perhaps more than any other register of behavior. The simplest object constructs a whole world for the child: the doll creates an entire household; a laser gun creates the whole of outer space; a ball, the total stadium with crowds cheering. The child feels these constructions are so real that he may want you to get out of the way or recreate you to fit the reality of the things he is imagining. That is the positive side.

On the negative side, the predominance of nightmares becomes a powerful force. At ages three to five, a child will awaken and come charging into the parents' room for their help in dealing with an ongoing nightmare, even as it is being described at two o'clock in the morning. One parent described to me that he had to go kill a herd of turtles, beating them to death in the sheets because they were lumbering across the child's bed. Only then could the child get back in bed and go to sleep.

Psychoanalyst Ana-Maria Rizutto's work makes it evident that the first conscious God representation also appears at about two and a half to three years of age.[5] Thus, imagination may be the vehicle of powerful religious experiences during this time of development. In one case, a three year old was entranced as she watched a colony of ants going about their work. After a while she realized that she was so big and so close they could not see her. Then the direction of her gaze turned to the trees, the horizon, and the sky. She gasped and ran inside the house telling her mother, "We are ants in a giant's tummy." It may not have been God language, but it was an enduring God image for her, like the hidden presence of the kingdom, even as she entered troubled times later.

Also attributable to the power of the imagination during this time is the appearance of a different sort of transitional object, the invisible playmate. The invisible playmate may be so real that parents will have to set another place at the dinner table and even put food on the plate so that "Itsy" (the name of my invisible playmate) will have something to eat.

"Itsy" is not necessarily going to replace other transitional objects, but it will tend to do so. The more satisfying the invisible playmate is in dealing with emerging relationships to the important people in her life, the less she will need the blanket or the earlier transitional objects.

In general, in the semiotic sphere the child is negotiating to separate and interrelate the realm of inner fantasy and the external reality of physical, social, and cultural objects. What is at stake spiritually in the empowerment of imagination is the eventual capacity of the child to construct and believe in a vision, whether from God or from her own heart and passion. Outer reality and the critical capacity of intelligence, as it matures through the manipulations of objects in the outer world and through language as the objectification of the intrasubjective world, enable the child to tell the difference between a herd of turtles and "ants in a giant's tummy." If every vision is made to seem like a nightmare, the child will gradually lose the power of imagination to inspire hope and galvanize initiatives in response to the Divine Presence. On the other hand, when nightmares seem like visions, then the demonic has appeared in ways that suggest the distortions described in the previous stage. Although increasingly differentiated, the mutual enhancement of inner and outer prepare the way for discernment without reductionism.

Development of Morality and Intelligence

Morality is still heteronomous, but further differentiation of inside from outside and the projection of her subjective world let the child eventually imagine how others feel and see, and so a more sophisticated ethics can emerge. As heteronomous, the child is still very dependent on large and small, loud or quiet, in terms of violations of interdictions. If the child is asked, "Which of these is worse: to steal a cookie when you've been told not to, or to accidentally smash a tray full of your mother's best dishes?" she will still say the latter is much worse because it is loud, the violation is visible, and the big people will be very upset. The advance in this stage is that at its conclusion, the child will begin to identify with the parental model of good and bad, predominantly the model of the parent of the same sex. This partly relieves the stress of feeling the criteria are outside and standing over the child. Still, the norm for good and bad is not yet the child's own; it is the norm that is being internalized through identification.

These emerging new competencies are still limited from the standpoint of adult intelligence. In Piaget's description, the development of the child's intelligence at this period, the preoperational (that is, prior to and preparatory for logical and mathematical operations) period, is marked by the following characteristics.

Continuing Egocentrism

Egocentricism still pertains in this period, but the child is not as symbiotic, not as tightly bound to the mother in a dual unity as before. She is egocentric but moving out from within egocentric autonomy into initiative, so toward the world and worldviews and perspectives of others. Although the child is moving exocentrically overall, certain egocentric limitations on intelligence still hold.

Concreteness

In spite of the emergence of symbolic play and grammatical speech, the child's thinking and cognitive operations are still very concrete. Symbols have a concreteness, an inflexibility, for the child. When the child is recounting things mentally, she runs through events as if they were actually happening but does not do cognitive operations on the series. This is why in storytelling, the child will tell you everything that happened, with all sentences linked with "and then." There is no effort to separate out what is essential as the main theme. Thus, as Piaget has put it, the child's thinking is kind of a mental experiment in a run-on sequence of images and symbols very closely linked to concrete events and persons.

Maranda and Maranda's studies on narrative show that at this period. plot structure does not mean anything to the child.[6] Although the child will listen to stories and wonder what happens, it is merely a series of events, not the working out of a plot. For example, television movies are not plots but a series of tableau images. As Fowler notes, that is why you can take the child to the bathroom during the movie, come back, and the child does not sense that anything is missing, does not think that the plot has to be filled in.[7]

Concreteness of the preoperational period is also behind the animism, artificialism, and verbal realism of this period, as Piaget describes the child's construction of the world. In animism, everything is alive: trees are hurt when they are cut, flowers suffer in being picked, and the moon hides in the clouds when it is cold. The subjective and objective worlds are fused. The boundary between fantasy and reality has not been clearly and cleanly preserved. Artificialism has to do with the question of origin; the child might say that mountains are "little stones that have grown up," or

"God is a big man who made the mountains." She is again projecting human characteristics into actualities in outer awareness, transgressing boundaries unconsciously and concretely, the way we would do intentionally in the use of metaphors. Animism and artificialism clearly overlap at this period since the subject and object worlds are not yet distinctly differentiated by operational thinking. Verbal realism occurs when the child assumes that the word *moon* must refer to the moon and *sun* must refer to the sun, and we could not call the sun "the moon" or the moon "the sun." The symbol is separated from the referent, but it has not yet been established that the moon, for example, is an object in its own right, quite apart from its name. Nor does the child know that the names are objects with which we can think. Considering these preoperational ways of thinking, it is evident that in some cases, rigid adult ways of thinking do not move very far from this period.

Irreversibility

Reversible means mentally able to be returned to the point of origin. For instance, every mathematical and logical operation is reversible: $3 + 5 = 8$; $8 - 5 = 3$. But ask a little boy at this period, "Do you have a brother?" and the following exchange is likely to follow. He says, "Yes." "What's his name?" "John." "Does John have a brother?" "No." In another classic Piagetian experiment, lumps of plasticene are first rolled into balls of equal size, and the child agrees that they are equal. Then one of them is rolled into a sausage shape. Children at this period may agree that the two balls were the same size, but then they will say that either the sausage shape or the ball is larger. In either case, all will say that they are no longer the same once one ball has been rolled into the sausage shape.

Similarly, in another experiment with beads in which two different types of containers are set side by side, even though the children will watch closely as the beads are poured from one container to another, they will not be able to preserve the constancy of quantity as the beads are moved back and forth between the containers. They will say one is larger or one is smaller, depending on the shape of the containers, not on the quantity of beads.

Similar kinds of experiments may be carried out with just two pencils. Children will agree that two pencils are the same length, until you move one of them ahead of the other a little bit; then the one that is moved ahead is said to be longer. The child's thinking does not recognize that an action can be reversed and an object or an idea can be put back into its original position. Reversibility is a cognitive competence that must be in place before an object can be conceptualized "objectively" in its own right. Seeing "the other" in its "otherness" must be learned. It is the key to the development of the highest orders of intelligence.

Centration

The child's tendency is to center on one aspect of a perceived object or event and ignore the rest. His apparent inability to shift perspectives and put two or three aspects together is part of the irreversibility in the child's thinking at this time. In the case of the plasticene sausage, the child concentrates on "length" and says "more," and then on "width" and says "less"; hence, a comparison among objects that calls for constancy of substance as against appearance is not yet possible.

One amusing case concerns a mother who had two sons, ages four and ten. There were three pieces of cake left, and the mother, thinking the older boy should have more, gave two pieces to him and one to the four year old. A cry of protest went up from the younger boy, and the mother, in a moment of inspiration, reached over and cut his one piece in two. The four year old was satisfied.[8]

Thinking and Reasoning

The child thinks in states and stages rather than in terms of transformations. If a stick is held upright and allowed to fall on the table, the child does not conceive of intermediate positions, a sequence unfolding. Instead the child thinks only from one state to the next: upright to fallen.

The child at this stage shows an emerging capacity to use classifications, but no sense of how to arrange them hierarchically, using categories of inclusion and exclusion to work out a process of deduction. For instance: all Italians eat spaghetti; we are eating spaghetti; therefore, we must be Italian. I remember my daughter Tami coming up from the basement when she was about three years old and announcing that God was in the basement. When we inquired further, we discovered that feelings of God in family prayer reappeared for her in the basement. So God was in the basement. This is transductive reasoning.

This overall period is called intuitive or preoperational, since the child intuits emerging qualities of mature intelligence. Classification and logical operations are sensed, but not able to be grasped and used as such. The child struggles toward logical thinking in intelligence, the same way that he or she struggled toward grammar in speech. Concrete operational thinking emerges at the end of this period, at about age six.

The Psychoanalytic View of Psychosexual Development

The cognitive considerations all combine to express the initiative of the child as she thrusts herself into the world with imagination, language, and intelligence. However, Erikson has in mind relations to the primary love objects in the child's life—specifically, initiative in the sexual development of the child, emphasizing the movement of libido from the anal to the genital area, and the Freudian "phallic" or "urethral" stage emerges.

Freud named this stage for the male child because he theorized more in terms of men, including himself (although he treated more women). Thus, we must dismiss Freud's penis envy theory, which seems to apply only in severely regressed patients, if at all. It is better to follow Erikson's more sensitive (although still psychoanalytic) account, which says that in both male and female, the genital area becomes spontaneously aroused during this period; it is the period of first sexual awakening. Little boys may spontaneously get erections, and they may be made to feel either ashamed or proud or both. This is, in keeping with the play stage, a time when the penis is a hose, a gun, or any number of instruments expressing aggression and initiative. The little girl is experiencing vaginal sensations and wants to bounce on Daddy's knee or innocently masturbate in other ways. Both little boys and little girls are innocently "on the make," as Erikson puts it.[9] (Behind Erikson's thought is the basic psychoanalytic model for this period, an important point because this is where early psychoanalysis thought that religion began, even though there are many variations that have been developed beyond it.)

Genetic inheritance and socialization have begun to give specific sexual definition to the child, and now it is being established and acted out. This leads into the first phase of the classic psychoanalytic view of the oedipal conflict (or Electra conflict for women). In what is still the vastly predominant number of cases, the little boy, by virtue of his expanding imagination and sexual aggressivity, will fantasize that he is, can be, the mother's lover. She is or can be his wife.

The little girl similarly grows tender toward the father, taking care of him, insisting she can do it better. She will say, "When you come home, don't go be with Mommy; stay here with me." The parent of the opposite sex is the first love object, inflated with all the power of a fantasy that does not yet fully know the difference between reality and imagination.[10]

Then enters the archenemy of childhood fantasy, the incest taboo, and the confrontation with social reality violates the burgeoning sense of initiative and threatens to inflict guilt, not yet fully conscious but resoundingly felt. The father comes home and cuts into the relationship between the little boy and his mother. The little boy is both angry and afraid, which combine to make him jealous. That is, jealousy is a combination of fear of retribution and of anger at being replaced in the mother's affection.

The little boy cannot overcome the father, nor does the mother as a rule encourage this, so the spirit of the boy makes another major defensive move similar to what it did with negation and repression at an earlier period. The boy identifies himself with the father; he can not beat him, so he joins him. Thereafter, he "loves" his mother vicariously through his identification with the parent of the same sex. However, this is a guilty love, coming as it does as a personal correction to a socially prohibited desire, the incest taboo, which is rooted more or less deeply in the history of every known social system.

Notice the psychic economy in "identification." It is a total, though not final, internalized model for how a little boy is to become a man in society. To be sure, it does not last, but it provides an overall, generally adequate image of male behavior. This is greatly helped by the burgeoning imagination; both the jealousy and the fantasy combine to fix the model in the developing psyche of the child. Hence, he can identify and retain the identification for years to come, but what he learns about how to be "a little man" eventually becomes the core of the superego in adolescence.

The little girl has both an easier and a more difficult problem. It is easier because she does not have to leave the mother to identify with the parent of the same sex. Her jealousy does make her angry, and she wants the father for herself. However, unlike the little boy, she can stay close to the mother, identify with her, and come to love the father through the mother's love for him. The sense of separation, abandonment, and the awakening of the underlying sense of nothingness at the base of the ego need not appear for the little girl at this period as it must for the little boy in setting the course of sexual identity. Eventually, though, it becomes more difficult for the little girl to get herself and mother separated, so that the woman whom the little girl is becoming can be her own person, and the mother can be herself in relationship to her daughter. Thus, a little girl needs male affirmation to help her get out of the maternal matrix and become a distinct person on her own. Here Nancy Friday's early book, *My Mother, Myself,* has been helpful to some, though it is limited to those who find the psychoanalytic framework compatible. It is difficult, though necessary, for healthy maturity in a woman eventually to "turn back" and love the mother for herself as a distinct person in her own right, provided the mother is not trying to live her own life through the daughter or make the daughter pay for the mother's own lack of fulfillment as a woman.

As a general rule, by the age of six, the boy and the girl both recognize and more or less accept the incest taboo. The little girl overcomes her jealousy by turning back to her mother, incorporating the mother image into her own self-concept. The little boy does the same with the father, and both now have the foundation for superego and conscience. This is to say that the superego is the parental image of authority derived from this early identification process and laid down as a permanent fixture in the child's inner world. This is the first resolution to the oedipal/Electra conflict. It will appear again in adolescence for what will be, hopefully, a final resolution. This, then, is the first phase of the biphasic nature of psychosexual development in psychoanalytic terms.

Kohut's Theory

Probably the introjection of adult images is not strictly one-to-one, but a relationship between the two parents in which one figure predominates. The contemporary theorist Heinz Kohut argues that from infancy, the self of the child seeks two fundamental types of relationships with the "self objects" or key persons in his life.[11] First, the child needs to display evolving capacities and to be admired for them. This leads to a healthy sense of omnipotence and grandiosity, which comes usually from the mother and mirroring (including constancy of presence, nurturance, general empathy, and respect). Second, the child needs to acquire an idealized image of at least one of the parents, from which he should derive the basis for healthy and strongly held ideals and values. This may more commonly come from the father.

The nature of the personality is determined by the content of these two figures and their relationship to each other. Failure on one side can be compensated for by the other. If both sides fail, the result is a narcissistic psychopathology ("secondary narcissism," in classical terms) characterized as a defective sense of self and an inability to maintain a steady level of self-esteem.

The cause of psychopathology in Kohut's view is not due to a lapse in parental relationships here or there, but to a chronic or traumatic loss on one side or the other. The contemporary social situation, marked by the breakdown of family values and coherence, is partly responsible for the rise in narcissistic disorders. Also, in his position, the relationality between the mother and father is especially important. The relational kinesis here is of potentially great spiritual significance. The developing person needs to be able to constellate the whole parental situation, including absences, losses, imbalances, and special strengths, as part of constructing and composing the self and its world.

The exocentric advance of the human spirit in this construction and composition can be seriously arrested when parental incoherence prevails. I observed one woman whose neurosis became disabling whenever her parents separated and threatened divorce. This occurred because they came together to take care of her when she got ill. This enabled her to recompose her world in terms of their unity in concern for her. Although this is a case of arrested development, it illustrates the more general principle that argues for the two lines of development in Kohut's view of self to be understood as distinct but relationally definitive.

Guilt and Shame

For Erikson, initiative versus guilt is the critical conflict in ego development to be resolved in this period.[12] Guilt gains preeminence when initiatives are frustrated without affection and abusively cut off. Chronic transgression and retribution awakens a deep sense that one has an underlying fault (as in geological fault) that makes surface faults appear. Psychoanalytically this deep sense of fault is based in the incest taboo, which is classically rooted in the inherited history of the human race. This means that the primal sense of guilt is rooted in the child's reprehensible incestuous longings, so guilt and sex are inextricably connected, and initiative is inevitably cut off.

If initiative gains the upper hand instead, the virtue that is accomplished in this period is purpose. Purposiveness then becomes a characteristic strength of the ego. The cultural and institutional forms that are expressive of and maintain the positive resolution of this period are theater and ideal prototypes. These are public images that manifest in imaginative ways the high purposes of the society and give public expression to both the visions and the nightmares of the adult world.

Some of the classical differences between guilt and shame distinguish the negative side of this stage from the negative side of the previous stage. Guilt, on the one hand, is based on the internalization of values, especially via identification with parents, and transgression of those internalized values. Shame is based on disapproval from outside, a reaction to ridicule or scorn from others. Guilt is a feeling of wrongdoing; shame is a feeling of inferiority. Guilt appears where a limit is transgressed; shame is a failure to measure up. Guilt says, "I am no good"; shame says, "I am weak."

Guilt is a transgression, a crime, a violation of a specific taboo or legal code by a voluntary act; shame is a wound to one's self-esteem, a painful feeling or sense of degradation brought on by having done something unworthy of one's previous idea of one's own excellence. Linguistically guilt is associated with a failure to pay; shame, with a wound or covering up. Note once again the contradiction in the social interpretation of these notions. "Shameless" is a term of opprobrium—you ought to have some shame; "guiltless" is an honorific term implying innocence. Psychologically and developmentally, the deeper weakness or wound is shame, not guilt, though when we think theologically, we will see that guilt is still the deeper notion.

Theological Implications

It is thought in the psychoanalytic tradition that the oedipal/Electra struggle is a reenactment of a primal drama that leaves human nature guilt ridden and obeisant to a primal father projected into heaven. This, in psychoanalytic terms, is the basis for the theological concept of original sin and the reason that believers must continually repent and repeat the rituals of their faith by which they are justified. If we do not, we feel guilty. Religion is the ritualistic effort to undo the sense of being deeply faulted, but we never can correct the fault itself.

What follows is a brief sketch of the primal drama from which all persons have presumably inherited this primal fault. Freud assumed that he could read back into primal history from specific cases, so this discussion first recounts his classic case of Little Hans.[13]

Little Hans and Freud's View of Childhood Sexuality

The case of Little Hans is the classic study of childhood sexuality, conducted by Freud in 1909. The entire case was carried out by mail between the father of Little Hans and Dr. Freud. Little Hans, at age five, had a phobia of horses. In particular, he was frightened of a big white horse that had a black bridle and a large "widdler," his euphemism for penis, and he was afraid that the horse would bite him.

The background is important. The mother caught Little Hans masturbating when he was three and a half and threatened castration by a physician as punishment if he ever did that again. This crucial episode in Little Hans's vast preoccupation with "widdlers" traumatized him. Also, his sister was born when he was three and a half. This was, for Little Hans, a mystery bathed in blood and confusion about storks. These two traumas, the mother's threat and the birth of little sister, are associated in Little Hans's mind, arousing jealousy, a combination of fear of the mother's threat to his sexuality and anger at being excluded from this event of the sister's birth, something very important that Mommy and Daddy have, but he is not included.

Then we learn that the early fear engendered by the mother's threat becomes associated with the father, and the father becomes associated with the castrating physician in Little Hans's mind. The father had a big black mustache and was the "acting physician." Little Hans saw him at one point undressed, and was impressed with how white he was and with how large his "widdler" was. Subsequently, Little Hans developed his phobia of white horses with black bridles biting his finger off.

After writing letters to Freud and one visit, the father figured out that the two great wishes that Little Hans had were, first, that he could have a "widdler" as big as Daddy's, and, second, that he could be married to Mommy and have children. When asked one day if these were his desires, Little Hans said, "That would be lovely."

Confirmed in his desire and supported by the father, Little Hans went to bed, and then the next day he had two incredible fantasies, which he acted out. In the first, a plumber came and gave him new equipment, which meant that he had a "widdler" as big as Daddy's; in the second, he was married to his mother and had children, and his father was in turn married to his mother, the grandmother, so there was a double oedipal triumph in Little Hans's fantasies. After playing this out all day, he said on the following day that his "nonsense was gone."

Freud never saw Little Hans until he was nineteen years old. When he came to visit Freud, Freud asked him about the case, but he could not remember any of it. This is as it should be, since no one is supposed to remember the first phase of the oedipal struggle; it is repressed in a way that enables each of us to move on into the next stage and eventually rework it all in adolescence.

Freud on the Origins of Religion

From this case and other material, Freud drew his conclusions about the oedipal drama as a latent structure in the psyche. The pattern indicated by this drama is inherited by means of a "racial unconscious" (that is, an unconscious knowledge of the history of the human race laid down in each individual from birth), and the foundation of religion follows from it.[14] Here Freud, with the help of Darwin and certain other anthropologists, describes the ancient primal situation. There once was a primal horde headed by a giant male, whom I will call "Big Daddy." Big Daddy kept all the primal females to himself and drove all the young males off into the woods. What he did not figure on was that they got together out there and then came back and killed him. But then they felt so bad that they did not take any of the females for themselves and projected Big Daddy into the sky as god. That is how we got "god" and the "incest taboo."

Religion, then, is the neurotic behavior that refuses to acknowledge the primal history behind childhood sexuality or refuses to recognize the child's unconscious drives toward "murder" and "rape" (killing the father and taking the mother sexually), which confront the incest taboo and so create the oedipal complex. Then, like all other obsessive neurotic practices, rituals are used for repeatedly cleansing one's guilt, the source of which remains buried in one's primal unconscious. That is, one must continue to practice one's religion to appease a "god" whose infliction of guilt is chronic and unable to be extricated permanently without psychoanalysis.

Critiques of Freud's Views

Freud's view is bad anthropology. Margaret Mead, who was inclined to agree with Freud when she could, made it clear that his view is untenable.[15] It was Freud's fantasy, "the illusion of a past." This does not describe the origin of religion any more than does an obsessional neurosis.

Second, Freud did understand some things about religion, but he really understood only the sick part of it. That is, his view of guilt is the guilt derived from a punitive superego, which is punishing the ego implicitly for having inappropriate sexual and aggressive desires. At the same time, the superego is directing the ego on how to maximize satisfaction and ensure survival within the strictures and structures of a civilized social order.[16] This brings up a classical dilemma in Freud's thought. Apparently repression of sexual freedom and a measure of guilt is the price one must pay for a civilized society, but this makes civilization a form of neurosis not very different from religion. Freud affirmed the first and rejected the second due to a prejudice against religion rather than through an analysis of the issues at stake in this dilemma.

Freud understood religion as a misguided defensive maneuver designed to protect the ego from an overbearing superego while at the same time it actually entraps the ego in a neurotic system of beliefs and rituals. Surely that is the case sometimes, and when the gospel degenerates into law, then Freud's criticisms may be on target. That is, religious legalism is an instrument of social coercion based on fear and guilt, and it is designed to keep the ego in subjection to the mechanisms of social control without regard for the ego itself. Sometimes the law is necessary pedagogically, and surely limits are appropriate for a child of this age, but children must grow out of the overbearing control of the superego, or the ego will be crippled, often fixated at the level of an identification with the punitive figures hidden in the superego. Freud wanted to free the ego from any such external coercion; he wanted to strengthen the ego so that, in his famous phrase, "Where Id is, there shall Ego be."[17] This was his highly rationalistic solution to how persons could be both civilized and nonreligious. Freud the rationalist is not a credible position, even to neo-Freudians such as Erikson.

Third, what Freud did not understand is that the ego itself is a bondage. For all its liberating powers of language, intelligence, imagination, and moral judgment, it is based on a fundamental negation far deeper than the superego and human conscience. This takes us back to the significance of the Divine Presence as the Face of God. That is, the guilt we are concerned about theologically is not primarily the guilt of a socially constructed conscience; theologically, it is the separation of the person from God at the very point of ego formation that concerns us. Sin, the geological fault in the substructure of the psyche, inflicts the ego itself (Freud's solution to all problems) with a fundamental brokenness that it can never resolve. Moreover, all efforts at resolution only confound and deepen the fault.

When Luther speaks of "mortification," the convicting act of the Spirit of Christ upon us, this is not directed to the moral or ethical conscience but to the very existential substructure of what it means to be human.[18] This is why the judgment of God is always much deeper and excoriating than human judgment: if you are condemned by God, you are condemned not so much for what you have done but for who you are at the very core of your being. On this point, theology and development agree, you cannot do anything to justify yourself. All your doing carries the mark of an existential negation. So if God were to judge us, who could stand? But, as Luther so aptly put it, "the just God does not condemn us but justifies us."[19] That is, in Jesus we see the Face of God, and by his Spirit he becomes the center of human existence for us, transforming ego, superego, and conscience. Through him we are justified before God; we are literally changed so the ego is subordinated to the center who is Christ, and through him we can appropriate that justification which stands outside us in the nature and love of God.

Finally, if we are to examine human experience for an analogy to a healthy religion, we should not look, as Freud did, to neurosis; that only prejudices the case from the outset. If neurosis pertains at all, it is analogous only to sick religion. However, we can find in the very context of the case where Freud demonstrated the presence of childhood sexuality a far more adequate analogy, which will take us back into the primacy of the spirit in human development.

The dynamics of therapy in the case of Little Hans recapitulate the dynamics of the stage transition process. Here is the human analogue for healthy religion in the very case Freud wanted to use to prove the deep primal origins of the oedipal complex and the sickness of religion. Recalling the stage transition sequence—conflict, interlude, constructive insight, resolution, release of energy, and the verification or "proving out"—is to recall that the key turning points in this sequence represent the dynamic pattern of the human spirit.

In Little Hans's case, the stage transition sequence, now transposed from its embeddedness in development, is precisely what is followed in the therapeutic sequence. The conflict is stated by the father, but it is an accurate account so Little Hans enthusiastically accepts it and sleeps; here is the interlude where unconscious scanning takes place during sleep; the insight or constructive resolution is the two fantasies, which when they are enacted issue in the release of tension. "My nonsense is gone!" exclaims Little Hans. Then the proving out is the appropriate forgetting and moving ahead in development. The transformation in Little Hans's condition was the work of the spirit that was in him.

As this one instance illustrates, therapy in the psychoanalytic tradition generally relies heavily on a recapitulation of the dynamics of development at the stage transition level. This is to be expected if one has learned—indeed, has been internally formed by—a pattern for conflict resolution through the course of one's lifetime, stage after stage. It stands to reason that the same or similar pattern should be employed when facing conflict in other contexts.

Theological Observations on Freud's Views

What is most compelling about this discovery, at the heart of Freud's discussion of his famous oedipal conflict, is that a far more powerful and pervasive force than sexuality is at work in the development and formation of the human personality at this very period. This can be discerned by theology because of the long history of its efforts to speak meaningfully about this illusive phenomenon of the spirit. At this period of development, the child for the first time can take the initiative to create spontaneously meaningful worlds. So it is at this time that this patterned process may be transposed from its embeddedness in human development and then put into the service of conflict resolution in another context. In this case, the transposition is into a therapeutic context in which the process is aided by Freud and Hans's father. This transposition of the process, from being part of development to being the way in which a conflict that is arresting human development can be intentionally resolved in a therapeutic context, is a paradigm for transpositions that may take place across the whole field of human action, from the biological to personal, social and cultural arenas.

A second theological observation to note is that Freud implicitly affirms the dynamics of the human spirit as health producing and therapeutically sound. As such, this provides the human analogate for the dynamics of the Holy Spirit as *Spiritus Creator*. In Luther's treatment of this, the Holy Spirit creates *ex nihilo*, so the Spirit comes and convicts us of the nothingness that underlies human existence. This is the mortification aspect of conviction; it brings a person to the very end of his existence in order to recreate *ex nihilo* the personality according to the "alien righteousness" of Christ, the illumination and vivification. Freud unwittingly affirms the human side of the analogy of the Spirit, which is a key to healthy religion. This legitimates from a surprising source the human side of the *analogia Spiritus*.

Third, notice that in Little Hans's case, seemingly bizarre imagery had healing power. That is, even psychoanalytically, bizarreness is not in itself necessarily pointing in the direction of pathology. The question is whether the bizarreness actually resolves the conflict (Hans's fantasies) or dramatizes and intensifies it (Hans's phobia). In some instances, it may take a very bizarre image to undo a very bizarre conflict; the deeper the conflict is, the more extraordinary the resolving, construction, vision, or experience may have to be. If the conflict is very deep, like the existential separation of one's very being from God, then it may take a seemingly bizarre revelation, like the incarnation, death, and resurrection of God in a particular person at a particular time in history, to undo the depth of that condition. The basic test for the undoing of that conflict is whether it puts one back into the world in a way that allows one daily to embrace the underlying nothingness of human existence as the context for recognizing that all that is given, including one's own self, is nothing other than the gift of grace from that transforming God.

Fourth, the potential transposition of the transformational dynamics to other contexts outside development per se prepares the way for a transformation of conscience. At this developmental period, conscience is bound to the socialization of the child through identification with parental models. This identification, which lays the foundation for the superego, becomes the core of the adult conscience. However, this all gets radically revised when guilt is redefined Spirit-to-spirit as an existential separation from God. This transformation of values and self-evaluation will be taken up in the subsequent discussion of adolescence.

Fifth, Ana-Maria Rizzuto's criticisms of Freud's effort to locate the origin of religion and the image of God at the oedipal period are helpful in pointing out the psychological limitations of Freud's analogies.[20] She has attempted to document the emerging image of God by establishing a close connection between the child's developing image of God and the child's image of the parental figures. This is not, of course, limited to any particular period, so she envisions the child's imaginative construction as emerging in a developmental sequence that enables a god image to work like a transitional object, enabling the developing person to negotiate by use of the god image between self and the parental or love object world.

This intriguing thesis is helpful as a corrective to the reductionism of the early psychoanalytic model, but its own reductionism belies the title of Rizzuto's book, *The Birth of the Living God*. First, within the psychological realm alone, it fails to make the crucial distinction between a person whose god is created out of the self and parental images and one whose image of God is derived from an actual encounter with the living God to whom humans do not give birth. Although many of us already know from our work with and study of convictionally encountered persons (for example, Paul, Constantine, Augustine, Aquinas, Luther, Calvin, Pascal), whose parental images and god images do not agree with Rizzuto's hypothesis, this is a very important exception to her thesis.[21]

Theologically, of course, Rizzuto's approach, although helpful to a point, exactly reverses the notion of the image of God that only God can give. At stake here is not merely that this approach has no theological integrity, but that understanding the image of God in this way deprives the spirit of the person of the transcendence and the "beyond-one's-self" toward which it drives. Worship of one who is truly other is cut off, the logic of the spirit is truncated in its search for its own ground and destiny, and it is turned back into its own imagination where "god" becomes at best an aid to social adjustment. Again, this is more than unfortunate; many of the psychological ills of our time exist precisely because of a reductionistic death leveled against the drive of the human spirit to find its reason for being, that is, to find a reason to live.

If we draw all these theological implications and considerations together, from the spiritual integrity of persons in relation to the Spirit of God to the liberating power of conflict-resolving visions, it adds up to the developmental origins of an act of worship. Rather than being driven by primordial lust and violence, development is driven by the human spirit toward the worship of God, an expression of the highest form of human behavior.

As Wolfhart Pannenberg points out, cultic play, the context of worship, has its developmental origins in the games and role playing of children where the imagination flourishes and the human spirit thrives in the creation of new and meaningful worlds. Cultic drama is not a game in the sense of arbitrary pretense. The totality of new meaning that the individual child experiences as play becomes increasingly corporate and anticipates the way in which cultic drama ignores the proportions of everyday life so as to stand apart and give meaning to the whole of life from a position beyond it. As Pannenberg put it, "Cultic play is the organizing center of the shared world and of its unity. . . . In this respect, Christian liturgy is sacred play, at the center of which is the supper that sums up the ministry and destiny of Jesus and links the created reality of human beings and their social life with their eschatological destiny.[22] This celebration makes the particular and personal lives of individuals part of that history and its destiny.

The central issue at stake in this period is not sex role identity, but the quest of the human spirit for being-outside-oneself; sexuality is but one aspect of it. This spiritual drive gives rise to culture and ultimately to worship of a God who, though being truly Other, at the same time provides ultimate meaning for the concrete particulars of everyday life. Then worship is not a neurotic flight from a threatening past but a creative response to a future that is known in the present through the irrepressible transcendent and transformative capacity of the human spirit as it receives its power, identity, and the whole of the created world as a daily gift from God. Developmentally this drive is a longing that anticipates but does not yet know the Face of God until it is revealed in the image of God in Jesus Christ. This is a revelation that must be grasped and appropriated Spirit-to-spirit, as the awakening of the human spirit at this period of development makes evident.

Making this argument for the primacy of the spirit at this period does not mean that issues of sex, death, and aggression are to be ignored. However, it argues that problems in sexual identity formation are fundamentally spiritual, not sexual. Something like this is frequently said in a way that ignores the human spirit and simply denies any credibility to the psychological side of such issues. However, it is said here in a way that is as deeply rooted in the human psyche as it is rooted in the human spirit's relation to the Spirit of God. When theological concern for issues of sex role confusion or conflict between male and female sex roles in society cannot be discussed with intelligence and compassion as fundamentally spiritual, the question will inevitably disintegrate into one sex against another. The force of death, which is always intertwined with sexuality, fuels the aggressive and defensive distortions of the view. Such sexual debates are begging the question because it is far more difficult to come to terms with God at the core of one's spirit than with sociocultural constructions of sexuality.

It is to Erikson's credit that he does not see the sociocultural expressions of this period primarily in terms of sexuality but in terms of contemporary forms of cultural play, even though he stops short of recognizing that this period is unto the worship of a God who is irreducibly beyond us. God is the only object who is irreducibly Subject, and so establishes a ground for the spirit as it continues to be the creative source of human development. Apart from such a ground, the human spirit will at best make creative approaches to the death and ultimate nothingness that haunts spiritless debates about sexual identity and sex role confusion. Failure to deal directly with the deeper questions means that more superficial issues will have to carry the emotional load that belongs appropriately to the overwhelming questions of human development: What is a lifetime? and Why do I live it? All other issues should find their place relative to our approach to this question.

NOTES

1. C. S. Lewis, *The Great Divorce* (New York: Macmillan, 1946).

2. This illustration and parts of the following discussion are derived from an interview with social psychologist Roger Brown: John de Cuevos, "No, She Holded Them Loosely," *Harvard Magazine* (September–October 1990).

3. Lev S. Vygotsky, *Thought and Language* (Cambridge, Mass.: MIT Press, 1962).

4. Roger Brown, *Social Psychology* (New York: Free Press, 1986), p. 345.

5. Ana-Maria Rizzuto, *The Birth of the Living God: A Psychoanalytic Study* (Chicago: University of Chicago Press, 1979).

6. Elli K. Maranda and Pierre Maranda, *Studies in Folklore and Transformational Essays* (The Hague: Monton, 1971).

7. James W. Fowler, *Stages of Faith: The Psychology of Human Development and the Quest for Meaning* (San Francisco: Harper San Francisco, 1981).

8. Robert Kegan, *The Evolving Self* (Cambridge, Mass.: Harvard University Press, 1982).

9. Erik Erikson, *Childhood and Society* (New York: Norton, 1963).

10. Nancy Chodorow, *The Reproduction of Mothering: Psychoanalysis and the Sociology of Gender* (Berkeley: University of California Press, 1978), and *Feminism and Psychoanalytic Theory* (Berkeley: University of California Press, 1989); Nancy Friday, *My Mother, Myself* (New York: Dell, 1981); Elizabeth Fishel, *The Men in Our Lives* (New York: Morrow, 1985).

11. Heinz Kohut, *Self, Psychology, and the Humanities* (New York: Norton, 1985).

12. Erikson, *Childhood and Society.*

13. Sigmund Freud, "Analysis of a Five-Year-Old Boy" (1909) and "On the Sexual Theories of Children" (1908) in *Complete Psychological Works of Sigmund Freud* (London: Hogarth Press, 1956).

14. Sigmund Freud, *Totem and Taboo* (London: Routledge and Sons, 1919).

15. Margaret Mead, lecture to students and trainees, Menninger Foundation, 1962.

16. Sigmund Freud, *Civilization and Its Discontents* (London: Hogarth Press, 1957).

17. Sigmund Freud, *Ego and the Id.*

18. Regin Prenter, *Spiritus Creator* (Philadelphia: Muhlenberg Press, 1953).

19. Ibid.

20. Rizzuto, *Birth of the Living God.*

21. This objection and its implications have been documented statistically in Timothy Engelmann, "Religious Experiences: Psychiatric Status, Religiosity, and God Images" (Ph.D. dissertation, Yeshiva University, 1994).

22. Wolfhart Pannenberg, *Anthropology in Theological Perspective* (Philadelphia: Westminister Press, 1985).

8

THE SCHOOL-AGE CHILD

WORK AND THE AMBIGUITY OF ACHIEVEMENT

FROM THE FIRST MAN, Adam, there is the divine commandment to labor: "to dress and to keep" the Garden of Eden (Gen. 2:15). Originally work is intrinsic to the way we are made, not a curse imposed by God. As God labored and then rested, so humans, made in the image of God, will also labor and rest. Work is instituted in paradise as a way by which humanity participates in the action of creation. This is not *creatio ex nihilo*; only God can bring into being that which is not. It is the creation of new things and meanings that are designed ultimately for the glorification of God in Jesus Christ.[1]

The brokenness in human nature described in Genesis does not change the fact that human nature is intrinsically made to labor, but it does change how we value the work that we are made to perform. A psychological reflection of this condition, which lies so close to the basis for how work is understood in the Western world, is Erikson's designation of this developmental period as industry versus inferiority. It is not industry versus apathy (although the apathy rubric does appear in his discussion of this issue); it is work, and its inner connection with human worth that is at stake.

Socially, culturally, and historically, this convergence of worth and work brings into developmental focus the characterological revolution fostered by the Reformation. Max Weber's classic sociological study, *The Protestant Ethic and the Spirit of Capitalism*, attempted to demonstrate that Protestantism, especially Calvin's doctrine of the elect, fostered entrepreneurial energy, success in business, and economic development, giving rise to capitalism.[2] The elect were those chosen by God from the beginning of time for salvation, and no works or achievement of any magnitude could change this eternal decree. This might have encouraged a kind of fatalism, but in fact Calvin's view of predestination does not have that effect because no one knows whether he belongs to the elect. This might make the whole thing irrelevant, but Calvin claimed that the elect could be recognized by outward signs, including not only self-denial and devotion to duty but also business success and prosperity. In time, under the influence of secularization, the significance of future salvation has given way to the more immediate gratifications of prosperity. The communicant has been replaced by the consumer, but there remains an almost sacred necessity to attach one's personal worth to one's work.

When the school-age child enters this developmental period, the underlying long-range issue is whether the child's innate capacity to put ends and means together and to construct worlds of real things and meanings will bring value to him as a person, or whether it will make him feel incompetent, inferior, and so worthless as a person. This is a judgment brought on him not just by his family or his schooling, but by a long tradition of how personal worth is assessed in Western culture.

Theologically this is a historically grounded and culturally perpetuated distortion of how human worth is to be assessed. But even theology has its own corrupt version of this distorted argument: since God ordained from the beginning that human beings should work, effectiveness in work has a sacred quality that can legitimately become a basis for assessing the worth of persons. The corruption lies in shifting the grounds of assessment from God to the public arena, where achievement is highly prized in its own right. Theologically, in the eyes of God you, the person, are worth more than anything you can ever achieve. Thus, the only proper basis for the assessment of human worth focuses not on achievement in the public arena but on the spirit of the person and the conformity of that spirit to the Spirit of God as revealed in Jesus Christ. This does not mean that achievements are irrelevant, but they are relevant primarily and ultimately only to what God is doing in the world to conform persons to the humanity of Jesus Christ through his Spirit.

When work and worth are confused, as they are in an achievement-oriented society, achievement becomes addictive because it is trying to solve a problem it was not originally designed to solve. The obsessive quality of the achievement-addicted personality is not evidence of maladaptive social adjustment; it is, rather, a highly successful appropriation of precisely what the society affirms and accelerates. The appropriate theological critique is not designed to take achievement out of life, but to take the obsession out of achievement. This is to the end that human worth may be established on its original grounds of the love of God for each person manifest to us, Spirit-to-spirit, in Christ. To put worth first and make it primary is to transform the cultural meaning of work into its original significance as participation in creation in responses to God's initiative.

This returns us to the necessity for focusing on the spirit of the developing person and the deeply embedded longing of that spirit for its ground in the Creator Spirit of God. Splitting off the development of the ego and the rapid expansion of its capacities for constructing realistic worlds of things, meaning, and values gets intense reinforcement during this period of development. Thus, it is of crucial importance to see how this occurs and discover the hidden sources of transformation of the human spirit operative from ages six to eleven.

The Ego Builds on Amnesia

This period from six to eleven years of age is sometimes designated the school-age child. Although children often begin school earlier, partly to free parents and partly to give the child a head start in an achievement-oriented society, strictly formal education, matters of mind, and genuinely social adaptation only now come into focus. The establishment of repression as an irreversible barrier between present life and early childhood, and a consequently firm distinction between subjective and objective reality, has now taken hold.

For the child's emerging ego, the infant past has been left behind, a victim of childhood amnesia, which typically sets in at about age three or four. Only rarely, apart from any clinically induced experiences, do we have memories of our life before the age of three. The rationale behind this may be that the child's emerging ego autonomy, which gets its earliest form at age three, moves ahead by negation, excluding the past as an act of defense. Another factor contributing to this amnesia is language; the full-blown grammatical emergence of language at age four makes the present world for the child a new and very different world, unlike the prelinguistic past. Thus the ego that makes schooling possible is moving into the center of psychic organization at the expense of deeper primal longings associated with the face phenomenon.

This stage is initiated by the first (temporary) solution to the oedipal/Electra struggle by age five. Typically, this is accomplished by identification with the parent of the same sex. Here may be the most decisive break with the past, as the child now moves into society at large.

The Two Worlds of the Child

Identification is only a partial solution to socialization for the child, which may be why the child's world is now divided into two parts. One way of naming the two parts is stated by James Fowler, in which he suggests mythical and literal differentiation.[3] On the literal side is a socially controlled, thinking ego that tends to be rational, schooled, and linear. A private inner life of imagination and play, submissive to adult authority, is on the other side. In the mythical world, the adult is still in charge, with the child having fantasies, engaging in imaginative behavior, and thinking analogically. Ronald Goldman has spoken of the development of religious thinking from childhood to adolescence and described this two-world situation by saying that the child is both an empiricist and a myth-maker.[4]

For the child, the two worlds do not seem to be contradictory. He goes back and forth between being an empiricist and a myth-maker, and seems to notice no dichotomy. He seems to be exploring both sides of the bicameral brain, experimenting with varieties of ways of combining and recombining them. At the end of this stage, by age eleven or twelve, the two worlds converge and are able to reinforce and enrich each other.

The chief way the child explores, correlates, and holds together the two worlds during this period is through narrative. This, of course, combines order with fantasy. As Fowler puts it, this is the basis for "world coherence" for the child. World coherence eventually matures into systems, ideologies, and metaphysics. This is, of course, educationally extremely important. By this time, children can begin to participate in the story as preparation for participation in history and the history of the universe.

In Erikson's terms, the main epigenetic task is the development of the cognitive and interpersonal competencies required by schooling, putting ends and means together to accomplish socially and culturally prescribed and desired goals without suffering put-down and rejection for his efforts. As this period unfolds, the child will develop confidence in his cognitive competencies, a way of adapting to the external world, which will work to satisfy not only adult demands but also the intrinsic demands of reason, fairness, and social organization at a peer level. All of this is designed to prepare the developing person to become a working member of society.

Motivation in Work

Why does work, the drive in the child to construct the world of things and meanings, appear at this time? More precisely, what motivates work? The classical psychoanalytical explanation views work as sublimated sexuality. The real pleasure of work comes at the end of the process, when the job is done. That is, beginning to work, one terminates pleasurable activities, faces the project, builds up concentration in gathering, fixing, and constructing real things, and finally feels the relief of the burden and relaxes and enjoys more explicitly self-indulgent pleasures. It is pleasure seeking diverted into job completion. This is possible during this period because sexuality has been repressed through identification—or so it is argued psychoanalytically.

Other researchers, such as Ives Hendricks, argue that work is as "natural to us" as the development of intelligence.[5] We construct the world and care for it in a way that gives satisfaction from beginning to end. In this view, the job is its own reward, and it is typified in craftsmanship.

A behaviorist, with B. F. Skinner's cause-and-effect analysis, argues that rewarded behavior is repeated. If the conditioning process is properly scheduled, Skinner can teach pigeons to play Ping-Pong and rabbits to play piano. We work because it is rewarding, and we work more the more the reward, but it is, of course, mindless. Nevertheless, Skinner's view is especially relevant to an achievement-oriented society when it is recognized that the achievement obsession is a result of reinforcement based on winning. The unfortunate consequence is that eventually the achiever is motivated primarily by finding a contest or another opponent to face and to overcome. The self-destruction in this pattern for individuals and for a winner-take-all society is completely ignored, making the work motive mindless.

Theologically, we may see how the human spirit can combine and intertwine all such motivational explanations, but theologically persons work not for reward, intrinsic pleasure, or sublimated sexual gratification. Work, as we will develop the notion here, is motivated by persons' being given a vision of what God is doing in the world. Psychological interpretations are all from behind, from within, or from below, but motivational dynamics in the Spirit are uniquely from the future. Theologically, motivational dynamics can reverse the flow of time from the past into the present and on to the future; in the spirit, the flow of time is from the future into the present to change, heal, restore, or transform the past for the sake of the coming future. The vision embodies "work prepared ahead of time" for one to perform; thus, St. Paul is "obedient to the heavenly vision," and Pauline works are then performed in the spirit of transforming the past in obedience to what has already been accomplished ahead of time in Christ. Work is proleptic participation in the final consummation of all things in Him.

Working in a Social Context

The child "works" not only on things and meanings, but also on herself, on getting her psyche together, relating past to present and future. One's personal story begins to emerge now for the first time. This can emerge partly because a basic image of the self has been provided by identification. That is, the ego has some socially acceptable baseline from which she can begin to objectify her past with continuity and begin to construct her own story.

For Erikson, the dominant developmental struggle of the ego is not work alone; it is characterized by the tension between industry and inferiority. This implicitly puts the notion of work in its larger social context and recognizes that competence to do work emerges in the context of a changing social conscience. In Western society, one's work is not a neutral activity; one's personal worth is definitely tied to it. Competence, in the context of conscience, means that this period is focused not only on whether to work or not, or whether it is pleasurable or not, but whether your capacity to work and produce will establish your worth as a competent person in the eyes of society.

During this period, there is in the child a broadening ethical sensitivity. The identification that will give rise to superego and conscience is becoming generalized and becomes ego ideal. That is, authority figures other than parents begin to be part of the child's developing sense of social conscience. The child realizes that parents are not omnicompetent or even the best adults around, so the child begins to construct her own sense of what sort of ideal figures to emulate. Hence, ego ideal is built up from an identification, but it becomes the ego's reconstruction of the ideal, rather than the view imposed by parental-type figures. Through identification, the core of the social conscience is in place, but its social implications are still in flux. The child of seven or eight is keenly aware of what is "mean" or "unfair." At the same time, the child may be very careful to suppress crying, to not be "made fun of." On the other side, the child is very susceptible to praise and signs of approval.

Thus, the question of industry takes place in the context of a heightened sense of social approval and potential disapproval. So the question is, Can one work and get approval, or, in the absence of approval, must one come to feel that one's competencies and oneself are inferior? In spite of the increasingly strong influence of schooling, the primary influence in determining the answer to this question is the child's primary group, usually the family. The primary group is the face-to-face group that constitutes the reinforcement of superego figures and "our group" or "those like us." One's own family as a subsystem in the larger sociocultural milieu in which schooling takes place retains primary influence for better or for worse, even into adolescence.

The Emergence of Role Taking

In the previous period, early family dynamics focus for the child on the oedipal/Electra conflict, and the diversion of primal intimacy drives into the formation of the superego through identification with parental figures. However, the drive for intimacy and its corresponding force, which moves toward death and aggression, do not disappear. They merely go underground and seek indirect expression as controlled by the superego, which is in the process of being generalized and becoming a socially constructed conscience. The resolution to the difficulty posed by repression and sublimation is partly engendered by advances in intelligence. Specifically, the child now learns to turn earlier capacities for play and imitation into the construction and enactment of roles. Here again, the human spirit creates a resolution to the conflict between the human need to be in direct interpersonal relationship with others and at the same time not violate the boundaries of one's individuality.

The capacity to adopt the role expectations of one's social group is the social version of ego construction in the ongoing struggle to balance autonomy and belonging. What began as the intervention of the mother to terminate nursing, moves to intervention against bodily impulses to defecate, and then to intervention against sexual aggressive drives toward intimacy. What has been focused on parents and family is now focused on school and an increasing circle of relationships that inhibit through role structure and correlative social expectations. In each instance, the human spirit has created an alternative to social intervention, which essentially says no to the impulses of the developing person and constructs a way to give those impulses indirect expression. However, because these solutions are compromises and indirect, they are only provisional; there remains in the developing psyche a longing for a totally adequate solution signified by the face-to-face mirroring relationship and its power to order the cosmos and give assurance of love to the individual.

Role structures, which are the core of social organization at all levels, are effective in part because they establish balanced distance between persons, and because our expectations of each other and our boundaries set against each other can be made explicit. Accordingly, goals that ensure survival and satisfaction on a social scale can be attained; thus, institutionally constructed role patterns work like a corporate ego. At this time the child learns conscientiously to fulfill her role expectations in the family, and this transfers to the larger social milieu—secondary socialization, so called. Just recall the familiar admonitions: "We do not treat each other that way in *this* family," or "She is your little sister and you are her big brother, and you should see that she gets at least one turn before you take your fourth turn on the swing."

Role structures, extensions of the repression that lies at the foundation of the ego, are an elegant solution to the problem of failed intimacy in view of the necessity for social interaction and the need for long-term survival. They effectively govern relationships, but they fail to satisfy the deepest longings for intimacy of an unstructured and immediate sort. That is partly why all societies, in their natural wisdom, provide socially acceptable contexts for "liminality," as anthropologist Victor Turner has named it.[6]

Liminality refers to interludes in which social role structures can be temporarily suspended and interactions among persons can take place on a more open-ended, interpersonal basis. Examples are socially sanctioned acts of worship, intimacy in marriage, beer drinking hoopla of the crowd at athletic events, or breaks during a lecture. Periods of liminality relieve the tension that builds up in a role-structured situation and, in a reciprocal fashion, reinforce one's capacity to take and maintain a role and play into role systems that give us a functional corporate life.

In the primary group, this rhythm between role-structured social organization and liminal interactions—openness to each other—must be sensitively preserved. Too much liminality leaves the child without a sense of boundaries, and too much role structure leaves the child with too much repressed emotion.

On the seriously negative side of this picture of the ego's expanding development into social roles and role systems, the inferiority reaction may take several different forms. Feeling the pressure to "get it right," the child's sense of inferiority may take the form of sensitivity and hesitancy in trying out new projects. Children at this age (about seven years old) really *think* before they speak, in contrast to children in the earlier years, who characteristically have something to say on any topic. They contemplate, if you like, but frequently, precisely because they are thinking, may have to say, "I don't know." Constant put-downs may make an "I don't know" into a "I can't know" mentality; easily hurt and withdrawn, either into oneself or into a stronger schoolmate, children at this age are just beginning to develop remarkable competencies by which they can recognize the complexity of the world and of themselves. This, which bodes well for future strength, temporarily makes them vulnerable to an insensitive world.

Such vulnerability may move into a profound sadness, inferiority, and eventually a neurosis. The child described by Arthur Janov in *The Primal Scream* is an example.[7] At this age, for the first time, the child begins to recognize the story of her life. The child begins to put it all together and works over what has happened. In the Janov case, a little girl about six and a half years old was caught in the rain and lost her way walking home from school. A kindly woman brought her in and dried her off, set her before the fire, and gave her a cup of tea. But to the woman's great surprise, when she left the room for a moment, the child suddenly got up, put on her coat, and ran back out into the rain, crying. The child eventually disclosed that she had been treated there so kindly in an unexpected way that it made her realize that, by contrast, her own life was shrouded in sadness. When she went home, she had to take care of a sick and disabled mother, and never had been treated as this woman had treated her, with a fireside cup of tea. Recognition of sadness in one's story can be a source of the inferiority that may appear at this time.

Also, the feeling of inferiority may take the form of chronic procrastination. Being hurried to school and constantly evaluated by standards that are not matched by standards of parental or teacher attentiveness may engender procrastination.[8] This may be a reaction against being hurried. But in the school situation, it may also represent a desire not to be evaluated. Often late work is face-saving because if it is put off, then one imagines that he could have received a better grade if work had been submitted on time. A regressive possibility is that the child uses the failure to do the work, or get work in on time, as a way of gaining lost attention and affection. That is, it may be a demand for ascriptive worth as against the pressure to achieve.

Inferiority and Achievement

The work principle may assert itself not only as an emerging capacity based on an instinct, but as a reaction formation. In this case, there is a repression of real feelings, which are the need to be loved for just being there, not for what one can do. Then one pours into the need to work all the energy that one would rather put into loving and being loved, so as to earn hugs and kisses (recall again the dynamics of the reaction formation). One does the opposite of what one really wants to do with all the energy with which one wanted to do the first thing.

This pattern follows from early independence training, identification with achiever parents, and an emphasis on work as a basis for worth established by family and school. The achievement-oriented child is socialized into an achieving society in which he learns not a sense of industry balanced by recognized and acceptable limits, but a hypercathected work principle in which he flees from the fear of inferiority through accumulating achievements and finds life dull if there is no competition. Inferiority in feelings of being loved and being lovable provoke the reaction formation and consequent overdetermined need to achieve.

This is the formula for an addiction. We say "drugs are people," but because they are in fact not people, then more and more drugs need to be taken. So it is with achievement. Achievement and the worth derived therefrom is not love, so the exercise of competence in the context of competition becomes an addictive solution to the primal loss of the face-to-face love relationship. The achievement addiction is a functional solution to an existential question of worth.

This addiction sets in in a very subtle way. I remember when I first found myself unwittingly drawing my daughter into this addiction. I was in the kitchen making coffee early one morning, and Tami, who is irrepressibly conversational and overflowing, came bubbling into the kitchen. I did not pay much attention to her; I grunted and groaned about getting started in the morning and making it to school in time. Then, finally, she said, "I tied my own shoes this morning," at which point all my activity stopped. "You did!?" I finally looked at her and appreciated her. But what I did without realizing it was tell her she was more important for what she could do than for who she is and for her just being there.

This is where the achievement addiction gets started, and it lies behind some of the pressures that are recognizable in the Ivy League mystique. The resulting addiction is a socially applauded and socially accelerated form of self-destruction. This is a dramatic illustration of how the drive for adaptation can actually kill you. The achiever is, by definition, "more planful, purposeful, tense, domineering, and cruel."[9]

Achievement is especially dangerous if it is achievement under pressure of latent anger or resentment or compensation for chronic rejection and social disapproval. That is, the loss or deprivation of the kind of love that appreciates you just for being there can affect your heart, and you may suffer the medical consequences of the loneliness of the achiever. This is the kind of achievement that can kill you. The tragedy is that achievers cannot love.

In an unpublished study done on Harvard students in the 1960s by psychiatrist Armand Nicoli, Nicoli said hundreds of students were interviewed. These are, of course, extraordinary students, but they had a high dropout rate due to drugs. The question he asked these highly competent students who had nevertheless dropped out, was, "You have some of the finest young minds in the world, so why do you want to fry your brains?" In essence they answered, "We want to feel something." It is a difficult task in our society to develop a capacity for excellence in anything and still preserve a sense of the whole person. It is ironic that inferiority in terms of personal worth could be so disguised in its opposite, which is the pride of accomplishment.

The Mechanisms of Defense

As the ego gets more socialized, it has to harden its defenses, so now all the classic forces of defense begin to get more fixed in the psyche. (It is important to mention these here since they will help us later to pinpoint the changes that take place in the eventual transformations of the ego.) Since primary repression is reinforced through identification at the beginning of this period, other defense mechanisms of the ego are built up on the strength of this repression. Consider *isolation*. Little Hans might remember the birth of his sister, but he would isolate this memory from all its attendant connections with his own oedipal struggle. Isolation built on repression is a systematic way of accomplishing unconscious forgetting in a selective fashion.

A second defense mechanism is *regression*. Here the child falls back into early phases of development in the face of threat, or to ward off an anticipated threat the child may play sick, become petulant, or be demanding in a way that deals with some imminent problem, perhaps being left by the parent. But other forms of regression are in the service of the ego, for example, sleep.

Another defense mechanism is *fantasy formation*. This is usually an asset since it will play into future-oriented behavior, but it may simply dull the pain of present reality and allow the child to turn his back on whatever interferes with adaptation.

Sublimation is a notion borrowed from chemistry. A solid turns into a gas without going through the liquid state. A prizefighter may discover in therapy that he sublimates aggression toward his father into prizefighting, and the little boy may sublimate aggression toward the father by being a class bully.

Denial is another defensive maneuver. ("I am not yelling," he yelled.) The simple denial of the existence of an unpleasant, painful aspect of reality is usually an overdetermined negation of what is manifest. The related defense mechanism is *reaction formation,* in which one does just the opposite of what one really wants to do with all the energy one wanted to do the first thing. This is illustrated by the earlier point in which one achieves as a reaction formation to the absence of the desire to give and receive ascriptive worth.

Projection is the attribution to another of one's own wishes or impulses. The child who cannot tolerate his feelings of hostility toward his brother believes that his brother is hostile to him. This also occurs in the heat of an argument when Tami says to me, "You hate me!"

Introjection occurs when one is disillusioned with a needed person. The introjection defense takes the form of inwardly appropriating the fault. "It is my fault that Mommy can't take care of me and drinks all the time. It's because I'm worthless; that's why they don't like me." Here the child would rather lose the battle for competence than lose the needed love figure.

All of these maneuvers are designed to aid in the battle against the engulfing of the new ego by unconscious forces that might be triggered by his own interaction with the social environment. In the normal situation, a child may use any or all of these from time to time, but they are flexible and correctable. By conversation and lots of storytelling, acceptance, and lowering of anxiety, the rigidity and even the need for these defenses dissipate. The theological significance of a transformed ego is that these defenses are themselves transformed and they become means of caring.

Piaget and Cognitive Development

We turn now to the cognitive aspect of development in this period, so we shift out of the motivational and interpersonal context into the development of intelligence, as Piaget describes it. This is doing in the cognitive domain what the developing person is doing in the domain of the ego and interpersonal relationships. Basically what has happened is that the child has acquired the cognitive competence of conservation of quantity, quality, and position. The object is now able to be cognitively conserved, and it works as a corrective to the egocentrism of perception. Objects are now perceived as separate and distinct from the observer and are not only conserved in their own right but also in their relationship to each other. Hence, the child can begin to develop and think in terms of systems and interact according to role patterns. The child is moving significantly out of egocentricity.

Up to this time, the child might buy his mother something that he would want—a small toy train for her birthday, for instance. After this time, the child can begin to examine what the parent would like and get something appropriate for her. This is illustrated in a classic study by Piaget in which a child is seated at a table, three dolls are seated around the table, and three mountains of different size are on the table.[10] Before this period of time, age seven, the child cannot see the mountains from any perspective but his own. But after this time, the child can begin to describe how the mountains will look to doll 1, to doll 2, and to doll 3.

This means that role structures may be consciously and cognitively grasped and transposed to various contexts. Role play emerges as the solution to the love struggle of the previous period—its hurts, guilts, and jealousy. Role then becomes a social version of repression, but in this cognitive development out of egocentrism, role structures can be created and maintained with accuracy and intelligence.

Roles as a means of defense can become highly rationalized. Role structures, so fundamental to institutional life, get stereotyped and detached through being rationalized. The individual can thereby be alienated from his work. It is a short step from rigidity and rationalization in role structures to Karl Marx's concept of alienation of the worker from the stuff and substance of his work.

Objectivity and Relationality

A general aim of this period is not only to establish object constancy but to establish constancy in oneself, that is, self-objectification, over a period of time and in the midst of change and changing circumstances. This is to gain control over one's life and the objects in one's environment. This manifests itself in the advancement of conversation. Earlier, the child engaged only in simple monologue, then collective monologue. Now the child can shift rapidly back and forth between one point of view or another. Hence, real dialogue is now possible, and so it is also possible for shared goals to be established. Cooperation and capacity to invent games, set rules, and work out patterns of fairness are possible. To play and invent games, one must be able, of course, to conceptualize the roles of others. During this period, the rules are first very rigid and concrete, like verbal realism or earlier constructions of grammar, but gradually they become more flexible.

In her book, *In a Different Voice,* Carol Gilligan makes some interesting observations about comparisons between boys and girls during this stage.[11] It is typical, she says, of little girls to be more interested in relationships than in the rules, while little boys will construct the rules and debate them for a much longer period of time than little girls will. In stressing relationship, little girls will confront a difference about rules and either drop the game or quickly compromise. If you argue about the rules, they say, "We're going to play our own game." Gilligan argues for the importance of the predominance of relationship. In a quaint conversation she describes a little girl who says to a little boy, "Let's play next-door neighbor." The little boy says, "No, I want to play pirate." And the little girl says, "Okay. Let's play you're the pirate next door."

Development of Intelligence

According to Piaget, concrete operations now emerge. This entails the emergence of the essentials of Aristotelian logic and the consequent capacity to perform mathematical operations. Orderly thinking is now an intrinsic motivation. Consider the classic illustration of the syllogism: Socrates is a man; all men are mortal; therefore, Socrates is mortal. This represents the use of classification, which appeared in the previous period, but now the child can recognize the appropriate use of such basic principles as inclusion, exclusion, and the law of identity. The emergence and construction of the basic principles of logic is analogous to the emergence and construction of grammar for the sake of speaking in a coherent and orderly manner.

Concrete operations manifest the striking capacity of the child to transpose symbolically sensorimotor connections between and among objects into logical and mathematical operations. What was done early on only by means of hands-on manipulation of objects has now taken on a purely symbolic form. Genuine thinking has begun. Nevertheless, concrete operations are still oriented toward concrete things and events in the immediate present. The child from ages seven to eleven tends to think as if his only task is to organize the immediately present objects or ideas. He has limited capacities for extrapolation and reflects on his own thinking only when it is necessary and in special cases. At age nine, concreteness manifests itself in that the child is usually intensely interested in memorizing concrete facts about great events. The world records in the mile run, pole vault, speed boat racing, and the like, as recorded in the *Guiness Book of*

World Records, will be more engaging than reflection on meaning. When the child does think, he does not raise his own thinking to an object of consciousness, but uses the principles of thought in a prereflective way to solve given problems. Thus, he may become intensely interested in computer programs and other technological puzzles. Nevertheless, a notable shift has occurred. Language now serves intelligence; intelligence is not under the control of the flow of language, as it was earlier. At this age, thought is stronger than language.

To develop this a bit further, reflect on the way in which logic emerges and is constructed in Piaget's theory. It develops out of physical or sensorimotor interactions with the environment, so it is possible to see that in mental operations, we have an abstract and symbolic expression of things done physically. I recall Julie, at age three, very quietly and intently tearing open sugar packs as we sat in the restaurant. She divided the piles and did the same thing repeatedly, adding more piles to the ones she already had. What is she doing? It is a sensorimotor approach to mathematics. Physically we combine; that is plus. Physically we separate out; that is minus. Physically we repeat several times; that is multiplication. Physically we divide; that is division. Physically we place things in order; that is greater than and less than. Physically we substitute one thing for another; that is equals. So by the period from ages seven to eleven, sensorimotor and preoperational or intuitive thinking has matured into a structured, coherent, and integrative cognitive system. Thus, the child of seven, when asked an unusual question or one that he is not prepared for ahead of time, does not tumble into confusion but has a systematic way of reflecting on the question to attain an answer. Notice that as logical operations develop, knowing something is being increasingly separated from the perceptual world. Intelligence now has its own basis for knowing, represented supremely in the formation of a mathematical or logical operation. Knowledge becomes increasingly based on the invisible and intangible, and it finds its foundation in logical mathematical coherence.

As this occurs, one can begin to understand the interesting comment by Oxford mathematician Roger Penrose, author of *The Emperor's New Mind.*[12] He said that only when he had almost finished thinking did he put his thought into numbers. Confidence in one's thought, albeit invisible, and the power of the invisible to explain the visible is what is emerging here. Even mathematics itself can be very misleading if one merely follows the logic of numbers. It is into the invisible and incalculable that thinking takes the human mind, not as if to get beyond thought, but rather to get into the essence of thought itself, for which numbers are one remarkably ingenious form of expression.

At this period of time, the child enters with intelligence into the commonsense universe, so brilliantly explained by Newtonian physics. Here cause and effect, basic laws of motion, the logic of induction, deduction, evident and self-evident reasoning, all taking place in Euclidean space and clock time, are accepted as unquestioned presuppositions. The child can think in terms of systems and the interconnected variables that constitute video games and computer technology. This is on the mathematical road to grasping the structure of group theory and number theory, but during this period, thinking remains in the concrete sphere of natural phenomena and rational numbers (whole numbers and fractions).

Piaget sees this limitation as the continuing effect of egocentrism. That is, the school-age child cannot yet recognize that thought has a reality of its own. Piaget also believed that what was taking place here was reflected in the history of science. A case in point is Pythagoras, who was convinced that rational numbers could explain all natural phenomena. This supposition blinded him to the existence of irrational numbers. It is said that one of his pupils, Hippasus, came to realize that the square root of two could not be expressed in either a whole number or a fraction because it is what is now called an irrational number. Pythagoras was not pleased with this revelation because it called his entire philosophy (based as it was on the concrete connection between whole numbers, fractions, and the physical universe) into question. But since he could not refute Hippasus's claim by logic, he sentenced Hippasus to death by drowning. If the history of science is reflected in the personal history of the developing mind, it is well that its prejudices and some of the violence that has accompanied its evolution have been modified in the transmission.

The concreteness in the child's mind at this time is a limitation due solely to the immaturity of the child's intelligence. However, there are signs of higher orders of thought emerging as the child begins to anticipate abstract thinking that can take thinking itself into account.

Interlude: Two Types of Order

This phase in development, when the order in the mind of the child is beginning to cohere with the order of the universe, is the appropriate time to recall the discussion in Chapter One regarding patterns of correlation between the study of human development and the study of the history of the universe. Consider the recent news that Andrew Wiles has found the Holy Grail of mathematics, a solution to Fermat's last theorem. Fermat's theorem is based on the Pythagorean theorem in geometry (which means "to measure the world"), which says of right triangles what every school child knows: $x^n + y^n = z^n$. That is, in a right triangle the sum of the squares of the legs equals the square of the hypotenuse. Fermat's theorem was that this formula works only for the exponent (^{2}); it will not work for any other whole number. Fermat's theorem has proved correct for every example anyone has ever tried; even in this computer age, only the number (2) satisfies the terms of the formula. However, negative examples, regardless of how many, do not constitute a mathematical proof, and a definitive and final proof was called for. In his jottings in the margins of Diophantus's *Arithmetica,* Fermat claimed that his observation on Pythagoras's theorem was mathematically demonstrable, but he did not have space to put it down. Since he did not write it down anywhere else, it has continued to baffle mathematicians for over three hundred years.

However, at the age of ten, Andrew Wiles, now a Princeton mathematician, took a trip to the local library, discovered the problem, and was informed that no proof of Fermat's theorem existed. Fermat's theorem had broken all records for unsolved mathematical problems, and it was a problem Wiles could easily understand. But Wiles, like Piaget himself, was intelligent beyond his ten years of life. He was at that moment so fascinated and deeply engaged with the problem that he worked on it for the next thirty years; during the last seven years of his quest, he went into isolation. He revealed his secret calculations to no one until he presented them in 1993 in the auditorium of the Isaac Newton Institute in Cambridge, England, to a room full of astonished mathematicians. Although he had to correct part of his proof later, he had essentially broken the back of the enigma and made mathematical history.

The mathematical order of the universe is being learned for the first time during the school-age period, and when Wiles seized on Fermat's last theorem with such intensity at the age of ten, he was exhibiting the power of an enigma to grab the intellectual imagination in a way not possible before the dawn of concrete operations. The development of intelligence in its next higher stage, formal operations, will take the enigma much further, and finally to its resolution. The more important point to be made here is that while Wiles was discovering the mathematical order hidden behind Fermat's enigma, he was exhibiting the order of knowing hidden in every act of discovery.

The dynamics of transformation, which are embedded in every transition in human development, are able to be disembedded from the matrix of human development and made intentional at least by the age of five. This pattern, which describes the therapeutic process that cured Little Hans, applies also to scientific discovery. Here again the intense engagement with a conflict over a period of time triggers the psychic search for patterns and prototypes. This is followed by bisociative connections that come by surprise, as insights or "revelation," as Wiles called them, which favor the intensely engaged and informed mind. This is followed by a sense of relief and release, the "Eureka!" response, and then the proving out for both coherence of the proof with the terms of the problem and correspondence with the concerned public.

The story of Wiles's discovery follows precisely this pattern, including "illumination" and "revelation," which moved him emotionally beyond words. His story exhibits on an abstract level the power of the human spirit to unearth hidden orders of meaning and so overthrow frames of reference that had previously proved incommensurate with the reality under investigation. So dramatic is this story of the human spirit, with its transformational plot, that it has been produced for television by BBC under the title *The Proof*. The fundamental point here is that the order of transformation as exemplified in scientific discovery is different from mathematical order, but it is built into human nature as the key to the other orders of creation, all of which become intelligible by essentially this same pattern.

Einstein and Piaget

When Piaget was at the Institute for Advanced Study in Princeton in 1928, Einstein challenged him to study the child's understanding of space and time prior to this period, which begins at age seven. The striking discovery was that Piaget's findings suggested that prior to this period, children have a view of space and time that is closer to relativity theory than after this period, when they learn the essential canons of the Newtonian world. Apparently this period of concrete operations entails some intuitive losses, which have to be reappropriated at a higher level of complexity later on.

Thus, thinking back to Julie and the sugar packs, the development of higher-order mental operations is not only derivative from psychophysical behavior; that behavior is created by the human spirit in a way that embodies the structure of the universe in relationship to which human consciousness and intelligence have arisen. Recall Einstein's comment pointing to the "subtle spirit" at work in us: "The most incomprehensible thing about the universe is that it is comprehensible."[13] It was Piaget's aim to make the incomprehensible at least a bit more intelligible by showing how intelligence itself develops.

Story and History

During this period of development, the child gains a sense of story and history. This is what allows her to integrate her world by means of narrative structure. According to a study done by Elli K. Miranda and Pierre

Miranda, at about age seven the child can grasp her own history, or at least has a sporadic sense of it.[14] In relationship to observed or heard narratives, the child can preserve opposites but not the plot. That is, the child can grasp good guys and bad guys, white hats and black hats, but not the whole narrative. At age eight the child's concepts of objective history can appear in dramatic form. The basic plot is simplified, but it is grasped as a plot, though the full structure is not there. At age nine, the child, now more together conceptually, can develop a time line, complete the plot structure, and get the idea of a historical sequence. At ten, the child can do all of these even better and with greater facility. Again, narrative supplies the coherence of the child's life and is the basis for constructing personal meaning.

Plot structures very often, if not always, have a conflict resolution pattern. They begin with a conflict and work through to a resolution. This is a viable way to construct the world because this is a narrative version of the way in which the child is constructing her own life. Narrative then is another way of raising to consciousness the stage transition process as a way of organizing the life of the child.

The therapeutic power of narrative is illustrated by Richard Gardner in *Therapeutic Communication with Children.*[15] Gardner takes children who are neurotic or depressed and invites them to come to what he calls a talk show. They will be invited to tell stories, and as they do so, the sensitive analyst will notice how the stories are reflective of the mood, attitude, and depression of the child. Often Gardner will say, "That's a very interesting story, but let's see if we can change the ending." So he retells the story and changes the ending to tell the child that there is another way to live and understand herself, another way to establish meaning and world coherence.

Moral Judgment

By the age of seven or eight, there is a shift from expiatory punishment and heteronomy to reciprocity. This is the language and understanding of Lawrence Kohlberg, whose classic sequence needs to be understood first as standing in the Piagetian tradition.[16] Kohlberg's studies on the development of moral judgment are structuralist in that they are hierarchically interpreted in six invariant stages, arranged two by two under three general categories: (I) premoral, (II) conventional, and (III) postconventional. In premoral judgment, the two subcategories, or stages, are (1) heteronomous and (2) instrumental exchange. In conventional, the two subcategories are (1) fulfilling expectations of others (nice girl, good boy) and (2) law and order. In postconventional understanding of moral judgment, the two subcategories are (1) social contract and (2) universal moral principles. Given this scheme, moral judgment at the period between six and eleven years of age is potentially at (I)(2) and has a long way to go.

This sequence is invariant, but the stages do not progress automatically with age (as they do in the case of Erikson's stages); thus, one may remain at stage 2 for a lifetime. Each stage must be acquired by working through the conflict with reality that is implicit in confronting the complexity of a moral dilemma with an inadequate frame of reference (again, the stage dynamic appears as conflict resolution through the constructive work of the human spirit in transforming and transcending the initial stage and the elements). Progress through the stages is marked by moving out of egocentrism toward individuality and universal moral principles (such as Kant's categorical imperative or Plato's idea of justice). Finally, according to the principles of structuralism, one cannot understand more than one stage above one's own.

Kohlberg's method of research was to elicit reflective judgments from his subjects on hypothetical moral dilemmas. The most familiar dilemma is the case of Heinz, whose wife was dying of a rare disease. He lived with her in a remote mountain village, which cut him off from any modern medical care. However, the druggist in his village had discovered a cure for this disease and was charging $2,000 for the amount needed to cure Heinz's wife. Heinz did not have that much money, and the druggist refused to lower the price. The dilemma is, What should Heinz do? There is no right answer, but what Kohlberg wants to study is how persons think when they work out that response. For example, if they respond according to a universal moral principle, they are stage 6, but if they respond in terms of what "a good husband" should do, then it will be stage 3.

There are two major difficulties with this approach. The first is philosophical, and the second resides in the male bias that pervades the assumptions of the scale. The philosophical problem emerged when Kohlberg was studying Harvard students during the 1960s. They frequently scored at stage 6, but they often said, in effect, "So what?" The difficulty was that there is no place within the scale where the subject answers the crucial question, "Why be moral?" Kohlberg added stage 7, which is somewhat ambiguously related to the rest of the scale since it is more difficult to assess the relative egocentrism of religious beliefs and metaphysical positions.

To examine the male bias here, we turn to Carol Gilligan and her critique of the Kohlberg scale. She argued that the male bias so slanted Kohlberg's research that women most commonly ended up at stage 3 and that the result was really more appropriate to the socialization and development of males. As a result, she did research using real situations, interviewing women who were facing the issue of abortion, and attempted to structure the analysis of moral development in a different way. As a result, in her early article published in 1970, she came up with the following scale: Stage 1, orientation toward individual survival, with the transition moving moral judgment from selfishness to responsibility; Stage 2, goodness as self-sacrifice, with the transition from goodness to truth; Stage 3: morality of care and nonviolence. Her understanding of the maturation of moral judgment was also focused on the movement out of egocentrism, but instead of aiming at an individual rendering universal moral judgments, her scale was oriented toward a relational notion of care.[17] Notice also that Gilligan, as well as Kohlberg, had failed to address the question, "Why be moral?"

Gilligan's later research has departed from any scale and become much more embedded in the social and interpersonal interactions, which yield, among other insights, that women in our society tend to be "confident at 11, but confused by 16."[18] She has recognized that during adolescence, women discover that the larger society into which they are emerging is not really constructed in ways that are amenable to their values—for example, the high value placed on relationality rather than regulation, aggression, and individualistic forms of achievement. Consequently, young women tend to go underground; often they recall the precise time in their adolescence when they realized this was necessary. Gilligan's therapeutic approach to this situation is to teach young women to play and affirm themselves, to recover some of the imagination and creativity they had built up in themselves before the age of eleven. In language used here, we can see that the approach is to recover the spirit of the person—the capacity to play and make one's composition of the world truly one's own creation.[19]

In her most recent research, Gilligan has begun to study the development of boys from the early oedipal period to adolescence. She is questioning the socialization of young boys who, at the age of six, feel they now have to be "one of the boys." She claims that this socialization in young boys in Western society muffles the very best quality in them: their sensitivity. No one can deny that she has carried out her claim to the primacy of relationality for women, and she may be able to demonstrate the universality of her claim as she listens to the voices of young boys. However, she says that everything turns on love, work, and gender: "How we work and how we love. And what's more basic than that?"[20] This sounds like the Freudian utopia where persons reach the capacity to *"lieben und arbeiten.*" Once a structuralist is not always to be a structuralist, but certain things are more basic than love and work, such as God and death. I want to appreciate Gilligan's contributions, but they decidedly need to be reenvisioned through theological perspectives.

Theological Perspectives

The theological perspective on the developing capacity to take roles and thus establish institutional life draws out the ambiguity of this new achievement of the ego. Roles are the developmental solution to the individual-belonging struggle that appeared very early. They are designed to protect us against too much intimacy and help us cooperate in doing work. On the one hand, the corporate life, which perspective taking and role construction (which emerges in this period) make possible, is surely an advance against egocentrism in thought, communication, and work. On the other hand, for all their power to socialize us, role structures are, at best, only an approximation of authentic Christian community.

Such community is epitomized in the biblical concept of koinonia. This can be defined with the help of theologians Paul Lehmann and T. F. Torrance as the communion-creating presence of Jesus Christ.[21] The spiritual presence of Jesus Christ becomes the relationality among persons, so that their interaction is simultaneously profoundly intimate and thoroughly functional. Such a communal relationship is like that which always accompanies the bestowal of the Spirit and creates a unique context for understanding the work-worth relationships. When Jesus bestows the Spirit on the disciples in the upper room, he gives them a task. When the Spirit is poured out at Pentecost, those who receive it go then into the world to proclaim the good news.

The first observation to be made here is that the gift precedes and is the condition for taking up roles and doing a job. It is not the case, as it is in the natural course of human development, that roles are a condition for dealing with intimacy and doing work. Intimacy in the Spirit is the condition that redefines roles and all the work that is to be done in the service of the spiritual presence of Jesus Christ.

This implies further that the institutional church is a socially constructed reality based on roles and role systems, which are the outgrowth of, not the condition for, koinonia. To be sure, these two, the koinonia and the institutional church, will always be found together and dialectically related, as the Chalcedonian understanding of Christ would dictate, with the spiritual presence of Christ exercising marginal control over the institutional forms that are created to express it.

What occurs in the natural course of human development once again cries out for a resolution that is higher than what the ingenuity of the human spirit can create, even in its most profound constructions. In the context of the Chalcedonian model, we do not understand that theological answers are brought in to meet human needs, but it is rather the reverse: human needs get their definition and take the form that they do because they already exhibit a longing for a lost reality that is tacitly presupposed by the anguished struggles of the human spirit to find its original ground. Human needs for resolution to such deep conflicts as the existential dichotomy between individuality and belonging are the shattered reflection of a reality that we tacitly know is there but have absolutely no access to it. Theological responses to such existential dichotomies are ways of articulating what has been revealed regarding the lost, forgotten, and otherwise unknowable reality that makes sense of the contorted creations of the human spirit.

To speak of koinonia as the resolution to the individual-belonging dichotomy is to say that the corporate reality created by the spiritual presence of Jesus Christ is itself an expression of the definitive corporate reality that long preceded, as eternity precedes time, the appearance of any koinonia. The theological notion describing the perichoretic relationality in the inner life of God was first formulated by the Cappadocian theologian Gregory of Nazianzus (329–389).[22] This can be understood by recognizing *peri* as meaning "around" or "at all points," as in *perimeter,* and *choreo* as meaning "to proceed" or "to make room," as in *choreography.* The Latin church fathers translated this as *circumincessio,* meaning that there is a moving around within the Trinity such that among the persons there is a mutual interpenetration at all points without any loss of identity. Individuality and mutuality are simultaneously affirmed, and the members of the Trinity can exchange places or mutually indwell one another without changing their identity. Thus, the unity of the Trinity *is* the relationality, and the relationality *is* the unity. Further, each one implies all three, yet the distinction of each from the others is not lost. Thus Basil, another Cappadocian theologian, could speak of a koinonia of the Spirit with the Father and the Son, and at the same time find in that koinonia the very unity of the Godhead. That God *is* Spirit (John 4) and that the Spirit is also one member *of* the Trinity (John 17, Eph. 2:18, 4:4–6) is not an internal contradiction. The potential confusion is resolved if it is recognized that it is inherent in the nature of the Spirit to be relational and at the same time in relation to relate to itself. That is, God both *is* Spirit and *has* Spirit.[23] This understanding of the divine nature discloses not only the ultimate ground for the koinonia at the core of the body of

Christ as the church, but also accounts for the deep, blind restlessness in corporate human life for some resolution to the individual-belonging dichotomy.

Similar to the way in which Andrew Wiles knew at the age of ten that there was in his soul a solution to Fermat's enigma, we all know that the resolution to our existential enigmas awaits discovery through revelations the Spirit can bring to us. Unlike Wiles, we cannot by any rigor of human effort attain those resolutions; they are gifts that precede the task and accompany it along the way. Again, the analogy between human spirit and Holy Spirit pertains.

In ecclesial context, the koinonia and the institutional reality of the empirical church will always be found together and dialectically related, but there can be no question that the life of the koinonia must define and direct the socially constructed reality of the empirical church—not the other way around. If this theological perspective is lost, then the consequences are a professionalized ministry and an enculturated church. That is, the whole ecclesiastical order is nothing more than a sacralized extension of the ego.

This can be portrayed in a phenomenon I call ministerial syndrome. In one of James Fowler's conversations with a physician, he asks, "What are you when you are not an M.D.?" The doctor stops, thinks a moment, then says, "By God, I'm always an M.D."[24] He had lost his person to his role. Now, all ministers worth their salt know they are not locked into their socially constructed ministerial role, "by God!" But there is this phenomenon of ministerial syndrome.

Many persons go into the helping professions, and ministry in particular, because for the most part they are sensitive, caring people. But such people usually get hurt; in order to avoid the pain and keep on in ministry, they construct a persona of kindness, a mask that looks just like them when they are being most kind and caring. Their most genuine caring selves are then reduced to a role. And like all other roles, it is designed to get them close enough to make contact and do a job, but stay far enough away so as not to get hurt again. The minister then becomes an imitation of her own best self. Meanwhile, her most genuine feelings, inspirations, and passions all dry up behind the mask. The result is either to drop out or to continue a shallow, professionalized ministry.

In order for koinonia to surface in and through a ministry, roles have to become reversible. One must be able to take them off and enter into a full presence of God in passionate prayer, or into the full measure of another's deepest concerns so as to "weep with those who weep and rejoice with those who rejoice." Yet one must be able to perform institutional responsibilities without losing touch with the passion of one's faith.

When roles become reversible by the transforming work of Christ's Spirit—reversible, that is, in the sense that you can take them or leave them—then the standard defenses of the ego are accordingly transformed. Thus, secondary repression, instead of rigidifying and shrinking the ego boundaries, becomes, through transformation by the divine presence, "patience and self control"; projection, instead of putting one's own feelings into another to hide from one's self becomes empathy, putting oneself into the other for the sake of feeling in oneself what the other one feels; denial, instead of being a partially conscious, partially unconscious effort to avoid the reality of a situation, becomes forgiveness—a forgiveness that forgives and forgets that it has forgiven; all regression is in the service of transcendence, fantasy formation becomes the vision of God, introjection becomes vicarious suffering, isolation becomes concentration, and reaction formation becomes the capacity to return good for evil. Then the transformed ego can be put into the service of the koinonia in which we mutually create each other in our particularity through our mutuality.

The second theological implication for this stage of development concerns the transformation of conscience through advancement in moral judgment. What is the transformed conscience? It occurs when the superego yields to what Calvin called "inner integrity of heart"; "con-scientia" is knowing within oneself by and with the spiritual presence of Christ that, in any given context, one may act freely and with integrity, or to act with integrity is to act freely.[25] Conscience presupposes relationality, so it goes in search of a fitting context that mirrors its transformed condition. One may understand this briefly by restating the decalogue in terms of "need." That is, since the Lord God is one God and is my God, I do not need any other gods before him; I do not need to bear false witness; I do not need to commit adultery; I do not need to steal; and so forth. It is in the koinonia, as the context of conscience, that we find not merely human support and encouragement for this, but we enter into the presence of God in and with the presence of another or many others. What supports and renews us is not primarily the other people, but the living presence of God as a shared reality. In this we are confirmed in our assurance that we do not need to separate ourselves from God by any compensatory act. Thus, koinonia becomes the context of the transformed conscience. Recall Freud's dictum that conscience is the price we pay for the advancement of civilization. Paul Lehmann's rejoinder to this claim was that koinonia is the price we pay for the advance of conscience.

In this third theological perspective, I must refer to Margaret Krych's work.[26] She is a Lutheran on the faculty at Gettysburg Seminary in theology and education. She was assigned the task by her congregation to "teach justification by grace through faith" to this age group, ages eight to eleven. This is right at the time when children are learning developmentally justification by works, so she took this as a test case for her dissertation.

She began by adopting Tillich as her major theological position and reenvisioned Tillich's correlational method of question and answer—the gospel supplies theological answers to existential questions—as transformational. That is, through the mediation of Christ, answers supplied by the gospel transform the existential questions of our lives and give us new being in Christ. In this theological context, she could see that justification by faith was transformational.

Translating this into human development and theology for children at this age, she took the premise that narrative is the way children establish their world coherence. Transformational narratives would tell stories about the transformation of the child's whole world when the mediator in the story was Jesus. An example of a transformational narrative in which Jesus is mediator is the story of Zaecheus.

The goal was not merely getting the children to learn transformational narratives. It was to awaken in them, by way of these stories, the dynamics of transformation per se. This was to move them proleptically and propaedeutically into the dynamics of transformation by the presence and power of the Holy Spirit. This would be moving them into the very dynamics of justification by faith, which is possible only because they have these dynamics built into their very nature through the stage transition pattern. Through narrative, Krych transposed this pattern, which transposes into therapy and scientific discovery.

Krych's educational method was to use a broken narrative approach similar to that used by Richard Gardner in therapy with children. Before beginning the instruction, she created a very pleasant and supportive setting; then she would tell them the first part of the story: Jesus came to town, and there was this very unpopular little tax collector up in a tree trying to look over the heads of the crowd. Now what is Jesus going to do?

All kinds of answers followed, in which it was shown that Jesus was punitive, associated with conscience and superego, among other things. Then she read the rest of the story, and it was shown how Jesus brought about the transformation of Zaecheus. Again and again she read stories, broken in the middle, and demonstrated the transformational nature and power of Christ.

By the end of the six weeks of class, these children were writing their own transformational narratives making Christ the mediator, and they were self-involved. One little girl drew a picture to illustrate the conversion of Paul, but she, being blond and blue-eyed, drew Paul as a blond-haired, blue-eyed little girl. And nobody laughed. They knew these transformational narratives were about them and their relationship to Jesus, who transforms and thereby justifies them.

The striking thing about this is that she managed to teach an existential form of transformation as a propaedeutic for teaching justification by faith in Christ at a time when ordinary socialization patterns of the ego are teaching justification by works. This reveals the superior, underlying power of transformation—the dynamics of the human spirit in stage transition and as operative in and throughout the life span.

Much more must be said about the work-worth relationship in the context of theology and human development, but this discussion sets some of the background. Later stages of human development will call forth other aspects of this critical connection for persons and for Western culture.

NOTES

1. Dietrich Bonhoeffer, *Ethics,* ed. Eberhard Bethge (New York: Macmillan, 1955), p. 74.

2. Max Weber, *The Protestant Ethic and the Spirit of Capitalism,* trans. Talcott Parsons (New York: Scribner, 1958).

3. James W. Fowler, *Stages of Faith* (San Francisco: Harper San Francisco, 1981).

4. Ronald Goldman, *Religious Thinking from Childhood to Adolescence* (New York: Routledge, 1964).

5. Ives Hendricks, *Facts and Theories of Psychoanalysis* (New York: Knopf, 1958).

6. Victor Turner, *Dramas, Fields, Metaphors* (Ithaca, N.Y.: Cornell University Press, 1974).

7. Arthur Janov, *The Primal Scream* (New York: Dell, 1972).

8. See David Elkind, *The Hurried Child* (Reading, Mass.: Addison-Wesley, 1981).

9. Urie Bronfenbrenner, "The Effects of Social and Cultural Change on Personality," in Neil J. Smelser and William T. Smelser, eds., *Personality and Social Systems* (New York: Wiley, 1963). This was subsequently confirmed in personal conversation (1970).

10. Jean Piaget, *The Psychology of the Child* (New York: Basic Books, 1969).

11. Carol Gilligan, *In a Different Voice: Psychological Theory and Women's Development* (Cambridge, Mass.: Harvard University Press, 1982).

12. Roger Penrose, *The Emperor's New Mind* (Oxford: Oxford University Press, 1989).

13. See Albert Einstein, *Out of My Later Years* (New York: Bonanza Books, 1956), p. 61. See also James E. Loder and W. Jim Neidhardt, *The Knight's Move* (Colorado Springs: Helmers and Howard, 1995).

14. E. Miranda and P. Miranda, *Structural Models in Folklore and Transformational Essays* (The Hague: Mouton, 1971), pp. 30ff.

15. Richard Gardner, *Therapeutic Communication with Children* (New York: Aronson, 1976).

16. Lawrence Kohlberg, *The Philosophy of Moral Development* (New York: HarperCollins, 1981).

17. Carol Gilligan, "In a Different Voice: Women's Conception of the Self and of Morality," *Harvard Educational Review* 47, no. 4 (1977): 481–517.

18. Francine Prose, "Confident at 11, Confused at 16," *New York Times Magazine,* January 7, 1970, pp. 20–46.

19. Recent follow-up research by Carol Gilligan, *Meeting at the Crossroads* (New York: Ballantine Books, 1992).

20. Michael Norman, "From Carol Gilligan's Chair," *New York Times Magazine,* November 9, 1997, p. 50.

21. Paul Lehmann, *Ethics in a Christian Context* (New York: HarperCollins, 1963); and T. F. Torrance, *The Trinitarian Faith* (Edinburgh: T. & T. Clark, 1988).

22. See especially the summary in Harry A. Wolfson, *The Philosophy of the Church Fathers* (Cambridge, Mass.: Harvard University Press, 1956), pp. 418ff.

23. Loder and Neidhardt, *The Knight's Move,* chap. 2.

24. James W. Fowler, *Life Maps: Conversations on the Journey of Faith* (Waco, Tex.: Word Books, 1978).

25. John Calvin, *Institutes of the Christian Religion,* trans. John Allen (Philadelphia: Westminster Press, 1936), Bk. III, ch. 19.6.

26. Margaret A. Krych, "Communicating 'Justification' to Elementary-Age Children: A Study in Tillich's Correlational Method and Transformational Narrative for Christian Education" (Ph.D. dissertation, Princeton Theological Seminary, 1985).

PART FOUR

THE RELEASE OF
THE SPIRIT

9

ADOLESCENCE IN PSYCHOLOGICAL PERSPECTIVE

FIVE AXES OF YOUTH IDENTITY

WHEN THE FETUS grows too large for the womb, it pushes out into the world and begins to forge its own definition of itself and of the world into which it has come. As it was with little Julie, so it is, more or less, for all other children; birth is an astonishing, wonderful, and dangerous time. Adolescence is like that. Having grown too large for the space available at home, the young adolescent begins to move out to make room for herself, or at least to have a room of her own. In many respects, it is getting started again and confronting those same earlier issues in a much more conscious and intentional way. The space available now is the entire universe, and the boundless potential the adolescent senses is a truth about human existence that she is just beginning to understand.

In Chapter One, I spoke of four themes that connect the study of the universe with the study of human development. In adolescence, for the first time, these themes, which have implicitly guided this book thus far, become an intentional part of the core struggle of this period. These themes are (1) the inevitability of order, (2) the eventual emergence of disorder, (3) the possibility of new order, and (4) the relationality that underlies all forms of order and their explanations. In adolescence, these themes become personal, explicit, and formative, both because of the great advances and the great dangers of this formative period.

Up to this time, the human spirit, primarily through its construction of the ego and the superego, has consistently created forms of order designed to sustain the developing person in the face of incipient destruction.

However, all these forms of order were compromises and half-adequate solutions, trapping the human spirit behind the lines of its own defenses. The spirit, restless with its limited successes and its corresponding failure to liberate itself without entailing further entrapment, now breaks free in the strange new powers of adolescence. In effect, all previous solutions to the major issues of the first ten years of life undergo an upheaval that thrusts the developing person into the abyss of nothingness underlying the ego, and calls that person into transformation. For better or for worse, both the ultimate emptiness and the possibility of new order and meaning are imposed on the developing person at this time. What begins now is a conscious and intentional quest for the adolescent to put it all together in a new and more comprehensive way in the ever-threatening context of potential meaninglessness. As with all other instances of transformative reconstruction, multidimensional relationality is the context out of which the human spirit generates new forms of order and meaning. Adolescents, from chums to cliques to gangs, congregate to get a grip on their own many-sided potential for both entropic destruction and new order.

The overall topic for this period in the context of this book is the release of the spirit and its discovery of its eternal ground—or its ostrich-like flight from nothingness into resocialization. All aspects of the first decade of life get a radically new appraisal and reappropriation in view of the necessity for gaining an identity in the complex and often threatening sociocultural and interpersonal milieu of which adolescents are now aware for the first time.

From the standpoint of the status quo sociocultural milieu into which adolescents are being socialized, it is sometimes said that the adolescent suffers from every psychopathology known to humanity: depression as aggression directed against the self; manic-depressive mood swings; obsessional guilt and compensation; hysteria that appears after long periods of concentration; suicidal thoughts as displaced aggression against one's caretakers; and megalomania, in which the adolescent will now resolve the world's problems. It was really adolescents whom Talcott Parsons had in mind when he said that each new generation is a barbarian invasion that has to be overcome by the power of socialization and enculturation.[1] Of course, if the adolescent suffers all of these ills at some time, he does not usually have any of them all the time. The point to be made here is that extremity is mainline adolescent behavior.

A recent *Rolling Stone* headline read, "The Disease Is Adolescence: And the Symptoms Are Violence, Suicide, Drugs, Alcohol, Car Wrecks and

Poverty."[2] The headline focuses the deep irony in such negative assessments. These are not the symptoms of adolescence any more than they are the symptoms of contemporary American and Western society.[3] From the standpoint of the larger social system, adolescent behavior is often best understood as a symptom of the larger society, not primarily an invasion of it. In effect, adolescents disclose in bold type and vivid colors the latent patterns of social disorganization that lurk always under the surface of polite society. In confronting adolescent behavior, adults must confront outwardly what they are continually dealing with internally in their personal family and institutional lives. That is, adolescent behavior is a two-edged sword; what appears to be social nonconformity is often a dramatization of the underside of large-scale social conformity. The greater danger to the human spirit in this is not from the adolescent side but from the sociocultural side: the fear of nonconformity on the part of status quo society will not so much redirect or transform the human spirit, but, if possible, suppress or break it so it will conform without complaint.

It is partly due to this potential standoff between the burgeoning adolescent spirit and the sociocultural drive for continuity and resistance to self-disclosure that there are two fundamentally different ways to go through adolescence. The first includes both male and female, and focuses on ego development. This is the traditional developmental approach. The second is distinctly religious and calls for a theological interpretation. It will be discussed in Chapter Ten. The first will build up an understanding of the ego around certain key axes, each amounting to a reworking of one of the previous developmental stages. To achieve a balance of inevitable extremes is generally the developmental aim in the formation of ego identity. The second will discuss the transformation of the entire ego struggle by the power of the Spirit, a transformation not developmentally possible before this period. In this, the spiritually transformed person will be able to take the critique of her social milieu into her own identity and follow a vision of a better society.

Background and General Issues

Chronologically, adolescence extends from ages eleven to seventeen and on. (Some say that American society is perennially adolescent, so perhaps adolescence may functionally extend throughout a lifetime.) Generally this period is broken into three parts chronologically: early adolescence up to age twelve, middle adolescence from ages thirteen to fifteen, and late adolescence from ages fifteen to seventeen and on. The functional distinction is that the younger adolescent generally ceases looking backward and reworking a familial past; the older adolescent begins to look and move toward the future.

Three observations seriously qualify any face-value acceptance of Erikson's understanding of this stage as identity versus role confusion. The first is that the young person is making a major transition in development, with the disequilibrium as intense as any other since birth. This means that he will both want to hold on and let go and will need a transitional object. Kegan claims that this will be the "chum" or "best friend."[4] This is the one who is like me—one whose needs and self-esteem are exactly like the needs and self-esteem of my own, but which will be transformed into a part of me—no longer who I am, but something I have. At this stage, chum and I are in-between talking, all the time talking to each other, but not about things we discuss with family and parents.

Why so much talking? Because the theological potential of this stage is emerging as each one senses the underlying void that is opening up as each moves out into an unknown future to which she is biologically, socially, and culturally destined. Adolescents sense with greater comprehension than ever before the truth about human existence: it comes to nothing; in and of itself it comes to nothing! They are trying to bridge the distance with words, the way they did when they first learned to speak and pointed to get words to reach across the gap between themselves and others.

A second mitigating influence is the common observation that a period of affiliation appears as part of this transition. Whether one is male or female, there is an affiliative stage in which males and females tend to associate exclusively with peers in same-sex groups. This affiliative sub-stage is like an extension of "chum" in the context of an emerging sexual identification.

The third mitigating consideration is the feminist critique. Criticism of the Eriksonian sequence that moves from identity to intimacy is, from the woman's perspective, reversed. That is, the woman tends to find her identity in the context of intimacy, partly because of the long-standing priority given to relationality as against individuality among women, and partly because differentiation from the maternal matrix need not be so decisive for the young girl who is becoming a young woman as it is for the boy who is becoming a male youth. This not only has developmental roots, but the sociocultural indexes governing male and female behavior call for this, though cultures vary in what constitutes male and female behavior.[5]

I propose to examine the issues at stake in the formation of an identity or in getting one's own voice, and I will modify Erikson's approach here and in the next stage, trying to be sensitive to the way relationality is a necessary context for identity, as well as identity being a basis for intimacy and in-depth relationality. As Robert Kegan points out, it is a misunderstanding to set individuality in some absolute way over against belonging. One may well make decisions for and about oneself in the context of belonging; such decisions will not be made by oneself. But decisions made by oneself may well be with a keen sense of one's belonging or connectedness.[6] The search for one's voice is also wrought out of relationships and from within their midst. A claim on one's own voice in the context of multiple relationalities, including the relational self, and for the sake of caring about these relationalities is viable and important for both male and female development.

Identity and Its Axes

Building on Erikson's premise, a working definition of identity is as follows: Identity is a consistent sense of oneself. That is, identity establishes self-consistency from one social and cultural environmental context to the next, and allows for a balance between resistance to adult conformity, on the one hand, and subjective self-absorption, on the other. Identity means also that the inner sameness and continuity sensed in oneself is matched by one's meaning for others. The body axis, the ideological axis, the authority axis, the love axis, and the work axis are the principal axes on which identity is built. On all of these axes the adolescent ego is striving for a balance that transcends the extreme of rigidity on the one hand, and diffusion on the other. When balance is achieved, diffusion becomes flexibility, and rigidity becomes reliable ego boundaries.

In opposition to identity, Erikson uses the term *role confusion,* suggesting that the opposite of identity moves primarily in the direction of diffusion, but rigidity in a stereotyped role pattern or in a negative identity is another failure of identity formation which moves to the opposite extreme of diffusion. *Role confusion* might be interpreted to mean both, but I will lay out the issue in terms of rigidity and diffusion in order to gain some greater specificity.

In the adolescent's development as human spirit, the spirit simultaneously centers the person and moves exocentrically toward a potentially infinite horizon. However, the unredeemed human spirit most often reaches outward and finds itself caught up in ongoing styles of life waiting to lay captive to the spirit and bring it under some prefabricated pattern of socialization. The achieving society, for example, lies in waiting to short-circuit the dynamic outreach of the spirit, shielding it from the nothingness that haunts the ego and filling the emptiness with competition and productivity. And there are others that take quick advantage of the transcending exocentricity of the human spirit and its incipient sense of groundlessness. Thus, an identity is constructed between the borders of one's preteen years and the powerful lifestyle patterns dominating the sociocultural milieu.

Bodily Axis

According to one recent report, the childhood brain remains supercharged until age ten or eleven.[7] Then the metabolic rate begins to fall, until it reaches the adult rate at about age thirteen or fourteen. The basic pattern is that neurons, axions, and synapses are at first overproduced in the embryo; then there is what is described as massive cell death. By adolescence, the main outline of adult brain activity has been sculpted into the neuronal design of the brain. Perhaps, it is argued, by changing hormonal conditions, the mature brain gets sculpted out by nature, so higher-order brain activity may emerge now that excess connections have been eliminated. Note that so-called massive cell death does not mean loss of intelligence; in fact, in adolescence, intelligence reaches a higher order of refinement than ever before.

The basic bodily changes that appear in adolescence bring about an upheaval in psychological space and time. Recall that the concepts of space and time come from bodily interaction with the environment in Piaget's sensorimotor period. The sense of space comes from reaching and touching, coordinating various schemata: eye and hand, ear and hand, and so forth. Space is constructed out of the action of the body in its relation to the environment. So is time, as rhythms of night and day, feeding and sleeping and waking, gradually differentiate a primal sense of duration, giving rise to a view of time. Because the body is so fundamental in developing space-time coordinates from the beginning, the rapid change in bodily development in adolescence produces a radical change in the organization of space and time.

If we begin with space, we can divide the issue between subjective space and objective space, and recognize a parallel here between diffusion and rigidity, with the stronger temptation to rigidity on the objective side and the stronger temptation to diffusion on the subjective side. The interplay here is very fluid, but the aim is lived space that transcends the distinction between subject and object and creates a differentiated unity.

This becomes increasingly difficult as adolescents realize that there is no ready-made space for adolescents qua adolescents in the social system. As a result, a lot of extreme behavior erupts, which is the norm for mainline adolescence. The adolescent is making space where there seems to be no space—with noise, green hair, pierced body parts, consuming enormous quantities of food, and wearing clothes that are out of size, either over-sized or almost missing. One of my colleagues working with adolescents said she had to give up her study of them because she could not tolerate their music. Apparently their power to claim space is effective. Inner space and outer space are then in fluid interaction.

This is not, however, just a matter of adjustment. Space is a powerful force, a matter of life and death, especially now in adolescence because one is old enough to fight for it. In his classic work, *The Territorial Imperative*, Robert Ardrey describes the naturalist who tried to mate two leopards. He put the male's cage next to the female's cage and let the two animals interact until he felt that there was a developing affection. Then he opened the door between the cages. When the female went into the male's cage, the male struck her and killed her. Ardrey's argument is that space is more powerful than sexuality.[8]

Other studies show that animals, given all they need except sufficient space, will die. Here one can refer to T. E. Hall, *The Hidden Dimension*,[9] where he discusses how all creatures live in a "space bubble." Intrusion into the space bubble or overcrowding engenders violent reactions. Studies of angry men in Megargee and Hokanson's *The Dynamics of Aggression* show that these angry men have about a three-foot space bubble.[10] When anyone gets within three feet, powerful autonomic responses begin to occur: they perspire, the pupils dilate, and the fist clenches—all just to make the point that territory can be a matter of life and death. At risk of imprisonment, teenagers with spray-paint cans, known as taggers, claim space by drawing their names on city walls, and gangs kill or maim to preserve their territory.

For adolescents, like infants, the space in which they have been raised has become too small, so they must "get out of here." But since they are unaccustomed to the body they have on their hands, they must construct space in relationship to inside and outside impulses and demands.

Furniture was clearly not made for adolescents; they can sit seven different ways in a chair or on the table and the chair is for the feet. Outside limits tend to be assimilated into inside impulses.

Subjective space is very fluid. My daughter Kim, at the age of twelve, invited me to see a very big and powerful man who was her teacher at that time in the seventh grade. It turned out that Mr. Cirrello was a relatively short man, but he had a very big voice and was very active. The physical size was exaggerated according to his subjective impact on her.

The adolescent may be able to do a full gainer off the high board and then stumble over his feet getting out of the pool. Space fluctuates with mood, personal history, and culture. When the mood is elation, then the sky is the limit, and one is "high." In the case of depression, as in a teenage alcoholic who described himself going through a tunnel, or in anxiety, which means "narrow space," the space contracts.

There are also important cultural variances. From culture to culture, interpersonal space is constructed differently. In some cultures, it is considered friendly to bathe the other person in your breath; in others, the norm is never to look at the person you are talking to. In many sectors of contemporary American culture, there is increased mobility, contingency, and fragmentation, so homelessness or wandering becomes the norm. Thus, space is fragmented, and finding a secure space is increasingly difficult for adolescents. Multiculturalism and pluralism mean fewer cultural markers are in place to help the struggle for psychological space to gain solidarity for one's identity. Notice again that what appears to be the problem of youth is also a symptom of the society at large.

Theologically, space, in its ultimate perspective, is not contingent on any of these factors. Space is a powerful force, and that powerful need must be satisfied. It is indeed a matter of life and death. But the transformation of space occurs when one realizes existentially that Jesus is the promised land, as W. D. Davies developed this theme in his book *The Gospel and the Land*.[11] Jesus is all that the promised land was supposed to be. He is the vine; he is the one from whom we drink the living water and never thirst again. In him the promised land is transformed into the Kingdom of God, the reign of the Spirit of Jesus Christ. I mention this to keep in mind a major thesis of this book: the theological reality, which is only reflected in the human, is ultimately definitive for every aspect of human development. Thus, only the transformed identity is "normal" identity.

Let us now turn to time: the reconstruction of temporality and the formation of identity. Augustine's description of lived time, that is, the present of things past, the present of things future, and the present of things present, is a good example of the integration of the objective structure of chronology into the subjective sense of the flow of time.[12] Lived time is the equivalent of lived space. Once again, the subject and object distinction is a helpful way to interpret the development of the form of time in identity. During the period of concrete operations, the child has learned to tell time and has come to believe that clocks have a kind of absolute quality about them. With pressures to "be on time" coming from every sector of human life, from school to bus to meetings to home or work, even waking and sleeping, the emphasis is to be on time. So the temptation to objective temporal rigidity is ever present in our society and cultural context, but the subjective sense of time erupts irrepressibly.

As with space, mood makes a difference in subjective time. In elation, as in boy-girl relationships, for example, time is open ended ("now is forever," "this will last forever"). Tami, who is always in a state of elation, is never affected by chronological time, especially when she is on the telephone. Always there is another, "Oh, and I have to tell you . . ." In depression, on the other hand, time has run out. "I'll never amount to anything," some of my students say. "Calvin wrote his Institutes before he was twenty-nine; Hegel wrote *The Phenomenoloqy of the Mind* when he was twenty-nine. I'm twenty-eight, and I haven't written anything yet" (he was right about Calvin, wrong about Hegel). Depression shrinks and distorts time; even the facts are distorted by the mood.

Less fluid, but mood related, are Philip Zimbardo's studies of the dominant time frame or deep sense of time in which adults come to live.[13] The dominant time frame here is correlated with the conflict and crises in one's life. Those who have had major crises but have not resolved them tend to live predominantly in the past. Those who have had relatively few major crises tend to live predominantly in the future. Those who have had crises but worked them through live in a balanced view of time free for the present.

Adolescents are in the process of forming the dominant time frame in which they will live. Unresolved issues from the past and ignored at this time will often go underground, but thereafter fix one's time frame back into one's past. The accumulation of conflicts resolved and unresolved engenders deep running developmental time; however, this is not the same as lived time. The lived time of the adolescent tends to be immediacy. The immediacy of experience is the preferred experiential time frame. "Proximal time" is the way some name it, a Now that leads into an undefined future by means that are equally undefined for getting there. Under the surface, however, the dominant adult time frame is taking shape.

Pathologies also develop around the failure to work out a balanced view between subjective and objective views of time. Chronic procrastination, for instance, and work paralysis are an eruption designed to lay a claim on one's own time against the pressures to conform to objective time frames. More serious pathologies may also appear. In the classic film *David and Lisa*, David, dominated by his mother's pressures and demands, at one point smashes a clock, as if to destroy objective time against which he felt his subjectivity was being crushed.

As before with space, the psychological search is for a balanced equilibration for subjective and objective time. However, theological time is neither subjective nor objective, nor merely a balance. Theological time is *kairos,* the fullness of time. A balanced view of time may be a prerequisite for fully understanding kairos; that is, the balance preserves the psyche from subjective absorption and from objective defensive rigidity. But theologically, kairos, as the fullness of time, is normative; balanced views of time are in expectation of or waiting on the fullness of time. This is something we say we sense in the Spirit, which is not surprising since there is in the rhythm of the human spirit a buildup toward insights, toward the culminating moment of illumination. Here subjective and objective time come together in a way that not only transcends the balanced ego but puts the ego back into the world with a heightened expectation of what the Spirit of God may do next.

Thus, the space-time coordinates of the adolescent's lived world emerge from the changing body in relation to the physical, social, and cultural environment, and they in turn give shape to the adolescent ego. The reworking of the body, and the way in which the body compels the adolescent spirit to reconstruct space and time, all work toward adaptation. However, implicit in this struggle are strong theological potentials that point toward transformation by the Spirit of God.

An example of space undergoing transformation in the fullness of time is the case of Michael. In a previous chapter, I referred to Paul, whose ministry in gangland on the streets of San Francisco won him the respect of some of the most dangerous youths in the neighborhood. This was a remarkable achievement. The gang where Paul's ministry occurred not only never bothered him, but they protected his car and his place of ministry from vandalism.

One day Michael walked into Paul's place quivering and shaking. He was a Hispanic youth about fifteen years old who had no permanent home. Sometimes he slept where his father lived, sometimes at a friend's place, sometimes on the street. Michael was a tagger who drew his name in beautiful colors on every available wall, bridge, or building where he could find the space. He had also painted his name all over his body. In fact, he was obsessed with putting his name everywhere, but he knew that painting his name and always running from the police was driving him crazy. The buildup of tension had finally reached "the fullness of time."

Paul took Michael to a Hispanic Pentecostal church, and he was converted. His love of Jesus and his joy in the gospel was overwhelming to him. The Creator Spirit had acted, and he was a new creation. But his human spirit was not yet transformed; he still felt he needed to paint. So Paul and his wife found walls where the police would let him paint. But as Michael's identity had been transformed, so had his sense of space. This was evident in that now he painted in beautiful letters "Joy," Peace," "Jesus," and down in the bottom corner he wrote "Michael." His paintings were so beautiful that photographs of them were printed up as postcards and sold as a source of income for him. This is a very graphic image of a dialectical identity; I-not I-but Christ was the new structure of his identity, and it came in the fullness of time, transforming his lived space. In the fullness of time, Jesus had become his territory, "the land" for Michael.

Ideological Axis

The attempt to build a system of ideals that one can live by is a reworking of trust in the context of adolescent thought and religion, and is greatly enhanced by the maturation of intelligence from concrete operations to formal operations. The main theme of formal operations is thinking about thinking. One can now begin to theorize and construct one's own systems of ideas.

By virtue of the transcending capacity of the human spirit, human intelligence is given a heightened sense of totality. That is, increasingly one is able to believe that intelligence can exhaust the sense of totality, as implied in the earliest phases of intellectual development. At this period, for the first time one may begin to sense the remarkable connection between how we think and the shape of the universe.

More specifically, after about the age of twelve, the child can and will begin to put concrete problems and solutions together and construct abstract theories. This represents the emergence of hypothetico-deductive thinking. This is the final, decisive move out of egocentrism insofar as intellectual competence is concerned, but it is also accompanied by a heightened intellectual narcissism, so that even in this last move out of egocentrism as intelligence, there is still a residual form of it—an egocentrism of new enthusiasm and sense of omnipotence of reflection.

The essential competence acquired at this time is that the adolescent can go through the basic textbook steps of conventional scientific thinking. One can (1) sense a problem; (2) intellectualize, that is, abstract and propositionalize the essential elements of the problem and formulate it; (3) construct hypotheses, that is, intellectually construct solutions to the problem, make deductions, and explore possible consequences; (4) mentally examine the hypotheses, anticipate conclusions, and select the most likely hypothetical solution; and (5) devise an empirical test and perform it. If this test fails, one goes back and repeats the same procedure. The adolescent mind does not collapse into a prereflective or preformal operational level of thinking.

This cognitive development fits well with what is occurring, according to Erikson. The emerging competence makes the formulation of an ideology possible, and the developing struggles of the ego make it necessary. Ideology is a genuine hunger that calls for an interpersonally constructed worldview, a place in the concrete world. Thus, ideology becomes an anchor of identity and displaces the family as the notion of trust is thereby reconstructed. One believes in the ideology and will live by it, and from that standpoint one *has* a family but does not *belong* to it.

The ideological hunger of this period brings adolescents, male and female, into devout commitment to causes. This ideological development first borrows from others and only later becomes one's own, but the adolescent is continually in the process of constructing an ideology, a worldview, a sense of cosmic meaning and the place of humanity in it. This is an effort to put a face into the emptiness of the universe to overcome the cosmic loneliness that now appears in the upheaval of the adolescent ego. Adolescents are uncompromisingly loyal to causes and make superb advocates and proselytizers. Hitler's youth movement, as well as the buildup of Mao's China, made demonic use of this ideological hunger and the adolescent's capacity for totalistic value commitment. In Mother Teresa's Calcutta, the ideology of charity is the exact opposite. I was moved by watching young white English and American students bathing and feeding the Untouchables, as if they knew intuitively they must come to terms with death in the context of love in order to know what it means to be truly alive. In Erikson's terms, "fidelity" is the consequent virtue of the ego to be acquired at this period.

Value commitments made during this time seem to have remarkable staying power. Robert J. Lifton's studies of protean behavior are germane at this point. His several books, including *The Life of the Self* and *The Protean Self,* [14] describe a postmodern lifestyle. This style is named after the Greek god Proteus who would not prophecy; he would not disclose his identity, changing from blood, to a stick, to a bull, but never being himself. However, some have suggested that by the time one reaches the age of twenty-nine, there is a return to the ideological perspective and values held at seventeen. [15] This is not to prove but to suggest that the ideological hunger in us is very deep—as deep as the need to find a foundation for trust since one is gradually separated from one's earliest context of trust, even if in the interim (seventeen to twenty-seven) one practices cynicism and a hermeneutic of suspicion. Rigidity of ideology occurs when ideology is adopted from an authoritarian standpoint engendered by the fear of punishment, or it is one that is born out of any ideological conformity and fear of facing adolescent crises.

Diffusion of ideology appears in protean behavior, whose patron saint is Jean Paul Sartre.[16] His dictum that we are "condemned to freedom" is license to disregard conscience as heir of the superego and become whoever you want to be whenever you choose.

In either case, the basic hunger is for a fundamentally religious ideology or theology because this alone covers all the dimensions of existence that the adolescent is confronting and supplies a new foundation for trust. That is, only an ideology that deals with one's own death and potential nonbeing in the light of that which is truly transcendent and holy will be strong enough to meet the intensified needs of this period.

In the case of "Mary," as Fowler recounts her story, she discovers in her early twenties, after a failed suicide attempt and in the midst of an LSD trip, that God is a real, solid, and inviolable reality. When she comes off the LSD (like so many young people in the sixties came off drugs and found the drugs to be impotent after that) she discovers experientially what her family of origin never gave her: a reason to live. It is eventually her brother, Ron, who gives her the God definition of that reason in biblical terms. The Spirit of God had acted at a level deeper than mother love to give life in a way that eventually transformed her entire family constellation.[17]

The Christian ideology not only provides an adolescent reconstruction of trust; it does what the original trust could not do: provides a reason to live and affirms life itself, not by repression but in the face of death itself.

Here it may be useful to remember the theological debate between Wolfhart Pannenberg and Hans Kung (explored in Chapter Five). Both of these theologians wanted faith to be based on basic trust. However, exactly the opposite is the case. Basic trust as reworked in this period must, from a theological standpoint, come to be based on a spirit-to-Spirit relationship in which basic trust is transformed into a convictional reality.

Authority Axis

As the adolescent is beginning to feel like a peer with adults, she reworks the relation between big people and little people, and so reworks the basis for control and authority. The developmental history of this issue should take us back to the first time it became focused at the age of two. Later (at ages three to five) identification with the parents then led to the formation of the superego, by which the laws of social reality are written on the adolescent psyche. During adolescence, the superego goes underground and is replaced in consciousness by a sense of conscience. Preparatory to this, the developing young person has felt increasing equality with peers and subsequently with adults. Out of this period of time, the ego ideal develops at a peer-level context and continues throughout adult life. According to James Younnis's study, adults become people and potential peers only after the age of twelve.[18] This development corresponds to the submersion of identification with the parents and the conversion of the superego into a psychological conscience.

There is a basic threat developmentally and dynamically in becoming as big as the big people. Everyone has some ambivalence about growing up, being big, and potentially replacing the big people. How one deals with this is largely the result of one's developmental history, but the working out of this is finding a balance between a rigid superego and diffusion of a sense of authority. This balance means in part that one acquires the capacity to move to a leader or follower position without loss of self-esteem either way.

The authority issue is especially poignant because we can find here two socially acceptable ways to move, either to the rigid side or to the diffused side, and one's sense of conscience will be skewed accordingly. The first is the authoritarian option—the rigid side; the second is the protean option—the diffuse side. Both represent a failure of identity along the authority axis, but both are nevertheless socially acceptable and affirmed in major sections of society.

The characteristics of the authoritarian personality are (1) a preoccupation with the distinction between strong and weak; (2) those like us, those not like us; (3) conventional values—unconventional values; (4) inside is weak (subjective)—outside is strong (objective); (5) given to stereotyping and superstition; and (6) preoccupation with all deep, dark, dirty things that are going on in the world (and there *are* deep, dark, dirty things going on in the world, but the authoritarian is especially driven to find them out). As Roger Brown suggested, we all know these people even if we do not know the continuing studies on this personality type.[19]

Essentially what happened developmentally is that for different reasons, the adolescent on the way to becoming authoritarian has identified with the dominant superego figure out of fear of punishment. Thus, by becoming authoritarian, he directs aggression at followers or subordinates, leaving the ego helpless to negotiate adjustment except in strictly black and white terms, right or wrong, with no mitigating middle. Two cases illustrate different aspects.

First is a controlling, manipulative mother and an explosive father who was also a minister. He was not able to discipline his son properly because the mother, under the rubric of protection from the father, controlled and wanted to absorb the son. The emergence of the authoritarianism in the son was mixed with a good deal of paranoia, but for him things were only one way, and bad things were very likely to happen if he was not careful. Evil should be severely punished. Once on Forty-Second Street in New York City, I went with him and watched him growl angrily under his breath at people of dubious sexual identification. He eventually went into one of the socially acceptable places for authoritarians: the ministry.

In this second illustration, a student came to me after a lecture on this topic and said, "I am one of those." Describing a home scene of arbitrary punishment in which his father, a part-time gambler, exercised control and authority entirely within his own internal frame of reference and needs, he set forth the developmental foundations of his son's personality. Unable to beat his father, the boy joined him and identified with him as a way to avoid the constant anxiety of being blindsided and punished for unknown and unpredictable reasons. He left seminary to join the military, one of the other major socially acceptable positions in society for authoritarians.

Other loci in society are the police force and secondary school administrators, where authoritarians are found in socially affirmed positions. To come to an authoritarian resolution to certain professional demands is not necessarily to become an authoritarian personality, nor is it true that all persons in these positions are authoritarian. Nevertheless, the rigid authoritarian solution to the control issue will narrow the scope of conscience and skew identity formation in socially affirmed ways.

On the other end of the authority axis is diffusion. Here is where most sociological studies of youth culture frame the contemporary adolescent picture as "the problem of youth." Both represent society as a whole, that is, as a symptom, and they struggle to find an identity that their culture often cannot help them find because their culture mirrors their adolescent struggles too directly. The socially acceptable lifestyle that emerges with the diffusion of authority, and that diffusion taken in as an aspect of the adolescent personality, is the protean style of life described earlier.

Here the social milieu, in which the "Nowhere Generation" or "Generation X" or "the Slackers" find themselves, lends itself to continuous change. Broadly speaking, Lifton speaks of psychohistorical dislocation in which there are high mobility and interpersonal fragmentation and very few reliable psychological, economic, or intellectual markers. Youth, particularly lower- and middle-class whites, are condemned to wander within and between multiple blurring boundaries and spaces marked by excess, otherness, difference, and indifference. In a postmodern world of the protean personality, space and time are condensed by the information highway and MTV into "speed space," and virtual reality technologies provide a kind of endless play of random access.[20] Thus, meaning is always en route, and the media become the substitute for real experience. Sometimes one cannot remember whether something really happened or he saw it on MTV.

The Reverend Don Barnhouse, who a few years ago did the editorial commentary for the *Delaware Valley News* (New Jersey and Pennsylvania), said people would come to the television studio to see the anchorman and meet the "real" John Vacenda. But when the red light went on and he was on the air, they turned away from him to the monitor; that was the "real" John Vacenda that they knew. Barnhouse also said that in the church where he subsequently pastored, there was a prayer group who was asked to pray for "Alice." Who was Alice? A woman in one of the soap operas who was having trouble.

The protean personality produced by psychohistorical dislocation, flooding of imagery, the blurring of socially constructed boundaries, and the devaluing of human life (begun with the nuclear era) is nevertheless an enigma to herself. Lifton's studies show the double-bind nature of this diffusion of authority and loss of conscience. The protean has both a deep ideological hunger and a cynicism about every ideology, a cry for nurturance but a rejection of all caring persons. The illusion is that one can mold oneself into any type of personality one wants to be. "Dying and rising" is the protean motif.

In the space of about five years, one may drop out of college, hit the San Francisco scene, go to Jerusalem and study orthodoxy, but then come back and go to business school, and after a year or so in a training program return to do studies for high school counseling. In all of this, there is no conscience or sense of a loss of continuity. The patron saint for the protean personality is Jean Paul Sartre, whose dictum that we are "condemned to freedom" means that all authority is to be ignored for the sake of self-expression. In his autobiography, he says that he "readily subscribes to the verdict of an eminent psychoanalyst who says he has no superego." What lies behind this is parenting of an absent sort, or the kind of parenting that understands so much that the parent stands for nothing.

Thus, on the authority axis, the adolescent identity seeks a balance between the two extremes of rigidity and diffusion, even though society finds both extremes to be acceptable in spite of the fact that both clearly manifest symptoms of self-destruction. One indicator of the balance takes the behavioral form of manifesting flexibility in leadership-followership

roles; thus, one can shift roles appropriately and have no sense of loss
inflation of self-esteem either way, but handle both types of roles respon-
sibly with continuity of selfhood.

Love Axis

In the normal course of development, an essential aspect of identity
includes a period of affiliation with one's own sex. The overwhelming
power of sexuality that emerges in the pubertal period is both a thrill and
a threat, so at first there is a tendency to group with one's own sex. The
anxiety about approaching the opposite sex with feelings of intimacy is
partially dealt with by these affiliative groupings in which the opposite
sex is not encountered but can be discussed at great length.

The correlative reality here is the adolescent experience of loneliness.
Loneliness has a deep root in the early sense of abandonment and as a
profound awareness of one's own groundlessness. Harry Stack Sullivan,
the famous psychoanalyst, said he could bring anyone to recall a repressed
experience with the exception of loneliness, because it is too close to one's
own death.[21] Sex as a solution to death is heightened by loneliness. In adolescence, young people are, for the first time, conscious of and experience
the primal void that has silently haunted human development for the first
decade of life. As in their search for an ideology, adolescents long for the
buried face, and they will try to make others fill that void. Intimacy and
accurate love is a desperate need, since the adolescent feels cut off from
his family and does not yet belong anywhere else.

However, as with all other burgeoning competencies during this period,
there is a tendency toward exaggeration at first. The period is marked by
an emergence of secondary narcissism; thus, when sexual identity generally fits the sex role assigned by society, the male must be supermale,
according to the indexes of his culture, and the female must be stereo-
typically woman, according to the stereotypes of the culture in which she
is maturing. Stereotypes have powerful effects and shape the emerging
sexual aspect of identity in terms of their extreme proportions.

Sexual identity in regard to the indexes of one's culture and society
should get set here; otherwise, the lack of fit will also appear at this time.
The media here are a powerful influence, often portraying an ethic of
meaninglessness that subverts love and links sex to violence in a way that
comes close to dramatizing the primitive instincts of eros and thanatos.
This breaks down the constructive capacity of the psyche to establish a
stable ego identity and a genuine love relationship. Thus, the media move
adolescents in the direction of diffusion.

As Erikson says, the optimal male-female situation is talking, playing, and talking, intense emotional exchanges and talking; when the relationship becomes dependent on the physical aspect, it is a dying or dead relationship. The reason is that at its roots, sex is nothing more than nature's answer to death; in itself, it has no other meaning. It cannot give constructive meaning to a relationship; the relationship, spirit-to-spirit, must and will give it its meaning even if the spirit is the specter of death. If there is no relationship at the level of "spirit," there is no meaning. Of course, the goal is that sex become expressive of the love between persons in which each discovers and embraces not a body but a person in her or his particularity. When it is not that, it becomes a deepening sense of loneliness, often agonizing, and proximate death, even suicide.

Adolescents take quite a while to recognize the limits of their narcissistically invested stereotypes, partly because the media dramatize caricatures and seem incapable of portraying maturity in either men or women. Eventually persons may become free for their sexual identity independent of the stereotypes, but only in the middle years can one genuinely discover, accept, and incorporate the presence of the opposite sex in oneself, such that a balanced relationship in the psyche can occur without sexual confusion.

At the ego level, resolution to the sexual identity question means an inner recognition of one's sexual nature in congruence with the sex role assigned by one's social context. This is a recognition that normally takes place in the context of one's opposite, in which the opposite is neither feared nor absorbing but is reciprocally an essential part of one's own and the other's self-definition.

But now we must turn at least briefly to discuss the increasingly evident fact that women go through adolescence in ways different from men. Sexual identity here emerges differently for girls than for boys. Because of the menarche in women (the beginning of menstruation), there is a clear-cut biological time in the woman when she moves from being a young girl to being a young woman. This is not so clear for the young male, since erection, masturbation, and ejaculation may have been present for some time before adolescence. The median age for menstruation is thirteen, but the normal range is from ten to seventeen, and 80 percent of young women start the menarche between the ages of eleven and fifteen. The psychological impact of menstruation can range anywhere from traumatic to indifference to positively proud.

Because, as Nancy Chodorow puts it, the development of the young woman is triadic, the role of the father in this period of time is important since the male figure needs to see, recognize, and accept the young woman with all the strength menstruation implies, and foster pride in what she can do that he, of course, can never do.[22] On the maternal side, menstruation tends to thrust the young girl into the maternal matrix. She may be less likely to be herself if she is frightened by her new powers, and threats that she "better not get pregnant" can make her want to repress the whole thing. That may mean an unconscious identification with the mother that is never dealt with. It is important here that this aspect of sexual formation be recognized and affirmed, but not become a declaration of one's destiny.

This issue contributes to the poignant and problematic psychological and social situation where a woman must struggle to get her own voice, as against the many voices urged upon her by a male-dominant society. Although this is more of a psychosocial than a physiological matter, the latter makes a significant contribution. But the woman basically finds that being a woman in society is not what society is all about. The woman's voice is suppressed, and there are specific moments when most women realize that they "must go underground." That is, they must stifle their resistance and their own initiatives in order to conform to some very negative social expectations. We live, as Mary Pipher says, in a look-obsessed, media-saturated, "girl poisoning" culture.[23] Despite advances of feminism, escalating levels of sexism and violence, from undervaluing intelligence to sexual harassment in elementary school, cause girls to stifle their creative spirit and natural impulses, which ultimately destroys self-esteem. Surprisingly, young girls often blame themselves or their families, not recognizing that it is in the world around them. So for women, rigidity means severe repression of their own voice and, very likely, of their own sexuality.

This may eventuate in an anorexic or bulimic condition. Diffusion means that sexuality is a matter of repeatedly acting out in order to hold on to relationships or to please men in male-female interaction. This, however, quickly ends in boredom, as Robin Norwood has pointed out in her book, *Women Who Love Too Much*.[24] In one case cited there, a woman who has acted out sexually a great deal consults Norwood in order to settle down and find someone to marry. She succeeds, but at night she lies by her husband and feels bored. Strikingly, Norwood, who has no theological axe to grind, leads this woman to the awareness that she is not bored and desires more sexuality; she is bored because she has a deep fear of being known "in a biblical sense."

All of this points to the alternatives suggested by some women theorists that identity emerges from relationships; intimacy, "hard dialogue, [and] deep connections" make for the formation of the feminine identity.[25]

However, the patterns that Mary Field Belenky describes in *Women's Ways of Knowing* are remarkably like a recovery of one's spirit after having it suppressed and shoved underground.[26] The move from silence to "received knowledge," listening to the voices of others, to "subjective knowledge," the inner voice, to the "quest for self," to the voice of reason, to "separating and connecting the voices," to constructive knowledge, "integrating the voice" describes the redemption of the human spirit: the power to create and compose one's world in one's own terms.

Finally, a word should be said about the complex issue of homosexuality. From the standpoint developed here, one may be able to see that there is no such thing as a homosexual. There are only persons who have this resolution to the sexual aspect of their identity. In my work with persons who have come to talk about this part of their lives, it is evident that they have not, and seemingly cannot, come to terms with the pervasive sense of negation that haunts their personal history. One with whom I worked for some time and who eventually married and had a family said that homosexuality, as he experienced it, was a form of necrophilia, a love of death. This comment illuminated for me a situation I had dealt with earlier, where I helped a young man come to terms with his homosexual feelings. At first he felt relieved to talk about it, but later he began to have violent nightmares in which some dark force crashed into his bedroom and terrified him before he awoke. It has appeared to me in subsequent work that it is doing such a person no favor to say that homosexual expression of this aspect of his identity is just one choice among others. If he is not attacked in the night through his dreams, he will turn the powerful negative at the base of his psyche on others—heterosexuals, the church, society at large—or on himself in depression and dependency.

The principal point of my observation is not an attack on persons who practice homosexuality, but it is in opposition to what this practice does to persons. The issue forces us to realize that homosexuality is not ultimately fundamental to anyone's nature; it lives too close to death for that. The condition of homosexuality is, however, provocation to look deeper and discover that the real issue is not sexuality at all. It is intimacy. All unredeemed sexuality is already an admission of death into the human condition, but the denial of the love of death, which often appears in the substructure of the homosexual mind-set is especially pernicious. Rather than sexuality's becoming a solution to death, sexual love nurtures death. Moreover, it conceals its love of its own self-destruction under the aggressive claim to legitimacy and liberation, shutting down the deeper, genuine longing for intimacy in a biblical sense.

A careful examination of sexuality reveals that no one's identity is ultimately determined by sexuality; rather, it comes from their walk in the Spirit of God. Whatever permits Spirit-to-spirit intimacy in that walk is gracious, and it empowers and truly liberates the human spirit. Moreover, that intimacy works toward the transformation of the whole person, including the sexual aspect of identity. Thus, even that which walls off such intimacy may undergo transformation by the work of God's Spirit, who longs for intimacy with us more than we do with God.

One study in the *American Journal of Psychiatry* corroborates my work in counseling and will make this point more concretely.[27] Eleven white men, it reported, changed their sexual orientation from exclusive homosexuality to exclusive heterosexuality, through participation in a Pentecostal church fellowship. The importance of ideology, expectations, and behavioral experience was noted. Cognitive change appeared first, then behavioral change, and finally intrapsychic reorientation. Thus, even when homosexual behavior was transposed into a personal identity, a change was not thereby inhibited.

What is at issue here is the way in which sexuality is a proximate and deficient longing for a deeper intimacy that only the spiritual life can provide. Only in this context can one be thoroughly known in a biblical sense by another. The fear and power of this, I believe, can be recognized and appropriated only as a gift of the Spirit in koinonia.

Work Axis

The latency period may accentuate this developmental thrust toward outer compensation for inner loss. The reaction formation in favor of achieved worth, as against ascriptive worth, comes to focus here once again. According to a recent study, the major conflict between high school adolescents and parents is around grades, future plans, and achievement in society, not about sexuality and not about values in general. This misemphasis can be fatal.

The *New York Times,* on October 1, 1995, carried a story about Scott Coteau, a high school senior who excelled in athletics, particularly football and weight lifting. He was a quiet, soft-spoken fellow, very popular with his peers, and an excellent student. He had received letters of acceptance from top Ivy League colleges and offers of scholarships as well. He carried index cards with him that contained verses of encouragement and inspiration to moral behavior and high achievement. He lived with his father, who was divorced from his mother, and was living with another woman. His mother lived in the same town on the opposite side of main street. They rarely, if ever, saw each other.

One day Scott was missing at home and from school. They found him hanging from a tree in a nearby woods with a bullet in his head and the gun on the ground. In a kind of bitter irony, someone said, "Scott was always very thorough." Scott's story is a paradigm case of the point that achievement is not a reason to live. Most developmentalists will blame the mother or the father, but there is a deeper issue here that has to do with Scott's spirit.

Theologically, the church knows a power that runs even deeper than mother love, so the failure to communicate to him a ground for his spirit as spirit, an alternate reason to live, is a failure of the church, a failure to bring the spirit of Christ to bear on the spirit of developing persons, whatever their situation.

What happened to Scott did not just happen in his senior year. It was building up in him from early on, and it was in this period that he focused in on the idea that achievement might be a way to fill in the emptiness of his life. After all, no one in this society is going to tell him he should not "go for it!" The spirit of the person creates the person; the spirit of the achiever is trapped in its own creation as it was trapped in its creation of the ego at the beginning of life. To set the human spirit free, it takes the Creator Spirit who proposes to take up in itself the nothingness and the seductions of death and bring forth new life, as in the earlier case of Lucy.

If it is not sudden death, it may be a gradual suicide of the human spirit. Social psychologist Maccoby found that many top executives were "perpetually adolescent" in their drivenness to "make it big" in a highly competitive, winner-take-all society.[28] The tragedy in this is that the achiever empties himself of inner resources. His only serious motivations come from external challenges and the drive to win; the motivations of his heart are almost unknown to him, and he rarely asks the spiritual question, "Why do I do this?" He is instead deeply preoccupied by the game at hand. When a group of highly successful churchgoing laymen were asked such theological questions as, "What is the meaning of life?" "What happens after death?" "What is the meaning of evil?" and "What is the nature of God?" they had virtually nothing to say because they had not invested any time in thinking about these issues for themselves. They could readily identify with the anxiety expressed by the executive who said, "I just hope I die before I lose my reputation."

On the opposite side of the achiever lifestyle, a rigid entrapment in winning, is the potential for work paralysis, a form of diffusion on the work axis. Here the wealthy, tough-minded, achieving father has produced a brilliant but radically unmotivated child who would rather do anything, like sell Kewpie dolls on Times Square, than become the tense, buttoned-down achiever that his father is. Their violent arguments are a polarization between the rigidity and diffusion of the work axis of identity. The boy is claiming ascriptive worth outright, which enrages the father, who has denied himself precisely what the boy is claiming, so he, the father, could achieve. Each one points to the undesirable condition of the other as a standoff on the issue of work and human worth. Keep in mind that the goal here is not to take achievement out of life; it is to take the obsessiveness out of achievement, so that achievement is not made to do something it was never designed to do. It cannot produce human worth in, of, and by itself.

The polarity here is that for decades, the work ethic has prevailed in a highly schooled society, and lifestyles are formed around it. But in the contemporary adolescent scene, work is less endowed with all the meaning once given to it by the Protestant ethic. As Henry Giroux says, the motif now is not "workers unite" but "workers relax." Polarization is clear here in which the rigidity of the achiever stands over against the diffuse Kewpie doll salesman in Times Square; they each are opposite sides of a negative identity in relationship to the work axis.

The adolescent may best find the balance between rigidity and diffusion on the work axis by moving to a higher understanding of work, one that breaks out of the double-bind between ascriptive and earned worth. Theologically, this struggle is a broken image of a true calling. One is free to achieve in the context of a calling because in that context, achievement has nothing to do with self-justification. One is "doing the works prepared ahead of time for one to do," but one is not free to prove one has such a calling by achieving. This is the perversity of the Protestant ethic. God may show favor to the elect in their work, but to work to prove one has God's favor is theologically perverse.

For a calling to break the double-bind in the work-worth tension, it does not simply move things into the theological realm, begging the question. Rather, it negates the negative assumption about human nature that it is somehow condemned and needs to work its way into acceptance. A calling does this by granting full and complete acceptance from the beginning, so now work may be a response to God's grace rather than a way of proving one has it, or an attempt to get it—usually from the wrong sources (parents, family, one's professional guild, or society at large). None of these sources can bestow the grace needed to set one free to work on the absolute assurance of worth. Only a calling from God can do this.

This concept of calling is twofold, as suggested by the twofold meaning of the term: to name and to summon. When the caller is God, then to name is to bestow a nature on the person, and that person becomes the possession of the name giver. Thus, Jesus uses the name Peter to assign to Simon his nature. But it is also the case that Jesus summoned or called persons such as Peter to follow him. This suggests the twofold work of the Spirit, who first bestows the gift of grace, giving a person the name, the new nature of Christian, and then assigns a task, which is to follow Christ and so live out the implications of one's new nature.

It is when we ask what this latter claim means that we can begin to see the concrete implications of calling as a task. The *locus classicus* for discussing this is I Corinthians 7:20 ("Let each of you remain in the condition in which you were called") and following. Three points need to be made in this connection. The first is that Paul does not intend that one remain where one is in personal, social, and cultural circumstances, as if that were the way to be obedient to God's calling. One must be obedient to God, not to the circumstances of the call. What this does mean is that each one is called according to very particular and concrete qualities of one's own person, which may or may not include one's immediate circumstances. God has made you his own in your particularity and your specific situation, and he has given you particular gifts and opportunities. Obedience to God means that you do not *have* to change such things in order to be obedient to the calling. Nor can anyone else's call be yours. Given the transformation implied in one's new name, a call is personally particular and circumstantially concrete.

The second point is that obedience to God's call implies freedom; otherwise the call would be coercive rather than liberating. The one free choice is to surrender one's freedom to the only One who can give it back every day of one's life. All other choices are bound by circumstances, genetic and personal history, social and cultural determinants. Absolute human freedom is an illusion of disconnectedness, but to receive the call of God is to be set free for the freedom of God.

Third, the essential feature of Paul's claims in I Corinthians, Chapter 7, for this discussion centers on the two Greek words (*hos ma*), "as if not" verses 29–30. Here we read that marriage, mourning, rejoicing, possessing, and working in the world are to be carried out by Christians "as if they did not."

It has been argued that Paul counsels this way of being in the world because he thought the eschaton was immanent in his own lifetime. Since that proved false, this counsel is irrelevant. However, in the Spirit, as we have interpreted it so far, it is clear that Paul's counsel here is a liberating word that translates into behavior what is already implicit in the dialectical identity created by one's being made into a new creation. That is, one is given a new nature, I-not I-but Christ. The task that follows is to do everything "as if you did not" because in the Spirit everything is a gift, not ultimately contingent on anything you do. The dialectical balance between engagement and disengagement is in temporal terms the familiar tension between "already" and "not yet" in realized eschatology. To dismiss this counsel as an expression of faulty eschatology is to confuse the two dimensions of time, reducing the eternal to the chronological with no attention to kairos. Paul's counsel is to stand ready for the fullness of time, while remaining fully in chronological time. Thereby, nothing but your calling can take possession of your spirit.

Thus, in terms of worth and work as an axis in identity formation, to be called by a new name is particular and liberating, and it establishes a dialectical identity by which one can work and achieve, but only "as if one did not." This not only eliminates the prospect of working to gain a sense of worth, but frees one to do the work prepared ahead of time for one to do. But, consistent with the dialectical structure of one's identity, even these works are done as if one did not, but they are done within the concrete and personal limitations and potentialities of one's condition when one was called. One does not have to change oneself or one's situation to be obedient; one needs only to be obedient to the Caller and then allow the original situation to change if and when God chooses.

The Adult Guarantor

One of Erikson's major contributions to resolving the dilemmas of adolescent identity is his reference to the category of the "adult guarantor," exemplified in what Staupitz was to young man Luther.[29] Usually such persons are not the parent; this person is close enough to the adolescent's age to participate in his world, but at the same time guarantees that authentic adulthood is possible.

One example of an adult guarantor is Lynn Grey, the leader of a group called City Kids, an open house on the streets of New York. Kids wander off the streets into this house, and the first question Lynn asks them is, "Can you change your world?" Of course, the answer is "no" and complete oppression. But by the time he is done with them, they will *sing* that they can change their world. He has a video showing these youngsters who have come off the streets, singing that they can change their world, on a special show hosted by Phil Donahue and attended by major figures who have changed their world, such as Jimmy Carter.

A second figure is Bill Kyte, who was a seminary student in Princeton. He could walk down the street and start conversations that changed the lives of the young people who were hanging out on various corners of the streets and doorways. It was his gift and his task, and it seemed to come easily to him.

My impression is that adult guarantors are called; they manifest a transformation of authority into authenticity. This is a transformation of conscience where inner integrity of heart in the koinonia context is the source and ground of right and righteousness. It is not just that you change your world; you change it in accordance with the way Christ is changing it and in conformity to his nature.

An Integrative Vision

In the following chapter, the large-scale theological claims on the adolescent period will be spelled out, but the following illustration will help to concretize what has been discussed about this first way to go through adolescence and some of its theological potential. Although I have stressed patterns in ego development, each axis of an identity has theological potential. In the following illustration these axes were all drawn together around a somewhat unusual calling.

My sister Kay was a troubled young girl living in a middle-class family in which there seemed to be no trouble at all. The day would be beautiful and things would be in good order, and then Kay would show up at the table, and her big blue-green eyes would suddenly start to fill up with tears and she would run from the table and go play in her room with her paper dolls. This occurred long after paper dolls were an appropriate pastime. This was something that occurred off and on until the time she was about fourteen, with trouble in school and a genuine sense of discontent and oppression within a family context that seemed otherwise almost optimal. When she was fourteen, our father was taken ill with brain cancer.

Nine months later, the night before he died, Kay and I took a walk in a light rain above the crest of a hill around a lake in Austin, Texas. As we walked, we looked across the lake through the lights and saw on the other side, remarkably, a Christ-like figure carrying a burden. We were both transfixed, but I was a philosophy major and tried every way I could to change my angle of perception, but to no avail. I then asked her, "Do you see what I see?" She said nothing except a hushed, "Yes." After a while the rain increased, and we went back to the house, but just as we reached the door, she wheeled around, stretched out her long arms, smiled a beautiful broad smile, and cried out, "I just love everybody." After that her whole life changed; she sailed through her academic work, entered the theater with the idea of bringing God into it, did a one-woman show in Carnegie Hall, and was remarkably and permanently changed.

Her calling had been given to her in a vision, but she was summoned to bring Christ into the theater. She was immensely creative and talented, writing her own material. She went to Hollywood, did television, and wrote her masterpiece, an integration of the lives of several religious persons. It was very hard, but always there was the vision; obedience to the heavenly vision was how she listened to the Caller. But she was continually ripped off. Her material was stolen, and she died at the age of thirty-nine. Even in dying, her great love of God and the power of the vision gave death to death; in love she was married to the Lord for life and for life after death.

Notes

1. Talcott Parsons, cited by William Baxton, *Talcott Parsons and the Capitalist Nation State* (Toronto: University of Toronto Press, 1985).

2. *Rolling Stone* magazine.

3. Kenda Creasy Dean, "Youth Ministry as the Transformation of Passion: A Practical Theological Analysis of Youth and Their Ministry to American Mainline Protestantism (Ph.D. dissertation, Princeton Theological Seminary, 1997).

4. Robert Kegan, *The Evolving Self* (Cambridge, Mass.: Harvard University Press, 1982).

5. Nancy Chodorow discusses this thoroughly in the early pages of *Feminism and Psychoanalytic Theory* (Berkeley: University of California Press, 1989).

6. Robert Kegan, *In Over Our Heads* (Cambridge, Mass.: Harvard University Press, 1994).

7. *New York Times*, "Science Times" subsection, 1997.

8. Robert Ardrey, *The Territorial Imperative* (New York: Atheneum, 1966).

9. T. E. Hall, *The Hidden Dimension* (New York: Doubleday, 1966).

10. E. I. Megargee and J. E. Hokanson, *The Dynamics of Aggression* (New York: HarperCollins, 1970).

11. W. D. Davies, *The Gospel and the Land* (Sheffield, England: JSOT Press, 1994).

12. Augustine, *Confessions* (New York: Modern Library, 1949).

13. Reported by Daniel Goleman, "Perceptions of Time as Key Psychological Factor." In *New York Times*, subsection "Science Times," Dec. 30, 1986.

14. Robert Jay Lifton, *The Life of the Self* (New York: Simon & Schuster, 1976), and *The Protean Self* (New York: Basic Books, 1993).

15. Discussion of self-process and protean man is included in *The Acquisition and Development of Values: Perspectives on Research* (Bethesda, Md.: National Institute of Child Health and Human Development, 1968).

16. Lifton, *Life of the Self*.

17. James W. Fowler, *Stages of Faith* (San Francisco: Harper San Francisco, 1981).

18. James Younnis, *Parents and Peers in Social Development* (Chicago: University of Chicago Press, 1980).

19. Roger Brown, *Social Psychology* (New York: Free Press, 1965).

20. This picture is painted vividly by Henry A. Giroux in several of his writings, for example, *Border Crossings* (New York: Routledge, 1994), and, with Peter McLarin, *Between Borders* (New York: Routledge, 1994).

21. See also James E. Loder, *The Transforming Moment*, 2d ed. (Colorado Springs: Helmers & Howard, 1989), pp. 83ff.

22. Chodorow, *Feminism and Psychoanalytic Theory*.

23. Mary Pipher, *Reviving Ophelia* (New York: Putnam, 1994).

24. Robin Norwood, *Women Who Love Too Much* (Los Angeles: J. P. Tarcher, 1985).

25. Carol Lakey Hess, *Caretakers of Our Common House* (Nashville, Tenn.: Abingdon Press, 1997).

26. Mary Field Belenky, *Women's Ways of Knowing* (New York: Basic Books, 1986).

27. E. Mansell Pattison and Myina Loy Pattison, "Ex-Gays: Religiously Mediated Changes in Homosexuals," *American Journal of Psychiatry* 137, no. 12 (December 1980): 1553–1562.

28. Michael Maccoby, *The Gamesman* (New York: Simon & Schuster, 1976).

29. Erik H. Erikson, *Young Man Luther*.

10

ADOLESCENCE IN THEOLOGICAL PERSPECTIVE

COMING INTO THE PRESENCE OF GOD

THERE ARE TWO ways to move through adolescence. The way described in the previous chapter is the sociocultural solution, which essentially and effectively extends the ego's defenses and its struggle for survival and satisfaction. It is difficult to overestimate the power of the sociocultural milieu in which adolescence appears. Accordingly, conversion during this period will often tend to be resocialized, in effect blessing and sanctifying the process of socialization. In fact, a genuine conversion cannot be reduced to the by-product of the social system. Rather, it ought to be seen as an entrée into the deeper roots and spiritual potential of the personality. When the personality is resocialized following conversion, the conviction is repressed, and the extraordinary spiritual potential of the adolescent is buried, just as the ego and its earlier socialization buried the face and its inherently religious significance. But suppose it does not get buried and begins to thrive, releasing the spiritual potential of the person. What then?

This leads us into the second way to move through adolescence: that which Erikson describes as *homo religiosus*.[1] Usually this phrase refers to a kind of generic religiosity, or sense of the sacred, that characterizes all human nature. The way Erikson uses it refers to figures in whom this generic religiosity has become definitive for the totality of their lives. Since there is no such thing as *homo religiosus* in a vacuum, *homo religiosus* is inevitably going to appear in some historical and cultural context. Thus, each culture and religion has its own version of *homo religiosus*. However, as with Torrance's view of natural science, so it is with the sciences of human nature. From the standpoint of the Creator Spirit in Christian theology, *homo religiosus* is not merely a Christianized version of religion in general. It is a transformation that transfigures the life span, creating a "religiousless Christianity," as Dietrich Bonhoeffer once put it.[2] The Divine Spirit dramatically and powerfully penetrates and permeates the whole person so that he is consumed by the Divine Presence. Regardless of what point in one's life span such a realization may occur, the totality of the life span from birth to death is brought under the power and purposes of God. This realization occurs in the fullness of time so that the present embraces both the past, which is reenvisioned in the light of the Divine Presence, and the future, which has come into the present as a prolepsis of what is yet to be.

From this vantage point, we can begin to reconsider adolescence—indeed, the whole scheme of human development—from a theological vantage point. We can see that the typical periodic upheavals in the life span are upheavals of the ego's structure of reality—upheavals of the negation that lies at the base of the ego and a spiritual cry to behold the face, the Face of God. From birth to adolescence (early or later in college years) to middlescence, on toward senescence, development is on the side of total transformation, recentering the personality beyond the ego in accordance with the exocentric drive (that is, out of egocentrism) of the human spirit, yet without doing away with ego functions. In a universe that is about fifteen billion light-years old (if the big bang theory is correct), a lifetime is scarcely long enough to be called a predeath experience. It is as if these periodic upheavals of the ego's defenses are at work in us, within this brief period of a lifetime, lest we miss the point. Each upheaval directs us away from partial, inadequate, adaptational solutions toward knowing and being known by the Author, the One who made it all. Until we get the point, time is short; when transformation is total, then time is also transformed, and the chronological arrows of time that govern contemporary cosmology and the stages of human development are enveloped in eternity. Temporal sequence is reconfigured as a "single day"; stages and phases are instances in an all-embracing Now.

The theological discussion of human development necessarily involves two distinct views of time. The more common conception of these two views is to think of eternity as entering chronological time from somewhere beyond. However, in a conversion that puts down roots and becomes the foundation for the Christian way of life, there is a figure-ground shift in the common view, and the converted person envisions time from the standpoint of eternity. This is not a disembodied, otherworldly journey, but it is rather that all time is gathered into a single comprehensive vision of one's place in creation. It is the fullness of time in a comprehensive present that takes up and transfigures all that went before and what is yet to come.

When Jesus speaks of the revelation of the coming kingdom of God, he speaks of the moment at night when lightning suddenly opens the way through a dark landscape. The time-binding power of the illuminating moment is not the invention of the existentialists or a religious contrivance to confound linear views of time. It is a universally recognizable phenomenon in which the fullness of time, kairos, is irreducible because its disclosive power exceeds from the outset the temporal assumptions behind any reductionistic analysis, precisely because reductionistic analysis is linear, analytical, and chronological. Consequently any such analysis of the Now begs the time question from the outset.

On the other hand, the Now does not eliminate chronology. It uses it, transfigures it, and confirms its essential concreteness and implicit spatiality (one thing after another), but chronology is not the figure in the picture anymore. It is the background, the secondary fact, in relation to which the vision of the whole takes on specific contours, structure, and pattern. This means that any chronological phenomenon, including human development, becomes for such an illumination the background against which the foreground notion of God stands out. As in the transfiguration of Jesus, time and history do not disappear, but they are dramatically and powerfully drawn into an illuminating light that discloses not only the present of the fullness of time but also the power of the moment to embrace the full amplitude of time. In the transfiguration, Moses and Elijah, the law and the prophets, are taken up in the illumination of Jesus, which in that moment reveals the glory from which he has come and the glorification to which he is going. The passage of time and history is not eliminated; it is transfigured as eternity envelops all of time, as created reality is taken up in the uncreated reality of the One through whom all things are created.

Such an observation is not without its special bearing on adolescence, because it is precisely this vast view of things that the adolescent, prior to resocialization, is supremely prepared to recognize and attempt to appropriate. The only greater vision or perspective beyond the grandeur of the cosmic order is the vision of the One who made it all, and the unique adolescent, who will not move through this period until she has had that vision, has seen the Face of God—that one has the makings of *homo religiosus* transformed and transfigured by the Spiritual Presence of God.

By taking this route through adolescence, one withdraws from standard, mainline socialized solutions to identity, reality, or ideology, and insists on finding his own roots for ego formation. Consequently, there is a moratorium taken on resolving the identity question. One goes into some form of seclusion from society at large—the monastery, the commune, the forest, the graduate school—and prolongs answering the question "Who am I?" until he can get an answer to "Why I am."

In order to bring this account of the transformation of a lifetime down to cases, I will examine two figures: Kierkegaard, briefly, and the case of "young Man Luther," a reexamination of Erikson's classic psychohistorical study in the light of my approach in this book. In the case of Kierkegaard, the focus is on the inner workings of such a transformation; in the case of Luther, transformation is in the psychohistorical perspective.

The Case of Kierkegaard

Kierkegaard's conversion gathers up his past, transforms it, and sets up the perspective in his person that will issue in his prodigious authorship. Because this transformation is so suffused by the Divine Spirit and gathers up the past in a fullness of the present that sets the course for the future, it represents a transfigured vision of the transformation of a lifetime.

Kierkegaard's conversion is recorded only in his journal and does not appear anywhere else in his writings.[3] Yet it is in some respects the experiential premise of them all. The 1838 entry for "May 19, 10:30 A.M. (The Saturday before the 5th Sunday after Easter)" reads as follows:

> There is *an indescribable joy* which glows through us as unaccountably as the Apostle's outburst is unexpected: "Rejoice, and again I say, Rejoice."—not a joy over this or that, but full of jubilation, "with hearts and souls and voices": I rejoice over my joy, of, in, by, at, on, through, with my joy—a heavenly refrain, which cuts short as it were our ordinary song; a joy which cools and refreshes like a breeze, a gust of the trade wind which blows from the Grove of Mamre to the eternal mansions.

Although this entry is full of rich imagery, its evidential message is that imagery cannot contain the event. It is, as Walter Lowrie suggests, like Saint Paul's experience when he was "caught up into Paradise and heard things that . . . no mortal is permitted to repeat" (II Cor. 12:4).[4] The experience seems to rupture the boundaries of every image while at the same time new images rush in to try to contain it. This is important to notice since here is an example of the otherwise elusive notion of transparency, which plays such an important, yet ineffable, part in Kierkegaard's thought. The self is truly itself only when it is "transparently grounded in the Power that posits it."[5] The notion refers to an unmediated relation to the Divine Presence for which even imagination—understood as always able to surpass reason—has no adequate visions.[6] Nevertheless, images rush like a torrent into the light of transparency, as if to shield his eyes when he is surprised by a sudden burst of divine sunlight.

Thus, joy expresses the "glow" of light (as in "awakening," Kierkegaard's later description of this event). The Apostle Paul provides him with a personal analogy to a place in the light, as the joy and the light seem to pulsate back and forth through his soul, "over, of, in, by, at, on, through, with," each new preposition catching some new facet of the ineffable source; and then, as if each preposition were more but still not enough, it is immediately superseded by a new surge of illumination. Then glowing shifts to singing, and song gives way to a breeze that cools and refreshes. From the glow that bursts with joy to the breeze that cools, a full range of ecstatic experience is covered by the One who comes to Kierkegaard the way he came to Abraham in Genesis 18:1: "The Lord appeared to Abraham by the oaks of Mamre, as he sat at the entrance of his tent in the heat of the day." The climactic image on which Kierkegaard's imagination finally settles is one in which Abraham, sitting in his tent, beholds outside an appearance of the Lord, to which he runs with excitement and joy.

Notice the biblical context. At this time Sarah's conception of Isaac is promised, and Abraham runs to meet the Lord; the covenant of the flesh through Ishmael has been replaced by the covenant of God's own promise through Isaac. Through the flesh God will overcome the power of the flesh, for ninety-year-old Sarah will bear a son. However, there is no mention of Kierkegaard's tradewind in the Genesis text; wind is apparently Kierkegaard's metaphor for the presence of the Lord. For him, the wind of the Spirit brings cooling; it reconstellates the world and one's place in it, so that now, contrary to all evidence of the flesh, even decrepit flesh becomes a bearer of the eternal promise of God. Why this image?

If we read back from the imagery, we can get some idea of what in Kierkegaard's personal history preceded this event and what aspects of the event might be attributable to the past. The image on which Kierkegaard settles is one in which the presence of God enters to break a false covenant with the flesh. The child, Ishmael, born out of wedlock, could not be the bearer of God's promise. God would miraculously bring forth from the flesh a covenant child through the union of Abraham and Sarah. Legitimacy would be established by a miraculous act of God, and the false covenant would be dealt with graciously, but Abraham's human invention could not be the bearer of God's eternal decree.

The parallel here to Kierkegaard's own situation is surely indicative. Until shortly before this awakening, he had been a licentious rebel, struggling through a prolonged identity crisis. Young Søren felt he was the heir to a curse on his family, and he rebelled radically, leaving home and living a dissolute life as a university student. Unwittingly at the time, he was acting out a repetition of the source of the curse from which he was fleeing. The curse was presumably a secret, explicitly hidden from Søren, but the secret had secreted into the family life in many ways. His father's melancholy and grief at the death of his wife was extreme and oppressive, and the death of several children by his second wife (Kierkegaard's mother) added to the weight of the curse. All in all, the family context had a severe and prolonged effect on Søren.

The curse apparently stemmed from the father's cursing God when he was a desperately lonely lad tending sheep on the Jutland Heath, and from his sensuality that eventually led him, after his first wife died, to sexual relations with the housemaid, who was also a relative of the family. He was then forced to marry this very simple but pleasant and generally happy woman because she was four months pregnant. It was from this second marriage that Søren was eventually born as the seventh child. Søren's father finally confessed the secret of his curse, supposedly manifested in his worldly success (since the world is the province of the devil), along with his guilt, to Søren on the occasion of the young man's twenty-fifth birthday, on May 5, 1838.

The effect of the eighty-two-year-old father's confession on Kierkegaard was overpowering relief and reconciliation. It went both ways, son forgiving father and father forgiving son. Kierkegaard wrote a prayer after this reconciliation in which he thanked God for an earthly father who would bring him to an understanding of his heavenly Father, and he prayed that his earthly father would "find more joy in being for a second time my father than he did the first time."[7] By reconciliation, the aging father had in a sense begotten his son again.

It was after this reconciliation, and shortly before his father died—all in the same year, 1838—that Kierkegaard had his remarkable conversion experience. The imagination tells Kierkegaard's own story in a biblical image that replaces illegitimacy (Kierkegaard as Ishmael) with a miracle of new birth (Kierkegaard as Isaac), and it establishes him as the bearer of the promise of God and an heir to his father's faith that God would lift the curse and bring forth blessing from his children. Thus, divinely established legitimacy replaced illegitimacy, and promise replaced curse.

It is crucial to notice that the imagery follows the joy, and the joy itself is inexpressible. There can be little doubt that Kierkegaard felt himself to be visited by the transparent presence of God's Spirit. That Spirit had reconstructed his own person as profoundly as if he had been a ninety-year-old woman who conceived a son, and it put him into the world in a new relationship to it, to his family, and to his calling. Most important, it made him heir of a divine promise rather than bearer of a demonic curse.

It might be said from a strictly cause-and-effect analysis that in his unconscious, Kierkegaard has conjured up biblical legitimation for the transformation of his troubled identity from derelict university student to beloved son. His reconciliation with his estranged father is the real source of the joy, and what we have here is theological and biblical legitimation that overcomes guilt, excuses the past, and puts Kierkegaard and his father in the mainstream of what God is doing in the world. This interpretation not only fails to account for several aspects of the event, but starts from a premise that violates the data at the outset.

A more adequate account sees two fields of force in creative tension.[8] The presence and power of the Divine Spirit sweeping down on Kierkegaard, filling him with the joy of the Lord in an ecstatic transparency is the first. The second is the dynamic field generated by the human spirit by which a flood of images and descriptive terms attempts to gain a grasp on the ineffable visitation of the Spirit. The resolution is accomplished when the biblical image appears bisociating the divine and the human using biblical language, which is essentially Christomorphic, and introducing the wind as the transparent image of the Divine Spirit, in which the fields combine to conform Kierkegaard to Christ. The reductive account tends to falsify the experience, not accounting for the wind and discounting the powerful consequences this experience had over the past and the future shaping of Kierkegaard's life.

This is not to spiritualize a naturalistic event; it is to recognize the transformation of the natural in the service of a more adequate explanation of the whole. Naturalistic aspects of the experience are the identity struggle of the young man with his authoritarian father, the multiple deaths and oppressive sense of doom the family curse laid on the young man, and the ambivalence toward his mother whose innocence and simplicity prefigures Regina, Kierkegaard's life-long unfulfilled love relationship. All of these dynamics are expressions of the human spirit in its exocentric drive to find the Other in whom it can be grounded and in relation to whom it might find freedom of expression and the power to love. All the dynamic patterns in Kierkegaard's family constellation represent failed attempts of his passionate spirit to overcome his version of the dark side of human development.

On the human side, this spiritual experience represents the upheaval of defensive dynamics and a reconciliation with his father, which centered in deep, wrenching confession and tearful forgiveness. What this account makes plain is that all that led up to it was not primarily a work of the human spirit; it was an act of God's Spirit that reaches its culmination only in this transforming moment when the human spirit and all its previous struggles are so permeated by the Divine Spirit that the two become one in "the transparency" that eliminates despair and grounds the self in faith. It should be emphasized that the Divine Spirit does not extricate the human spirit from its concrete matrix in human development, but reconstellates the specific forces and figures in that matrix with the biblical imagery that implicitly unites the human and the divine in a differentiated unity. The great achievement of this event is not just the human reconciliation or the emergence of the appropriate biblical imagery, but the underlying relationality between the human spirit and the Divine Spirit; this is the form of Christ emblazoned on the existence of the young man for the rest of his life. When this occurs, then thereafter there can be no end of the passion, the intensity, the inner conflict, the implicit joy, and the drive to love that characterize anyone in whom all natural religiousness is transfigured by the spiritual presence of Christ.

Before Kierkegaard died in Frederik's Hospital, November 18, 1855, he left a profound impression on those who visited him. Walter Lowrie records the following. A relative, Henrietta Lund, in a book entitled *Memories of Home,* wrote, "Never in such a way have I seen the spirit break through the earthly hush and impart to it a glory as of the transfigured body on the resurrection morning."[9] Trols Lund, Henrietta's half-brother, only five at the time and later a distinguished historian, wrote of his visit with Uncle Søren: "He took my hand in both of his—how small they were and thin and palely transparent—and said only, 'Thanks for coming Trols; and now farewell,' but these simple words were accompanied by a look, the match of which I have never seen. It shone out from a sublime and blessed splendor which seemed to me to make the whole room light. Everything was concentrated in those eyes as the source of light: heartfelt love, blissful dissolution of sadness, penetrating clearness of mind and a jesting smile."[10]

The Case of Luther

The paradigm case for *homo religiosus* in Erikson's writings is his treatment of *Young Man Luther.*[11] Although Erikson's treatment of Luther from a psychoanalytic point of view has been widely discussed, it has been as thoroughly rejected as it has been thoroughly appreciated.[12] Nevertheless, this study of Luther is an example of the human spirit (tacitly present in the psychoanalytic interpretation) at work to transform personal, interpersonal, and sociocultural clashes and influences into a meaningful worldview against severe odds. Luther's passion was great and intense, especially in a man of genius, but his human spirit alone could not account for his power to change the course of history as he did. Whatever errors of fact and lack of theological understanding may mark Erikson's treatment, this work is an excellent example of the dynamic of the human spirit's animating, empowering, and illuminating a young man in a prolonged identity struggle, first within himself, but more profoundly with God.

Erikson's treatment provides a unique opportunity to bring theological motivation under the power of the Divine Spirit to bear on human motivation as seen by one who records with such insight the struggle of a young man's soul. By taking account of Luther's doctrine of *Spiritus Creator,* we can do some of the interdisciplinary work missing in Erikson's treatment and negate some of the negations of Luther's theological self-understanding which he, Erikson, tends to employ.

In Erikson's interpretation, Luther took the extremities of adolescence to their limits and through a prolonged identity struggle radically exposed both the potentials and the latent disasters of this period of development. In Erikson's terms, this is an account of a young man's becoming a great man.

Luther was born in 1483. November 11 of the year 2000 will be Luther's 517th birthday—so old and yet so very contemporary. At the age of seventeen, in 1501, he entered the university at Erfort, and he finished his M.A. at the age of twenty-one. On the road to law school, he was nearly struck by lightning, and it was a convicting experience that caused him to enter the monastery in 1505. He became a priest and celebrated his first mass with considerable trauma. He fell into self-doubts, the "fit in the choir," in 1507 at the age of twenty-three. At the age of twenty-eight, he received his doctorate of theology and delivered lectures on the Psalms at the University of Wittenberg, where he experienced "the revelation in the tower" in 1512. In 1517, he nailed his ninety-five theses on the church door at Wittenberg. He was thirty-two years old.

The question now for Erikson is, What makes this intense young man a great man? Before entering the monastery in 1505, Luther was under the driving and authoritarian influence of Hans Luder, his father, a copper miner. Luther's ambitious father had sacrificed to give young Martin strict schooling because he wanted him to study law, a profession that was a springboard into administration and politics in a society that was beginning to awaken to the Renaissance world that would eventually celebrate human achievement. As Roger Johnson has pointed out, if you read the text carefully, you will see that Erikson overstates the case, and at one point he confuses Luther's father with his uncle, Little Hans, making the father brutal beyond the evidence.[13] Little Hans was supposed to have killed a shepherd and was, at least implicitly, a violent man. It seems in Erikson's interest to make Luther's father a potentially violent authoritarian figure.

According to Erikson, Father Hans moved into the kitchen and took young Martin from his mother's friendly, loquacious companionship and began his discipline early. The rich verbal exchanges that Martin had with his mother are very important for his later emphasis on "the Word." Remember, word is the key to bridging the emptiness of abandonment in early childhood. Young Martin complied with his father until he finished his master's degree and started back at Erfurt to begin his studies in law. Then the lightning bolt that struck and nearly killed him occurred. He cried out to his father's patron saint, "St. Anne," and, without returning home, he went to the Augustinian monastery.

It is not hard to see that the dynamics of authoritarianism and achievement obsession in Martin here are coming apart as the life and death crisis of the lightning bolt opens up the buried struggle in the young man. This is not introducing a new crisis; it is the exposure of an unseen crisis tacitly known from birth, but it is now at the surface, waiting to be consciously grasped.

That Martin cries out to his father's patron saint is significant in that the lightning bolt now divides him from his father and his father's obsession with his son's ascendancy in the emerging modern world. St. Anne is over his father, so she must protect Martin against the wrath of his father, which he anticipates as he breaks with twenty-one years of conformity. She is to restore love from the father, which Martin actually wants, even though he fears his father. In achievement-oriented terms, he will no longer earn the love he needs; he will claim it outright from God. This means an undoing of the reaction formation of achievement orientation as the defense system that undergirds the ego itself. As a result, young Martin is thrown headlong into the sense of abandonment that underlies the ego, precisely the disaster that the reaction formation and the incorporation of negation that early ego development was designed to prevent.

This is possible now at this age, because in the upheaval of adolescence, the whole structure of the ego is up for reexamination. Consequently, that which lies just under the surface of the ego—the sense of nothingness and abandonment, the cosmic loneliness for all that the primal experience of the Face connoted—now comes to the surface. The negative side of control, bad conscience and fear of social exclusion and inferiority, must be addressed if the boundaries of the ego are opened up to the presence of the Face of God. Reworking ego development means reworking its negative side and its history.

Luther enters his studies for the priesthood with this struggle in his soul or psyche. Luther does not confront his father until the father is invited to attend Martin's first celebration of the mass, the equivalent of a graduation ceremony for a young priest. Martin is traumatized. As Erikson sees it, having his punitive father behind him in the congregation and confronting the Holy Father in front of him (this, by the way, is not a modern-day grape juice and crackers affair for a monk at this time in history), the combination of the awesome Holy Father represented in sacrament and the abandoning and abandoned father in the congregation was too much when, after all, he was to mediate between them! He had a paralyzing anxiety attack during his celebration of the first mass, but he finally did get through it.

The anxiety attack no doubt contributed to his father's saying after the mass that he strongly suspected that the lightning bolt was a demon, not a stroke of grace at all. Only after much cursing and anger did Father Hans accept his son's religious vocation. Martin had, after all, picked the Augustinians, an intellectual and ecclesiastical elite order in the monastic world.

This set the scene for the "fit in the choir" in the year 1507. It comes to focus on Luther's intense repetition of *"Non sum! Non sum! Ich bin nicht,"* in response to the text of Mark 9:17–24: "Master, I have brought thee my son which hath a dumb spirit." Jesus's response is, "All things are possible if you believe. Do you believe?" "Lord, I believe. Help then my unbelief!" The text contains the story of an ambivalent father and a son possessed of a demon—too much like Luther's own situation. This, for Erikson, is the climax of Martin's identity crisis, because now the "I" must be reclaimed by Jesus Christ independent of the earthly father.

How can such a reclamation take place? Erikson describes this in terms of psychodynamics. Luther will get rid of the oppressive burden of the father's influence on his calling by splitting his ambivalence toward the father. That is, he desperately wants his father's approval for what he, Martin, knows he has to be and do; he genuinely loves the father and wants that love returned. Yet he is violently oppressed by the father's suspicion that he is demon possessed and his demands that Martin enter into the society of justification by works. Consequently, Luther's repeatedly reiterated plea was that he be allowed to look at God face to Face. This is a demand that he get to the source and ground of his humanity, deeper than his family of origin. In his famous repetition of "I have been baptized" in his opposition to the devil is a claim again to a deeper than family, deeper than society and culture, origin for his identity. This is a sign that he belongs to a different family, a different bloodline.

The final splitting of the ambivalence toward the father is not accomplished until 1512, when Luther has his famous experience of a revelation in the tower. These are his words as he reviewed in his mind Romans 1: 17, "For therein is the righteousness of God revealed from faith to faith: as it is written, the just shall live by faith."

> These words "just" and "justice of God" were a thunderbolt in my conscience. They soon struck terror in me who heard them. He is just, therefore He punishes. But once when in this tower I was meditating on those words, "the just lives by faith," "justice of God," I soon had the thought whether we ought to live justified by faith, and God's justice ought to be the salvation of every believer, and soon my soul was revived. Therefore it is God's justice which justifies us and saves us. And these words became a sweeter message for me. This knowledge the Holy Spirit gave me on the privy in the tower.[14]

Note that psychoanalysts do not overlook the shift in control taking place on the privy. But they do not know what to do with the more important part, which is the Holy Spirit.

It is in the tower experience that Luther affirms that Jesus Christ is the Face of God, and this shifts his understanding from the just God who condemns to the just God who justifies. This is the basic figure-ground shift that allows Luther to split the ambivalence he has toward his father. This splitting makes the heavenly father gracious, and the evil father is projected in two directions. One is spiritual—to the devil, the father of lies, who becomes the evil presence (the dumb spirit now cast out), and the pope, the evil earthly father who, like the natural father, demands "works" as indulgences and so cuts off the Face of God in Jesus Christ. This sets the stage for 1517, the ninety-five theses on the Wittenberg door, and the launching of the German Reformation. Thereafter, Luther was frequently attacked, and subsequently at Worms he uttered his famous declaration, "Here I stand. I can do no other. God help me. Amen." This becomes the archetypal opposite for Luther of "*Ich bin nicht*," I am not, and marks the move from his being a young man to his becoming a great man.

Erikson sees all this taking place within the limits of the human spirit; thus, he develops his psychological understanding further. His explanations are helpful and illuminating on the human side but not sufficient, because he does not deal effectively with Luther's theological self-understanding. Nevertheless, let us examine Erikson's explanation. Christ becomes the core of Luther's identity, says Erikson. Having split the ambivalence with the father, he, Luther, is now able to be identified with the good son, the righteous son of the heavenly father. He, in effect, "etches his own countenance into Christ's face." In the Bible, Luther recovered the loquacious mother whom he could acknowledge, who was wedded to the Heavenly Father by inspiration of the Spirit. Now he, Luther, can be his mother's son without fear of intrusion. In the Bible he found a garrulous generosity of grace and nurturing from which he could derive strength and himself speak. This is a transformation of the maternal image. The oral, verbal connection, together with Luther's claim that he had to be "reborn out of the matrix of Scripture," "*ex matrice Scripturae nati,*" leads Erikson to make the etymological connection of matrix with *mater,* and recognize Luther's bond with Scripture as a reunion with his mother.

But even if this works, it is only the positive side. The negative side is that from the time Martin entered the monastery, he was plagued with anxiety, guilt, and the fear of death and damnation. For this reason, his confessions to Staupitz, who served as his adult guarantor, were his struggles with God, his *anfechtungen.* Staupitz once said he wished Luther could just confess lust or pride or something that could be forgiven, rather than the complex struggles he was having with justification and salvation.

This points to the adolescent totalism carried into the extremity of *homo religiosus.* In effect, in Luther's struggle there could be no satisfactory solution to the *anfechtungen* that did not deal with the whole of the life span, from birth to death, from beginning to end. In Erikson's terms, Luther had to know not only *who* he was, but *why* he was, and he had to have the why before he could accept the who. This is, in language we have used here, a profound move into the nothingness that lies coiled at the base of the ego.

This is why Erikson's scheme cannot hold Luther. Luther had to have a solution to the final crisis of development, integrity versus despair, which occurs decisively when one confronts one's own death. He had to have an answer to the meaning of his entire existence if he were to affirm his identity. Again, in Erikson's terms, Luther had to be able to affirm "life itself in the face of death itself." This is the "all or nothing" and "the meaning of meaning it." Therefore, Luther, like Kierkegaard, has a prolonged identity crisis, and he declares a moratorium on resolution until he can solve both identity and integrity at the same time.

In any psychological interpretation, it is important to listen carefully to how the person himself says how things in his life have occurred. It is a distortion of science not to permit the phenomenon to say how it will be studied and known. Here is where Erikson's approach, intriguing as his analytical interpretation may be, fails to take sufficient account of Luther's own way of saying how these events came about. Erikson's view, at best, traces the ingenious defensive maneuvers of the human spirit, but that is not enough. So we turn now to the theological side of Luther in Luther's own terms.

For Luther's own account of his personal history, we will rely primarily on *Spiritus Creator* by Regin Prenter, an account of Luther's doctrine of the Spirit.[15] The *Spiritus Creator* is Luther's way of speaking about the Holy Spirit's transformation of his existence. From our developmental position, this is a total transposition of transformation outside the sequence of human development. This is the opposite of the reductive pathological position that Erikson takes, and it claims that the transformational dynamic, the engine of human development, is at best a reflection of the work of the Holy Spirit. This is not to bring the Holy Spirit in *deus ex machina,* but it is to disclose the underlying reality of which development is an expression. To grasp this requires a figure-ground shift of immense magnitude encompassing the whole of one's lifetime.

How does the Spirit declare its priority? According to Luther, the *Spiritus Creator* begins in inner conflict. The core of that conflict is guilt, but not psychological guilt. The Spirit does not convict us at the point of the superego, but it is existential guilt. At the very origin of our existence we are convicted by the Spirit. It is the work of the Spirit first to heighten the dichotomy between life and death, to slay ego-centeredness by exposing that it is fundamentally based on nothing and nothingness. It is gracious to be convicted of sin and to understand where one really is in relationship to God. This is the mortification of conviction and the way the Spirit begins a work in our lives. Developmentally, conviction takes place with respect to the lost face, not anything else or any other standard. The anguish that follows is the struggle to work back through one's developmental history to deal with law and love, with the hidden and the revealed, with the alien and the proper, with the cross and the glory; this is all to work out the significance of the inner conflict of guilt inflicted by the Spirit in an act of conviction. In Luther these are the temptations, the *anfechtungen,* the struggles with God.

The Spirit mortifies in order to redeem by the Word. This is illumination. The Scripture, like a loquacious mother, becomes the bearer of Christ to the convicted person. But here Luther deviates sharply from Erikson's description. Christ, for Luther, is always "alien righteousness," that is, ego alien righteousness. There is no identification of Luther with Christ. Luther sees the Face of God in Jesus Christ, but he does not etch his own face into Jesus Christ. It is clearly a dialectical identity for Luther in which the acting ego is passive before the righteousness of Christ. It is an I-not I-but Christ position. Thus, the illumination in the Word of God is that the Word is the bearer of the presence of Christ—the living Word of God; one is here addressed by him through whom all things are made. This is as it should be, since words convey interiority and come finally to silence in perfect communion. In the presence of God, conveyed through the Word of God, one comes finally to hold one's tongue, *favete linguis* (Kierkegaard). Yet identity is not lost, only dialectically sustained, as Christ's presence make us present to him.

This yields the result—not condemnation and not self-justification, but the just God justifies. He becomes sin for us so we may become the righteousness of God. Thus, Christ as the Face of God becomes the cosmic ordering, self-confirming presence of the Loving Other. There follows from this a release of the tension built up in the original conflict and in the *anfechtungen,* and Luther is then, as someone said, "fired on the world with a velocity not his own."

The outcome is new action: the proliferation of Luther's writings and the beginning of the German Reformation. All of this Luther saw as the work of *Spiritus Creator,* not, as Erikson claimed, the work of a pathological mind adjusting to the pathology of its times, governed by the normativity of developmental stages. Luther said, "The Spirit has a grammar of its own."[16] Thus, the grammar here is one recognizably transformational, only now the Holy Spirit is transforming all subordinate human transformations—a transformational logic by which the life span itself is transformed. This, I suggest, is a sketch of Luther's own way of interpreting how the young man moves toward being a great man.

The issues at stake are threefold:

First is the truth question. If one believes in the reductive truth of psychoanalytic understanding, then one must agree that Luther's personal story portrays a struggle with psychopathology. However, even within the context of psychoanalytic interpretation, it is more important to take Luther's self-understanding seriously than it is to reduce outright his self-understanding to the analytical system. It is to Erikson's credit that he acknowledges that Luther cannot be contained within his eight-stage system, but he tends to say this is the result of Luther's struggles with his psychopathology rather than an expression of his spiritual life. However, Erikson is ambivalent; he seems to recognize that being *homo religiosus* (in Erikson's usage), Luther would ipso facto be larger than the eight stages of ego development. How Luther could be both below and above Erikson's normative picture of ego development is not clear. This is precisely, in Erikson's own treatment, what calls for the theological interpretation given above.

The second issue is Luther's understanding of identity in Christ, which Erikson misunderstands and thus gives evidence of the inability of the psychoanalytical approach to grasp the substance of Luther's self-understanding. The biblical concept of a dialectical identity that is reflected in Luther's self-understanding automatically marginalizes identity as primarily a matter of ego formation. If the developmental history of the ego is interpreted as it has been in this theologically oriented discussion, then it is clear that any resolution to the identity question must involve a recentering of the whole person around a spiritual center that simultaneously nullifies the negation at the basis of the ego and preserves ego functioning as an expression of the ego as transformed. Without a theological perspective, this is incomprehensible except in reductionistic terms. However, within a biblical-theological perspective, no other understanding of human identity is fully adequate to meet the conditions that confront human existence for the first time in adolescence and can be worked out only through a prolonged identity quest.

Finally, the nature of the pattern by which Luther saw himself transformed is the pattern of the Creator Spirit—not the pattern set by any stages of human development, but the pattern in the dynamics by which those stages are created and themselves transformed in the course of development. Erikson goes a long way toward introducing a concept of the human spirit into the life and thought of a figure who wanted generally to denounce the human spirit, but as Luther said, the human spirit "is a dark room, like the holy of holies in the temple where God dwells in the darkness of faith without light."[17] Erikson's analysis bears this out; the human spirit cannot grasp theological truth, but it does bear the marks of its origin once the veil of the temple is rent and the light of the Spirit of Christ permeates the darkness. But until that light breaks in from the redemption wrought by Christ on the cross, even those marks are unrecognizable. However, in the light of the Creator Spirit, it is possible to see in the human spirit generally, and in Erikson's treatment of Luther specifically, a kind of fundamental theology in which the human longing is finally brought to the light as a longing for the reign of the Spirit, the Kingdom of God.

Thus, Erikson succeeds in setting up helpful prototypes, patterns, and analogies on the basis of which the Holy Spirit works to bring Christ out of the remoteness of history and establish him concretely as the center of Luther's life. But, constructively, Luther's self-understanding by way of the logic of transformation and the work of the Creator Spirit transforms all of the transformations that can be grasped by the psychology of development and puts them into the Christomorphic relationality between the divine and the human spirit.

Now the ego, its stages, and all of its developmental competencies are put into the larger context of transformation (the logic of the Holy Spirit) rather than vice versa. Prior to this understanding, transformation is embedded in human development and brought forth intentionally for specific contexts and occasions. Now that this transformation by the Creator Spirit has occurred, human development itself is embedded in transformation.

Finally note two implications of this. The first is that since Luther leaps out of the stages—goes from identity to integrity—all subsequent stages of his ego development, intimacy, generativity, and so forth are now going to be interpreted in the light of the ultimate transformation that has brought Luther's total life under the power of the Spirit. The second is that we need to note that many more persons undergo this transformation of the ego and recentering on Christ than we realize, but not all are geniuses such as Luther. Many have experienced this transformation and lived it out, but they may not be able to be prophetic for their times as he was.

Transformation in Multiple Contexts

The transformational pattern embedded in human development throughout the life span can be transposed into intentional action in many different contexts covering the whole field of human action. It can be transposed into psychotherapy. This makes therapy a form of redevelopment, not only in the sense of a reconstruction of the past but in the reappropriation of the dynamics of the spirit. It can also be transposed into life-shaping narrative, as Richard Gardner and Margaret Krych have shown.[18] Paul Anderson, in his acclaimed study, *The Christology of the Fourth Gospel,* has shown how this pattern shapes biblical narratives.[19] It is also transposed into scientific discovery, as Andrew Wiles's story illustrates; but there is a long line of evidence to support the primacy of transformation in scientific discovery from Archimedes to Einstein. It is transposed again in anthropology, as in the studies by Anthony Wallace in "Revitalization Moments"and as in Claude Levi-Strauss's interpretation of mythology described in *Structural Anthropology*.[20] It is also the basis for the political theory of Princeton professor Manfred Halpern, where "Transformation and the Source of the Fundamentally New" is the basis for healing broken relationships on all levels.[21] Transformation is the pattern in cosmological events that redirects the course of entropy in open systems, as Ilya Prigogine demonstrated. However, the supreme transformation, which includes but transforms all these transformations of creation and the human spirit, is the transforming power of the Creator Spirit who is at work to transform and redeem all of God's creation. This is the grand, irreversible theological figure-ground shift in which our entire developing life, the whole of the life span, the totality of one's own existence, moves into the background, and the Creator Spirit becomes the central figure, the definitive reality. The human spirit in all its proximate transformations is now ultimately grounded as spirit in God's Spirit. This is the glorious liberty of the children of God.

Because of their totalism, their deep ideological hunger, their heightened awareness of their potential nonbeing, and their sense of urgency about the meaning of life, adolescents are especially capable of the kind of commitment and "fidelity" in self-sacrifice that life in the Spirit calls for. Apart from a sense of identity, commitment may come too easily and be misleading, but given clarity about the object of faith, Jesus Christ, and the transformational work of his spirit, the struggle to work out *who* one is only in relation to *why* one exists at all forges an identity of theological proportions. This person understands well the biblical injunction, "Work out your salvation with fear and trembling for God is at work in you to will and to do for his good pleasure." This is a high-risk undertaking for the sake of the greatest possible reward: to know Christ and him crucified and resurrected.

So is this grand figure-ground shift the answer to our twofold question, "What is a lifetime?" and "Why do I live it?" No, but this is the primary condition for coming to an adequate answer. When Archimedes said, "Give me a place to stand and I will move the earth," he was not only talking about the power of leverage but supplying a metaphor for what happens in a transfiguring transformation of a lifetime. Whether one comes to this realization suddenly or gradually, the Creator Spirit is the place to stand and from there gain leverage for committing the entire life span to the passion of one's faith in Christ, and the doing of works prepared ahead of time for one to do.

What are those works? They are the works of love that must be done with the whole heart, mind, soul, and strength. To this we now turn because it is here that the answer to the dominant question of this book may be found.

NOTES

1. Erik H. Erikson, *Young Man Luther* (New York: Norton, 1958).

2. Dietrich Bonhoeffer, *Letters and Papers from Prison,* ed. Eberhard Bethge (London: SCM Press, 1971).

3. Søren Kierkegaard, *The Journals of Søren Kierkegaard,* ed. and trans. Alexander Dru (London: Oxford University Press, 1938).

4. Walter Lowrie, *A Short Life of Kierkegaard* (Princeton, N.J.: Princeton University Press, 1942).

5. Søren Kierkegaard, *Sickness unto Death,* trans. Walter Lowrie (Princeton, N.J.: Princeton University Press, 1941).

6. This is the crux of the difference between Kierkegaard's experience and that of Magister A. P. Adler, whose visions Kierkegaard studied so closely. Kierkegaard's imagery retained a metaphorical or parabolic quality, but Adler's were literal to him. The effect of the latter is that there is no space for choice, mind, or love.

7. Kierkegaard, *Journals.*

8. Wolfart Pannenberg, *An Introduction to Systematic Theology* (Grand Rapids, Mich.: William B. Eerdmans, 1991), pp. 43–44.

9. Henrietta Lund, *Memories of Home,* cited by Lowrie, *A Short Life.*

10. Lowrie, *A Short Life,* pp. 210–211.

11. Erikson, *Young Man Luther,* p. 34f.

12. See Roger Johnson (ed.), *Psychohistory and Religion* (Philadelphia: Fortress Press, 1997). Professor Johnson has brought several important perspectives to bear on Erikson's study.

13. Ibid., p. 138.

14. H. Grisar, *Luther,* trans. E. M. Lamond, ed. L. Cappadelta (London: Kegan Paul, Trench, Trübner), VI p. 506.

15. Regin Prenter, *Spiritus Creator* (Philadelphia: Muhlenberg Press, 1959).

16. Martin Luther, *Werke,* vol. 39:2 (Weimar: H. Böhlau, 1883), pp. 104–105.

17. Martin Luther, cited by Hendry, *The Holy Spirit in Christian Theology* (Philadelphia: The Westminster Press, 1956), p. 98.

18. Richard Gardner, *Therapeutic Communication with Children: The Mutual Storytelling Technique* (New York: Science House, 1971); Margaret A. Krych, "Communicating 'Justification' to Elementary-Age Children: A Study in Tillich's Correlational Method and Transformational Narrative for Christian Education" (Ph.D. dissertation, Princeton Theological Seminary, 1985).

19. Paul Anderson, *The Christology of the Fourth Gospel* (Valley Forge, Penn.: Trinity Press International, 1996).

20. James E. Loder, *The Transforming Moment,* 2d ed. (Colorado Springs: Helmers & Howard) 1989, p. 159, n. 1.

21. Manfred Halpern, "Transformation and the Source of the Fundamentally New" (paper presented to the American Political Science Association, Chicago, September 1, 1974), and unpublished book manuscript on this same theme, placing transformation at the center of political theory. Firestone Library, Princeton University.

11

YOUNG ADULTHOOD

RISKING IDENTITY IN THE SERVICE OF LOVE

IN *WORKS OF LOVE*, especially his commentary on I Corinthians 13:7, Kierkegaard writes, "Love believes all things and is never deceived."[1] In the case of Helen, recounted in Chapter Three, her discovery of the love of Christ became the most profoundly intimate event of her life. The intimacy of Christ's love had the power to redefine her entire existence; her outlook on life, her relation to herself, and her capacity to relate to those who had abused her changed dramatically. It was the Christ known in the power of the Spirit who held her in his arms and danced around the room with her, who redefined all of reality for her. Her experience begins to explain Kierkegaard's dictum, "Love believes all things and is never deceived."

It is tempting in reading this statement to think that lovingly to believe all things would be utterly naive, the height of romantic foolishness, the frivolity of inexperience, or the blindness of being smitten. But as Kierkegaard explains, this is a misreading, because the accent of one's attention has fallen on being deceived, not on love. This misdirected attention reflects the eye of a self that first sees mistrust, guards against every form of betrayal, before "love" of some sort is permitted expression. That is, the could-be lover is already self-deceived, living in mistrust, practicing the one and only form of betrayal that can defeat true love: self-deceit. That is, love redefines reality, and it has this power because it is the presence of the eternal life of God in the heart of the believer. One loves from the heart, but it is more profoundly true that love creates the heart of the believer in and through the believer's repeated choice in love to believe all things. To believe all things is grounded in a prior belief in God's eternal love, but to guard against deception warily is to bring oneself down to the level of the deceiver; to believe in deceit and deception is to be recast in the image of love's enemy.

The power of Kierkegaard's argument depends on being grasped at the core of one's existence by the pure love of God. This supreme intimacy occurs by the power of God's Spirit at work in one's innermost self, by one who knows one is loved by God. This means that everything else is seen in the illumination of that love. The only possible deception of such an ultimate love is self-deception brought on by mistrust and a preoccupation with detecting deception in the world. Intimacy, then, is the key to understanding Kierkegaard's claim, and Helen's case is an example of how deeply the Spirit of God must reach into the personal history of the person to convey the love that can never be deceived, except by the lover herself.

Clearly Kierkegaard's dictum does not make sense to a well-socialized ego. As long as the ego is the center of the personality, the underlying "no" that enters the personality in the first year of life will create ambivalence and defense against the quality of love Kierkegaard is describing. The love of which Kierkegaard speaks is the expression of a transformed ego; it is the love that returns good for evil, loves the enemy, and does not seek vengeance but forgives even before forgiveness is asked. It is the love expressed by a transformed ego, a dialectical identity.

We must now turn to the developmental foundations of young adulthood in order to return in the conclusion to see how the transformation of development, as viewed from within this period, yields the potential for such a love.

From Eighteen to Thirty

The period of young adulthood extends approximately from age eighteen to thirty; at last the Freudian utopia may be reached. This is the period in which one finally is able to *leiben und arbeiten*—not as simple as it sounds. Genital love is referred to here, and work is productiveness, but in Freud's ideal, they go together. There is not to be a schizoid separation between sex and work from his standpoint.

Whether one agrees with Freud or not, interplay and interaction between sexuality and productiveness in work is a major developmental issue at this time. This is a dialectic between two fundamental polarities. The need for love may hinder the capacity to work, and a work obsession may hinder the capacity to give love. Psychoanalytically, maturation in ego formation occurs as these two powerful motivational forces support each other.

Erikson carries this further to say that sooner or later what is at stake in young adulthood is the willingness to risk fusion of one's own identity with another—to risk being absorbed into her or his world, or being the one who is the absorber. Broader and wiser than Freud's focus on genital intimacy and productivity, Erikson suggests an alternative word, *encounter*, so that the fear of ego identity loss in love or work is the main threat, but intimacy through encounter is the principal gain. This means that in any real encounter with another person, one faces possible threat of despondency or depression and an urge toward isolation, the negative side of the epigenetic task of this period. For example, being a "good sex partner" in sexual relationships may prove to be more depressing than satisfying. "Performance" that is in flight from being "known" and "knowable" in the biblical sense is en route toward isolation. Sexuality that is schizoid—sex without involvement—under the illusion of being genuine intimacy, will create ambivalence and depression, and move persons, at best, toward a kind of titillated isolation. The fantasies and scenarios that would invade sexual union often defeat sexuality as a practice of person-to-person intimacy: either fantasies of the idealized partner or fantasies of the idealized climax, or even the societal demand that one feel free and enjoy this may actually hinder the process. I am reminded of the woman who, in therapy, finally spoke up and said, "You mean I have to do what I want to do?" This captures the irony of the attempt to predict and control spontaneity.

Working out genuine mutuality in sexual relationships is part of the intimacy task of this period and a sensitive indicator, but it is not sufficient. The threat is loss of self-worth acquired in identity; frigidity, impotence, or schizoid participation may come as profound blows to an identity that seemed intact. In a sensitive paper written by a mature woman in my class a couple of years ago, she described her first intercourse on her marriage night. Her husband considered this to be some sort of a victory or conquest, but for her it was an experience of awesome threat. Suddenly the powers of life and death became very immediate and very significant for her. In this case, intimacy began to look like the beginning of bipolar isolation, except they did communicate and discover and accept the mutuality of difference, which was simultaneously awesome, fearsome, and wonderful. Sexuality *may* be a sensitive indicator of one's capacity for intimacy, but it is not necessarily so. One of the cases I observed during my training was of a couple in the midst of a messy divorce, but they nevertheless had excellent sexual relationships. Clearly we have to look deeper than these indicators of intimacy that characterize the Freudian, neo-Freudian approach, so we turn again to a study by

Thomas Oden, a theologian, and his book, *Game-Free: The Meaning of Intimacy.*[2]

Intimacy, says Oden, focuses first on the Latin word for inner or innermost, which is *intimus,* the innermost character of a person. In other languages also, Oden says, the term means "most internal, the most internal quality." Recall from the case of Helen in Chapter Three that if one senses the *intimus,* the innermost character of a person, then one knows the core or center of that person: "What it means for me to be me." Here, where one may feel most secure, is also where one may be most intimidated. Notably, etymology may link intimacy to intimidation through the Latin root of *timor,* meaning "fear." This suggests the familiar title of the book *Why Am I Afraid to Tell You Who I Am?*[3] Hence, the move toward isolation is quite logical in the light of the deep ambivalence we have about our innermost or core self.

Intimacy was of special interest to Oden because of exploratory research he did in relationality. He found that in a significant number of cases, when intimacy as defined above occurred, there was a sense on the part of both persons that a third presence was accompanying the exchange. The phrase, "It's bigger than the both of us," was not mere sentimentality; the relationality seemed to take on a life of its own.

This is not an invitation to mystical conjuring, but it is to be seen alongside others who talk about intimacy in terms such as an "interpersonal trance." Ervin Goffman and Wolfhart Pannenberg, in his book *Anthropology in Theological Perspective,* described a truly good conversation as an interpersonal trance in which the relationship seems to transcend and sustain the persons involved.[4] Here there are no explicit rules being followed, no game plan, nor is there any loss of integrity or personal countenance on the part of either party in the relationship. Indeed, individuality in the sense of particular personal worth is heightened after such encounters.

When such encounters occur continually over a relatively long period of time, then the sort of intimacy that overcomes isolation and does not merely deepen it in the direction of role-structured distance or narcissistic self-sufficiency is being accomplished. Furthermore, if we begin with the general view of intimacy as the quality of relationship in which the relationality itself takes on a life of its own and overcomes each one's anxiety at being known, then we are looking at an experiential foundation of covenant in a theological sense. That is, the developmental struggles of this period, seeking intimacy with integrity, can be seen as implicitly a quest for covenant in Christ. But no covenant is ultimately possible in strictly developmental terms because, in such terms, the quest must begin and end in the human ego. Thus, the stuff and substance of intimacy psychologically must be taken up and transformed by the Spirit of Christ so the intimacy we most deeply long for may be found in our life in the Spirit of Christ with the people of Christ.

Cognition in Young Adulthood

If intimacy versus isolation marks this period for Erikson and the psychodynamics of development, how can we describe this period from a cognitive side? What is the Piaget equivalent here? Since for Piaget studies in the development of intelligence reached their peak in adolescence, how do we develop cognitively in the postadolescent years? It is here where the work of James Fowler is most helpful, especially his books *Stages of Faith* and *Life Maps*. Fowler's research was done primarily in the company of Lawrence Kohlberg, Carol Gilligan, and others. (He is now at Candler School of Theology at Emory University, and has moved from his previous appointment to ethics and social theory.) His method of research was the life interview, one of the most valuable aspects of his work. The stages, as he develops them, are illuminating as stages of ego and the capacity of ego to construct meaning. But they are not stages of faith in any biblical or theological sense.[5]

There is, first of all, in the picture of development as Fowler lays it out, a triangle that moves between self, other, and shared centers of value and power. This triangle is the basic structure of faith, but because faith is continually in process, we are really talking about "faithing," the repeated reconstruction of the structure of faith. Figure 11.1 contains the seven variables and the six stages.

As with Piaget, Kohlberg, and other structuralists in this tradition, the movement from stage 1 to stage 6 is a movement out of egocentrism. The various stages are not automatic, as they are with Erikson; they must be attained, as with Piaget, Kohlberg, and early Gilligan. Note also that we are interested in structure here, not in content; faith does not have any definitive content, only structure. That also is typical of Piaget, Kohlberg, and early Gilligan in their respective fields. The same strictures that apply to Kohlberg apply to this model: the stages are invariant and cannot be skipped. Furthermore, no one can really understand two stages above one's own position. Another interesting point is that Kohlberg found that people who have just moved to a higher stage have a certain disdain for those at the stage they have just transcended. Given this description of faith and faith development, we need to look at some of the basic issues involved in this very popular understanding of faith and why it is better

Figure 11.1. Fowler's Structural Model.

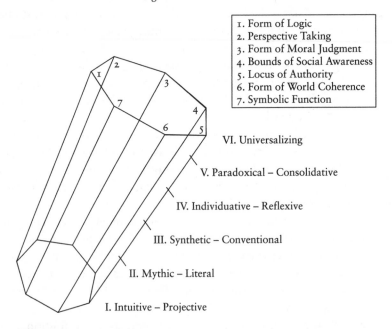

Figure 1

SCVP

Self   Other

Figure 2

1. Form of Logic
2. Perspective Taking
3. Form of Moral Judgment
4. Bounds of Social Awareness
5. Locus of Authority
6. Form of World Coherence
7. Symbolic Function

VI. Universalizing

V. Paradoxical – Consolidative

IV. Individuative – Reflexive

III. Synthetic – Conventional

II. Mythic – Literal

I. Intuitive – Projective

understood as an approach to the developmental potential of the human ego, rather than "faith" development.

The fundamental question is what developmental phenomenon Fowler is actually studying by use of his interview method. More pointedly, how is this to be understood as faith development in any definitive biblical or theological sense?

My predisposition would be to say that the main title and subtitle of Fowler's book should be reversed to read instead *The Psychology of Human Development and the Quest for Meaning: Stages of an Aspect of Faith*. It seems to me that Fowler's work is a sensitive, insightful study of the ego's competence in structuring meaning, and it is only potentially but not necessarily related to faith in a biblical or theological sense. Fowler wants to concentrate on the human aspect of faith, but the decisive question is how Fowler's constructs relate to biblical understandings of faith. To focus the sort of issues that emerge from such a question, take a page from Gerhard Ebeling's study, *Word and Faith,* and draw out some of the discrepancies between Fowler's view and the synoptic accounts.[6] Ebeling first says that faith gives certainty to existence. It is taking sure steps, but with no road visible, hoping although there is nothing to hope for, refusing to despair although things are desperate, having ground under us although we step into a bottomless abyss. The source and substance of such faith clearly reside beyond the ego's capacity to construct meaning.

The second aspect of Jesus' understanding of faith is directed toward the future; indeed, it really brings about the future. That is, faith has to do with an event. Faith directed toward so-called facts is faith only insofar as a future opens up in the light of these facts. As an event, faith is an act of creation, including but always transcending and transforming any given state of equilibrated development.

Third, faith is understood as power. It is really participation in the omnipotence of God, but by means of human weakness. Mountains and mustard seeds are no more strikingly contrasted than when Jesus claims that faith the size of the latter will move anything the size of the former. Faith as power comes forth precisely in the face of human powerlessness; hence it is seen not as an exercise of human potential but of existential participation in God's power, participation that discloses human power as weakness.

Fourth, faith comes forth in the encounter with other people. Preeminently this occurs in the encounter with Jesus but also in encounters with other persons who are graciously empowered to invoke faith. Here it is notable that faith has its origin in a divinely endowed, humanly embodied authority to evoke that response personally. The rise of faith depends on encounters with witnesses of faith. It does not develop as an organ of the human personality arising automatically from person-environment interaction.

Fifth, faith is concrete rather than general and abstract. Faith masters and overcomes particular, concrete situations on the basis of the transcendent ground of its existence. Faith is something exceptional. It does not appear as the inevitable subjective design of particular situations, but repeatedly proves or authenticates itself in situations. Faith is not a phenomenon automatically present to supply the general structure of awareness; it is everywhere and anywhere accessible and effective in shaping the future of concrete particulars.

Sixth, faith saves. That is, *pistis* (faith) and *soteria* (salvation) are characteristically associated in the synoptic gospels, but the manner of their interaction is exceptionally fluid. Whatever the manner and form of their interaction, the point is that with the arrival of faith on the scene, the decisive encounter between God's action and human affairs has occurred. Massive facts will now have to yield. The cause of the future has been espoused and the old—all that comes from the past to discourage the present—has been declared to be past. Where there is faith, then and there at the point of encounter, existence becomes whole and is healed, not as an expression of human fulfillment but by and for the purposes of God.

The question, perhaps, is not unanswerable, but it is so far unanswered: How does Fowler relate his understanding of faith to these basic aspects of the synoptic view, to say nothing of the Johannine and Pauline material, where there seems to be so much disparity? Fowler acknowledges this problem but in *Stages of Faith* never deals with it.

A second group of questions might be labeled methodological and refers to areas in which Fowler's position does not seem to be sufficiently self-conscious or self-critical. First among these is the intrinsic difficulty in making the developmental sequence normative; this difficulty focuses on the problematic standpoint of the observer. If one asks, Where would anyone have to be, in the system's own way of accounting for things, to be preeminently interested in stages and the staging of the whole of human development? it seems unlikely that one could be beyond stage 4. If this is the case and, if one were to move into stage 5 and paradoxicality the stages would become ambiguous; in stage 6, universality, they would appear to be of minor interest and not definitive of anything. Indeed, insofar as they were thought to be definitive, they would be representative of an error with respect to the stage 6 normative way of constructing meaning and being. But the normative goal of Fowler's sequence is precisely this: universalizing. What kind of a model is it that sets up a normative goal that, if it is attained, would expose the model itself to be inadequate and in error? The problem by which Fowler's system seems to contain the seeds of its own falsification apparently lies partly with a failure to clarify the faith standpoint from which faith itself is being observed and partly with making universalizing the normative goal for faith development.

In terms used in this book, the stages Fowler describes are the creative achievement of the human spirit as it strives for universality phase by phase, moving out of egocentrism toward a universal comprehension of all things. The human spirit exhibits here what it shows in all its other manifestations. In the effort to construct a stadial order that appears rational, coherent, and comprehensive, it has tacitly used the deeper order of transformation. Each stage is constructed by a creative act of the human spirit, but, as with all other such creations, the ground and direction of the creative act remain unclear. The unclarity lies partly in the fact that since these are stages of ego development, the negation that underlies the ego is repressed, and the concern for the dark side of human development plays no part in the developmental process until middle adulthood.

This is unfortunate not only because it fails to provide an adequate picture of the whole but because so much that is important to developing persons gets deleted in the name of faith. If we look at Fowler's case of "Mary," it is evident how important the negative aspects of her life story were to the story as a whole. Moreover, it is in response to these potentially traumatic events that Mary becomes a spiritual person in a definitively theological sense.

Nevertheless, Fowler helpfully describes the cognitive domain of the young adult as formal operations (Piaget) used in a dichotomizing fashion. That is, the young adult's developing ego at this period is not taken up in idealism in a way that typifies adolescent ideology, but is rather at work to construct her own ideological perspective in a way that carves out a cognitive space for her place in the world, associating with communities that are ideologically compatible with the explicit system of beliefs and practices she is constructing for herself. This "individualistic reflexive" approach to the cognitive domain makes the young adult a demythologizer, attempting to see through symbols and images to their meanings. Although the view of hard structures, as employed by Piaget, has become a style of thinking in Fowler's scheme, the accuracy of his description seems sound and helpful. Indeed, Fowler's own system seems to exemplify very well what is described as normative for this period of human development.

The Dream

This developmental period would be a bit sterile if it were not for something David Levinson calls "the dream."[7] In fact, in the best scenario for ego development in this period, one's cognitive development and self-.chosen communities and relationships in which cognition matures are at work to articulate and live out the emerging dream, "a vague sense of self-in-the-adult-world." The understanding of dream here is like a vision of the future that gathers up deeply felt personal feelings and translates them into images of oneself in the adult world "out there," the world one is entering as a young adult. Thus, the dream has a transitional quality; indeed, like a transitional object, it combines what *is* the present personal situation with what is open to oneself in the adult world of the future. As with transitional objects in the earlier years of development, the dream is a symbol of the space to be traversed on the ego's way into the early thirties.

The dream is the creation of the human spirit whose unremitting drive is to ground human existence in its source and ground as spirit. According to the principle of coherence in the logic of the spirit, it is all important that the dream be one's own, not one handed down from one's parental past or imposed by the social and cultural order into which one is moving developmentally. The dream is conjured up as a resolution to the developmental conflicts of the ego at this period: an occupation, intimate relationships, marital adjustment, parenting, and lifestyle. If the essential integrity of the dream as it expresses one's innermost passion about one's self and the future can be preserved, through modifications and revisions that inevitably come, the human spirit remains alive and is a continuously constructive power in one's life. It is as if the cognitive development Fowler describes is a left hemisphere analysis, articulation, and expression of the right hemisphere's myth-making, dream-conjuring capacity; but the order of priority lies with the dream as the image or insight precedes the interpretation in the transformational logic of the spirit. Thus, the primary authority in one's life as a young adult is the integrity of the dream, whether it is obeyed or not; to disobey is to pay a high price, as we will see.

Psychoanalytically, the imaginative power of the dream recalls the play period, from ages three to five, when the child constructs real worlds out of the stuff of the imagination. The sexual and aggressive aspects of that period are in the dream by which one expects to beget a future by aggressively taking possession of one's place in the world. The major difference is that now one's sense of an identity is one's own, so whatever reality may be conjured up by the dream must include the reality of one's own selfhood, as well as all the reality checks implicit in the several axes that comprise that identity.

In terms of Erikson's description of the core developmental struggle between intimacy and isolation, intimacy for a young adult amounts to the shared dream. Intimacy means being with one who can share, enjoy, and enrich one's dream. In Levinson's language, this includes "special persons" who help one to feel the depth and power of the dream as realistic and as one's own, and "mentors" who share the importance and potentiality of the dream for connecting with and influencing the "world out there."

But in and through all these interpretations, it is the human spirit that works to draw up hidden resources from the depths of psychic organization, which reflects the place of human nature in all of creation, to bring about new patterns of coherence and meaning, and to point to the ultimate order, the Author of creation, who is the source and destiny of the Spirit-to-spirit relationship.

One young woman recalled that when she was about four or five years old, she went with her parents to the Roman Catholic church. She would sit in her pew with her little legs, too short to hang over the edge, sticking out straight in front of her, and watch the proceedings. At last she announced that when she grew up, she was going to be a priest, whereupon she was quickly informed that it would be impossible. But the dream had taken root and did not die even in the face of the inevitable opposition. Even as she was about to complete her preparations for a promising career in organic chemistry, the dream was reawakened. Her professor, whose competence she greatly admired, would string out equations across the boards of the classroom, and then from time to time would stand back and exclaim, "Isn't God amazing!" It was in his class that she realized that if she were to be true to the deepest root of her dream, it was God, not the string of equations, that most profoundly moved her. Thus, with all the intensity and passion that she might have become a scientist, she became an ordained minister, administering the sacraments in the Protestant tradition. I am sure she will never cease in her intellectual quest to bring theology and science together, as if to allow the root of her dream to continue through all creation.

The formation of moral judgment during this period also needs to be considered. The young adult is most likely governed by an intuitive sense of justice in his moral judgments, but this is also a period of exploration, of new values for one's own life now that some ego integrity has been established. Thus, Fowler says such a person whose ego is maturing on schedule will probably be something of a "contextualist." Early in this period, the young adult "encounters" (Erikson) a major source of tension in his exploration of the views and values of other young adults, thus exploring other possible ethical stances and defending and developing one's own. This gives rise to "the explicit system" and one's defense of the dream.

On this point, Sharon Parks in *The Critical Years* was helpful in describing a convergence between Carol Gilligan and James Fowler on the formation of moral judgment during this period.[8] Parks describes an emerging contextual relativism and provides typical cases. She sees the college-age young adult as moving out of adolescence through a dialectic between "authority-determined" judgment and "unqualified relativism." The emergent competence, she says, is a contextual relativism in which the idealism and the relativism are combined and woven into the complexity of the experience of the young adult. This represents a departure from inherited or assumed conventions, and thus the young adult begins to compose the world in his own terms, keeping self, world, and ultimate reality in a lively interplay with ongoing experience. Emerging from this will be a conceptual pattern or explicit system, which is at first tacit but drives toward explicit formulation.

Following Fowler, persons at this age typically find symbols, myths, and rituals to be useful if they can be translated into clear conceptual, empirical, or pragmatic concepts. The emphasis here is on the power of the interpreter and rarely on the opposite power of the symbol to interpret the interpreter. This reflects the intensity of this period and its characteristic drive to test identity competencies against every "reality," so as to hammer out, create, and craft one's place in and among those realities.

These considerations are on the positive side in which the human spirit is working toward the development of a healthy intimacy. If we now look at the negative side, we must turn to isolation, to use Erikson's term. The etymological root is the same as *island* and refers to someone who lives an insular life primarily in terms of psychological organization.

Isolation may be indirectly related to childhood by way of the dream; that is, the dream is not one's own. Let us say it is the dream of a warm but ambitious mother; then the explanatory aspect of this stage will work overtime, and illusory patterns of intimacy may follow. In the case of James Tracy in David Levinson's studies, a great deal of relatively meaningless sexual acting out occurred in his early adult years, until he found a mentor who supported him in his own dream, which was to be a business executive, instead of his mother's dream, which was that he be a military leader. He also found a woman who shared and supported the dream. The result of the wrong dream was a long period of isolation from himself and from intimacy with others, including his own wife and children, and from occupational fulfillment.[9]

On the other hand, the dream may be obsessively one's own and the extended ideology of a "negative identity." In the case of a young man who must gain power and earn money because he was raised in the home of a poor orthodox priest who had little or no influence in his parish, the drive will be a repression of the need for any intimacy, since it may detract from the ideological security against childhood traumas that he needs. Hence, the result will be isolation of a type familiar to the achievement-oriented personality.

Isolation may also be directly related to parental patterns. Here I have reference to Oden again and the games people play with each other in intimate relationships and so remain isolated from being known in a biblical sense. Here is one of my own cases, a young man who could never get angry with his mother. She managed out of a combination of helplessness and demand to make him feel impotent, so he came to rely heavily on masturbation. He married a woman who had been raised in a strict religious home by a father who tried, without success, to break her will. When she refused to cry when he tried to beat the devil out of her, he finally gave up. She thought of herself as unattractive, although she was actually quite pretty. Sexual relationships were frightening for her since they conjured up images of male violence. They married because both wanted, but also sought to avoid, intimacy.

Here is a typical conversation to show the way in which the games they played kept them isolated from the intimacy they sought. They are getting ready to go to bed early, so a sexual relationship looks imminent. She says, "I'm going to wash my hair." This makes him angry because he needs to try to prove his potency. He waits, and when she returns, she says, "Did you empty the garbage?" at which point he explodes, and she says she cannot see why he is so mad. All she said was . . . She goes to bed alone; he stays up late, watches television, and masturbates, which intensifies his isolation. Notice the close connection between isolation and the potential for violence. All games have a kind of payoff. The payoff here is that they get a kind of intimacy without threat. They would rather have anger, a kind of an inverse form of intimacy, than anything that is genuinely open and positive. This perverse form of intimacy will result only in mutual isolation.

Eventually he follows what he thinks is his dream, which is to have a hard-hitting urban ministry, and she tries to follow and support him, but for him it is too closely linked to a negative identity. That is, he is overcommitting himself to the opposite of what he fears may be the truth about himself: he is weak and ineffectual as a man and as a person. They do get to the place where they can understand and discuss this style of mutual isolation, but they cannot break the pattern. He eventually has an affair with a divorcee who was his secretary and who was, in fact, against marriage. The couple then were divorced. Eventually, two or three years after we broke off our counseling relationship, he came back to talk, looking for a spiritual basis for reconstructing his life. It was at last the right question, because spirituality is an intimacy deeper than all of the dynamics in which he was so enmeshed.

In isolation the human spirit, so entangled in its constructions of defenses and its efforts to manipulate the environment, cannot create a world outside the egocentrism imposed by anxiety and flights into self-deception. The spirit has no choice but to move the person deeper and deeper into a well-defended isolation. As a consequence, the cry for a way out is a cry of the human spirit for a ground beyond itself. Isolation is not from people or relationships; it is fundamentally the entrapment and isolation of the human spirit itself. The alternative is true intimacy, Spirit-to-spirit.

Intimacy in Theological Perspective

My first case in therapeutic training was a Mrs. Sandberg, to whom I introduced myself as "Dr.," even though I was just beginning my studies. It was such a remarkable encounter that it was eventually published.[10] I really did not know what to say, so I just listened to her as she poured out all kinds of lurid sexual episodes, apparently trying to engage my attention by saying shocking and potentially embarrassing things. Not knowing exactly how to respond, I just said, "Ummm." Finally she said, "You're pretty smart, aren't you? You're not going to say anything until I say what's really important." At that point I replied, "Yes." But I did not know how else to respond, so I asked, "Have you ever had an experience of God?" She suddenly became very quiet and well focused. She then told me a parable about her life: that she was like a honeybee who had taken on too much honey and had lost the power to fly. The centeredness, the calm, and the peace that came over her was striking. It was striking even to the psychoanalyst who was in charge of her case. He told me, "I don't know what it was you did, but do it again. It's of great help to her." The point is that the spiritual presence of God is able to establish genuine intimacy at the point where other forms of intimacy have gone terribly wrong.

As a second example, consider the case of Willa, a young adult who was hospitalized and classified as schizophrenic "undifferentiated type." She was an unwanted child who caused her parents to get married. She was alternately abused and neglected as a child by her parents, who were both alcoholics and potentially violent. She was very bright, but everyone took advantage of her because she had no sense of intimacy or balance in relationships. She had homosexual and heterosexual relations with ministers, doctors, and others who were supposed to help her. She was in the second year of graduate school when she finally broke down and could not finish her examinations.

In the hospital where she was placed, she sat for hours in the chair, rocking her doll, "Bill," and staring into space. Then she would get up, act in a bizarre manner, dance around, talk to herself, hassle the nursing staff for information about her record, and then go back and sit in her chair and rock her little doll. The head nurse on her floor told me that they expected Willa never to leave the hospital. One day, however, while she was sitting in the chair, someone came up behind her, put arms around her, and said, "The silence is not empty; there is purpose for your life." She turned around, but there was no one there. The power of the experience began to build sanity and, as she said, the stronger the experience, the more she could distinguish illusion from reality.

Of course, she could not ever convince her Freudian therapist of the legitimacy of her experience. So she played his game and got out of the hospital in about three weeks, when they had thought she would never be able to get out at all. She came to talk and was eventually baptized and returned to the profession for which she was training. The intimacy of the Spirit runs deeper than family violence and neglect, and has immense restorative power.

Here is a third case, of a young woman, raised Roman Catholic, who was hospitalized for borderline schizophrenia and depression. One day in the hospital, she saw a man strapped to a bed, his arms outstretched, facing upward to the ceiling, his feet tied to the bottom railing, and screaming. What she saw in this man was the cruciform presence of her Lord, so she went to minister to him, to quiet him, to comfort him, and in comforting and quieting him she was in her spirit ministering to Christ. It was then that she was able to return to soundness of mind, and to leave the hospital.

The most powerful intimacy comes from the presence of the Spirit of God. It may be mediated, as in these cases. The spiritual presence of Christ is not dependent on the development of the ego, but it is a sanity-producing intimacy that does call forth interpersonal affirmation and openness in a psychological and spiritual sense. This is, of course, the satisfaction of the deepest longing of a person for presence implied in the significance of the primal longing for the Face, the Face that will not go away. This satisfaction occurs at a level deeper than the psychological *intimus,* the innermost being of the person. At the very point where I know what it is for me to be me, I discover that it is the spiritual presence of Christ that knows better than I do what it is for me to be me. This realization produces the potential for freedom for intimacy at other levels.

This new potential occurs because the recentering of the psyche on the Face or the Face representation, the presence of God, overcomes the two main threats to loving: the fear of absorption and the fear of death or annihilation. This transformation works to free the person to give love because now one does not need anyone else to be that Face. One does not need anyone else to satisfy that longing.

The fear of absorption and fear of annihilation derive from opposite ends of the life span. In absorption, intimacy has become suffocating. The fear is that one will be drawn into the lifestyle, family patterns, personal needs, demands, and expectations of the other one to such an extent that one's own freedom to be oneself will be stifled, if not shut down completely. This happens only when the potential lover wants the other one to be for him the Face that will not go away, a double-bind that issues in the anguish of being absorbed. In order to make sure the human face does not go away, the lover must continually stifle attitudes, behavior, and genuine initiatives that may alienate the presence of the other one. This does not liberate the lover with a sense of confidence that love is supposed to give; rather, it binds the lover in patterns of regression that alienate him from himself. He cannot let his spirit be made captive to such a bind. So, alas, he cannot allow himself close enough to let love happen because he can sense that it will kill his spirit by suffocation. Yet his longing continues.

On the other hand, annihilation is isolation in devastating extremity. To love the other one may make it possible for him to destroy her. When a marriage relationship burns out and he says simply, "I have had enough. I cannot live with you any more. I am getting a divorce," then she may say, "If you leave me, it will kill me." But he really *has* had all he can take, so he says, "That's emotional blackmail. You've manipulated me for the last time." But suppose she really means it, and it does kill her or kill her spirit, and she dies from sheer isolation of abandonment. She cannot give way to love and give the other one the possibility of killing her. The stakes are too high. This is the second main threat to love: annihilation by abandonment.

But if by the intervening power of the Creator Spirit, Jesus Christ becomes the Face that will not go away, then neither he nor she needs the other one to be that Face. Absorption is not a possibility because he belongs completely to Christ, so now he can love without the fear of absorption. And suppose again that the spiritual presence of Christ has become the Face of God for her; then the ego has been displaced, it is no longer the center of the personality, so now she cannot be killed. She has already died to the ego's defenses and any obsession with survival. Since she has already died, he cannot kill her, so she is free to love him.

In this particular context, love implies a nonpossessive delight in the particularity of the other one. Usually one wants to possess what one loves, but that sort of love can easily be deceived; or one wants to put the beloved in some category. In Kierkegaard's ironic parable, the woman knows her husband does not love her, but she consoles herself with the thought that he is "a great man."

But love that depends on complimentary categories is not love. Love is not possessive and earnestly desires the fulfillment of the unique particularity of the other one. This is not obscure to the lover who has known love through the spiritual presence of Christ; indeed, this is precisely how one has experienced the love of God—intimately, knowing better than I do what it means for me to be me and in liberation, as in "for freedom Christ has set us free," so I am possessed only by the One who sets me free.

Now we must ask certain questions of this notion of love. If we ask first what is the ground of such a love, we can say that the form love takes in us is prefigured and grounded in Christ when we are joined to him by faith. In contrast to ways discussed in Fowler's understanding of faith during this period of development and in fundamental agreement with Ebeling's discussion, we can say that the dialectical identity, I-not I-but Christ, is a highly condensed version of the inner structure of faith. What Fowler discusses and insightfully understands is the expanding competencies of the "I" to understand itself in relation to itself and its world; it is an expansion of ego consciousness and competence. However, if we follow Ebeling's discussion of faith in the synoptics, then we can see that faith is bestowed by the grace of God across the fundamental abyss that separates the human from the divine. In effect, the grace of God in Jesus Christ has, by the power of the Creator Spirit working in us, transformed the human ego, setting it free from the negation that underlies it, negating that negation and simultaneously recentering the psyche on the indwelling presence of Christ. The ego, now free *from* its defensive posture, can be free *for* the full exercise of its competencies. It is the expansion of competencies that Fowler's work seeks to describe, but the essence of faith resides in the divine-human relationship, not in the developing competencies of the ego.

As Daniel Day Williams writes in his discussion of love in the Reformers, the love of God comes through the Holy Spirit, who freely bestows grace on us, which is received by faith. But reception in faith restructures the personality, creating a dialectical identity.[11] Thus Calvin writes: "Now we shall have a complete definition of faith, if we say, that it is a steady and certain knowledge of the Divine benevolence towards us, which, being founded on the truth of the gratuitous promise in Christ, is both revealed to our minds, and confirmed to our hearts, by the Holy Spirit." Moreover, the relation of Christ to the Christian, as constructed by the Creator Spirit and appropriated by faith, is such that we are being transformed into his image: "Christ is not without us, but dwells within us;

and not only adheres to us by an indissoluble connection of fellowship, but by a certain wonderful communion coalesces daily more and more into one body with us, till he becomes altogether one with us."[12]

As Williams continues, describing the history of this understanding, he says that later orthodoxies sometimes lost the significance of the remaking of the person through one's relationship to the spiritual presence of Christ. Later pietism sometimes sentimentalized the relationship, making it depend on emotional responsiveness, doctrinal correctness, or moralistic striving. More recent attempts, which shift the whole matter to the expanding of ego competence, eliminate the inherently relational structure of faith in a cognitive direction. However, the dialectical identity of the remade person is a bipolar relational unity of the whole person, and its inherent relational unity is maintained by the grace of God, which is God's love toward us. This love becomes effective for us in that "wonderful communion" of which Calvin spoke and which is experienced corporately in the covenant community of the body of Christ, the koinonia.

Thus, the ultimate ground for such a love is the love of God for us as revealed in Jesus Christ and his atoning work on the cross. But this is not a ground for the expression of any love except that which stems from a transformed ego. Through the eyes of faith, other loves may point toward God's love for us in Jesus Christ, but in themselves they may just as easily point in the opposite direction, toward idolatrous, romanticized, sentimentalized relationships that are only expanded forms of self-centered love. But is this to be said of the love of beauty, the love of learning, the love of a child for the parent?

This moves us to the second question: What is the developmental history of love? In his discussion of the several metaphors for the atonement, Williams finds that none of the theories of the atonement has taken as its point of departure and its key an analogy to the reconciling work of love. He then proceeds to interpret "actual reconciliation" in human terms as a basis for further understanding of the reconciliation between God and humanity. Valuable as this is and as are all the traditional theories of the atonement, a different point of departure could be the work of the Holy Spirit by which the atonement is made more than actual—indeed, redemptive for us.

If we cast the issue in this frame of reference, then the transforming power of the Creator Spirit in relation to the human spirit becomes the issue, and the restoration of the image of God becomes the experiential aim of atonement. It is possible to say that in the atonement, God shows his love to us in the fact and in the way a particular man lived, died, and was raised from the dead. Furthermore, the conflict between God and humanity has been so profoundly resolved that all creation has been transformed through him. In the transformational language of the spirit, Christ is the mediating reality by which the ultimate conflict between God and humanity is, at least proleptically, resolved. Exactly how that mediation took place, or precisely how the nature of the conflict is conceived, and what was necessary to mediate the essential terms of the conflict, will determine which metaphor of the atonement will be most adequate to carry the issue deeper. The essential point is that through the atonement, God in Christ made love the definitive power in and over all creation.

The developmental history of love connects love to transformation; that connection is threefold. First, given that the work of the Creator Spirit is to create, maintain, and deepen "a certain wonderful communion" with the in-dwelling presence of Christ, and in so doing the Creator Spirit is transforming us into his likeness, it might be said that the aim of transformation is to create in us the love relation with Christ. More profoundly, it could be said that transformation through the mediation of Christ is the way of love.

Second, since the human spirit is also transformational, it is continually doing within the limits of its human domain what the Creator Spirit does in ultimate terms. The ultimate aim of the human spirit in its quest for the Face of God is also love, but its love will always be marked by the dark side of human development from which the human spirit by itself cannot extricate itself. The lower forms of love, such as eros, phileo, and caritas, are all efforts of the human spirit to create on its own what only the Creator Spirit can create in the selfhood of the believer. The developmental history of love is a history of many diverse loves circumambulating around the center: the agapic love of God in Jesus Christ. All other loves conjured up by the transformational dynamics of the human spirit are like the human spirit itself, groundless and in a state of longing for the ultimate form of its proximate expressions.

Third, this is not to ignore the current criticisms of the "impossible possibility" that one might be able to give love sacrificially with integrity. It is quite correctly argued that to talk about sacrificial love by itself as an ethical norm is an invitation to oppression and abuse. Like the discussion on the atonement, this is potentially an extremely broad discussion. In at least one widely read criticism, it is said that agape is a form of love that is lower than "equal regard."[13] Agape as sacrificial love is not the highest form of love because sacrificial love is unto the end of living together in mutuality and cooperativeness. In this argument, it should be stressed that "equal" regard is not "identical"; each one is a singular and unique individual, but each has a dignity as a child of God. Also, love as equal regard is not dependent on reciprocity for its existence because one should love the enemy with the same love as one would love any other person. Indeed, one should love oneself in a similar manner, as the great commandment declares when it says, "Love your neighbor as yourself."

This view is helpful in criticizing any tendency in persons to glorify the significance of self-sacrificial love or to oppress others with this notion of sacrificial love. However, because the argument here is so highly rationalistic, it clearly has no space for the inner moral disposition of a person to be governed by anything more than an ego-centered personality. The biblical understanding of a dialectical identity is foreign to the argument, so as a result, the aim of sacrificial love as moving toward community, mutuality, and cooperation sets up an aim that might better be analyzed and interpreted by a social psychologist or a sociologist than a theologian.

The argument that a different view of the moral agent—the dialectical identity in which the Spiritual Presence of Christ dwells within us and daily we become more and more at one with Christ—is of no significance to the argument, but theologically it is of the utmost significance. The "equal regard" in the trinitarian life is koinonia, held together by the Spirit, and the koinonia, the communion-creating presence of Jesus Christ, is not an option for the ego-centered personality, but transformation into that communion is always an option.

What seems evident from the standpoint of the dialectical identity as moral agent is that agape is not the highest form of love *because* it is self-sacrificial but because it is *holy* and *pure* and has the power of purity in its encounter with the impurities in creation, including death. Thus, the transforming power of love has its integrity not in sacrifice but in the purification of any context where the impurities of human existence have stifled the human spirit, choking off the prospect for experiencing the communion-creating presence of Jesus Christ.[14]

The primary concern here is neither the broad theological topic of the atonement nor the debates that center around a love ethic. It is that when human development in a theological perspective is brought into such discussions, the issues get significantly reformulated. In this instance, the developmental question of intimacy versus isolation gets purpose and meaning in relation to the love of God in Jesus Christ. In turn, intimacy gives some direction to the theological understanding of the presence and power of love.

The developmental history of love can be understood by taking up the cross and resurrection as a model of love, and looking back through the development of the personality from the young adult years. Repeatedly, from stage-to-stage in every register of behavior, the human spirit has cre-

ated new constellations of meaning out of conflicts and various distur-
bances of developmental order. Transformation embedded in human
development and the eventual transformation of human development as
a whole enact the way of love at the level of the human spirit and according to the model of cross and resurrection. Thus, the struggle of the
human spirit during at least the first two decades of life is a struggle to
release the power of love into the world through the self and to achieve
the kind of relationality that will finally ground the human spirit in the
Creator Spirit, and ground our human loves in the love of God in Jesus
Christ. To recognize one's developmental history as a love story seemingly
foredoomed to unfulfillment is important for recognizing why, when love
is so widely affirmed as essential to our nature, it is so difficult to do, and
why the proper practice of love is so important.

Thus, we turn to the third question: How is love practiced? In discussing the practice of love, we can begin by understanding the convergence between Iranaeus's recapitulation theory of the atonement and the
deepening of intimacy as the key to releasing the power of love into
human context. Iranaeus's view of recapitulation implied that in the incarnation and atonement, understood as one continuous act of the love of
God, the human race could now properly reappropriate its origins, starting with Jesus as the second Adam.[15]

A succinct way of stating the contrast between the first and second
Adam set forth in Romans 5:12 and I Corinthians 15:45–49 (also verse
22) can be found in the Carmen Christi, Philippians 2:5–11. Ralph Martin sets it up in his book, *Carmen Christi,* pages 163–164, as follows:[16]
The first Adam, made in the divine image, thought it a prize to be grasped
at to be as God. He aspired to a reputation and spurned being God's servant, seeking to be in the likeness of God, and being found in fashion as a
man (of dust, now doomed), he exalted himself, became disobedient unto
death. He was condemned and disgraced. The second Adam, in whose
image the first Adam was created, was the image of God. He thought it
not a prize to grasped at to be as God, and made himself of no reputation. He took upon himself the form of a servant and was made in the
likeness of men; and being found in fashion as a man (Rom. 8:3), he hum-
bled himself and became obedient unto death. God highly exalted him
and gave him the name and rank of Lord (pp. 163–164).

In effect, in the second Adam, the conditions of the first are exactly
reversed. Translating this into developmental terms, the "no" that underlies the ego is exactly reversed by the "yes" expressed in the Face of God
and all that implies. It is the transformational work of the human spirit
that seeks, in futility, to restore the dominance of the Face. It is the

Creator Spirit who grounds the human spirit and makes it more than effectual—as the second Adam who ontologically preceded the first Adam is greater than the first. The "yes" is far larger than the "no," so the "yes" does not merely negate the negation, but opens up human existence to the full stature of Christ. This openness is preserved and empowered through life in the koinonia, where the practice of love through the deepening of spiritual intimacy over time cancels the ultimate isolation of human existence from its source in God's love.

Here we see again the deepest human longings given theological context in order that that context can account for what happens in human development before and after a transformation of the ego, and so that transformation may be located in history and the redemption of all creation.

In the beginning of human development, there is a reenactment of the "qualitative" aspect of Adam's original sin that determines the entire course of one's personal history.[17] It is now possible to argue that through the transformation of human development in Christ, one's developmental history may be reappropriated and so be restored to the source of its deepest longing: to behold the Face of God. Thus, one may experience in adult terms the child's fulfillment in beholding the face of the nurturing person: the cosmic ordering, self-confirming presence of the loving Other. Indeed, the practice of love in the Spirit of Christ is a reappropriation of the developmental history of the "I" in the dialectical identity bestowed on the believer in faith. This is not an exercise in self-analysis, but it is the practice and deepening of intimacy in the context of the communion created by the Spiritual Presence of Christ. What has given birth to the dark side of human development through each one's qualitative participation in the old Adam is redeemed through the transformation of the ego and sanctified through the practice of love in the koinonia.

In doing marriage counseling, I sometimes speak about "thinking married" as a way of stressing the primacy and power of relationality. A couple may come and want "to work on their relationship," and that is probably commendable, but the real power in the marriage lies in letting the relationship take on a life of its own. Then the relationality defines the persons, not the other way around. This is perhaps the most practical reason that married couples should pray together, so they can take the risks required in entering into the intimacy of prayer and so their relationship can get a life of its own. The more profound reason is that by doing so, they permit themselves to experience in small form the inner life of the church, the koinonia, as a human reflection of the inner life of God. However, all that may be involved in such a serious call to a devout married life is not sufficiently clear. Accordingly, I have suggested the following model as a way of bringing the theology of human development to bear on the questions of intimacy in the context of grace. Of course, marriage only supplies a relatively small sample of what happens on a much larger scale in the Pentecostal power of Christ's Spirit.

The model of intimacy by which persons are drawn out of incipient or growing isolation is given in Charles Hampden-Turner's book *Maps of the Mind* and in his earlier book, *Radical Man*.[18] He described a series of steps that persons in relationships could take to empower their interaction and strengthen their sense of identity. He found that those who could take these steps in a relationship correlated with persons who had high scores on Kohlberg's scale and with those who were able to break free from the cultural constraints in Stanley Milgram's experiment on conformity.[19] When he first designed this model in the early 1970s, he was a guest lecturer at Princeton University, where his views could be carefully scrutinized. I have attempted to fill out his model developmentally and theologically, since by itself the model is incomplete.

Developmentally, I have reenvisioned the model as the systematic reappropriation of Erikson's stages in the only context that could possibly support this kind of move for the sake of appropriating one's full and complete redemption in Christ: the communion of the koinonia (see Figure 11.2). I have restated the model here in language as close as possible to Hampden-Turner's original conception, but I have added the developmental rubrics to indicate how the model outlines revisiting and reappropriating decisive stages in ego development, but now in the context of grace and ego as transformed. Double helix describes the interaction and locus of the meeting in love as a gift of the spiritual presence of Christ.

Spiritual Presence of Christ

This is an interactive relational model that by itself, without its theological context, could be psychologically dangerous. Regression in interaction such as this on purely human grounds could lead to an inflated ego identity or deep despair. What makes it work as a mutual deepening and personally enhancing interaction is the matrix of grace in which the identities involved are dialectical and the distance is already bridged by the Spiritual Presence of Christ. The interaction then is a matter of appropriating what is already present and alive and at work. Thus, this pattern of interaction releases the Spirit more fully into the relationship, increasingly giving it a life of its own. In such a context, the model suggests a way of practicing intimate interaction within the context of the koinonia, thereby

Figure 11.2. The Practice of Love in Koinonia.

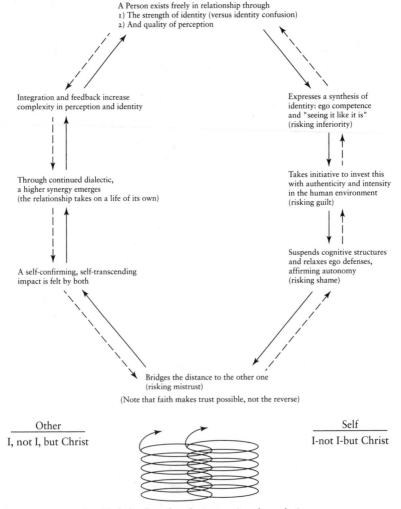

Based on the Spiritual Presence of Christ

A Person exists freely in relationship through
1) The strength of identity (versus identity confusion)
2) And quality of perception

Integration and feedback increase
complexity in perception and identity

Expresses a synthesis of
identity: ego competence
and "seeing it like it is"
(risking inferiority)

Through continued dialectic,
a higher synergy emerges
(the relationship takes on a life of its own)

Takes initiative to invest this
with authenticity and intensity
in the human environment
(risking guilt)

A self-confirming, self-transcending
impact is felt by both

Suspends cognitive structures
and relaxes ego defenses,
affirming autonomy
(risking shame)

Bridges the distance to the other one
(risking mistrust)
(Note that faith makes trust possible, not the reverse)

Other
I, not I, but Christ

Self
I-not I-but Christ

Double helix describes the interaction through time

practicing and deepening the power of God's love in human life. Eight
phases are described on which the following observations should be made:

1. One moves into an interpersonal encounter by risking expression of
   one's ego identity in Christ, beginning with one's developmental
   competencies in the presence of the other. Intimacy is not attained

by passive vulnerability, hiding competence, divesting oneself of initiative and autonomy; rather, these must be brought into the love relationship if intimacy is to be achieved and if the emerging relationship is to overcome isolation, achieve trust, and so empower faith as a corporate reality.

2. The model says that the capacity for intimacy in grace is dependent on the capacity of the transformed ego to reverse its patterns of defense, and recover strengths and weaknesses through interpersonal interaction. That is, one must learn to become a child without ever losing or diminishing one's adult ego capacities. Increasingly faith consciousness expands to include the whole of the life span in love; one begins to see an entire lifetime through the eyes of God.

3. This recapitulation of one's developmental history requires that in the context of such an encounter, one will face and embrace the negative aspect of each phase in one's developmental history on the fundamental assumption that the Spirit of Christ undergirds, heals, and restores any disclosures that may prove to be painful. This is *not* to say that intimacy, according to this model, is simply disgorging one's dark side to another person. It is to say that one reenvisions one's past through the eyes of faith, corporately confirmed, that is, through a relationality of love whose present existence proleptically embodies the nullification of the dark side of one's past. As one who has already died in Christ does not fear death, so the faith-to-faith intimacy in encounter with the other increasingly nullifies all that might hinder that "wonderful communion."

4. Reinforcement from the other one strengthens this effort of love and makes greater intimacy possible through the synergy of two persons joined in faith by the Creator Spirit. Rejection may turn back the human spirit and temporarily delay the move into greater intimacy. In the positive case, the consequence is that ego identity is strengthened in Christ.

To summarize, the redemption wrought in Christ is appropriated through a personal and interpersonal recapitulation of one's own lifetime as formerly a bearer of the brokenness of the image of God and a perpetrator of the long-standing self-inflicted curse upon the human spirit. Through this model, what Iranaeus envisioned historically is hereby reenacted in the course of personal history, beginning at the point where our history connects directly with the qualitative nature of Adam's sin. Adam is born in us, and we live out the Adamic condition. Our redemption by God's love through the incarnation and atonement restores to us our true nature in Christ through his Spirit. We now live out the life of faith in love as we reappropriate our personal history in light of and by the power of his presence. Thus, we actualize that "wonderful communion" of which Calvin spoke. As Christ is born in us, the old Adam, the man of flesh and death, is replaced by the spiritual man; what began in flesh and death now becomes spirit and eternal life (I Cor. 15:45ff.). Bringing personal history and salvation history together in this way makes theology and human development mutually illuminative; each informs the other, but the theological side has an ontological priority in this Christomorphic relationality.

Ultimately the practice of love through deepening intimacy in Christ allows persons to be drawn by the spiritual presence of Christ into the inner life of the Trinity. The ultimate ground for this model is the Trinity understood perichoretically. In Chapter Three, we discussed this classical term for the inner life of the Trinity as follows: *peri,* "around, or at all points," as in *perimeter*; and *choreo,* "to proceed or to make room," as in *choreography.* The Latin Church fathers translated this *circumincessio,* meaning that there is a moving around within the Trinity such that among the persons, there is mutual interpenetration at all points without loss of identity. Individuality and mutuality are simultaneously affirmed, and members of the Trinity can exchange places without changing their identity. By means of perichoresis, the Trinity takes on an inherently relational quality such that the unity of the Trinity *is* the relationality, and relationality *is* the unity. The practice of love in the intimacy of the koinonia promises to actualize in human terms this Trinitarian reality. The case of Helen, at points where prayer took on a life of its own, illustrates this point most effectively.

We now may be prepared to return to Kierkegaard's dictum, "Love believes all things and is never deceived," and ask what underlies such a statement. There are, of course, several aspects to Kierkegaard's commentary *Works of Love,* but looking closely as this single comment will disclose his basic stance.[20] In spelling out what is behind this cryptic claim, five assumptions can be formulated. First, this is the statement of a transformed ego; from the standpoint of faith, love can be all that this dictum claims. Second, this refers to the pure love of God, not loves created by the human spirit in its frustrated longings for fulfillment. However, it is a pure love that can be appropriated and lived out by the human spirit in communion with the Creator Spirit. Third, this love is transformational in its character and its power. This love is not merely an ethical norm, nor is it a disposition to do good, or a work of the human will "screwed to its sticking point." This love is alive in the person through the spirit of the person in communion with the Spirit of God. It is not *a* force; it is *the* force by which everything in all creation is moved, changed, transformed, and redeemed. Fourth, to say that it believes all things is not to say it is gullible. It is to say that it has full awareness of all that is going on, including the deceits perpetrated against it, but as love, it exposes, as in a harsh white light, that deception is in fact an exercise in nihilism, so it comes to nothing. The startling juxtaposition of Judas departing to betray Jesus and Jesus saying, "Now is the Son of Man glorified," is a paradigm of the futility of deceit in the presence of love. Fifth, from this paradigm, it seems perfectly clear that love can be deceived only by the lover himself. *Isolation* is the developmental term used to describe self-deceit at the ego level, but isolation is more profound when it is alienation from the spiritual truth about oneself. It is well known that there is a close connection between personal isolation and the human propensity to violence. The hidden life of Judas is the prime example. Intimacy in God's love is the ultimate answer to violence.

If Jesus had exposed, condemned, and ostracized Judas, he would have betrayed his own nature; he would have stooped to Judas's level, and the power of love literally to redefine reality would have been dissipated in his taking up Judas's fundamental posture of self-centered interest for personal gain.

Finally, it must be said that such a love is comprehensible only as one practices it in a purifying relation to the other one and to the ground of that love—that is, only as one practices the deepening of intimacy at the one point where intimacy is of ultimate significance in the koinonia.

"What is a lifetime?" and "Why do I live it?" now are answerable in terms of the immense love of God. Love is the ultimate statement about God's nature, so any doubt that might be expressed in the question, "Why love?" with the kind of love described above in mind, is not answerable because it is not a meaningful question. It would suggest that there is something higher than the nature of God by which we can justify affirming God's nature as it comes to us in Jesus Christ. It is, of course, impossible for the creature to evaluate the creator, the finite to measure the infinite, humanity to judge or justify God. Love must always be its own reason.

Thus, the fundamental move toward an answer to the two questions behind this book is to reposition the questioner from an ego-centered existence to a Christ-centered existence. This is the only way one can begin to come to an answer. The question asked strictly from within the ego's stance already contains the ambivalence that always ends in, "No answer is sufficient." If asked from within the love of God mediated to us by his Spirit through Christ, then an answer is forthcoming: My life is an incomplete act of God's immense love toward God's creation; it is an act that is completed only as I return with my lifetime that same love to God and to God's creation. "Why do I live it?" I live it because this love redefines life itself for me; in the koinonia, life becomes love. There, life itself is reenvisioned and redefined as the struggling raw material from which love is fashioned by the grace of God. Thus, I said in the beginning of this book that the two questions are the same because an adequate answer to one implies the answer to the other. Both questions find resolution in God's love. To raise the question in the abstract as an untransformed ego and apart from God's love is to foreclose on an answer and to end, at best, in Camus's meaningless moral struggle against death. In the order of creation, love precedes meaning and purpose and is the substance of their power to shape and direct a lifetime. This is true for the order of human development and remains true throughout the life span. This truth concerning the primacy of love does not depend on any level of ego development; the pure love of God is the nature of the "absolute unity of being" around which human development circumambulates for seventy or eighty years—or until it recognizes that this is indeed the nature of the case. It takes a universe and more to create a human being, but it is now, as one may be "filled with all the fullness of God," that one can grasp the theological reality that the universe is the obverse side of God's immense love for humanity and for each singular individual.

NOTES

1. Søren Kierkegaard, *The Works of Love*, trans. David F. Swenson (Princeton, N.J.: Princeton University Press, 1946).

2. Thomas Oden, *Game-Free: The Meaning of Intimacy* (New York: Harper-Collins, 1974).

3. John Joseph Powell, *Why Am I Afraid to Tell You Who I Am?* (Chicago: Argus Communications, 1969).

4. Pannenberg on Goffman in *Anthropology in Theological Perspective*, p. 371.

5. James E. Loder, "Conversations on Fowler's *Stages of Faith* and Loder's *The Transforming Moment*," *Religious Education Journal* 77, no. 2 (March–April 1982).

6. Gerhard Ebeling, *Word and Faith* (London: SCM Press, 1963), chap. 7.

7. David Levinson, *Seasons of a Man's Life* (New York: Ballantine, 1978), chap. 6. Also see his *Seasons of a Woman's Life* (New York: Knopf, 1996). This latter book was written with Levinson's wife, Judy, who completed the book after her husband's death in 1994.

8. Sharon Parks, *The Critical Years* (San Francisco: Harper San Francisco, 1986).

9. Levinson, *Seasons of a Man's Life,* chap. 6.

10. Hans Hofmann, *Religion and Mental Health* (New York: Harper, 1961), chap. 37.

11. Daniel Day Williams, *Spirit in the Forms of Love* (New York: Harper-Collins, 1968).

12. John Calvin, cited by ibid.

13. This discussion is developed at length in Don Browning's *A Fundamental Practical Theology* (Minneapolis: Fortress Press, 1991), pp. 158ff. This is based on an article by the Roman Catholic theologian Louis Janssens, "Norms and Priorities in a Love Ethic," *Louvain Studies* 6 (1977): 207–238. It is also used in certain branches of feminist literature; see Carol Lekay Hess, *Caretakers of Our Common House* (Nashville, Tenn.: Abingdon Press, 1997).

14. David Willis, *The Holiness of God* (forthcoming manuscript). The understanding of holiness as pure love is the thesis of this remarkable study of the divine nature.

15. Gustav Wingren, *Man and the Incarnation* (Philadelphia: Muhlenberg Press, 1959); J. F. Bethune-Baker, *Introduction to the Early History of Christian Doctrine* (London: Methuen, 1954), p. 333ff.

16. Ralph Martin, *Carmen Christi* (Grand Rapids, Mich.: Eerdmans, 1983).

17. As discussed in Chapter Four, in Kierkegaard's *Concept of Anxiety*, trans. Walter Lowrie (Princeton, N.J.: Princeton University Press, 1947), we participate in Adam's sin qualitatively by reenacting in our development the inevitable self-alienation from God implicit in ego formation. In this way, we are like Adam universally. But we are unlike Adam quantitatively. That is, the results of our human separation from God accumulate, making further enactment of qualitative sin more likely in later generations. Original sin, then, is inevitable but not necessary since transformation is possible.

18. Charles Hampden-Turner, *Radical Man: The Process of Psycho-Social Development* (Cambridge, Mass.: Schenckman, 1970). Hampden-Turner has recently developed this model alongside others, but none has a theological baseline such as we have constructed here.

19. Stanley Milgram, *Obedience to Authority* (New York: HarperCollins, 1974). Milgram studied whether persons would resist an authority, even if the authority told them to endanger the life of another person. Milgram said he would take the blame if anything happened. A startling number of subjects were quite willing to do so.

20. Kierkegaard, *Works of Love*.

12

THE MIDDLE YEARS

EGO TRANSITIONS AND

TRANSFIGURATIONS OF THE SOUL

TWO OF THE WORLD'S great masterpieces, which portray the extremities of good and evil, begin at this midpoint in the life span. Dante opens the *Divine Comedy* with the line, "Midway in the journey through life, I found myself lost in a dark wood strayed from the true path."[1] Goethe's Faust finds that although he has studied philosophy, medicine, and law thoroughly, he is fundamentally no wiser than the poorest fool, feels his life is wasted despite his achievements, and makes a pact with Mephistopheles in his attempt to salvage it.

Historically, many notable figures have entered into a pact with God at this point in their lives, and undergone conversions. After the age of thirty, Wesley, Pascal, Loyola, Calvin, and (all the way back to) Constantine entered into a covenant with God to salvage their lives and so changed the course of history. Midlife conversions that have far-reaching consequences are almost as legendary as adolescent conversions. What is going on here, developmentally and theologically?

An Overview

David Levinson, in his study of the adult years for both men and women, has determined that the period from ages thirty to sixty can be divided into segments of approximately five years each.[2] Although this span does need to be divided and studied in smaller chunks, we will assume that Erikson, Jung, and Fowler are correct in suggesting that there are dominant themes in the formation of psychic life that run all the way through these middle years. The broad-scale themes we have employed to describe the overall unfolding of a lifetime (order, entropy, new order, relationality) apply during this period as well. Entropy becomes conscious and recognizably inevitable; the order of transformation in the human spirit retains the capacity to reverse or redirect the course of entropy, giving rise to new being within, and dramatically altering a wide range of relationships—circumstantial, historical, and theological. This thematic overview can be specified by subthemes: Erikson's focus on generativity versus stagnation, Jung's view of archetypes and individuation, and Fowler's cognitive focus on dialectical thinking.

Psychophysical Evidence

The physical changes become increasingly pronounced as these years unfold. By the middle of the middle years, the hair is getting gray or sparse or both, wrinkles appear in the skin and the skin itself is sagging, the abdomen has a new inclination to expand into the world, the eyes develop a certain blur, vision and hearing are not quite as sharp, old injuries reappear and become painful, knees stiffen, back pains appear, and other more serious problems also arise. Men of forty to fifty are particularly subject to coronary occlusion, especially if they are the A-type personality, that is, one for whom achievement is an aggressive drive for respect and ascendancy. After age fifty, a heart attack is less likely to be fatal since the heart builds up alternate pathways if the large vessels occlude. Women are more subject to malignancy, breasts need to be checked regularly, and gynecological examinations are advised on a yearly basis. At the turn of this century, few women lived long enough to go through menopause, but now there are at least thirty-one million women undergoing or in menopause in the United States. As menstruation tapers off or ceases abruptly, a woman may experience waves of hot flashes, unexpected sweating, blotches, fainting, dizziness, upset of emotional equilibrium, and occasional depression.

In one study, the conclusion was that men also have a psychophysical equivalent of the menopause, depression, and lower-level functioning. For both men and women, it is time to surrender narcissistic gratifications from bodily exertion and expression as the body itself begins to decline. It is generally a time to take stock. It is an arithmetical awakening when one realizes that this is a midpoint in life. Having grown up for thirty, forty, or fifty years or so, now one must realize what it means to grow down. This physical decline puts the evidence of dying in the mirror every day. Most commonly, we turn inward toward the inevitability of irreversible losses in the future and the mourning of those in the past. The question now becomes: "How much time do I have left?" Your children, or students, or younger associates all seem to assume that your life is essentially over, or at least set for the duration. One's own parents are very old, dying, or dead by this time. One's self-image is at stake: the question of where one had hoped to be by this time as opposed to where one actually is becomes important. All this enters into and lurks behind the question of "How much time is left, and did it mean anything anyway?"

Two Typical Syndromes

In this connection, there are two familiar psychological patterns, both of which are depressive forces and foster the turn inward that characterizes personal stock-taking and healthy ego development. These are paradigmatic syndromes in that they bring to focus a number of issues typical of the middle years.

The first is the motivational and emotional paradox of promotion depression. Now you are at the point of attaining that for which you have striven throughout your career, and you have attained that coveted position, you may become depressed. Why? There are several possible answers. One is that the future is now closing in. For some, of course, this is a great relief, and they can begin to plan within the finite limits of life. But for others, this amounts to the loss of a future, plus the fact that they are burdened with new responsibilities. One may rather suddenly find that one is a member of the old guard. It increasingly dawns on me with surprise that I am now the senior faculty member in my department and that I have taught at this seminary almost as long as any other member of the entire faculty. If I were inclined to be depressed, I suppose this would not be a healing realization.

A second answer is that it did not bring with it the change in your being you thought it would. This is similar to the pursuit of degrees that presumably will get you to the place in life you want to be. You get your college degree, and then you have to get a master's degree, and then you have to get a doctorate, and then you have to specialize because none of these degrees quite get you to where you need to go. This is like being addicted to a promotion; when there is no further promotion, the result is depression. One well-known religious author confided that often the only way he could get to sleep at night was to think about his next promotion. There is never any topping off for that kind of addiction.

But there may be a deeper underlying dynamic, according to Freudian and neo-Freudian thinking. To gain the position of responsibility as the senior person is now at last to effect the replacement of the parent—the father type or the mother type. This is the person or type he sought to replace at the beginning of the oedipal period. During the oedipal period and the reworking of it in adolescence, he learned both directly and indirectly never to try to supersede the authority. So unconsciously, success in making the replacement brings not pure exhilaration but also underlying depression because, responding to old fears of parental retaliation, he punishes himself for this hubris involved in his success. I know of one outstanding tennis player, highly ranked in California for many years, who could not beat his father, a fifty-five-year-old professor. When he finally did, he said he lost something that was in fact more important to him than the tennis match.

But the reverse may also be true. That is, rather than succeeding in replacing the father, it seems more likely that he realizes that indeed he has not replaced the father as he saw the father from a childhood standpoint. At that time, the father was omnipotent, but in the new position, he must work hard; the father seemed to be in control of his world, but for him his powers are diminishing. Whichever way the dynamic works, the person cannot continue with the ego's ongoing construction of meaning as before. He is thrown back decisively on self-evaluation. Not only is he not what he thought he was, but his vision of what he was to become is at least partly illusory. So depression at this time represents a loss of an illusion of a future and confrontation with the paradox of this era: the prime of life is now bounded by inevitable loss and death. Add to this that the younger generation is saying, "Times are changing, and you are set in your ways. Also you have failed at certain key points. Now, if you will just bless us for taking over and showing you these insights, we can move ahead to solve problems you have not even thought of." Again, the inner dynamics call for a reexamination of one's developmental history, which has led one up to this point.

The urgency here is that one does not just sit and think about this after reading one's alumni magazine with particular attention to the obituary section. The necessity for thinking about this, and the turn inward, is right there confronting everyone in the middle years day after day. Contrary to Thomas Wolfe's famous phrase, it should be said, "You must go home again," in the sense that you must reconsider and reconstruct your personal past in the light of emergent new conditions.

The second syndrome is becoming less prominent as women become less identified with home and move toward the pattern described by the first syndrome. Nevertheless, it does describe a pattern for women who do choose to stay at home and those who are forced to do so. This may be more of a problem for a Barbara Bush than, say, a Hillary Clinton. For women, the so-called empty nest syndrome begins to appear alongside the emerging signs of the climacteric. For the man, this period may occur alongside his own struggles with depression and may be aggravated with regret that he did not spend more time with his children when they were home. On the other hand, this may be a "free at last" experience. As the old fellow said, "Life does not begin with conception or even with birth; it begins when the children leave home and the dog dies."

Renegotiating Relationships

In our contemporary era, the empty nest syndrome seems to be followed by the "glutted nest" syndrome, as daughter and son-in-law want to come home, move back in, and so forth, and the parents enter the "sandwich generation," where parenting never ends. We who are parents now must take care of our parents as well as our own adult children.

Assuming that parents do succeed in moving their children into larger society, they now must look at each other and rediscover who they are all over again. Marriage as life together must now be more or less radically renegotiated, remembering that the physical changes in a woman may be more decisive, and symptoms of menopause may be at least disturbing, if not actually requiring medical help. Considering that the indices of our society do not favor the aging process in women or men, the sexual aspect of marriage will have to be renegotiated. It is, of course, not true that the sexual desire declines after menopause. It actually may liberate sexual relations, since there may be greater ease and spontaneity at this time—that is, provided the husband can participate fully, since in most cases after fifty, male potency may decline, even though interest does not. One is reminded about the aging gentleman who was chasing a young woman around the table at a party, until he forgot why he was doing it.

These patterns in aging are designed to make us stop and take notice, to turn inward so we can turn outward in a new way with new resources. Failure to stop, take notice, and renegotiate the contract means entrenchment in established roles and overcompensation as old resources dry up. This is what Erikson calls the issue of generativity versus stagnation.

Consider the following case of mine. This woman's husband has made it hard for her to be a person in her own right. He is married to his profession (he is a physician), and he had left her at home and dominated and controlled her rather affluent life. In response, she became an intense mother and suffered overcompensation symptoms. That is, she used the climacteric to manipulate his attention, and when his sexuality declined, she pressed herself on him in order to gain vengeance. Neither one realized that the other one was the key to stagnation in a social role system. He worked obsessively, losing touch with his own humanity; she compensated by overdoing the role he had forced her into.

I was convinced that they did care about each other; however, they did not know how to give each other sufficient voice. They did not know how to talk about the situation so that they could renegotiate the marriage relationship. I was amazed that when I asked him if he had ever told her that he loved her, he replied, "Not for a long time." The key was that he thought that he was doing his best and was showing her that he did love her by his hard work and provision for her life, but he could not say he loved her. When he realized how much he wanted to tell her directly that he loved her and finally did so, she was astonished. She felt something strange was happening and asked him to repeat it several times. This was the beginning of their discovery of the care they had for each other, and renegotiation became possible.

The turn inward at the ego level means reassessing one's developmental history, discovering one's own voice, and using new resources to reenvision the future. In Levinson's language, what is involved is termination, individuation, and initiation: termination of the old self-stifling patterns of defeat, frustration, and guilt that bind one to the past; individuation, a Jungian term that can be succinctly stated in the phrase "becoming one's own person"; and initiation, which means drawing on new resources for constructing a future—not only one's own, but for subsequent generations. In general terms, this is what the doctor and his wife began to do.

Middle Years Stagnation

The significance of the Eriksonian way of setting up this period may now be clear. "Generativity versus stagnation" means that there is a decisive hiatus in the middle years. Middlescence, like adolescence, is a major developmental turning point. Powerful forces gathering strength and associations through the course of a lifetime make one resist change. A study done on some twenty men, some who were top executives and all members of the same church, showed that they were unable to move beyond their business or professional responsibilities, and yet gave evidence that those responsibilities were sapping their spiritual strength.[3] This is "the boiled frog syndrome"; it is possible to boil a live frog without its leaping from the pot if the heat is raised to the boiling point gradually and with sufficient discretion. However, devolution and stagnation are not destiny; the alternative is generativity.

Stagnation is not just a matter of having some bad habits that are hard to break. One way to characterize the inclination to stagnation, so that we can sense why it is such a powerful temptation, is to use the classic model of games, designed first by Eric Berne and later picked up by Thomas Harris in *I'm OK, You're OK* and discussed at some length in the earlier cited book by Tom Oden.[4]

In essence, over the years people build up unconscious drives that are working in one direction, an accumulation of unfinished business with any number of important people in their lives. But consciously at the ego level, they are working in an opposite direction. As the ego's control diminishes with age, the underlying conflict surfaces and becomes deeply stressful. The result is that intimate relationships (husband and wife, parent and child, siblings and relatives) get into double-binds of life-and-death significance.

One such game is, "See how hard I tried." Remember that games are established between closely related persons who are important to each other, so they lead to defenses against the recognition, acceptance, and regeneration of the other person. "See how hard I tried" is a game in which the husband takes care of his wife and works to achieve, but he does this in response to her ambitions and her pushing. At a deeper level, he wants her to take care of him. The mother stage is not surpassed; the feminine side is not incorporated. So he plays out his side of this game. She, on the other side, admires him only so long as he is achieving and looking powerful, but under the surface the one person she really admired was her father. He will go into his forties and fifties very tired and angry, and will even work toward a heart attack (which may, significantly, come at night, when he gets his wish, to please a Freudian psychiatrist) or ulcers in order to show how hard he tried. The net result is that she now has to take care of him because he is in some way or another disabled. Did he win? No. Both lost. This is a picture of stagnation because development is arrested by the double-bind.

I once worked with a minister who was a good preacher but had lost the strength of his voice and now could only whisper. His voice had been a strong masculine organ used effectively in preaching, and it called forth his wife's admiration. He was in other ways a small man, physically and in some mannerisms. What he really wanted was to regress to being cared for by a mother. He could not accept this consciously; therefore, after retirement he developed a symptom in which he lost his voice. He kept going, but said in effect, "See how hard I've tried." Again, this game ended in stagnation in which both lost.

Games can be played as well between parents and children. Here is a father who waits up for his daughter to come home and loudly criticizes her for coming in so late. She, on the other hand, stays out too late in order to get the criticism. Argument always ensues, and each goes to his or her room and slams the door. This is the result of a latent physical attraction between them. Without ever confronting it, father and daughter work out a socially acceptable neurotic pattern of interaction, but it is stagnating for each of them and for their relationship. The name of this game might be "Why can't you just love me?"

Stagnation can take place through denial and the deepening of vocational obsessions. Developmentally, the work axis has not been effectively resolved. This is usually accompanied by depression, obsessiveness, intensified dichotomous thinking, some paranoid feelings about work and love, and developing resentments. The name of this game might be, "You won't get the best of me!" This may be illustrated by a manager and owner of a small business who had a heart attack, but he could not cut back on activity because he feared that a younger colleague and the doctor were in collusion to get him out of the business. He went back to work too soon, worked too hard, and died. The situation reflected back to a competition he had with a younger brother that he had never resolved.

In other cases, overcompensation may drive one to rush to the opposite extreme. This is another form of stagnation. One may call the game, "I'm just as good as I ever was." Here age attempts to act young. A mother, jealous of her daughter, competes and tries to win her boyfriends, even goes to bed with her boyfriends at times. The film *The Graduate* made high drama of this possibility.

Here is a man who tries to make out with young women, sensing the decline of his powers. Often this is a nostalgia for an unfinished adolescence and never working out the love axes of his adolescent identity.

Middle Years Generativity

Even without the double-binding dynamics of stagnation, the advance of the middle years makes it evident that the negative side of human development is going to win in its battle against the ego. The ego now appears clearly as the tragic hero, destined to fail from its inception. This is not to eliminate the ego; rather, from this standpoint of the middle years, it may be possible to see the ego as "a truth-producing error" that is decisively called into transformation at this period of time in development.

The shift into generativity may be sudden and powerful, or gradual and emergent.

On the sudden side, consider the story of the founder of the Fuller Graduate School of Psychology, Lee Travis. A generation ago, he was one of the most highly esteemed psychologists in America. In one survey during the early part of his career, of all the hundreds of psychologists in America, he was ranked twelfth. Clearly he was widely known and widely respected. When he reached the age of fifty-nine, he discovered that a church was being built up on a hill behind his home. He went up to see what the building was all about. He said that it was a beautiful setting, but it was too bad that this was a "monument to a superstition." When the church was finished and the services began, he decided he would go up and just see what this was all about. As he stood outside he said, in his own words, "I got zapped." He went back a second time. He had to stay outside the first time because there were so many people in the church, but he went in the second time, and he "got zapped again." It completely transformed his approach to psychology and to therapy.

He is the only psychologist I have ever known who enjoyed working with suicidal patients. For them, he said, the issue was very clear, and he knew what to do to help them. I lectured at a ceremony in which he was the figure of honor, and he made the remark that in the early days, they threw Christians to the lions. Now, he said, they simply push them aside, saying they are regressed or brain-injured persons. But this particular "regressed or brain-injured person" was the founder of the only school of psychology in America accredited by the American Psychological Association and associated with a major theological seminary, a truly extraordinary tribute to Lee Travis. The main point here is that Travis underwent a radical transformation toward the end of the middle years, and it brought about a dramatic change in him that proved to be generative for several generations of graduate students in theology and psychology.

If instead the change is gradual and emergent, then what will happen to the ego in relationship to the psyche as a whole? The argument here is that it will move toward generativity in a typically Eriksonian sense. Generativity refers to the positive prospect for the ego during these middle years. For Erikson, as Don Browning puts it, generativity is the ethical center of the descriptive system that has become normative for development.[5]

This way of putting it recalls the discussion from the previous chapter on normativity in Fowler's model. It raises the question, "How does Erikson, Fowler, or Kohlberg commit the naturalistic fallacy and get away with it?" How do you get a value out of a fact without importing a value scheme covertly into the argument? Kohlberg once wrote an essay entitled "From *Is* to *Ought*: How to Commit the Naturalistic Fallacy and Get Away with It," but Piaget, who makes the same essential move, is most persuasive when he says essentially that what comes naturally as adaptation is adaptation to a "good" reality; indeed, adaptation itself is a part of that "good" reality.[6] The wider, more complex, and more intelligent the adaptation is, the better it is because this is intrinsic to the larger, good reality that is itself in a continuous process of becoming. In other words, value is tacitly inserted at the outset.

Browning's assertion seems to make a similar point for Erikson. Development of the Eriksonian ego is automatically "good" from the beginning as it develops a concern not only for itself but care for the ego development of upcoming generations.[7] Generativity is the stage in ego development when the welfare of future generations becomes an essential part of one's own adaptational concerns. Thus, the ego at this stage is the ethical center of an otherwise descriptive account of the life span.

To be generative is a response to an instinctual power expressed in the ego through the virtue of caring. Generativity sums up the unity and tension between what is archaic and what is teleological (that is, for the future of humanity both in and beyond the individual's own lifetime). The generative person must both set the standard for the future and reach the younger generation where they are with his or her own feelings and sensitivities derived from his or her past history. In this it is evident that the generativity struggle is the other side of the identity struggle. This is the oedipal/Electra situation now looked at from the standpoint of the adult involved. It is as much of a complex for the adult as it is for the younger person, but the complex struggle for the adult is an issue of generativity. Given the advancing demise of one's own life, the rising concern is how to bring up the next generation on the positive side of the ego tensions described in earlier stages. The answer to developmental entropy is the next generation and a confident love of the future and of the as-yet-unborn children of the time to come.

The psychological core of the generative person is "I-thou," an interpersonal relationality that crosses generational lines. It extends from one-to-one to the concern for all the great adult institutions of society. Here we see the generative person operating to build up those institutions that foster the phases in human development. Thus, the generative person is concerned with religion, law, theater, technology, ideology, marriage, and family, all institutions that support the virtues or the ego strengths of hope, will, purpose, competence, fidelity, and love. Generativity represents a synthesis between personal and interpersonal insight and public responsibility, between the developing person and the social and cultural institutions that foster human development on its positive side.

The model that Browning gives of an institution that is inherently generative is a mother nursing a child.[8] He sees this as the paradigm of creative ritualization. Reciprocal needs of two persons are met as they should be in all such institutions. It is a practical activity, yet it has symbolic meaning; it is highly personal, yet it exhibits a style characteristic of a much larger group; it heightens a sense of belonging and yet protects personal distinctiveness; it is playful yet formalized; it provides a relatively unambiguous context in which to satisfy needs or later to live out life's ambiguities. These characteristics that pertain to the mother with nursing child paradigm, Browning argues, should be applied to all of the other great institutions: religion, law, theater, and so forth. This is a helpful way of looking at generativity, the positive side of this period.

Cognition in Middle Years

On the cognitive side of this period, it is helpful to return to Fowler's model in which formal operations move from "dichotomizing" in young adults to "paradoxical-consolidative" as the middle years unfold. As Fowler points out, this multidimensional dialectical style of thinking rarely occurs before the age of thirty for much the same reason that Carl Jung said no one could study to be a therapist at the Jung Institute in Zurich who was under that age. That is, one simply has not lived long enough to incorporate irreversible losses at the mature ego level. However, it should be noted that, consistent with Fowler's roots in Piaget and Kohlberg, this level of cognitive competence has to be achieved; it is not an automatic consequence of reaching the middle years chronologically. Nevertheless, reaching the age of thirty is ordinarily the condition for such an achievement.

For this level of cognitive growth to become one's own style of thinking about oneself and one's world, it is argued that one must know suffering and loss, responsibility and failure, and the grief that is an inevitable part of having made irreversible commitments of life's energy. This negative or dark side of human life is present from the beginning, but only at the middle years does it become patently plain that patterns of ego defense against this realization are gradually collapsing and giving way to the inevitable and ultimate triumph of negation that lies ahead. Fowler's description of cognition at this time is helpful because it is a recognizable style of thought that demonstrates the effort of human intelligence to take account of its own inherent limits and yet construct a comprehensive and coherent account of reality that includes those limits.

This recalls a psychological limitation of Fowler's thought. The negative side of development is present from the beginning, so any comprehension of the whole life span should be at least dialectical from birth on. Thus, what we see in the middle years is a surfacing of what has been the case all along. It is this that makes Erikson's description so compelling, and brings Robert Coles to note the Hegelian character of Erikson's description of ego development.[9]

It is important to recognize that the human spirit has begun the struggle with negation from the first months of life; now, negation places its stamp on the form and pattern of intelligence itself. It becomes the very way that self-understanding seeks to embrace its own life—its meaning and its purpose. What surfaced very powerfully in adolescence now emerges gradually within the ego's fading world. It is the spirit's transformational power and pattern that has driven development forward to this phase of life, and because the dark side of development can no longer be ignored, it is the incredible resilience of the human spirit that comes forward to create coherence and meaning when the disappearance of the ego is clearly inevitable. At the cognitive level, dialectic and paradox prevail as the ultimately irrepressible human spirit seeks a comprehensive and meaningful solution.

Emergence of Opposites

The emergence of opposites is the hallmark of the middle years. In each instance, a balance is attained by looking and searching inwardly, finding and accepting in oneself "the other" or the latent opposite. This means that a tension will be set up, and some resolution will be found, and on the ego level the resolution will be the creation of the human spirit and will move one toward generativity or more toward stagnation if the resolution fails.

Carl Jung: Life and Thought

We need to go deeper into the structures and dynamics that guide and govern this period of the middle years. To do this, I will turn to C. G. Jung's view of the transformation of the ego. (Note that Jung is the psychologist for the middle years, partly because he worked out his theories on himself after he had attained the middle years. Until this time, he claimed, no one was old enough to understand the significance of his thought.)

Jung's route is not merely turning inward but going there; it is an inward journey that lasts for the rest of life. To take this journey is to look for meaning in one's life by going deeper inwardly and surfacing with a new sense of self that transforms and transcends the ruptures and dichotomies in the ego of the middle years. To place Jung in context, we might say that analogous to the way in which grammar arises at about age four to give order to the plurality and diversity of language, and the way in which logic arises at about age seven to give order to thought, so now there is at least potentially an emergent order that might be called a grammar of psychological wholeness, "the Self." This allows the maturing person to give coherence to the vast array of his experiences and accrued assumptions about the self, all in the light of impending decline and death. This emergent order, as Jung sees it, is the archetype of the Self.

Jung's view of psychic life is larger than any psychological perspective we have examined so far. Thus, the significance of his thought extends uniquely into the scientific perspective. Since his explorations reach into and are intentionally related to physics and cosmology, it is useful to examine his significance in part from that perspective. This will also help to separate him from the esoteric and cultic perspectives into which his thought is sometimes drawn.

Jung's perspective on psychic life is a kind of field theory. James Clerk-Maxwell's contradiction of the mechanical shape of Newton's world opened the way for a field theory understanding not only of the natural but also of the human sciences. The consequence in the physical sciences was eventually Einstein's theory of relativity. The emphasis in Jung is on field theory when the field is characterized by multiple causality, relationality, and opposites in tension at the level of the collective unconscious. Deeper than the personal unconscious to which Freudian and neo-Freudian thought is confined, Jung explored interactional patterns of archetypical proportions inherited from the evolutionary history of the species. Explanation for Jung was multiplex and based on the psyche's inherent drive toward balanced wholeness.

The ideas of order out of chaos, and chaos theory in general, are in agreement with Jung's theories. Order out of chaos is an alternative to the second law of thermodynamics developed mathematically by Ilya Prigogine, who won a Nobel Prize in 1977 for showing that in open systems, entropy can become the progenitor of a new order. This advocacy of spontaneous self-organization in physics also points toward the scientific relevance of Jung's theories regarding the spontaneous emergence of coherent orders of meaning and selfhood.

In the anthropic principle, strong or weak forms, one can recognize that in the evolution of intelligent human life, the universe is becoming conscious of itself. This advocates a significant shift in how we ordinarily think, urging on us an advance in the expanding magnitude of consciousness, which again is a Jungian principle. The aim in Jungian therapy and the larger Jungian goal of individuation is not primarily to get a right answer or to resolve buried conflicts in the personal unconscious. Rather, it is to increase consciousness to the point of including the history of the species and its place in the universe. Jung's view of the psyche was as large as the history of the universe, and he is the only major psychologist to have written a book with a physicist of international acclaim in an effort to reach that goal.[10]

These three developments in the physical sciences seem to point toward the great potential in Jungian theories of psychic development. If we add the neurological sciences, we can note that recent developments in neurology make it necessary to think from the whole to the parts, as well as from the parts to the whole.[11] This is one of the major differences between Freud and Jung. Although both worked in both directions, Jung stressed the preeminence of wholeness, Freud the preeminence of the analytical parts. Also at a neurological level, Anthony Stevens's *Archetypes: A Natural History of the Self* contends that recent studies in neurobiology and ethology provide confirming evidence for the existence of Jungian-type archetypes that have evolved through natural selection.[12] If archetypes have evolved through natural selection, then Jung has been a Darwin of the mind who looked for homologous symbols cross-culturally and effectively argued that these are "habits" of adaptation developed over several generations to meet inevitable recurrent struggles of the psyche. Victor Turner, the well-known Chicago anthropologist, confirmed the explanatory value of Jungian archetypes, referring to "Great Mother" in some of his later writings.

Because of the uniqueness of Jung's thought and his towering influence among religiously interested psychologists and psychologically interested theologians and biblical scholars, it is important to examine his personal history as well as his theories. Indeed, the two are so closely linked it is much more difficult to understand his theory apart from his personal history.

Carl Gustaf Jung (1875–1961) was named after his grandfather, professor of medicine at the University of Basel.[13] Young Carl was the oldest child and only surviving son of a Swiss Reformed pastor. His parents had considerable marital difficulties. Various nervous disorders troubled his mother; his father was moody and apparently rather unlikable. The parents slept apart, and Carl shared a bedroom with his father. As he later recorded it, the little boy had many wonderful dreams, which he later recognized to be of archetypical proportions. He was torn professionally and could not decide among medicine, anthropology, archaeology, and the humanities. With the help of his dreams, from which he took guidance, there is a sense in which he ended up doing all of these together. As he went through medical school (where he was a brilliant student), he spent his spare time digging into philosophy and humanistic studies, and eventually developed a kind of archeology of the soul.

He became a psychiatrist at Burghölzli Clinic in Zurich and practiced for some time before he ever heard of Freud. His relationship with Freud led to a powerful friendship and eventually an equally powerful estrangement. He broke with Freud on the issues of symbolism, religion, pansexuality, and eventually the structure of the psyche. He discovered a deeper dimension of psychological organization, the other side of the psyche from Erikson and Freud: the collective unconscious (see Figure 12.1).

Most developmentalists focus on the ego, but Jung was concerned about the transformation of the whole personality, including the ego. This makes his work inherently religious. He said that no therapeutic success could be achieved after the age of thirty without the person's becoming religious. In a famous BBC interview series entitled "Face to Face," which recounted his life and work, he is asked at the end, "Do you believe in God?" He replied, "I do not believe in God. I *know*."

Figure 12.1. Jungian Model of the Psyche.

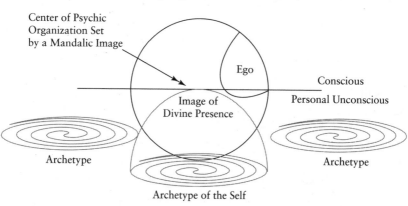

Jung's Personal History

Jung explained in his autobiography that his theory and practice came more from his self-understanding than from any other source. His turning points were often dreams, as one might expect from one who took the inward journey to its limits as Jung attempted to do.

The first example takes place at age three or four. It is his terrifying dream of an underground ritual phallus. Like a giant worm, it sat on a throne in an underground chamber. On top it had a single eye that stared motionlessly to the light. Just as he sees this huge thing loom up before him, he hears his mother's voice cry out, "That is the man-eater!" Overwhelmed with terror, he wakes up and later associates his mother's words with his having earlier been frightened by a Jesuit priest, a man dressed in black cape who, coming along a path toward Jung, caused the boy to run upstairs to hide under a beam in the attic.

Jung connects this to primal religious rituals: the transubstantiation in the mass, the eating of the body and blood of Christ, the God-man. Also sexuality and spirituality are linked, and sex is incorporated into a religious rite. Phallus is not so much linked to sexuality as to, *phalos,* which in Jung's view means "light," "shining," the eye looks up to the light, defining the spiritual meaning of sexuality. Even if it was terrifying for the little boy, the religious meaning seemed most powerful as Jung looked back on it.

Quite a dream for a three-year-old boy. It was so powerful that he could not forget it, and it made all his superficial instruction in Christianity from his father and his church seem superficial and irrelevant. In his own mind, he kept asking, "What about that underground thing?"

It is not surprising that it should make such an impact; recall that ages three to five is the time when imagination runs on high and nightmares have the power of reality. It is the deep-running significance of the content and the endurance of its impact that so impressed Jung.

A second turning point in which his theory was significantly influenced by his life's events occurred when he engaged as a little boy in certain ritual practices, quite unaware that he was replicating the rituals practiced by the Australian aborigines; also he used images of the early Greek gods. As Jung entered school age, about seven to eleven years old, he carved a little wooden man out of the end of his ruler, gave him an oblong blackish stone, and placed a scroll of paper with some writing on it in a pencil box and hid it in the attic. Why these objects? At the age of thirty-five, Jung read about the Australian aborigines and the primal symbols of the Greeks. In the aboriginal context, the churinga is an object of wood or stone considered sacred by the tribes of central Australia. It has an elliptical shape and bears designs. It is believed to represent either a spiritual devil or the embodied spirit of a totemic ancestor, and it is regarded as secret.

Asclepias, the element of Greek mythology in Jung's practice rituals, was the physician hero of Greek mythology, sometimes worshipped as the god of healing. A Telesphoros is a mini-God, a little cloaked god of the ancient world who stands on the monuments of Asclepias and reads to him, deciphering his text from a scroll. These observations, together with observing archetypal symbols in his patients' symptoms, compelled Jung to believe that there is a deeper untapped level of psychic reality. All of this is preliminary to the development of his theory. But before going into that, turn back to his autobiography.

In his twelfth year, Jung was knocked down by a schoolmate on his way home from school. He did not like school because his teacher had not appreciated his genius, believing that he had copied essays from someone else because they were too good. Embarrassed at school and then knocked down by a schoolmate and bumping his head on a curb, he said to himself, as he passed out, "Now I do not have to go to school anymore." Thereafter, whenever he tried to study, he had fainting spells, until he overheard his father say one day, "I don't know what will become of him. I lost what little I had. If he can't earn his own way, I don't know what will happen." Upon hearing this, Jung was motivated to get to work. He went to the library, started studying, stuck it out through three fainting spells, and finally began to feel better. "I am myself," he thought, as if a wall of mist were behind him. "There is an authority in me," he says. He now knew what a neurosis was: an unconscious preference for the pain of the neurotic symptom over the pain of freedom.

I must make reference to one other image, which depicts in a single picture Jung's approach and attitude to the church. He was at one time overwhelmed with the need to allow himself to experience a vision. The vision was that there was a cathedral and God was sitting on the throne (toilet, that is) above the cathedral. He let go a great turd and crushed the cathedral. Jung fought this thought and tried not to think it, but when he did not think it, it made him ill. It is easy enough to see this as aggression against his father and the institutional church. On the other side, it is important to see this opening up of Jung's relationship to God in the future, breaking through the ecclesiastical order that from Jung's standpoint was closing him off from the presence of God.

Now let us turn back to his overcoming the neurosis. The "I," which is "I am myself," which Jung affirms, is important, since he calls this his

Number 1, the equivalent of the ego in our model. The unconscious, personal and collective, and all its root symbolism is his Number 2. This is not a dissociation but an interplay operative in all persons, he argued. But not all persons give Number 2 freedom, as Jung did, to express itself. Jung felt his mother had the same duality, since her Number 2 was somber, imposing, and unquestionably authoritative. A later dream confirmed that Number 1 was the light, and Number 2 followed it like a shadow cast by the light against the mist. Numbers 1 and 2 should be kept in continual interplay from the Jungian standpoint. Like the ego and the archetype, both are necessary, and, in refutation of Freud who wanted ego to be all in all, neither should be allowed to engulf the other.

Following his student days, Jung's dreams helped him determine the direction of his career. Eventually he went into psychiatry and finally met with Freud. He spent 1907 through 1913 with Freud. When they first met, they talked for fifteen hours continuously. Jung was the crown prince of the movement, but when he broke from Freud, Freud reportedly fainted and Jung went into a profound depression. Jung's way out of the depression was through it, so he began to work on himself and with clients, asking himself what was really the basic myth by which he lived. Since he could not believe in the traditional Christian myth, he sought his own. He began to emerge from the darkness about 1918–1919, at the end of World War I. During this time, he was practicing psychotherapy.

Part of Jung's own therapy, by which he tried to extricate himself from his depression, was drawing, mainly elaborate circles with rectangles in them, which seemed to satisfy some sense of his selfhood. Frustrated one day, he drew one that burst open at the sides, and he realized that he was drawing cryptograms that had an archaic origin. He came upon *Secret of the Golden Flower,* a book on oriental religions, and other writings of other religions that disclosed the connection between the mandala he had drawn and its origins.[14]

"Mandala" means, according to Mircea Eliade, "sacred place."[15] It was drawn in the sand or on the ground in ancient Tibetan religions as an image of the world or cosmos. A cross was put in the middle of the world or the universe, and this was the place where theophonies or hierophonies would take place. It is the place where heaven and earth come together, the place where the temple should be built; hence, it is a symbolic pantheon, a sacred city, a consecrated space, and God will continue to appear there. This is the origin of the archetype of the Self, which, in evolving through the history of the human race, has moved from something described externally to something that appears internally in psychic organization.

Then Jung had his own archetypical dream of the Self emerging at the core of his psyche. This was the event that revealed to him the goal of his intrapsychic search and the beginning of the end of his depression. He had reached the center; he could not go beyond it. The dream was as follows:

> I found myself in a dirty, sooty city. It was night, and winter, and dark, and raining. I was in Liverpool. With a number of Swiss—half a dozen—I walked through the dark streets. I had the feeling that we were coming up from the harbor, and that the real city was actually up above, on the cliffs. We climbed up there. It reminded me of Basel, where the market is down below and then you go up through the Totengässchen ("Alley of the Dead"), which leads to a plateau above and so to the Petersplatz and the Peterskirche. When we reached the plateau, we found a broad square dimly illuminated by street lights, into which many streets converged. The various quarters of the city were arranged radially around the square. In the center was a round pool, and in the middle of it a small island. While everything round about was obscured by rain, fog, smoke, and dimly lit darkness, the little island blazed with sunlight. On it stood a single tree, a magnolia, in a shower of reddish blossoms. It was as though the tree stood in the sunlight and was at the same time the source of light. My companions commented on the abominable weather, and obviously did not see the tree. They spoke of another Swiss who was living in Liverpool, and expressed surprise that he should have settled here. I was carried away by the beauty of the flowering tree and the sunlit island, and thought, "I know very well why he has settled here." Then I awoke.

> On one detail of the dream I must add a supplementary comment: the individual quarters of the city were themselves arranged radially around a central point. This point formed a small open square illuminated by a larger street lamp, and constituted a small replica of the island. I knew that the "other Swiss" lived in the vicinity of one of these secondary centers.

> This dream represented my situation at the time. I can still see the grayish-yellow raincoats, glistening with the wetness of the rain. Everything was extremely unpleasant, black and opaque—just as I felt then. But I had had a vision of unearthly beauty, and that was why I was able to live at all. Liverpool is the "pool of life." The "liver," according to an old view, is the seat of life—that which "makes to live."

This dream brought with it a sense of finality. I saw that here the goal had been revealed. One could not go beyond the center. The center is the goal, and everything is directed toward that center. Through this dream I understood that the self is the principle and archetype of orientation and meaning. Therein lies its healing function. For me, this insight signified an approach to the center and therefore to the goal [see Figure 12.2].[16]

Note that the mandala is ethically neutral, as are all structures of grammar and logic. To illustrate this, recognize that a swastika, the symbol of Hitler's Third Reich, is also a mandala. Thus, there is no prescribed necessity that the god who emerges at the center of the mandala be a gracious god or convey the truth about persons. Jung's system is amoral; human wholeness built around this structure is neither good nor bad. In the same way that grammar or logic are amoral, the mandala is an amoral "grammar" or "logic" of the self.

Figure 12.2. Mandala Structure.

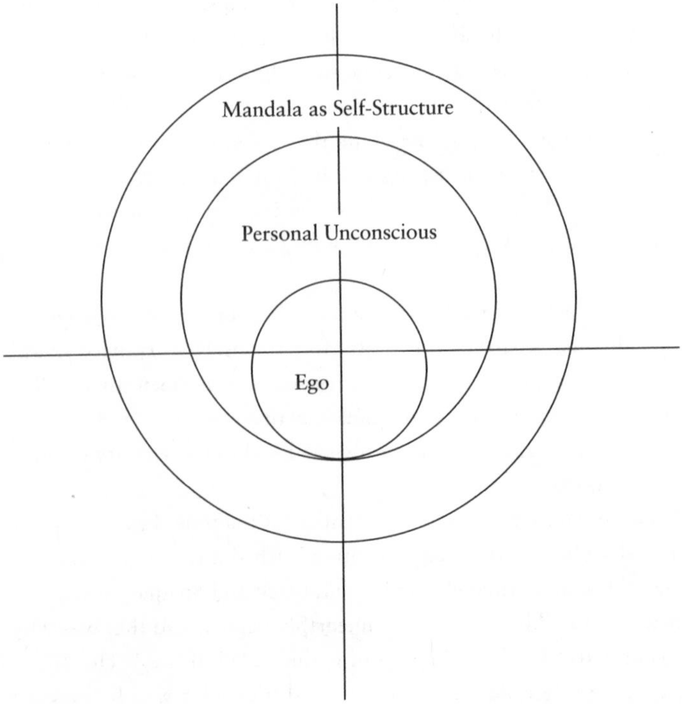

Mandala as Self-Structure

Personal Unconscious

Ego

Jung's Theory

There are five basic principles that can be set forth as an introduction to Jung's theory:

1. A fixed libido or energy quantum. Jung believed that we are endowed at birth with a certain quantity of psychic energy. It can be transformed and displaced, but it cannot be destroyed.

2. Enantiodromia, the law of opposites. The psyche as a whole drives toward balance or equilibrium between opposites—for example, the balance and equilibrium between conscious and unconscious, persona and shadow, anima and animus, and others.

3. The overall drive of psychic life toward wholeness. There is, in other words, a purposiveness in psychic formation that extends beyond causality. The future orients us toward wholeness, which exceeds any analysis of the past or the subparts of the psyche.

4. Equilibrium. This is sought by way of dreams; ultimately it is the image of the mandala that establishes equilibrium for the psyche. The power that moves us toward equilibrium is Jung's definition of "spirit," and spirit is understood as transformational in character, creating a differentiated unity, which establishes equilibrium.

5. Jung's introduction of a deeper region of the psyche called the collective unconscious or the objective psyche.

Archetypes are the primordial form of the psychic. They are an inherited potential for reconstructing solutions to present problems on the basis of the archaic past. These are perceived intrapsychically as pictures or images of basic instincts that are awakened through various encounters with the current external world. The image of the Great Mother, for instance, is occasioned by the encounter with one's mother and types of mothers in one's daily life.

The archetypes remain unknown and unknowable in themselves; indeed they are too powerful for us to see directly. There, we can "see" only images of the archetypes, with the images constructed out of the personal unconscious. The archetypes are like magnetic fields; when they are awakened, they often draw associated images to themselves with great power. Thus, "Great Mother" draws symbols, images, and other materials associated with "mother" into its field of influence.

When an archetype is overactive, it upsets the inherent drive toward equilibrium in the psyche, and it becomes the core of a complex. It takes on a life of its own and disturbs the ego's capacity to negotiate with the external environment. Thus, a "mother complex" can arrest development because the drawing power is too great to be balanced out in the psychic economy.

Jung's theory of symbolism and expansionist interpretations of dreams is an especially important aspect of how the archetypes influence the psyche. The power of symbol for the psyche depends on its capacity to unite or hold together opposites. The more extreme the opposition is, the greater is the power of the symbol. The psyche is continually at work to bring about symbols, images, and myths that will deal with ultimate existential dichotomies, such as life and death, good and evil, divine and human, male and female. The process of individuation is one in which many proximate images and symbols are employed to move one toward full equilibrium of these great opposing forces in one's psychic life. The process of individuation is moved forward by our psychic power, the human spirit, to resolve opposites in this fashion.

For example, here is a nun who is aging, and she is in Jungian analysis. She dreams that she is bound hand and foot, lying face down in a stream of water, slowly drowning. Then she realizes that she need only roll over, which she can do even while she is still bound. Now looking upward, she floats down the stream with confidence and release. Her bonds are her aging. She cannot do all that she wants to do, and the flow of life is killing her. If she looks upward, turning to God, what was killing her becomes gracious. The symbol releases energy into her psyche because she now does not fight to stay alive. The dream is realistic; it does not unbind her, but it holds bondage and freedom in a single picture in which an image of death is transformed into an image of life.

Another example is John Sanford's interpretation of Jacob's wrestling with the angel at Jabbok.[17] In Jungian terms, Jacob is wrestling with his shadow side: his guilt and fear at confronting his brother Esau. He wrestles until dawn and will not let the dark angel go until he blesses Jacob. The angel gives him a new name, no longer Jacob but Israel; and now, like Oedipus, he limps as a symbol of one who walks between two worlds. To wrestle through to one's wholeness is in Jungian terms to wrestle with God. This is psychologically illuminating, but not theologically helpful, since it reduces holiness to human wholeness.

The release of psychic energy into the system through this symbolic resolution has a positive purpose. It is not just solving a problem; it is moving a person toward wholeness, which can include the resolution to all the great existential binds in one's life. In other words, the psyche is drawn forward by the future as much as it is concerned with constructing resolutions to conflicts in the past.

The classic opposition that Jung thought needed to occur early in the individuation process, but not until after age thirty, was male-female. Each developing ego must find its sexual identity in the preceding years. But each psyche has in it both male and female aspects. Thus the developing female ego needs to discover and appropriate its contrasexual side, the animus, during the middle years; the developing male ego needs to discover and appropriate the anima, the feminine side of the personality. In earlier development, for example, the anima within the male drives him to relate to women in his environment, but in the middle years he needs to appropriate inwardly his own feminine side and allow the psyche to generate symbols and construct imagery that will bring the male and female sides of the psyche together in an equilibration without nullifying the sexual identity of the ego. In terms of classical mythology, the elevation of the beautiful Psyche into the pantheons of the gods alongside Eros is an account of the equilibration of male and female, which repeatedly recurs in terms of one's own personal imagery.

In the woman, as well as in the man, the equilibration takes place symbolically. Ann Ulanov provides this illustration of how one phase of individuation process occurred in one of her cases.[18] Here the woman cannot extricate herself to be fully her feminine self because of entangling relationships with both her mother and her father. In the dream, she and her male counterpart, representing the male side of herself, were swimming, and she got out of the water. But he dove deeply and brought up a cure for an incurable disease. He brought the cure to her and kissed her, saying, "I will love you forever." It is notable in Ulanov's analysis that the mother died of cancer, and her father's zodiac sign was Cancer. This is significant not because of astrological reasons but because of what she believed about herself. Implicitly the male figure in the dream frees her from the "disease" that pertains between her and her parents. He does this by giving her a deep, liberating image of male-female unity, anima and animus.

The ultimate aim of symbolism is transformation of the whole psyche by a self-symbol mandala structure that aims toward individuation. The key feature of the mandala is that it integrates polar opposites of existential proportions. Brought to the surface in one's life, these opposites are recognized and held in tension through symbols and images.

In the therapeutic process, preconscious images are made conscious to the person through a process that Jung called "active imagination," his alternative to free association in the Freudian school. The idea was that persons close their eyes, imagine something at a hypnogogic level, and allow the image to lead them. As the image leads them, they track it, and the move will be toward something that must be dealt with that stands in the way of wholeness or something that will open up personal wholeness to the individual.

When the numinous image of the Self finally appears, it is experienced as "a god," integrating personality and combining opposites in what is called a "mysterium conjunctionis." For Jung, whoever the god is, he or she will represent the Self. Every "god," then, is a symbol of the Self archetype. However, completeness or wholeness always implies imperfection; "Christ" may be a symbol of Self, and as such will appear balanced by Satan. Here one might even argue that Jung, as opposed to Erikson, is a better interpreter of Luther, whose faith held titanic opposites in paradoxical tension—at the same time justified and sinner, dead and alive, and so on.

Implicit in the process by which the mandala emerges in an image of the Self (and thereby the psyche is transformed) is the decentering of the ego. The significance of this decentering of ego and recentering on Self is never fully developed through the whole of one's life.

The archetype of wholeness is represented symbolically in the psyche long before the middle years. This is demonstrated by Rhoda Kellogg's work with children's art.[19] As a Jungian, she described the evolution of children's drawings of people as moving from large circles to just adding two stick legs on the side and two eyes in the circle, and only gradually filling in the body.

I was first studying this material when my daughter Tami was very small. Reviewing my notes, I noticed that she would watch me draw and, as I would swing a circle to begin a sketch, she, acting like someone awakened to a latent potential, started drawing circles and calling them "moons." I tell her that this is the origin of her "lunacy," but Kellogg would see this as a primordial sign of psychic wholeness emerging as early as eighteen months.

This connects with the research on the face material in an interesting way. After a while, Tami drew two eyes in the circle, and nothing else. This is indicative, since the minimal image of a face to trigger the smiling response in children is a circle with two eyes. In fact, Jolande Jacobi, another Jungian, argues in agreement with Jung that "the face" is an archetype of wholeness, following Justyn Martyr, who saw that even in the face is etched the cross of Christ.[20] In other words, the face is a symbol of the archetype of the self, the wholeness, the place where God will appear—as in Jesus' becoming the Face of God for us.

One further theme must be discussed before we turn to a theological discussion: Jung's unique treatment of time. One especially notable feature of Jung's thought is that all archetypes are in themselves timeless and may appear in different symbolic forms at different chronological times during life. That is, since Piaget has shown us that chronological time and Euclidean space are constructs of the ego and not necessitated in the final analysis by any external reality, it is all the more feasible to suspect that there may be other views of time experienced by the ego as timelessness or, in Jung's term, "synchronistic." The definition of synchronicity is an "acausal meaningful coincidence" that transcends the ego's boundaries of inside and outside, space and time, and at the same time is meaningful within the ego's constructs of everyday life.

Jung's familiar example is the story of the woman who, at her father's deathbed, saw a flock of yellow birds fill the trees outside her father's window. It was so stunning, unanticipated, and unrepeated that she never forgot the image. Years later when her husband, who had a weak heart, went to visit his doctor, she saw for the first time again a flock of yellow birds outside in the trees, and she knew that her husband had had a heart attack on the way to the doctor, and died. A telephone call confirmed her assumption. Jung's view of what it means, beyond the coincidence, is that it is a balancing out of life and death in the context, albeit mysterious, of the whole or totality.

My own experience of this type of synchronicity occurred in Bremen, Germany, when I was returning home from Geneva. I had to ship my Volkswagen from Bremen and, in order to do this, I had to take it to a particular shipping company. Before doing so, however, I had to visit someone in Hamburg. So I drove up from Geneva to Amsterdam, leaving barrels of material there because I would be taking the boat home to New York from Amsterdam. Then I drove the car across to Bremen, figured out where I would have to leave it, and drove on further to Hamburg. I saw the person there, stayed overnight, and drove back the next day, presumably in time to ship my car. My plan was to catch the four o'clock train from Bremen to Amsterdam, or I would miss the boat.

Everything went according to my expectations until I got stuck in the Bremen traffic. It took two or three changes of a light to move ahead through a single intersection. Finally I reached a red light where I was the next car to go, and the time was 3:40. I had to drop off the car and get back to the train station in twenty minutes, because I had been warned that the train to Amsterdam was never late. My prayers were now in great earnest.

As I sat there, someone in a little blue Volkswagen across the intersection to my right began to honk at me. I did not know what he was honking about, so when the light changed, I went ahead. I had traveled about twenty feet when he pulled around behind me, jumped out of his car, came up to my window, and said, "Do you want to ship your car?" I was stunned. I did want to ship my car, and I had run out of time. "Yes!" I said, and he hurriedly jumped in his car saying, "Follow me" (all this in perfect English, mind you). So off we went, roaring down a side street. I did not know where he was taking me, but it never occurred to me that this could be a carjacking. I followed him, and he took me to the shipping company, in fact, the right shipping company, because it turned out that I had planned to go to the wrong one. Furthermore, he was the associate manager of the shipping company. I told him, "Look, I've got to catch a four o'clock train. But how did you know?" He just laughed and said, "Here, fill out this form; I'll get a cab for you so you can get back to the train." And sure enough, he did—and I did. I got back to the station just before four o'clock, and still had to pick up my ticket. By the time I got to the train platform, it was about 4:10. There was no one there except one person, and I thought that surely I had missed the train. But on this particular day, the crack train that was "always on time" came in about fifteen minutes late. So I got on and rode to Amsterdam—and asked myself what had happened.

This was not a matter of life or death, but of providence and grace in answer to prayer. It is an important example of the transformation and transfiguration of synchronicity, making the impersonal concept of synchronicity into a personal reality. The suggestion that God can use, or not use, the archetype to answer prayer leads into the necessity for making some basic theological observations on Jung of both a critical and a constructive nature.

Jung and Theology

As we turn to the theological perspective on Jung, we should be reminded of Jung's increasing popularity in the marketplace, in part because his psychology overlaps religion. Morton Kelsey, Walter Wink, Roy Fairchild, John Sanford, and others want to reinterpret theological understandings in Jungian terms. But I am much more interested in reinterpreting Jung in the light of theology. Methodologically, this is to preserve the ontological priority of theology over psychology in the Chalcedonian formulation. Many substantive issues are at stake here if Jung is to contribute significantly to our theological understanding of persons.

First, Jung has made a very important suggestion regarding the shape of a lifetime. He has said that since the center of the personality is timeless, it is more accurate to envision development not as a linear progression of stages (Erikson), a hierarchy (Fowler), or even a kind of bell-shaped curve (Pruyser),[21] but as a circumambulation around the center. Recognition of the center involves the transformation of ego, such that the mandala structure displaces the ego as the center of the personality, keeping all aspects of the personality in equilibrium. So far, so good. But then we must move to the larger theological context in which human wholeness is to be understood.

Second, Jung tends to see human wholeness as the ultimate reality. As a result, he confuses the orders of being and knowing. The archetype, as a structural reality, is on a par with grammar in speech and logic in intelligence. As a result, it is a structure by which one comes to know one's personal wholeness; it is not a structure of being. The further confusion this creates is evident in Jung's essay taken from *Aion* concerning Christ as the symbol of the archetype of the Self.[22] For Jung, the basic order of ultimate reality is the Self archetype, for which Christ is a symbol. This puts Christ on an ontological par with Satan, the Christian symbol for evil, which is already surprising. But, then, Jung said he never understood revelation,[23] and transcendence for him was only transcendental, that is, an a priori structure of mind that conditions knowing. Thus, his view of Christ is a direct contradiction to Christian self-understanding where Christ is the one in whom all things cohere, because it was through him that all things were made. The archetype, then, is at best an epistemological approach to the nature and being of Christ in whom all things cohere. This criticism is not merely a Christian bias. It is in keeping with Jung's self-limitation to epistemology, and it is confirmed by Mircea Eliade,[24] the great historian of religion, that all the patterns in comparative religions may seem to be preparatory for the revelation of God in Jesus Christ; or, in language used here, they are magnificent strivings of the human spirit, moving to the outer boundaries of human existence, but one cannot get further unless one is met from the other side in the revelation of God in Jesus Christ. My point is not to administer a Christian put-down, but to say that as a scientist, Jung has radically misunderstood the data he sought to explain.

Third, what I just said still may not be sufficient to differentiate Jung's work from Christian understandings of human nature, so we must now note that for Jung, the presence of God and human wholeness are directly linked; it is through developing human wholeness that one draws closer to God. However, in Christian self-understanding, it is precisely in the weakness and brokenness of human existence that God comes to us. It is often when we are least whole within ourselves that God is most evident.

The Christian aim is not psychic wholeness, but holiness brought into our lives, whatever our fragmented condition, by the only One who is truly holy.

What then shall we have? Breakdowns to bring on the presence of God? In Paul's language, shall we sin that grace may abound? Of course not, because the presence of God does beget a sound mind; indeed, it is so good that one does not even want to sin any more. Holiness is not keeping the commandments; it is making them unnecessary. The Spirit of Christ will bring forth the sanity and sanctity of holiness, but psychic wholeness is not a precondition for this. Psychic wholeness is not a condition for the experience of God, nor is it any guarantee that one is closer to the God revealed in Jesus Christ. Another way to put it is that God's personal nature far exceeds, and is not contingent on, the impersonal structure of psychic wholeness.

Fourth, although Jung affirms transformation of the ego, he does not take sufficient account of the role of the mediator. That is, transformation of the ego may take place in several ways, but whatever way it takes place, the transformed person will bear the marks of the mediator. If one is transformed by a Marxist cell group, one becomes Marxist; if the mediator is Buddha, one becomes a Buddhist.

In Jung's thought, the mediating reality is the archetype of the Self, which seeks to equilibrate all aspects of the personality. Perfect individuation, the goal of the Jungian journey, ends in perfect equilibration. As if to exemplify this, Jung said he had a vision of his wife after she had died (he had many such visions), and she was perfectly equilibrated. True or not, the vision displays Jung's goal for human existence.

By contrast, Christian self-understanding drives toward the goal of giving love sacrificially with integrity after the pattern of Christ. This means the willing breaking of one's wholeness potential for the sake of another, a free choice that has nothing to do with oppression because it is an act of integrity and everything to do with Christ's free choice to go to the cross as an act of love. In this, a person recognizes that a lifetime is an incomplete act of love by God toward God's creation, and in such a realization life is transformed into love as one permits God's act to be completed in oneself. This, of course, may have little or nothing to do with individuation as a final aim in life.

Fifth, although I could point out that Jung is essentially a gnostic and does not understand the complexity of the Christian doctrine of evil he has drawn on, it is of some importance to make positive use of Jung's understanding of the psyche. Thus, in the earlier reference to Erikson's treatment of Luther, the emergence of the archetype of the Self might improve on Erikson's understanding of the ego as a basis for interpreting the great antitheses in Luther and theology.

Another great theologian, Hildegaard von Bingen (1098–1179), the first woman to be called a theologian by the Roman Catholic church, also used the mandala structure as a foundation for her theology.[25] She had visions of powerful, revelatory significance. She would describe them, and they were then drawn by one of her colleagues. Her theology then came forth as an interpretation of her visions.

Some replications of her visions are in Figure 12.3. They are an excellent example, I believe, of the transfiguration of the mandala archetype. Here Christ's being uses but far transcends the archetype as a way of knowing and refers us back to God's person, through whom all things (including archetypes) were made, and who is yet alive in and for each one of us in our own particularity.

Conversion and Spiritual Life

Many of the great conversions I noted at the beginning of the chapter took place during these crucial middle years. In these instances the pact with God was to permit God to complete his act of love toward his creation through them, for their redemption and for the redemption of the part of creation they influenced.

Pascal was thirty-one when he had his great night of fire in which he moved from "the god of the philosophers" and mathematics to "the God of Abraham, Isaac, and Jacob." Wesley was thirty-five when he had his Aldersgate experience, and his "heart was strangely warmed." St. Ignatius was thirty when he hung up his sword and had several mystical experiences of Christ, and was thirty-three when he laid the foundation for the Jesuit order. St. Teresa went into an Augustinian convent when she was sixteen, but did not consummate her union with God until she was sixty. Calvin's conversion, more inferred sometimes than explicitly developed, occurred when he was thirty. Augustine was thirty-two; so was Constantine.

At the other end of this period, Tolstoi was fifty-one when he was converted. Lee Travis, discussed earlier in the chapter, was sixty. What is taking place is that the ego finally comes unbuckled and enables one to free the longing in oneself for the Spirit of God and for the relationship to God. No one else describes the gracious overpowering of the ego by the Divine Spirit better than C. S. Lewis. And no other account makes it clearer that the experience of God is quite independent of an achievement of human wholeness. It happened first on a bus and then while sitting in

Figure 12.3. Transfigured Mandala Image.

his room at the age of thirty-one. In the light of Lewis's place in human development, read again his compelling account:

> I became aware that I was holding something at bay, or shutting something out. Or, if you like, that I was wearing some stiff clothing, like corsets, or even a suit of armor, as if I were a lobster. I felt myself being, there and then, given a free choice. I could open the door or keep it shut; I could unbuckle the armor or keep it on. Neither choice was presented as a duty; no threat or promise was attached to either, though I knew that to open the door or to take off the corset meant the incalculable. The choice appeared to be momentous but it was also strangely unemotional. I was moved by no desires or fears. In a sense I was not moved by anything. I chose to open, to unbuckle, to loosen the rein. I say, "I chose," yet it did not really seem possible to do the opposite. On the other hand, I was aware of no motives. You could argue that I was not a free agent, but I am more inclined to think that this came nearer to being a perfectly free act than most that I have ever done. . . .
>
> [Then later in his room in Magdalen College:] You must picture me alone in that room in Magdalen, night after night, feeling, whenever my mind lifted even for a second from my work, the steady, unrelenting approach of Him whom I so earnestly desired not to meet. That which I greatly feared had at last come upon me. In the Trinity Term of 1929 I gave in, and admitted that God was God, and knelt and prayed: perhaps, that night, the most dejected and reluctant convert in all England. I did not then see what is now the most shining and obvious thing; the Divine humility which will accept a convert even on such terms. The Prodigal Son at least walked home on his own feet. But who can duly adore that Love which will open the high gates to a prodigal who is brought in kicking, struggling, resentful, and darting his eyes in every direction for a chance of escape? The words *compelle intrare*, compel them to come in, have been so abused by wicked men that we shudder at them; but, properly understood, they plumb the depth of the Divine mercy. The hardness of God is kinder than the softness of men, and His compulsion is our liberation.[26]

How might we describe what is at stake here in these middle years? What is the point? First, the account given thus far of human development has shown how the ego periodically erupts to give us opportunity to discover the center of our existence in God. Second, when the ego lets go, we can for the first time step outside the whole of the life span and embrace it as a totality while we are still within it. The transfiguration of the ego is accomplished all at once, because it is now grounded in the One who encompasses both past and future and fills the present time. Such experiences move us well beyond any kind of psychic balance and toward transfiguration.

Transfiguration, as used here, may be briefly understood after the pattern of Jesus' transfiguration in which the human figure becomes transparent to the Divine Presence. To refer back to the Jungian notion of balance, male-female balance is not definitive in transfiguration; the relationality takes on a life of its own. Thus, the male-female balance is no longer definitive, but it is transfigured by the presence and power of the Holy Spirit, wherein the relationality that holds these polarities together and apart becomes the positive third term, the Spiritual Presence of God who redefines the polarities as participants in the divine love. Divine love disregards balance for the sake of compassionate suffering, regards sacrifice as holy, and "believes all things but is never deceived."

Good and evil are not balanced either, but are transfigured by the reality of the holy, which is beyond good and evil, and creates an innocence of evil for the sake of an all-consuming union with the Holy God described so dramatically by St. Teresa of Avila, St. John of the Cross, Meister Eckhart, and others.

Life and death are not balanced either, but transfigured because the preservation of life as we know it is not a distinctively Christian virtue. Thus, transfiguration frees us from the survival instinct and for the living of life at its extremities for the sake of deepening life at the center. Death is "without sting" since it has been already gladly embraced as the key to life through him whose presence is profoundly known as the One who gives death to death and so builds his church on "the blood of the martyrs." In a phrase attibuted to Kierkegaard, "When a king dies, his reign ends. When a martyr dies, his reign begins."

What we have come to see is that human development is the cradle of the human spirit. Human development is inherently incapable of answering the fundamental questions it raises, yet answers to those questions must be thoroughly developmental. Disembodied and timeless answers will not do. Jung has enlarged our view of human development and our understanding of the human spirit. Nevertheless, his view is still not large enough to supply the ground for the human spirit in the pure love of God. Moreover, what the middle years add to divine love intimately appropriated is the privilege of the contemplation of the nature and Person of God with the whole of one's existence.

Jung did not invent the *coincidentia oppositorum*, as he himself said, but he did not understand the theological, especially the Christological significance of this medieval teaching. For instance, Richard of St. Victor's twelfth-century treatise on contemplation, and Nicholas of Cusa's principal work, *De Docta Ignorantia* (1440), both depend heavily on teaching a unison of opposites as a way of moving beyond rationality and into contemplation. For Richard, several types of opposites appeared in and near the source of deepening contemplation: active-passive, empty-full, hidden-revealed, open-closed, presence-absence, unity-diversity, visible-invisible. For Nicholas, the contemplative comprehension of God is at once infinitely great and infinitely small; the center and circumference of the world; everywhere and nowhere; neither one nor three but triune. Jung's mistaking how we know for what actually is the case led him to map self-structure on to the universe and into the Face of God, but the opposites as Nicholas and Richard describe them are already embodied in Jesus Christ, and all come under the greatest opposition of all: the divine and the human as defined by his two natures and one person. This, in its inherent opposition, confutes the Jungian premise that what is historically human can provide the primary image for us of the nature of God. It is just the opposite; the divine nature manifested in history in the person of Jesus provides us with the primary image and the ultimate union of opposites, which embraces and redefines all others.

Thus, the relationality of opposites that appear to us as we contemplate the nature of God in Jesus Christ is not aimed at balance along the lines of an organic homeostatic model of the psyche. As Nicholas said of the intellect, the mandala is a whore that will prostitute itself to anything, as the swastika makes plain. But as opposites in the triune nature of God lead us into contemplation, we are transfigured. In Richard's terms, contemplation is a kind of angelic hovering in which the relationality of opposites takes on a life of its own, and one is drawn into the life of God—in a word, into a moment of transfiguration. The model of transfiguration is important as the fullness of the presence of God that binds space and time and relativizes all culture and enculturated religion. As with the transfiguration of Jesus, one comes down from the mountain to heal and die for God's beloved people.

It is the unique privilege of the middle years to add to an intimate appropriation of God's pure love, contemplation and participation in the holy, inner life of God. Out of such contemplation love can be poured out for the healing of the world and for the redemption of past generations and preparation for the eschatological future, both already embodied in the life of God. All of this and infinitely more was revealed to us in Jesus while he himself was yet in his middle years.

NOTES

1. Dante, *The Divine Comedy* (New York: National Library Company, 1909).

2. David Levinson, *Seasons of a Man's Life* and *Seasons of a Woman's Life*. The segments are as follows: ages twenty-eight to thirty-three, the age thirty transition; ages thirty-three to forty, settling down; ages forty to forty-five, midlife transition; ages forty-five to fifty, entering middle adulthood; ages fifty to fifty-five, age fifty transition; ages fifty-five to sixty, culmination of middle adulthood; ages sixty to sixty-five, late adult transition; late adulthood. It is important to study these divisions in their own right, especially since they apply to both women and men; the five-year cycle is in itself interesting in relation to the crucial importance of the first five years of life. This, however, is material for another project.

3. Thomas Robinson, "Church Migration of Mid-Life Transition in Men as a Factor for Wholistic Later-Life Spiritual Development" (D.Min. dissertation, Princeton Theological Seminary, 1994).

4. Eric Berne, *Games People Play* (New York: Grove Press, 1964); Thomas A. Harris, *I'm OK. You're OK* (New York: HarperCollins, 1969), cited by Thomas Oden, *Game-Free: The Meaning of Intimacy* (New York: HarperCollins, 1974).

5. Don Browning, *Generative Man: Psychoanalytic Perspectives* (Philadelphia: Westminster Press, 1973).

6. Lawrence Kohlberg, "From *Is* to *Ought*: How to Commit the Naturalistic Fallacy and Get Away with It," in *The Philosophy of Moral Development* (San Francisco: HarperCollins, 1981), pp. 101–189.

7. At other points, Browning talks about a "premoral" good (borrowed from Thomistic thought), which may be apt for this discussion. Over and above adaptation of the ego, certain virtues develop consistently out of successive stages. Thus, the virtue of hope is the ego strength that emerges out of the primary adaptational or "premoral" good of achieving a favorable balance of trust over mistrust in the first eighteen months of life.

8. Browning, *Generative Man*.

9. Robert Coles, *Erik H. Erikson: The Growth of His Work* (Boston: Little, Brown, 1970).

10. Jung collaborated with Nobel laureate Wilhelm Pauli to study "synchronicity," and they wrote a book entitled *The Interpretation of Nature and the Psyche,* trans. C. Hull (New York: Routledge, 1955).

11. This point is dramatically portrayed in the recent study *Inside Information: The Brain and How It Works* (Princeton, N.J.: Films for the Humanities and Sciences).

12. Anthony Stevens, *Archetypes: A Natural History of the Self*. This Darwinian way of appreciating Jung may not be the most adequate. What Prigogine's theories revealed was that the "old idea of survival of the fittest" is to be replaced by optimal stability creative of new order. In the recognition that nonequilibrium may become a source of new order, what emerges will have an organizational complexity that could not be anticipated or informed from original conditions. It is Prigogine rather than Darwin who may lend most scientific credibility to Jung. See T. F. Torrance, *Transformation and Convergence in the Frame of Knowledge,* p. 187.

13. Much of what follows is based on Jung's autobiography *Memories, Dreams, and Reflections,* recorded and edited by Aniela Jaffe, trans. Richard and Clara Winston (New York: Pantheon Books, 1963). For the interesting history of this text see Alan C. Elms, *Uncovering Lives* (Oxford: Oxford University Press, 1995).

14. Tung-pin Lu, *Secret of the Golden Flower* (San Francisco: Harper San Francisco, 1991).

15. Mircea Eliade, *Patterns in Comparative Religion* (Lincoln: University of Nebraska Press), p. 372f.

16. Carl Gustav Jung, *Memories, Dreams, and Reflections*.

17. John Sanford, *Dreams: God's Forgotten Language* (San Francisco: Harper San Francisco, 1989).

18. Ann Ulanov, *The Feminine* (Evanston, Ill.: Northwestern University Press, 1971).

19. Rhoda Kellogg, with Scott O'Dell, *The Psychology of Children's Art* (New York: CRM-Random House, 1967).

20. Jolande Jacobi, *The Psychology of Jung* (New Haven, Conn.: Yale University Press, 1943).

21. Pruyser's model for a lifetime will be discussed at some length in the following chapter. Basically this refers to the parallels between the helplessness in childhood and the return to helplessness in old age.

22. This essay is reprinted in Cary Baynes and F. C. R. Hull (eds.), *Psyche and Symbol* (New York: Doubleday Anchor Books, 1958), pp. 35ff.

23. C. G. Jung, *Letters* (Princeton, N.J.: Princeton University Press, 1973–1975).

24. Eliade, *Patterns in Comparative Religion,* p. 30n.

25. Hildegaard von Bingen, *Scivias* (New York: Paulist Press, 1990).

26. C. S. Lewis, *Surprised by Joy* (Orlando: Harcourt Brace, 1955), p. 224.

13

BEYOND 65

DREAMING DREAMS AND

TALKING WITH GOD

IN THE BOOK of the prophet Joel, the Lord said he would pour out his "spirit on all flesh." It was this prophecy that was fulfilled at Pentecost, and in Peter's sermon on that occasion "all flesh" meant not only the Jews but all nations (Acts 2:17). In almost the same breath, the prophecy discloses that by the Spirit, "old persons will dream dreams."

To say the elderly will dream dreams is not a description of dementia setting in, as if they were drifting further from reality. Actually, the tone of the passage is thoroughly positive, triumphant, and focused on God's version of the future; their dreams occur because they are drifting closer to reality. This part of the passage refers to the privilege of the aging person to allow dreams, often God's language to his people, to speak beyond the organic condition and the present perceptions of circumstances about the time to come.

A few years after my mother had retired and became a praying Christian woman, she had two dreams. In one, she perceived in the vagueness of the dream state someone holding out a child to her and asking, "What shall we name this child?" Without stopping to think, she said immediately, "New Life." This came, I am persuaded, as a response to her beginning to learn to pray after she was well into her late seventies. It was not like Sarah, but there was laughter here nevertheless.

The second dream came to her in her real-life role as a teacher of dramatics and play directing at the University of Texas. In this dream, everyday life was portrayed on a stage, and without warning or fanfare a veil was suddenly lifted from the front of the stage. She saw people who had died and some she had never seen before, and she realized this was heaven. It was already with us, among us, but it was veiled from our eyes. "It is so simple," she said. "Of course, that's how it is!" The eyes of the elderly may be dim in some ways, but in other ways, which have nothing to do with biology, they may glimpse reality better than our 20/20 vision can see.

Although she had been raised in a home where Christianity was at best a marginal possibility, she had learned in these later years to talk with the God who loved her, and he was giving her new life and a positive view of a future that was blessed and already present in a very simple and straightforward way. At the time of this writing, she is ninety-three and still going strong. Although she would say she is just getting started, apparently New Life was the right name for her new birth of faith and the outpouring of the spirit upon her.

Aging in Psychological and Social Perspective

Persons sixty-five years and older constitute the fastest-growing segment of the American population and are an increasingly large proportion of American society as a whole. Here are a few basic statistics:

Generally in 1900 life expectancy at birth in America was forty-nine years; today it is seventy-six. At the turn of this century, three million people sixty-five and older made up 4 percent of the population; by 1980 they made up 11.3 percent of the population; by 2000 it is predicted they will make up 12 percent of the population, almost thirty-two million people; by 2020, when the baby boomers are old, they will constitute 20 percent of the population.

If you are male and live to be sixty-five, on average you have fourteen and a half more years to live. If you are female, you have on average nineteen more years to live. If you live to be seventy-five and are male, you have nine more years to live; if you are female, eleven and a half years. If you live to be eighty-five and are male, you have five and a half more years; if you are female, you have seven more years. If you live to be one hundred and are male, you have two and a half more years; if you are female, you have three more years. The oldest well-documented case is a woman who lived to be 113 years old. Women tend to outlive men because they are biologically tougher, less susceptible to infection, disease, and illness; their system deteriorates more slowly, so dysfunction of kidneys, heart, liver, lung, and brain occurs more slowly on average. Of persons over age sixty-five, 60 percent are women. By the age of eighty-five, women outnumber men two to one.

Functionally it takes increasingly longer to get old in our society, but the basic divisions of late adulthood, sixty-five or retirement on, senescence and senility still pertain. Senescence is described as the time from sixty-five or retirement on when physical changes cause one to become reliant on others for sustaining the basic functions of life. Senility is when the brain no longer functions as a organ of adaptation.[1]

Aging in psychosocial perspective is provided by Paul Pruyser of the Menninger Foundation.[2] There is in our society a perpetuation of an "iconic illusion" of aging that suggests that this period, age sixty-five and older, is the last half of a Gaussian curve. Pruyser's more colorful way of putting it was as an old Victorian mantle setting: two empty vases with a clock in the middle winding down, as Figure 13.1 shows.

Aging then goes from one form of emptiness to another as time passes. Thus the aged person is a mirror image of the child, but in reverse. Consider these comparisons:

1. The child is a helpless organism, increasing in complexity toward self-sufficiency; an aged person is a self-sufficient organism devolving toward helplessness.

2. The child has increasing powers of mastery over objects in the environment and is increasing in security and self-respect; the aged person has decreasing capacities over the objective world and is becoming more insecure and losing self-respect.

Figure 13.1. Pruyser's Image of Aging.

3. The child has the security of dependency, moving toward independent survival; the aging person has the insecurity of needing, but
not being able to expect or accept, dependency as he or she moves
back from independence just to survive.

4. The child finds compensatory satisfaction in the working of the vegetative organism, eating, defecating, bodily narcissism; the aging
person has almost no satisfaction at the vegetative level by which to
balance dissatisfactions at the psychic level. Thus, we have a functional description of the iconic illusion.

An interesting comment on this illusion that pervades our society comes
from Simone de Beauvoir in her colorful descriptions of aging in *The
Coming of Age*. She wrote that the attitude of a society toward its aged
citizens is one of the best indications of the core values of that society.[3] So
the bell-shaped curve is not only descriptive but representative of what
we take to be normative in American society. That is, it looks descriptive
of the facts of the matter, but this is a culturally constructed illusion. It
merely portrays the values of a society that is preoccupied with youth and
achievement, obsessively celebrating what is new, what is the latest
change, speed, power, being "with it," all on the way of maximizing productivity. It is not surprising, then, that we tend to disregard or even disdain aging. The obsession with youth and productivity can more
accurately be seen as in part a flight from aging and, as Ernest Becker put
it, the denial of death.[4]

The irony in this is a social version of Jung's warning that what you
deny as going on inside you happens outside you as fate. For example, if
you deny your guilt, you increasingly believe people are accusing you and
blaming you. On a societal level, the obsession with youth drives us to
find ways to preserve youth against aging and death. The result is not that
people stop aging but that there is a rapidly increasing number of elderly
persons. The presence of the aged is becoming more and more of a political and economic force in American society and a burden on the youth
and the "productive" members of that society. It is ironic that billions of
dollars are spent on trying to stay young, and it has only increased the
number of those who are not young. So the increasing numbers of the
elderly come back to haunt a youth- and production-oriented society.
Thus, at one level, the life span derives its meaning from its sociocultural
context, but this irony suggests that the Victorian mantle image is not the
whole picture. Indeed, it is less than half correct, because it pays primary
attention to only one aspect, the dark side of the life span. That is, there

are in fact powerful positive outcomes to aging in this final stage. These must be taken account of.

Erikson argues that there is a way, even in this society, to come out ahead of the ironic illusion and overcome the irony. It is possible to gain a favorable balance of integrity over despair and acquire the virtue of wisdom, whose institutional correlate is "the collective wisdom" or the recognition that humankind is my kind. It is perhaps notable that Plato believed that philosopher-kings would have to be at least fifty-eight years of age or older if they were going to be able to exercise the wisdom necessary to govern the city state.

Looking at Erikson more closely, we can ask what is meant by his describing the final major developmental crisis of life for the human ego as integrity versus despair. Integrity is an accrued sense of and appreciation for the ego's proclivity for order and meaning over the years; it is an appreciation for the remarkable integrative capacity that for so long has been at work in him or her. This he describes as "the post-narcissistic love of the ego." This borders on what I have been describing as the transformation of the ego, since it implies a stance outside the ego and an appreciation of it as a truth-producing error. Though decentered, it still serves as Jung's Number 1, the agency we use for reality testing.

A second aspect of integrity is comradeship with distant times; a sense of cosmic order is inwardly felt. This is an appreciation of the universality of the human struggle, as reflected in one's own. Yet one's own struggle is appreciated as unique. "It was my way of doing it, and I would do it the same way again if I had to do it over."

Third is a new appreciation of one's parents. They were the origin of order and growth and now can be more coolly evaluated. Their failures and successes can be seen in a more balanced perspective.

In some, integrity amounts to the affirmation of life itself in the face of death itself, and integrity in the face of death will inspire trust in the value and worth of life. Consequently, it is often the grandparents, who do not fear death, who most adequately inspire a love of life in their grandchildren. Here we see exactly the opposite of the image portrayed in the iconic illusion. At the end of life, persons savoring the fullness of life give it to those who are just beginning. In Pruyser's imagery, we can now begin to put flowers in the vase on both ends of the mantelpiece.

Let's look briefly at a senior thesis done at Princeton University, "The Influence of Grandparents on Young Adults," by Tina Horner. In a questionnaire to eighty Princeton and Westminster Choir College students, Horner investigated persons of different ages, sexes, religions, races, and academic majors. Ninety-five percent reported that their grandparents had been very influential and important in their lives. Eighty-eight percent reported that their grandparents were important because they offered "unconditional love and support." The key word here is "unconditional." The next most common reason for importance was that grandparents contributed to identity development and social skills, that is, they served as role models, instilling a sense of roots and continuity, and possessing admirable characteristics. The final observation is that maternal grandparents were cited more often than paternal, and the maternal grandmother, the mother's mother, most of all. So contrary to our denial of death and the irony of the iconic illusion, it may often be that from points closest to death, we are most able to affirm life. From points in the midst of old age, we can most effectively encourage youth.

An interesting sidelight here is that some psychologists claim what folklore already knows: that young people of college age remember stories better if they are told by older adults than if the same stories are told by the same-age or middle-age persons. Discursive material is less well remembered if it is passed on by peers. This may be some indication of the archetypical power of the ancient storyteller, which in turn may cast some further light on Horner's thesis.

For Erikson, the opposite of integrity is despair. What is meant by despair? This plays into the iconic illusion. Fear, anxiety, apprehension, and frustration as one approaches death make one apprehensive about this being the one and only life cycle, and it has proved to be unacceptable and an accumulation of inferiority, role confusion, isolation, stagnation, and the like. Death becomes the climax of all the negatives. Time has run out, and the illusions one has tried to sustain have collapsed, fallen apart, and exposed the inner emptiness in one's person. A woman who used to greet me as I would come into the nursing home for visits would sit rocking and say, with empty eyes, "Hi, how are you? It's a nice day. Hi, how are you? It's a nice day. Hi, how are you? It's a nice day." She was beyond despair, in some ways mercifully. Despair is when you still have the illusion but you know it is an illusion. Despair is epitomized, perhaps, in the achiever's comments cited earlier in this book: "I hope I die before I ruin my reputation."

In the face of death, the despairing person can only express fear and attack life with disgust, regret, and demand. This is what lies behind the image of the domineering, chronically depressed, self-centered, paranoid older person.

Looking at what makes the difference between integrity and despair, we can elaborate each side of the picture with Pruyser's help. First are the factors in old age that bring forth a climax of negativity and despair:

1. Losses beyond simple physical decline. Loss of personal dignity means there is an erosion of self-worth; the self-concept is eroded by condescension, loss of esteem due to being a nonproductive person in an achievement-oriented society.

2. Loss of work. Workers tend to endow a job with a profound sense of vocation. Humanistic, ethical, and religious implications of work are important. Even though one may only seem to be a cog in the wheel, a vocation is participation in the creation of society and the societal order. The loss of work in Western society indicates loss of worth, even if one is not an achiever.

3. Loss of structure behind reality testing as a result of loss of work. Work structures time and space. Without the structure, fantasies go unchecked. The work enables actualities to be affirmed and enables one to take on responsibilities according to a preset pattern. When work goes, outer structure goes; some inner structure must take over, and this means that the concealment of despair is less possible.

4. Loss of independence. Early independence training in autonomy urges persons away from any kind of dependency in our society, as if to be dependent is to be weak or bad or lazy. Independence means management of our lives, and when the signs of this independent management are taken away, when we lose work or become dependent on others, then the control and direction of society is beyond us, and we begin to move toward despair.

5. Loss of time and what it does to enrich life. There is a paradox here. New chronological time is at one's disposal, but there is not enough time to finish long-term projects. The new time available is unstructured, and it is difficult to make it count toward projects that may have any long-term significance. Also, present time is painful. One may be inclined to forget one's hat, but remember youthful feats in great detail.

The sum of it is that one feels abandonment, which is what you would expect as the ego declines toward death. That which the ego was originally designed to conceal throughout the lifetime now surfaces with redoubled force like "the return of the repressed." Despair is the older person's version of the original loss of the face. No objects will remain; even one's own face, as the mirror shows, is passing away. Hence, despair is possible.

Whether one's lifetime capitulates to this has much to do with how one dealt with the void or negative proximate death experiences all through the life span up to this point. How heavy was the investment in stagnation, isolation, and so forth? If the investment was too heavy and there was no religious solution to the centrality of the ego and its failures, then the iconic illusion does become a reality. Thanatos finally has its way with the whole person.

But it is possible to develop differently, positively, in spite of the socially constructed conspiracies against aging in American culture. When integrity occurs and wisdom is manifest, here then is what happens.

A very important and fundamental competence that gains ascendancy in these later years is simplification. It is partly necessary losses that give rise to this new developmental competence, but it is, more important, the response of the human spirit to those losses by which one discovers this new competence.

The aspects of simplification are as follows. Concerning physical development and exercise, one can learn to accept less narcissistic rewards from physical exertion. One can lay aside the games that say, "I am just as good as I ever was," and recognize that such games are formulas for despair. Sexual rewards must be surrendered to loving and being lovable. I am here reminded of the older couple cited by Theodore Lidz in his book *The Person,* who when they wanted to make love would put on their best clothes, go out to dinner, and then come home at night and lie in bed just holding each other all night long. Since sexual relationships become increasingly less frequent, there can be some surrender of this to the greater satisfactions of love and holding. One has less need for ego stroking. We learn to need this less since it tapers off when achievement and production decline. It is possible to simplify one's ego needs, and this emerges, in the ordinary course of things, from generativity. Now one wants the younger generation to get all the strokes and rewards.

There is material simplification. Things are relegated more and more toward the margin of life as one ages. "You can't take it with you" becomes a code of life. Recognizably fewer and fewer things are really needed. I remember an elderly woman who used to bring us slightly tattered clothing and doll clothes from her childhood. She came from her retirement community and walked past our house on her way to certain university gatherings. These were things that she simply did not need any more and had let go of emotionally. She thought we might be able to use them. Even though they were useless to us, she was cleaning out her room in the retirement community, and she was gradually getting used to needing fewer and fewer things.

She stood in contrast to the woman who lived next to her in the community who held on to probably every tin can she had ever opened. The

stronger one's personal integrity is, the greater the power is for simplification. Integrity surrenders material objects as an expression of one's
acceptance of the loss of the physical body. Integrity does not cling to
material objects as compensation for bodily loss because it draws on its
own inner resources.

Pruyser's discussion cites the following psychosocial expressions of simplification. First, some dependencies can be accepted as wholesome. Some
of the drive toward independence has been overdetermined by society, and
wholesome dependence is a willingness to let the functional competence
of children or younger relatives serve you. Stubborn insistence on independence is despair when one reaches senescence.

Second, one may redefine one's status; one may redefine what it means
to "make it." Here we are in need of positive models of aging. Maggie
Kuhn, the founder of the Gray Panthers in Philadelphia, engaged older
persons in concerns for justice. Their small group meetings, which occu-
pied them in examining the welfare system, led them to concerns for
which they would never see the results. As they worked together, they
engaged in face-to-face relationships, and the value of what they did in
interaction exceeded their individual lives and so gave them a form of
transcendence. This enhanced their sense of worth and well-being.

Third, ego individuation is possible. That is, in Jungian terms it is
possible to grow in inner spiritual ways. The confrontation with one's
psychological opposites is a possibility for further maturation to the end
of life.

Fourth, one can begin to relax one's defenses. It is possible in these later
years to accept unpleasant and inevitable ambiguities in one's life. Also,
the negative results of a life can be accepted more philosophically and
without a reaction formation. One may simply say, "That's all past now.
I have made my share of mistakes, but it seems to have worked out." As
defenses relax, the human spirit can be released into the assurance of forgiveness and God's providential care.

Fifth, work can become an avocation, integrated into life. Work no
longer has to be separated from life or be definitive of one's personal
worth. One can now choose what work to do and make work an expression of genuine interest. Mrs. Peroni used to come and clean our house,
wash, iron, and do the dishes. The striking thing was that she was in her
mid-seventies, but abounding in energy. All during her productive years,
she had been an independent entrepreneur in Princeton, New Jersey; she
owned and managed a nursery and had planted many of the trees in town.
Finally she retired, and then she could do what she really wanted to do:

take care of a home. We used to say to her, "Mrs. Perone, you are terrific," and she would say, "I know." Energy and satisfaction abound from doing what one most wants to do.

Sixth, living in the present without an anxious future is a privilege of the aged. It can come as a great relief that you cannot accept the final responsibility for the future. This is not necessarily a negative reaction; it may be a religious insight. Therefore, the present becomes more precious and increasing in satisfaction since it may last three or four decades. The fullness of the present time is a developmentally prepared kairos if the human spirit is not trapped in despair.

Seventh, identification with the idealism of youth is the special privilege of the aged. The elderly can no longer be competitive, so all oedipal strivings and competition with the younger generation become irrelevant. There can be a delightful acceptance of the cycle of the generations, making the older person, "the grandfather" or "the grandmother," the best possible companion for the younger person. Grandparents who can invest themselves in the dreams of the younger generation without self-interest are themselves renewed.

Eighth, older persons may now write their credo. Gifted persons often in these later years can say what they really thought. Tough-minded scholars back away from the demands for retaining a professional image and formulate personal statements. One can see such statements in Wilder Penfield (*The Mystery of the Mind*) and Karl Menninger (*Whatever Became of Sin*).[5] It is the privilege of the aging person to state her credo with the transcendental immunity that comes only with having lived life fully to the end.

Ninth, inner thoughts and confessions now can be disclosed. A person may now want to come clean with what she always believed under the surface, and may want to own up to certain attitudes that have been held in secret. It is said that in his later years, Sinclair Lewis acknowledged that he wrote all his books to impress his older brother, and B. F. Skinner disclosed in an interview published not long before his death that he was afraid of dying.

All of these points are instructions for looking backward at the life span in order to look forward with integrity. Of course, one need not wait for aging to benefit from the wisdom of the elderly and, in benefiting, become better prepared for that time. What age permits is always the privilege of the convicted and transformed person, so there finally is no wisdom that is uniquely the property of the aged or elderly person. Rather, this wisdom, and much more, is incarnate in Christ. It is the outgrowth of the decentered ego, an ego in Christ that is able to embrace its own death and so allow the whole person to derive strength from this embrace. All of these expressions of ego integrity are potentially gifts of grace to be transformed and appropriated by faith. Indeed, all of development over the course of a lifetime, even in its final stages, moves toward a decentering and transformation of ego. Thus, a lifetime, with all its stages and upheavals, its losses and its satisfactions, its tragedies and its comedies, may sooner or later be recognized as a repeated quest of the human spirit for centeredness in the Divine Presence. Restored centeredness, Spirit-to-spirit, implies contemplation and the ever-deepening realization that every individual lifetime is a creative act of divine love, and what seems like ordinary life, even in the most common sense, is the ultimate love of God seeking ever fuller expression in the world.

Cognitive Potential in Later Years

In the universalizing style of formal operations, which characterizes stage 6 in Fowler's scheme of ego development, formal operational capacities are synthetic; simplified by being universally comprehensive (beyond dialectic), one feels that one is participating in the "One beyond the many," and there is a transnarcissistic love of being.

Here are a few lines excerpted and condensed from the only interview that James Fowler has for a stage 6 person:

I: At the present, what would you say gives your life meaning?

HE: God, the giver.

I: Do you want to explain that a little bit?

HE: Well, I think that is basic to Christianity, and understood well enough, God is the only person in this universe who is truly liberal; in the sense that he cannot receive anything, and he does not want to receive anything. God is the sheer giver and complete unselfishness. He is the God of love because he is the God of holiness.

I: What do you see as the purpose or purposes of human life?

HE: It's receiving from God what he wants to give. That is the purpose of human life. And we are constituted by an aspiration for union with God to the highest degree that we can receive him. That is what human life is all about. And we have that deep aspiration which is for God and for love of our neighbor, which is by a sacrificial love. "Sacrificial" does not mean giving up things: it means a unifying love which we receive only from God and his inner dynamism. And growth is in the realization that we do this not through our own power, but through the transformation of our spirit by the spirit of God.

I: Okay, so, you'd say—If I say, what are the beliefs or attitudes or values that dominate your life, it would be the value of love, and the purpose of being. . . .

HE: Well, the value of love that does not spring from my inner resources alone, but only through the inner transformation of the spirit. It isn't from God or Christ looked upon as a model; it is the realization of solidarity with him that he's available to give me a new life.

I: Are there some systems of religious beliefs that are truer than others . . . ?

HE: I don't—I think we are dealing here radically with mystery, and mystery is incapable of systematization. But I think the deepest, radical aspiration of every human being *is* a gift of God, and it is an impulse toward union with God and with our fellow human beings. Now in each one's situation, the use of all human resources, of intelligence and affectivity and sensitivity—that is a judgment . . . that each one has to make for him or herself. And I think that it is foolish to try to systematize that and to force everyone into a groove. But I think that the mystery of God's call is in everyone, either more or less explicit.[6]

It is sometimes thought that this interviewee, called an "insignificant monk," was Thomas Merton. Whoever it was, for Fowler it is not the precise content but the form of thinking that counts in establishing this level of reflection. In his reference to systematization, it is clear that the respondent's opposition to a system places him outside the scale according to which he is being studied, and this in itself moves him toward universalizing. This is Fowler's paradigm case for stage 6, and what I am calling now the cognitive aspect of ego integrity. Once again, chronology does not automatically call forth this cognitive stance, but it is evident that there is no potentiality for stage 6 until the person has reached stage 5. Indeed, stage 6 may be only a hypothetical possibility for the human spirit.

The Last Stage: Foretaste of Things to Come

One developmental step beyond later adulthood senescence and senility needs to be understood in the light of the wisdom revealed in Jesus Christ. I was reminded of it recently when we received a telephone call that my wife's aunt, who had been in intensive care and in a coma, had come out of the coma just as we had so earnestly prayed she would. She was vastly improved, but roaring mad because she did not want to come back from that "beautiful place" where she said she had "seen the Lord." She and the Lord met, but at a dividing line, like a step, up about two feet, and she asked him to help her up. But he said, no, she had to go one step further. And so she returned to this life.

Life-after-life experiences bring us close to home at Tennent Hall Princeton Seminary. William Tennent (1705–1777) had such an experience studying for his presbytery exams. He became so anxious, not about passing them but about whether he was saved, that he actually became desperately ill and to all appearances died. He was laid out on a board, and the funeral was planned. Indeed, just shortly before the funeral, a doctor noticed what he thought was a slight movement under the left arm of the body. He had them postpone the funeral for about an hour until he could investigate. Within the hour, Tennent sat bolt upright on the board and groaned at having returned to this life. It took him about a year to recover his Latin and his learning so that he could finally pass his presbytery exams and have an immensely productive ministry. But what he saw during that time while he was presumably dead made him absolutely convinced of his salvation and the reality of heaven. (Some people cite this experience to say that you cannot always tell whether Presbyterian ministers are alive or dead. I rather think that such experiences need to be carefully documented and studied.)

In the pattern that is typical of these accounts of life after an apparent death, these people recognize that they are out of his body, possibly accompanied by a kind of buzzing; they recognize that they are able to observe what is going on, but are doing this unobserved. They then pass through a dark tunnel toward a light. A figure of light may appear as a guide, and they will be led into the realm of the beautiful. The word *beautiful* is used most often by persons who have these experiences. Here they may see heaven or other persons and relations, and reach the point of decision where they are either able to choose to return or told that they must return. When they find themselves back in their body, they are unable to say how they returned.

Note the similarity to the birth experience with which this book began. But now it is enacted in full consciousness. Kenneth Ring's research in his book *Life at Death* points to the reality of these experiences, saying they are not hallucinatory or simply screen memories of physical birth.[7] If they are in any way linked to birth, they represent a transformation at the end of life of life's beginning.

Thus, the archetype of birth may get its fullest expression in death. We therefore may look backward on development from these experiences and recognize with those who do come back that what lies beyond death is designed to validate and strengthen the worth of this life. After our aunt got over being mad, she did as others who have had these experiences do. She came to affirm this life with a greatly heightened sense of its value, saying that much of what we think is important really is not, and so manifests the true simplicity of wisdom.

To get a more serious perspective on these experiences, consider a recent and thorough study on life-after-life experiences. Carol Zaleski, in *Other World Journeys,* compares contemporary versions of these experiences to those recorded in the sixth century by Gregory the Great, who kept an account of near-death experiences.[8] Zaleski notes that the two types of experiences share a similar narrative paradigm in which certain characteristics are held in common across the board:

1. Both are frankly dualistic.
2. The visionary finds himself in a liminal condition hovering above the scene of crisis.
3. The guide ("light") appears.
4. The topography of the other world is pointed out.
5. The message to the visionary is a call for the need for spiritual instruction.
6. The pivotal episode is the life review in which the visionary learns the weight of his soul.
7. Paradise is a beautiful comprehension of the whole.
8. The journey is interrupted and suspended, and the visionary feels compelled to return to this life.
9. Upon returning, the person is changed physically and spiritually.
10. The didactic aim is not designed to describe spiritual reality or to satisfy theoretical curiosity, but "to serve as a goad to transformation."

However, there are important differences. The older experiences had different content. They spoke of judgment and the second death; contemporary experiences speak about a good death. Older experiences speak about a feudal lord; more recent experiences speak about parental-type authorities. The older experiences convey doom; the more recent convey the experience as educative. The older experiences call for repentance; the more recent ones say not to worry, that life is for love and service. Therefore, the specific content of such experiences is likely the work of socially conditioned imaginations, says Zaleski.

The argument for the legitimacy of these experiences is not that they have unexplained features. For instance, the "light" is sometimes cited as the aspect that is inexplicable by any neurological interpretation. But that is a "god of the gaps" argument that simply leaves the issue open to further neurological research. Rather, the argument should be that these experiences are legitimate; they are healthy and intelligible, precisely because they are consistent with other manifestations of the transforming power of the human spirit. Their theological potentiality lies not in an inexplicable discontinuity but in their continuity with the profound sense of order we have observed over and over again in the human spirit. This is the order of transformation and discovery that is the foundation of analytic and discursive reason, the driving force of human development, and the pattern that the *Spiritus Creator* follows in the transformation of an entire lifetime. The sense of order at stake here is the inherent order and intelligibility of the human spirit.

The unique contribution these experiences make is that they greatly advance the scale on which the human spirit can operate, but the basic pattern of transformation, in both the content they convey and the form of the experience, is what they consistently express. As such, they suggest that the creative resources of the human spirit are far deeper and more profound than we have thought. These experiences parallel the visions of the prophets described by Anthony Wallace in revitalization movements, which we discussed in Chapter Three. Accordingly, the neurological explanation of those prophetic visions and of Helen's visions also apply here. That is, we are neurologically designed for just such experiences. Carl Jung's view of the psyche approached this as he moved from psychic organization to cosmology. However, Carol Zaleski's commentary on these experiences is quite insightful. After concluding that the difference between otherworld journeys in Gregory's day and our present day shows that these experiences are "through and through the work of the socially conditioned religious imagination," she says that they disclose a deep human need for "orientation." The need is to be positioned not only socially and culturally but also in the cosmic order.

In many respects, her discussion parallels the developmental argument of this book that in the human spirit there is a pervasive cosmic loneliness derivative from the loss of the face in the first months of life. In keeping with the transformational pattern of that spirit, she says that these visions are more likely to become prominent when a new culture develops, old cultures break down, or new perspectives alter our comprehension of the universe. Such "cognitive dissonance" (Leon Festinger and others) or breakdown of "mazeways" (Anthony Wallace) throw us into an unevaluated or desacralized universe. Given the nature of the human spirit, it is not surprising that such narratives arise in response to the conflict of cosmic disorientation. The spirit then searches out patterns and prototypes by which to map the cosmos and turn it into a home. Zaleski says it is as Gordon Allport taught us: there is a "ceaseless struggle to assimilate the scientific frame of thought within an expanded religious frame."[9] Thus, religious images and visions manage to give the desacralized scientific picture of the universe a feeling of familiarity, and we have a sense of belonging to it. It is, in effect, resacralized. When this is achieved, the visionary returns to this world healed and restored in himself and with others. He is now put into the world with a new perception of reality, which reorients the visionary and heightens the meaningfulness of this life and this world.

These experiences are the work of a greatly enlarged view of the human spirit, but thoroughly human nevertheless. The false problem introduced into much of this discussion is that it sets these experiences over against science. This is also the fault behind Allport's comment. Both the religious imagination and discovery in science are expressions of the one and same human spirit. Imagination is not merely an isolated faculty of mind, as Allport well knew, but it comes into play as an expression of the logic of the human spirit. Thus we may ask of these experiences what we asked of the visions that occur at the core of any version of the transformational process: Where does the vision come from?

The great chemist Friedrich A. von Kekule, sitting before the fire one evening in 1865, had a hypnogogic vision of snakes whirling about; then each took the tail of another in its mouth, and they whirled around together in one great circle. When he awoke "as if by a flash of lightning," he knew he had seen an image of the circular structure of the benzene molecule. This was a brilliant piece of prediction, since the idea of a circular structure of the molecule was unprecedented. He had been given a vision of something whose particularities and implications were fundamentally new, yet nevertheless real and awaiting articulation. When such an image has predictive and realistic visionary force, we must ask, "Where did the image become from?" Similarly, where do the life-after-apparent-death experiences come from? They often heal the visionary and make her more realistic about this life as well as the next.

In Chapter Three, we traced out the steps in spiritual formation at a neurophysiological level. This was not regarded as a reductionistic argument but rather that human nature is wired for much more profound experiences than the order of analytical or discursive reason might allow. It is only when the ego-centered, rationalistic view of enlightenment science is given permission to define science and nature that these experiences seem bizarre and unintelligible, and their origin therefore needs some special linear explanation.

On the other hand, if the postmodern view of science, which prizes the primacy of discovery, relationality, transformation, and personal involvement in knowing, holds as much credibility as the rational empirical aspects of modernist science, then the coherent, reorienting power of other worlds becomes as intelligible as any other act of creation or discovery in the arts or sciences. Otherworld journeys are not otherworldly, but they are unexpected and baffling images of this same astonishing reality and universe that repeatedly excites, challenges, and mystifies us. They have an inherent intelligibility, but we have yet to comprehend them except as extraordinary manifestations of the human spirit relentlessly in search of its ultimate ground.

We are so created and so deeply embedded in the universe at a physical level that we are neurologically capable of producing visions that gather up the drive toward unity and coherence in the universe, and simultaneously affirm our human particularity. The same spirit that is responsible for so-called discovery in science is responsible for otherworld journeys because it is able to draw on a tacit sense of coherence that pervades the universe and the human psyche and so to unify widely diverse and seemingly unrelated factors into meaningful wholes.

The human spirit is so constituted because we are created in both the image of the universe and the image of God, the view from below and the view from above. In naturalistic terms, the universe in us and in itself balances titanic opposites, such as expansive explosion and gravitational contraction, to produce an intelligible whole. At the naturalistic level, we are created in the image of this universe. However, since we are more than the universe, our mirror image relation to it points beyond the physical to the personal. Thus stems T. F. Torrance's case for a personal Author of the universe.

Theologically, we are made in the image of God. I have argued here that the core of that image is in the uprooted and disoriented human spirit, which will do art, science, religion, and philosophy endlessly until it finds an adequate ground for itself as spirit. Even the otherworld journeys recognize this incompleteness when they bring the visionary to a place where he or she must be evaluated and either moved on or sent back by the only One who can complete and fulfill spiritual longing. We must now turn to a more explicit theological perspective on otherworld experiences and their implications for the living of this life in the light of what lies beyond it.

Theological Reflection

If we ask how to look at these experiences from a biblical and theological standpoint, we must turn, as did William Tennent, to II Corinthians, chapter 12. Here Paul writes about "a man who was taken up into the third heaven, hearing things no man could utter, whether in the body or out of the body, he could not say."

Perhaps this is an account of Paul's life-after-life experience, but I am struck by the fact that this experience is mentioned only once in the New Testament and seems to be of little consequence. On the other hand, the Damascus accounts of his encounter with Christ are mentioned three or four times and are absolutely pivotal for his life and ministry. The Corinthian experience focuses on potentially disembodied experience that occurs somewhere beyond this life. But Paul's encounters with Christ focus on the way in which the Spiritual Presence of Christ was thoroughly embodied and seeks to create his "body," the church, in and for the world. Salvation is to be understood not as "out of this world" or for a disembodied spirit. Rather, to participate in the Spiritual Presence of Christ is to be thrust more profoundly into the body, and so into the concreteness and miracle of the created order. This is not an adaptational aim, but a transformational aim; to be in Christ is to be in what he is doing to transform all creation into conformity to *his* nature.

In an intriguing use of the transformational pattern raised to the level of the power of the Divine Spirit, biblical scholar Paul Anderson discussed John 6:16–21 in relation to Mark 6:45–52. In working out the difference, he nevertheless sees that the episode in both cases was a theophany in which Jesus' presence is the conflict-resolving, mediating reality that takes command of the natural order, either by stilling the wind or by moving instantly through space and time to the shore. My point with Anderson's carefully worked out exegetical study is that the theophany was not merely making things seem better; it actually altered the physical reality at stake. This is a paradigm for how the Spiritual Presence of Christ works through faith in the formation and transformation of the believer and his world.

The Spiritual Presence of Christ radicalizes space and time, and in so doing redefines death, the termination of our space-time existence, as a reality that is at *his* disposal. Thus, all that has been discussed in this book to describe how he gives death to death by taking it into himself on the cross now pertains. The point is not that he facilitates our adaptation to this world; it is that through us and by the power of our faith, the created order is to become "adapted" to *him*. Thus, embodiment is decisive for us in fulfilling Christ's purposes, but it is the transformed, transfigured, resurrected, and glorified *body* toward which the Creator Spirit points us. The human spirit's creation of other worlds may be wonderfully healing, restorative, and life giving, but this is still the human spirit in search of its origin and destiny. In the Creator Spirit, the person of faith is not looking primarily for a personal heavenly reward; rather, he is looking primarily toward the final consummation of all things in Christ as that consummation has been partially disclosed to faith as a foretaste. By this, the conclusion of life must be understood as a fulfillment and joyful completion of the process of development by which the human spirit, finally in agreement with the Creator Spirit, has put death to death in order that Christ may be all in all. As the image is restored to its original, it is evident that every lifetime is intended to be a work of God's love, but death completes the circle when not only is God's love returned through each of us but the lover in person, each of us, is returned in joyous reunion to God.

Meanwhile, we can savor the foretaste of the full consummation in Christ that faith provides. If we ask how that looks, we can recall Kierkegaard's familiar description of the knight of faith. This conclusion returns us to the argument stated in the Preface to this book.

A lifetime is set between two absurds, and the knight of faith has been taken up in the positive absurd that God became a particular man at a particular time in history so as to transform all things and all time according to his nature and person. The "knight of faith" *lives* in the sea-crossing theophany and so is engaged in the quiet passion of believing at every moment. Thus, he is fascinated that every particular is an embodiment of the universal, yet without losing its particularity; every event and interaction is a gift that is unique but embodies eternity; everything is truly possible but nothing is necessary—all "by virtue of the absurd." Who would not like to see such a knight for, by such a faith, death itself would have to yield. But as you read the following passage, remember that Kierkegaard's method is indirect, so the real point here is that the reader becomes the author of the text; that is, this account is designed to say to the believer, "Release the spirit so faith may be true to itself in you." Ironically, should Kierkegaard succeed in this, the reader could never own such a faith outright, lest its very force would elude him:

Here he is. Acquaintance made, I am introduced to him. The moment I set eyes on him I instantly push him from me, I myself leap backwards, I clasp my hands and say half aloud, "Good Lord, is this the man? Is it really he? Why, he looks like a tax-collector!" However, it is the man after all. I draw closer to him, watching his least movements to see whether there might not be visible a little heterogeneous factional telegraphic message from the infinite, a glance, a look, a gesture, a note of sadness, a smile, which betrayed the infinite in its heterogeneity with the finite. No! I examine his figure from tip to toe to see if there might not be a cranny through which the infinite was peeping. No! He is solid through and through. His tread? It is vigorous, belonging entirely to finiteness; no smartly dressed townsman who walks out to Fresberg on a Sunday afternoon treads the ground more firmly, he belongs entirely to the world, no Philistine more so. One can discover nothing of that aloof and superior nature whereby one recognizes the knight of the infinite. He takes delight in everything, and whenever one sees him taking part in a particular pleasure, he does it with the persistence which is the mark of the earthly man whose soul is absorbed in such things. He tends to his work. So when one looks at him one might suppose that he was a clerk who had lost his soul in an intricate system of bookkeeping, so precise is he. He takes a holiday on Sunday. He goes to church. No heavenly glance or any other token of the incommensurable betrays him; if one did not know him, it would be impossible to distinguish him from the rest of the congregation, for his healthy and vigorous hymn-singing proves at the most that he has a good chest. In the afternoon he walks to the forest. He takes delight in everything he sees, in the human swarm, in the new omnibuses, in the water of the Sound; when one meets him on the Beach Road one might suppose he was a shopkeeper taking his fling, that's just the way he disports himself, for he is not a poet, and I have sought in vain to detect in him the poetic incommensurability. Toward evening he walks home, his gait is as indefatigable as that of the postman. On his way he reflects that his wife has surely a special little warm dish prepared for him, e.g. a calf's head roasted, garnished with vegetables. If he were to meet a man like-minded, he could continue as far as East Gate to discourse with him about that dish, with a passion befitting a hotel chef. As it happens, he hasn't four pence to his name, and yet he fully and firmly believes that his wife has that dainty dish for him. If she had it, it would then be an invidious sight for superior people and an inspiring one for the plain man, to see him eat; for his appetite is greater than Esau's. His wife hasn't it—strangely enough, is quite the same to him. On the way he comes past a building site and runs across another man. They talk together for a moment. In the twinkling of an eye he erects a new building, he has at his disposition all the powers necessary for it. The stranger leaves him with the thought that he certainly was a capitalist, while my admired knight thinks, "Yes, if the money were needed, I dare say I could get it." He lounges at an open window and looks out on the square on which he lives; he is interested in everything that goes on, in a rat which slips under the curb, in the children's play, and this with the nonchalance of a girl of sixteen. And yet he is no genius, for in vain I have sought in him the incommensurability of genius. In the evening he smokes his pipe; to look at him one would swear that it was the grocer over the way vegetating in the twilight. He lives as carefree as a ne'er-do-well, and yet he buys up the acceptable time at the dearest price, for he does not do the least thing except by virtue of the absurd.[10]

NOTES

1. Factors that contribute to longevity are happiness and a sense of satisfaction; physical activity and outside interests; determination, that is, "sheer cussedness" and refusal to give up; having an accepted place in the community; higher level of education; higher IQ; marriage (if happy); readily available health care. Finally, notably, the moral factor is a crucial one. Here religion plays an important part statistically, perhaps more than any other institution. The trends suggested by the statistics cited here have been recently checked against those cited by Jack Rosenthal, "The Age Boom," *New York Times Magazine,* March 9, 1997. Factors contributing to decline are obesity; poor or impoverished diet; very rich diet; excessive alcohol; smoking; exposure to heavy pollution; poverty; work that is too exhausting; emotional stress; A-type personality; poor health care facilities; feeling lonely; and having a low morale.

2. Paul Pruyser, *Toward a Theology of Aging,* ed. Seward Hiltner (New York: Human Sciences Press, 1975), pp. 107–118.

3. Simone de Beauvoir, *The Coming of Age* (New York: Putnam, 1972).

4. Ernest Becker, *The Denial of Death* (New York: Free Press, 1973).

5. Wilder Penfield, *The Mystery of the Mind* (Princeton, N.J.: Princeton University Press, 1975); Karl Menninger, *Whatever Became of Sin* (New York: Hawthorn Books, 1973).

6. James Fowler, *Life Maps* (Waco, Tex.: Word Books, 1985), pp. 91ff.

7. Kenneth Ring, *Life at Death* (New York: Coward-McCann, 1980).

8. Carol Zaleski, *Other World Journeys* (Oxford: Oxford University Press, 1987).

9. Gordon Allport, *The Individual and His Religion* (New York: 1950), p. 132.

10. Søren Kierkegaard, *Fear and Trembling* (New York: Doubleday, 1954), pp. 49ff.

CONCLUSION

But do not ignore this one fact, beloved,
that with the Lord, one day is like a thousand years
and a thousand years are like one day.

—II Peter 3:8

THE HUMAN SCIENCES have traditionally studied and evaluated the human life span as it unfolds through time. This book has respected that tradition, but it has insisted that clocks and calendars cannot supply the definitive time frame for the study of a human life. By applying a theological view to human science accounts of development, we have seen that from the moment of birth, the transformation that characterizes the human spirit continually thrusts into the flow of clock time new orders of meaning and being. These emerge, erupt, and reconfigure all that develops according to linear views of the life span. Thus, the question is not only what may we expect of a person at a given age or stage, but where in a person's life is the transformational potential manifesting itself. In, through, over, and above so-called normal development the human spirit surges, struggles, sustains, submerges, and reemerges with the newness of life. The logic of the human spirit is the heart and center of every lifetime wherein duration and synchronicities combine in moments of kairos, where the fullness of time reshapes chronos, as the human spirit seeks ultimate agreement with its eternal ground in the unity of the inner life of God.

Theologically, all views of time come under the perspective of eternity, as is manifest to us proximately, in transforming moments of life-embracing significance. Such moments encompass the complete breadth of time in the fullness of the present and so redefine all of life for us; it is like "a single day" *sub specie aeternitatis*. To grasp the whole while still in the midst of relentless and unforgiving clock time ticking off the

339

segments of life is a gift of God's Spirit. By that Spirit, which grounds the human spirit, such a sense of wholeness is articulated in Jesus Christ who appears in the midst of history to redefine historical time according to the Triune oneness of the God revealed in him.

The theological perspective on human development has not only brought this study to focus uniquely on the life and logic of the human spirit and its search for ultimate ground in the Spirit of God, but, unlike the human sciences, it has also come to focus upon the pervasive negation of life that relentlessly haunts the human spirit and the unfolding of life through time. In birth, the human spirit is cut adrift in a sea of almost infinite creative possibilities, but with no answer to the questions of what is a lifetime and why live it. When it reflects upon itself, the human spirit stares into an abyss of potentiality without meaning; cosmological loneliness pervades every lifetime from the beginning, and increasingly it fills consciousness until in adolescence—or the middle years or old age—the magnitude of meaninglessness becomes stark and often overwhelming.

Long before French existentialism, Quoheleth, the author of Ecclesiastes, saw the power of nothingness and claimed that all of life is vain striving after wind. He was not speaking out of depression, despair, or a distortion of reality; Ecclesiastes is a clear-headed, sane, sober, and non-neurotic declaration of what is. This, I believe, is one of the principal reasons it is in the canon. We begin to die the moment we are born, and we cherish life; but this endearment of life, created and continuously sustained by the human spirit, is shrouded by its inevitable outcome in death from the outset.

In this context the radical, staggering claims of the Creator Spirit of God, mediated through Jesus Christ, take up both the affirmation of life and its inevitable annihilation in his cross and resurrection, the ultimate transformation. In Christ, death is put to death, and the transformation inherent in the human spirit is itself transformed by the Creator Spirit. This does not mean the faithful do not die; it means that death cannot hold them, so they will live again. Death does not have the final word, but, directly contrary to its fundamental intent, it contributes to the declaration of the power of God's Word spoken decisively in the resurrection of Jesus Christ to all those who can hear with the ears of the Spirit.

If through the course of a lifetime one recognizes that the logic of the Spirit cuts across our typical, sequential, and chronological account of things and draws on powerful resources hidden both in creation and Creator to construct and reconstruct a lifetime, the ultimate resolution that negates death itself is no great surprise. Death shocks, depresses, or seemingly presents a definitive finality only for a locked-in, chronological mind-set that has suppressed the continuous presence of the end of things under stage sequences, growth cycles, and adaptation to everything except its own termination. Those who have seen spiritual transformation in its wondrous and joyful intention to transcend linear expectations and repeatedly reconfigure life's set patterns, yet without loss of continuity in selfhood, have little difficulty in recognizing and accepting the analogy between this and the rebirth of life after death according to God's promise of resurrection and redemption for all creation beyond time and history.

Because transformation in the midst of time illuminates the transformation of all time and history, transformed persons are freed from the chronic underlying dread of proximate or ultimate negation. The haunting presence of non-being is dissipated; it no longer clouds perception, so each particular event, person, thing, and circumstance is filled with the eternal Presence of God (Knight of Faith). For faith, the mediator of the transformation is himself a finite person who is at the same time fully God without in any way being diminished thereby in his full humanity. Indeed, because he is fully God, the fullness of his humanity comes into perfect focus. By beholding him in faith, we can see the immense love that combines in a profound differentiated unity creature and creator, human and divine, time and eternity, and thereby annihilates from the outset anything that would seek to drive a wedge of nothingness or nonbeing between God and God's created order. Yet this unity in Christ only serves to heighten the uniqueness and the integrity of the polarities involved, as is always the way with love. As stated earlier, it takes a universe and more to create a person, but the sheer fact that creation has culminated in God-conscious persons makes of the universe not an impersonal cosmological entity but a stunning account of how much God loves us.

In actuality, human development is never experienced as a cycle or a sequence; it often feels more like a few decades of searching, finding, and losing an uncertain fulfillment. But in each person the search is a longing for the eternal intimacy of a love that may be grasped only unclearly and proleptically, but nevertheless profoundly, in the face of a beloved caretaker. At three months of age, before the sense of abandonment begins to dawn upon consciousness, the prototype of the face, the configuration of a gracious presence, is set down. Even in the absence of the face, the longing appears and persists. This anticipation cannot be fulfilled in human terms; indeed, every human effort to solve the dilemma posed by the abyss underlying development only intensifies the difficulty. When the longing for that intimacy is satisfied by the Spiritual Presence of Christ, the Face of God, then the answers to our basic questions may dawn on us. A lifetime is an unfinished act of God's love; it is intended that we complete that act by returning ourselves to God, directly and through others, in love. In this recognition, we discover that the fundamental data about us are not merely that we are alive and developing, incredible products of a vast expanding universe. Rather, as each life unfolds, gets torn open, stripped of its survival techniques and its passing pleasures, and discovers itself as spirit, then it appears from under the surface that we have been created for nothing less than the pure love of God, whose universe is our home.

INDEX

A

Abraham and Sarah, 235

Absorption, fear of, 265–266

Absurdity, 334

Accommodation and assimilation, 96–100, 101, 140, 154

Achievement: inferiority and, 181–183; and worth, 174–175, 181–183, 223–225

Achievement-oriented addiction, 141, 174–175, 181–183, 223–224; isolation and, 262; in Luther case study, 240; physical illness and, 283

Achievement-oriented society: motivation in work and, 177; United States as, 141

Active imagination technique, 303–304

Acts: 1:15, 111; 2, 111, 112; 2:17, 316

Adam: Jesus as the second, 271–272; sin of, 275–276, 279n.17

Adler, A. P., 249n.6

Adolescence: adult guarantor for, 227–228; affiliative stage in, 206; authority axis of identity in, 215–219; bodily axis of identity in, 208–213; calling of God in, 225–227; chronological phases of, 205–206; cognitive development of, 213–214; conversion in, 231–233; of girls versus boys, 220–222; *homo religiousus* approach to, 231–233, 246; iden-

tity formation in, 206–225; ideological axis of identity in, 213–215; love axis of identity in, 219–223; overview of, 203–205, 205–207; psychological perspective on, 203–229; psychopathologies of, 204–205; role confusion in, 206, 207; sexual identity formation of, 219–223; space and time concepts in, 208–213; theological perspective on, 228–229, 231–249; work axis of identity in, 223–225

Adult guarantor, 227–228, 243

Adulthood. *See* Later years; Middle years; Young adulthood

Affiliative stage, 206

Agapic love, 269–270

Aggression: negative, 139–140; positive, 139, 140, 147; in toddler period, 138–140

Aging, 317–326; factors of, that bring on despair, 321–322; positive models of, 324; Pruyser's image of, 318–319; social values and, 319. *See also* Later years

Alien righteousness, 116–117, 168

Allport, G., 82–83, 331

American Journal of Psychiatry, 223

Amnesia, of early childhood, 175–176

Anal expressive character, 140–141

Anal period, 133–138; character disorders of, 140–142

Anal retentive character, 141

Analogia spiritus, 35–36, 39, 109, 110–111, 112–118, 120; aggression in, 139

Analytic tradition, 20

Anderson, P., 247, 333

Anima and animus, 303

Animism, 156, 157

Annihilation, fear of, 266–267

Anthropic principle, 294

Anthropology, theological. *See* Theological anthropology

Anthropology in Theological Perspective (Pannenberg), 26, 27, 30, 254

Anxiety: as interpersonal organizer in infancy, 91–92; qualitative and quantitative, 123–124

Apostle and genius, 110

Appropriation, 88, 89

Aquinas, T., 169

Archetypes: of birth process, 83; evolution of, 294, 315*n*.12; in Jungian theory, 26, 78*n*.9, 293–295, 301–302, 304; overactive, 301–302

Archetypes: A Natural History of the Self (Stevens), 294, 315*n*.12

Archimedes, 248

Ardrey, R., 209

Artificialism, 156–157

Asclepias, 297

Aspect, A., 8

Assimilation and accommodation, 96–100, 101, 140, 154

Atonement, 268–269, 271, 276

Attachment, 86–87

Augustine, Saint, 34, 58, 67, 169, 210, 309

Australian aborigines, 296–297

Authoritarian personality, 216

Authoritarianism, 144, 280*n*.19

Authority axis of identity, 215–219; in Luther case study, 239–240

Autonomy: development of, in toddler period, 131–133, 145–147; illusion of, 130; longing for, 130; versus shame, 131, 135–138, 145–147; theological significance of, 145–147

Avocation, 324–325

Awakening stage of spiritual development, in counseling case study, 48–50, 65–66

B

Baken, D., 21, 85

Baptism, 42

Barnhouse, D., 218

Barth, K., 27, 29–30, 31–33, 34, 37, 38, 74

Basil, 195

Beauvoir, S. de, 319

Becker, E., 319

Behaviorism, 19–20

Belenky, M. F., 222

Bell, J., 8

Bellah, R., 39

Berger, P., 39

Bergson, H., 25

Berne, E., 287

Bettelheim, B., 101

Birth of the Living God, The (Rizzuto), 169

Birth process, 81–83, 106*n*.3, 107*n*.25; life-after-death experiences and, 328–329; negation and, 83, 134

Bizarre images, 62–63, 168

Blissful Birth, 82

Bodily axis of identity, 208–213

Body changes, in middle years, 282–283

Body (soma), 55–60

Bohr, N., 129

Boiled frog syndrome, 286–287

Bonding, 86–87

Bonhoeffer, D., 232

Brain structure, 5–6; transformation capability and, 56–60. *See also* Neurological systems

Breath of life, 111–112

Brown, N. O., 137

Brown, R., 151, 216
Browning, D., 37, 289–290, 291, 314n.7
Bultmann, 27
Bush, B., 285

C

Calling of God, in adolescence, 225–227
Calvin, J., 73, 78n.18, 169, 173–174, 197, 211, 267, 268, 276, 281, 309
Camus, A., 3, 278
Cappadocian theology, 195
Carmen Christi (Martin), 271
Centration, 158
Chalcedonian model: and bipolar, relational definition of Jesus Christ, 14, 37, 38, 120; and differentiated unity, 38; dynamic version of, 121; and koinonia, 195; and relationality between eternity and time, 76–77; and theology-human science relationship, 33, 35, 37, 39, 41–42, 306
Chaos, 7–8, 10
Character disorders, developmentally associated with toddler period, 140–142
Child, aging as mirror image of, 318–319
Chodorow, N., 220–221
Chomsky, N., 20
Christie, A., 97
Christological position, 29–30, 31–33; and coincidentia oppositorum, 312–313; on the Eucharist, 40; and interdisciplinary approach to human development, 37, 40–41, 54–55
Christology of the Fourth Gospel, The (Anderson), 247
Christomorphic position, 41, 60, 75–76; and Jesus Christ as Face of

God, 120, 121; and transformation, 247
Churinga, 296–297
Circumincessio, 195, 276
City Kids, 227–228
Claude-Pierre, P., 137
Clerk-Maxwell, J., 27, 32, 293
Clinton, H. R., 285
Cognitive development: during adolescence, 213–214; and ego development, 104; during infancy, 95–104; in later years, 326–327; in middle years, 291–292; during oedipal period, 151–153, 155–158; Piaget's stages of, 98–99; relational context of, 8; during school-age period, 184–191; theories of, 23–26; during toddler period, 131–132; in young adulthood, 255–259. See also Human development
Cognitive development theories, 20
Cognitive dissonance, 331
Coherence, 54, 55–56, 122
Coles, R., 292
Collective monologue, 152
Collective unconscious, 20, 26, 293–294, 295, 301
Coming of Age, The (de Beauvoir), 319
Community, 194–199
Complementarity, 13–14
Concept of Anxiety, The (Kierkegaard), 123, 279n.17
Concrete operations stage, 99, 186–188, 211–212
Concreteness, 156–157
Conflict, 88, 89, 105
Conflict resolution: in narrative, 191; and oedipal period, 167–169
Conformity and nonconformity: in adolescence, 205; in toddler years, 129–130, 147
Conscience, 161, 178, 197; development of, in adolescence, 216

Conservation, in school-age period, 184–185

Consistency, 121–122

Constantine, 169, 281, 309

Contextual relativism, 261–262

Continuity, 54, 74, 77n.2

Conversion: in adolescence, 231–233; examples of, 309, 311; of Kierkegaard, 234–238; of Luther, 238–247; in middle years, 281, 289, 309, 311–313

Conviction of sin, 114–115, 168

Convictional neurosis, 142

I Corinthians: 2:10, 35; 2:10–12, 36; 2:10–16, 3; 3:11, 30; 7:20, 226; 7:29–30, 226; 15, 86; 15:45–49, 271; 15:45ff., 276

II Corinthians: 3:13–18, 120–121; 4:5–6, 120–121; 12, 333; 12:4, 234

Cosmic loneliness: and life-after-death experiences, 330–331; and repression of significance of face, 94, 123, 124, 135; and symbolic construction, 104

Coteau, S., 223–224

Creating Minds (Gardner), 25

Creator Spirit: aggression of, 139; analogy of human spirit to, 35–36, 39, 109, 110–111, 112–118; and relationality, 41; and transformation, 41, 248. See also Spiritus creator

Critical Years, The (Parks), 261–262

Cross, 270–271, 340

Cultic play, 170

Cultures, manifestation of character disorders in, 141

D

Dante, 281

Darwin, C., 164, 315n.12

David and Lisa, 211

Davies, W. D., 210

Death: aggression and repression of, 139–140; denial of, 73, 319–320; fear of, and love, 265–266; and meaning of a lifetime, 4; and negation, 115; and original sin, 122; sexuality and spirituality and, 150, 170–171, 222, 223; transfiguration and, 312. See also Life-after-death experiences

Death instinct, 21, 84–86

Defense mechanisms, 183–184

Deferred imitation, 99, 103–104, 153

Denial: of death and aging, 73, 319–320; defense mechanism of, 184; stagnation and, 288

Depression, 204; in middle years, 283–285

Despair: defined, 321; factors in aging that bring on, 321–322; integrity versus, in later years, 320–326; and original brokenness, 124; and purgation, 67

Destrudo, 21, 84–85

Deutsche, H., 22

Dialectical identity, love of God and, 264–273

Dialectical thinking, 291–292

Differentiated unity, healing and, 38–39, 58

Diffusion: of authority, 217–218; of ideology, 214, 215; of sexual identity, 219, 221; of work axis, 224–225

Divine Comedy (Dante), 281

Divine Presence: and conversion in adolescence, 231–249; and intimacy in young adulthood, 264–266. See also Face of God

Divine Spirit-human spirit relationality: approaches to examining, 17–43; interactionist psychological theories and, 20–26; interdisciplinary approach to human development and, 36–43; in pastoral counseling case study, 46–77; theological anthropology and, 26–36. *See also* Relational unity

Does God Exist? An Answer for Today (Kung), 113

Dream, the, in young adulthood, 259–264, 262

Dreams: in Jungian theory, 296, 298, 299–300, 302; in later years, 316–317

Drive theory, Freudian, 21–22

Dynamics of Aggression, The (Megargee and Hokanson), 209

E

Eating disorders: and diffusion of sexuality, 221; feeling of "badness" and, 136–137; sociocultural causes of, 138

Ebeling, G., 257, 267

Eccles, J., 6, 8

Ecclesiastes, 340

Eckhart, M., 58, 312

Ego: defeat of, in middle years, 288–289; in Freudian theory, 22, 166; and love, 267; transfiguration of, 311–312

Ego chill, 115

Ego development: in adolescence, 203–229; and cognitive development, 104; exocentric centeredness and, 117–118; during infancy, 81–95, 102; intimacy versus isolation stage of, 60–62; negative side of, 73, 81–106; during oedipal period, 159–163; in school-age children, 181–184; versus spiritual development, 72–73; during toddler period, 131–145; transcendence and transformation of, 55, 72, 73–74; transcendence and transformation of, in adolescence, 231–249; in young adulthood, 252–255. *See also* Human development

Ego development theorists, 22–23

Ego redevelopment, therapeutic: interdisciplinary approach to, 72–77; prayer and, 62–64; psychodynamic approach to, in case study, 60–64

Egocentrism, 99–100, 156, 188; move away from, and stages of faith, 255–256; move away from, toward hypothetico-deductive thinking, 213; move away from, toward moral judgment, 190–194

Einstein, A., 7, 25, 32, 76, 129, 190, 293

Einsteinian universe, 32, 190, 293

Einstein's Dreams (Lightman), 41–42

Electromagnetic field, 27

Eliade, M., 298, 307

Emperor's New Mind, The (Penrose), 11, 187

Empty nest syndrome, 284–285

Enantiodromia, 301. *See also* Opposites

Encounters, 253, 254–255

Entropy, 293

Environmentalist theories of human development, 19–20

Ephesians: 2:18, 195; 3:19, 15; 4:4–6, 195

Epigenesis, 23

Equilibrium: in Jungian theory, 301, 308; theological critique of, 312–313

Ergotropic system (ET), 56–58

Erikson, E., 20, 22–23, 26, 31, 60, 86, 87–88, 90, 94–95, 113–114, 115, 117, 131, 132–134, 136, 140, 143–144, 150, 153, 159, 162–163, 166, 171, 173, 176, 178, 192, 206–207, 214, 220, 227, 231–232, 234, 238–247, 253, 255, 260, 261, 262, 273, 281–282, 285, 286,

Erikson, E., *(continued)* 289–290, 292, 295, 304, 307, 308–309, 320, 321

Eriksonian theory, 22–23

Eros, 303

Eucharist, social science versus Christomorphic interpretation of, 39–40

Ex nihilo, 115–116, 118, 168

Existentialism, 27, 29, 37, 135

Exocentricity, 5, 28–29, 33–34, 112–113, 232; and centeredness, 117–118

Ezekiel 37:9, 111

F

Face: absence of mother's, and negation, 91–95, 102, 124; as archetype of wholeness, 304; loss of, and despair in later years, 322; loss of, and guilt, 166; loss of, and shame, 143; as mother's presence, 90–91; as primal prototype of religious experience, 91, 110–111, 115, 124, 175; repression of significance of, 94, 95–96, 134–135

Face of God, 95, 118–122; Jesus Christ as, 118–122, 242; as love, 269; restoration of, 121–122, 242–246, 271–272; yearning for, 110–111, 170, 232. *See also* Divine Presence; God images; Image of God

"Face to Face" BBC interview, 285

Fairchild, R., 306

Faith: basic trust and, 31; Fowler's stages of, 255–259, 267; synoptic view of, 257–258, 267

Family: primary influence of, 179; role expectations in, 180

Fantasy, 62–63, 153–155, 159–160

Fantasy formation, 183

Farley, E., 37

Fermat's last theorem, 188–190, 196

Festinger, L., 331

Field theory, 293

Formal operations stage, 99, 213–214, 259, 291, 326

Fowler, J., 23, 37, 156, 176, 196, 215, 255–259, 261–262, 267, 281–282, 289–290, 291–292, 307, 326–327

Fowler's structural model, 255–259, 289–290, 291–292, 326–327

Freud, A., 20, 22, 23

Freud, S., 20–22, 23, 24, 26, 61, 62–63, 83–86, 93, 149–150, 163–171, 193, 197, 252, 253, 294, 295, 298

Freud and the Jewish Mystical Tradition (Bakan), 21

Freudian theory, 20–22, 83–86; on childhood sexuality, 149–150, 159–160, 163–164; critiques of, 165–167; on origins of religion, 164–165; on promotion depression, 283–284; theological observations on, 167–171

Friday, N., 160–161

"From *Is* to *Ought:* How to Commit the Naturalistic Fallacy and Get Away with It" (Kohlberg), 290

Fromm, E., 84

Fuller Graduate School of Psychology, 289

Fundamental-theological anthropology, 28

Fusion, 253

G

Galatians, 144

Game-Free: The Meaning of Intimacy (Oden), 254

Games people play, 262–263, 287–288

Gamow, G., 98

Gandhi, M., 23

Gardner, H., 25

Gardner, R., 191, 198, 247

Geertz, C., 39

Generation X, 217–218

Generativity versus stagnation: generativity axis of, 288–291; in middle years, 282, 285–291; stagnation axis of, 286–288

Genesis, 111–112, 123; 2:15, 173; 18:1, 235

Genius: and apostle, 110; nonconformity and, 129, 130

Geometry, 32

German Reformation, 242, 245

Gilligan, C., 20, 23, 186, 192–194, 255, 261–262

Girls versus boys: identity formation of, 206; moral development of, 192–194; play of, 186; sexual identity formation of, 220–222

Giroux, H., 225

Gisin, N., 8

Glutted nest syndrome, 285

Göbel, K., 11, 12

"God hypothesis," movement away from, 27

God images: development of, in oedipal period, 154, 169. See also Face of God; Image of God

God the Creator, and logic of the spirit, 9–10. See also Creator Spirit

Goffman, E., 254

Goldman, R., 176

Good-enough mothering, 87

Gospel and the Land, The (Davies), 210

Grace, 34–35, 267

Graduate, The, 288

Grandparents, influence of, 320–321, 325

Gray Panthers, 324

Great Divorce, The (Lewis), 149

Great Mother archetype, 294, 301

Greek mythology, 296–297

Greenacre, P., 81, 82

Gregory of Nazianzus, 195

Gregory the Great, 329, 330

Grey, L., 227–228

Groome, T., 37

Guilt: development of, in oedipal period, 159–160, 162–163; initiative versus, 162–163; versus shame, 143, 148n.17, 162–163

Guiness Book of World Records, 186–187

H

Hall, G. S., 19, 209

Halpern, M., 248

Hampden-Turner, C., 273

Harris, T., 287

Hartmann, H., 22

Hawking, S., 11, 12

Hebrews, Book of, 143

Hegel, G.W.F., 211, 292

"Helen" case study, 46–77, 118; analysis of, from neurological view, 55–60; analysis of, from psychological view, 60–64; analysis of, from spiritual view, 64–72; awakening stage in, 48–50, 65–66; course of counseling in, 46–54; illumination stage in, 52–53, 67–68; purgation stage in, 50–52, 66–67; reflection on, 54–72; unification stage in, 53–54, 68–70

Hendricks, I., 177

Hendry, G., 27, 34–35, 111, 112

Hess, C. L., 138

Hidden Dimension, The (Hall), 209

Hildegaard von Bingen, 58, 309

Hippasus, 188

History, sense of, in school-age children, 190–191

Hitler, A., 214, 300

Hofstadter, D., 11

Hokanson, J. E., 209

Holophrastic speech, 102–103

Holy Spirit: analogy between human spirit and, 35–36, 39, 109, 110–111, 112–118; presence of, in pastoral counseling, 47, 49–50

Holy Spirit in Christian Theology (Hendry), 34, 111

Homo religiosus, 231–233, 246

Homosexuality, 222–223

Horner, T., 320–321

Höwe, G., 70

Human development: in adolescence, psychological perspective on, 203–229; in adolescence, theological perspective on, 228–229, 231–249; alternative, non-interactionist approaches to, 19–20; archetypal approach to, 26; awakening stage of, 48–50, 65–66; birth experience and, 81–83; cognitive/structuralist theories of, 20, 23–26; ego and spiritual axes of, 72–73; hypotheses about, 72–77; illumination stage of, 52–53, 67–68; in infancy period, 81–106, 109–124; interactionist approaches to, 18, 20–26; interdisciplinary approach to, 36–43; interdisciplinary approach to, in case study, 46–77; language development and, 18; in later years, 316–336; in middle adulthood, 281–313; mirror relationship of, to universe, 6–10, 24, 56, 188–190, 203; negative side of, in infancy, 73, 91–95, 103, 104, 105–106, 109–126; oedipal period and, 149–171; open-endedness of, 83, 86; phases of, 87, 105; psychoanalytic theories of, 20–23; psychological approaches to, 18–26; purgation stage of, 50–52, 66–67; reconceptualization of, 74–77; at school-age period, 173–199; spiritual, 64–72; as stages versus inter-action, 18; theological approach to, 17, 26–36; in toddler period, 129–147; unification stage of, 53–54, 68–70; in young adulthood, 251–278. *See also* Cognitive development; Ego development; Spiritual development

Human freedom, 118; and calling of God, 226; foundation of, 130, 138, 144, 145–147

Human spirit: and adolescence, 203–204; awakening of, 48–50, 65–66; creativity of, 35–36, 63, 258–259; and Divine Spirit relationality, 17–43, 54–55; illumination of, 52–53, 67–68; in infancy period, 81–106; isolation and, 263–264; logic of, 9–10, 340–341; negation of, 81–106, 109–124; neurological systems and, 5–6, 56–60, 73; and oedipal period, 167–171; purgation stage and, 50–52, 66–67; relational unity and, 13–14; religious view of, 10–12; scientific and experiential view of, 5–10; study of, 4; theological anthropology approach to, 26–36; unification and, 53–54, 68–70. *See also* Divine spirit-human spirit relationality; Spirit

Hunsinger, D. van Deusen, 38

Hypothetico-deductive thinking, 213–214

I

Id, 21

Identification, in oedipal period, 160–161, 175–176, 215–216

Identity: adult guarantor and, 227–228; authority axis of, 215–219; bodily axis of, 208–213; and conversion, 231–249; formation of, in adolescence, 206–225;

ideological axis of, 213–215; love axis of, 219–223; and role confusion, 206, 207; space-time dimensions and, 208–213; work axis of, 223–225

Ideological axis of identity, 213–215; Christian ideology and, 215; diffusion of ideology and, 214, 215; rigidity of ideology and, 214–215

Ignatius, St., 309

Illumination, 115, 116–117, 233

Illumination stage of spiritual development, in counseling case study, 52–53, 67–68

I'm OK, You're OK (Harris), 287

Image of God, 109, 118–122. *See also* Face of God; God images

Imagination, 154–155, 260

Imago dei: in anthropological terms, 28; human spirit as, 111–112; and new creation in Christ, 36

Imitation, 153–154

Imprinting, 90, 121

In a Different Voice (Gilligan), 186

In Over Our Heads: The Mental Demands of Modern Life (Kegan), 45n.29

Incest taboo, 161, 162, 165

Incompleteness theory, 11–12

Individuation, 286, 294, 302–304, 308, 324

Industry-inferiority, 173–175, 178–179; role taking and, 180–181

Infancy: age eight to twelve months, 102–103; age four to eight months, 101–102; age one to four months, 101; age twelve to eighteen months, 103–104; anxiety as interpersonal organizer in, 91–92; birth process and, 81–83; cognitive development during, 95–104; creative work of, 89–95; creeping period of, 102; first month of, 100–101; Freudian theory and,

83–86; mother's face and, 90–91; mouth as primary organizer in, 89–90; negation in, 91–95, 103, 104; neo-Freudians views on, 86–87; "no" as interpersonal organizer in, 92–95, 103; psychological perspective on, 81–106; semiotic function in, 103–104; theological perspective on, 109–124

Inferiority: and achievement, 181–183; reaction of, in school-age children, 180–183. *See also* Industry-inferiority

"Influence of Grandparents on Young Adults, The" (Horner), 320–321

Initiation, 286

Initiative, versus guilt, 162–163

Insight, 88, 89, 105

Instinct theory, 84–86

Institutional church: convictional neurosis of, 142; koinonia and, 194, 196–197; ministerial syndrome and, 196–197

Integrity, 73; cognitive aspect of, 326–327; defined, 320; versus despair, in later years, 320–326; simplification competence and, 323–325

Intelligence: development of, in infancy, 95–104; development of, in oedipal period, 155–158; development of, in school-age period, 186–188; Piaget's approach to, 23–26, 34n.9, 96–104; and role taking, 179; and theological intelligence, 25. *See also* Cognitive development

Intensification model, 56–60, 65–66

Intentionality, 102

Interactionist developmental approaches, 18, 20–26; archetypal, 26; cognitive/structural, 20, 23–26; combined with theological, 36–40; psychoanalytic, 20–23

Interdisciplinary methodology, 36–43; characteristics of, summarized, 40–42; in "Helen" case study, 46–77; illustrations of, 38–40; position of, 36–38

Interior Castle (Teresa of Avila), 68

Interlude, 88, 89

Intimacy, 60, 64; with Christ, 69–70; and feminine identity formation, 221–222; versus isolation, 252–255, 262–264; koinonia model of, 273–275; meaning of, 254–255; presence of God in, 264–266; and relationality, 207; versus sexuality, 222, 253–255; as shared dream, 260; spiritual presence of Christ in, 273–278; theological approach to, 264–273; in young adulthood, 252–278. *See also* Love

Intimacy versus isolation, 60–62, 64, 252–255

Intimate language, 152

Introjection, 184

Intuition, in oedipal period, 158. *See also* Preoperational or intuitive stage

Invisible playmates, 154–155

Iranaeus, 271, 275

Irreversibility, 157–158

Isaiah 57:15, 34

Ishmael, 235

Isolation, 60–61; built on repression, 183; intimacy versus, in young adulthood, 252–255, 262–264; parental patterns and, 262–263

I-thou, 290–291

J

Jacob and Esau, 302

Jacobi, J., 91, 304

Jahoda, M., 20

Janov, A., 81, 83, 181

Jaynes, J., 5, 83

Jesus Christ: Chalcedonian definition of, 14; as Face of God, 118–122, 242; intimacy with, 69–70; presence of, in counseling case study, 50–52, 54–55; relationality of, 38; as the second Adam, 271–272; as Self archetype, 307; and Spirit-to-spirit relation, 10, 12, 17, 36, 42–43, 54–55, 118, 333–334; spiritual presence of, 273–278; wisdom incarnate in, 325–326

John: 1:1–14, 34; 4, 195; 4:1, 74; 4:24, 111; 6:16–21, 333; 16, 49, 54; 17, 195; 20:22–23, 111–112

John of the Cross, St., 312

Johnson, R., 240

Joy, in conversion, 236–237

Judas, 277

Jung, C. G., 20, 26, 78n.9, 83, 91, 281–282, 286, 291, 292–313, 319, 320, 324, 330; personal history of, 296–300; theological perspective on, 306–309, 312–313; theory of, 301–306

Jungian model of the psyche, 295, 297–298

K

Kairos, 212, 233

Kant, I., 192

Kegan, R., 23, 45n.29, 134, 206, 207

Keller, H., 28–29, 33–34, 104, 117

Kellogg, R., 304

Kelsey, M., 306

Kermode, F., 89

Kierkegaard, S., 11, 12, 27, 38, 110, 123–124, 125n.2, 245, 249n.6, 251–252, 266–267, 276, 279n.17, 312, 334–336; conversion of, 234–238, 243

I Kings: 17:21, 111

Knight of faith, 334–336

Kohlberg, L., 20, 23, 191–194, 255, 273, 289–290, 291
Kohut, H., 161–162
Koinonia, 194–199; practice of love in, 270, 272, 273–275
Kris, E., 22
Krych, M., 198–199, 247
Kuhn, M., 324
Kung, H., 113, 215
Kyte, B., 228

L

Langer, S., 89
Language development, 18; in infancy, 95–104; in oedipal period, 151–153; in school-age period, 187; in toddlerhood, 131–132
Later years, 316–336; cognitive potential in, 326–327; dreams in, 316–317; dynamics of aging and, 317–326; integrity versus despair in, 320–326; life expectancies and, 317–318; life-after-death experiences and, 328–333; psychosocial perspective on, 318–322; senescence of, 318; senility and, 318; wisdom in, 325–326. See also Aging
Law and order, 144
Leadership-followership roles, 218–219
Learning theory, 137, 177
Leboyer, F., 82, 106n.3
Lehmann, P., 194, 197
Levinson, D., 259, 260, 262, 281, 286, 314n.2
Levi-Strauss, C., 248
Lewis, C. S., 149, 309, 311
Lewis, S., 325
Libido, 21, 84, 301
Lidz, T., 323
Life Against Death (Brown), 137
Life at Death (Ring), 328–329

Life instinct, 21
Life Maps (Fowler), 255
Life of the Self, The (Lifton), 214
Life-after-death experiences, 328–333; legitimacy of, 329–330; theological reflection on, 333–336
Life/lifetime questions: absurdity in, 334; in case study, 49, 63–64; love as answer to, 277–278, 341–342
Lifton, R. J., 214, 217–218
Lightman, A., 41–42
Limbic system, 58
Liminality, 180
Lindbeck, G., 36
Little Hans, 62–63, 163–164, 167, 168, 183
Longevity, 317–318, 336n.1
Lorenz, K., 90
Losses of aging, 322
Love: as answer to life/lifetime questions, 277–278, 341–342; cross and resurrection as model of, 270–271; developmental history of, from theological perspective, 268–271; of God, 251–252, 267–273, 277–278; of grandparents, 321; nature of, 267–268; non-possessiveness of, 266–267; practice of, 271–273, 274; sacrificial, 269–270, 308, 327; threats to, 265–266. See also Intimacy
Love axis of identity, 219–223, 288
Lowrie, W., 234, 238
Loyola, 281
Luckmann, T., 39
"Lucy" case study, 85–86, 118–119
Luder, H., 239–240
Luhmann, N., 39
Luke 2:8–14, 112
Lund, H., 238
Lund, T., 238
Luther, M., 23, 114–115, 117, 166, 168, 169, 227, 234, 304, 308–309; life and conversion of, 238–247

M

Macbeth, 14–15, 142
Maccoby, M., 224
Magical Child, The (Pearce), 87
Mahler, M., 86
Male-female balance, 303, 312
Mandala, 91, 295, 298–300,
    303–304, 309, 310, 313
Manic-depression, 204
Man's Place in Nature (Scheler), 5
Mao, 214
Maps of the Mind (Hampden-Turner),
    273
Mark: 2:5, 38; 6:45–52, 333;
    9:17–24, 241
Marriage, 272–273; renegotiation of,
    in middle years, 285–286
Martin, R., 271
Martyr, J., 91, 304
Marx, K., 185
Maternal grandparents, 321
Mathematics, 11–12; and concrete
    operations stage, 187, 188–190
Mazeways, 331
Mead, M., 165
Mediation, 308
Megalomania, 204
Megargee, E. I., 209
Memories of Home (Lund), 238
Men: individuation of, 303; life
    expectancy of, 317–318; middle-
    aged, physical changes in, 282
Menninger, K., 325
Menopause and climactic, 282,
    285–286
Merton, T., 327
Middle years of adulthood, 281–313;
    cognition in, 291–292; conversion
    in, 281, 289, 309, 311–313; emer-
    gence of opposites in, 292; games
    played in, 287–288; generativity in,
    288–291; generativity versus stag-

nation in, 282, 285–291; Jungian
    approach to, 292–313; overview
    of, 281–292; psychophysical evi-
    dence of, 282–283; renegotiating
    relationships in, 285–286; seg-
    ments of, 281, 314*n*.2; stagnation
    in, 286–288; themes of, 282; typi-
    cal syndromes of, 283–285
Milbank, J., 39–40
Milgram, S., 273, 280*n*.19
Ministerial syndrome, 196–197
Miracle, 70–72
Miranda, E. K., 156, 190–191
Miranda, P., 190–191
Möbius band, 13–14
Moral development: Gilligan's theory
    of, 192–194; of girls versus boys,
    192–194; Kohlberg's theory of,
    191–192; in oedipal period, 155; of
    school-age children, 191–194, 197;
    in young adulthood, 261–262
Moral judgment, development of,
    191–194, 197, 261–262
Mortification, 114–116, 166, 168
Mother complex, 302
Mother Teresa, 214
Mother-child bond, 86–87
Mother-father relationality, 161–162
Motivation in work, 177–178
Mouth, 89–90
MTV, 218
Multiculturalism, 210
My Mother, Myself (Friday), 160–161
Mystery of the Mind (Penfield), 325
Mythical and literal differentiation,
    176

N

Narcissism: primary, 86–87; sec-
    ondary, 161–162, 219
Narrative: oedipal-age children and,
    156; school-age children and,

190–191, 198–199; therapeutic power of, 191; transformational, 198–199, 247

"Natural Theology of Karl Barth, The" (Torrance), 32

Naturalistic fallacy, 288–289

Negation, 81–106, 109–124; in birth experience, 83, 134; and death instinct, 84–85; and despair in later years, 322–323; and eternity, 340–342; in homosexuality, 222–223; inclusion of, in interdisciplinary approach, 73; in infancy, psychological view of, 91–95, 103, 104, 105–106; in infancy, theological view of, 109–124; manifestations of, 105; in middle years, 288–289, 291–292; suppression of, in theoretical approaches, 31, 83; in toddler period, 133–138, 139–142; in toddler period, constructive alternatives to, 142–144, 145–147

Neo-Freudians, 22, 84, 86–87

Neurological systems: at ages three to five years, 150–151; and life-after-death experiences, 332; at toddler period, 131; transformation capability and, 56–60, 73

Neurosis: and Freud's views on religion, 164–171; origins of, in school-age children, 181

New York Times, 223–224

Newton, I., 71

Newtonian world, 32, 188, 190, 293

Nicholas of Cusa, 313

Nicoli, A., 183

Niels, Bohr, 13–14

Nightmares, 154, 155

"No": of infants and toddlers to environment, 92–95, 103; parental/environmental, 91–92, 102; of toddlers, 139–140. *See also* Negation

Nonconformity. *See* Conformity and nonconformity

Norwood, R., 57, 221

Nursing child paradigm, 291

O

Object constancy, establishment of, in school-age period, 185–186

Objectivity, of school-age children, 185–186

Object-relations theorists, 22

Object(s): and concrete operations stage, 186–188; conservation of, 184–185; construction of, 101; imagination and, 155; permanence of, 101–102; and reversibility, 158; transitional, 133–134, 154–155

Obsessive compulsive behavior, 142, 165, 204

Oden, T., 254, 287

Oedipal period, 149–171; from adult viewpoint, 290; bodily development during, 150–151; cognitive and language development during, 151–153, 155–158; development of intelligence during, 155–158; guilt and shame during, 162–163; imagination during, 154–155; moral development during, 155; oedipal/Electra conflict and, 159–161; play during, 153–154; psychosexual development and, 159–171; self object relationships of, 161–162; theological observations of, 167–171; thinking and reasoning during, 158

Oedipal/Electra conflict, 159–161, 163–164; and origins of religion, 164–171; resolution of, 175–176; theological observations on, 167–171

Oedipus Rex (Sophocles), 149

"On Negation" (Freud), 93
One Triune God schemata, 74–76, 105
Opposites: emergence of, in middle
    years, 292; law of, in Jungian the-
    ory, 301, 312–313; theological
    view of, 312–313
Oral personality, 84
Oral stage, 84
Original sin, 109, 122–124. *See also*
    Sin
Other World Journeys (Zaleski),
    329–331
Overcompensation, 288

P

Pannenberg, W., 5, 6, 23, 27–31,
    33–34, 35, 112, 113, 117–118,
    122–124, 170, 215, 254
Paradigmatic figures, 23
Paradoxical-consolidative stage,
    291–292
Parallel play, 131–132
Paranoia, clinical, 141–142
Parks, S., 261–262
Parsons, T., 39, 204
Pascal, B., 169, 281, 309
Passion, 57–58, 67
Pastoral counseling: and differentiated
    unity, 38–39, 58; in "Helen" case
    study, 46–77
Paul, St., 144, 145, 169, 177–178,
    226–227, 235, 308, 333
Pearce, J., 87
Penfield, W., 5–6, 325
Penrose, R., 11, 187
Pentecost, 111–112, 118, 194
Perichoretic relationality, 195, 276
Person, The (Lidz), 323
II Peter 3:8, 339
Phenomenological method, 37
Philippians: 2:5–11, 271; 2:12–13, 36;
    2:16, 116; 3:16, 68
Philosophy of being, 37

Philosophy of culture, 37
Physics, Newtonian versus Einsteinian,
    32
Piaget, J., 8, 20, 23–26, 43*n*.43, 76,
    96–104, 117, 131–132, 140,
    153–154, 155–158, 177, 186–188,
    190, 191, 208, 255, 259, 290, 291
Piagetian theory, 23–26, 96–104,
    155–158, 184–185; theological
    underpinnings of, 24–26
Pipher, M., 221
Pippard, A. B., 11, 71
Plato, 192, 320
Play: of boys versus girls, 186; and
    cultic play, 170; in oedipal period,
    153–154, 171; in school-age
    period, 185–186; "the dream" of
    young adulthood and, 260; in tod-
    dler period, 131–132, 140
Polanyi, M., 77*n*.4, 113
Popper, K., 6
Postmodern lifestyle, 214, 215,
    217–218
Postmodernism, 45*n*.29, 332
Powers of Ten, 6–7
Prayer: in counseling case study, 47,
    50–51, 59, 62; psychodynamic
    approach and, 62–64
Predestination, 174
Predeterminism, 19
Preformationism, 19
Prenter, R., 114–115, 244–245
Preoperational or intuitive intelligence
    stage, 98–99, 155–158
Prigogine, I., 8, 107*n*.16, 248, 293,
    315*n*.12
Primal Scream, The (Janov), 181
Primal symbols, 296–297
Primary narcissism, 86–87
Principia Mathematica (Whitehead),
    11
Privatization of religion, 27–28
Procrastination, 181, 211
Project of 1895, The (Freud), 21

Projection, 184
Promised land, 210
Promotion depression, 283–284
Proof, The, 190
Prophets: model of intensification and, 56; nonconformity and, 129, 130
Protean behavior, 214, 215, 217–218
Protean personality, 217–218
Protean Self, The (Lifton), 214
Protestant Ethic and the Spirit of Capitalism, The (Weber), 173
Protestant Reformation, 173–174
Protestant work ethic, 225
Proteus, 214
Proving out, 88, 89, 105
Pruyser, P., 307, 318–319, 321, 324
Psyche, dynamics of, 21–22
Psychoanalytic approaches: in counseling case study, 60–64; to infancy, 83–95, 102; to Luther's conversion, 238–247; prayer and, 62–64; to psychosexual development, 159–171; theories of, 20–23; to toddlerhood, 135–136; to work, 177
Psychogenesis and the History of Science (Piaget), 26
Psychohistorical dislocation, 217–218
Psychological approaches to human development, 18–26; at adolescence, 203–229; alternative, noninteractionist, 19–20; applied to "Helen" case study, 60–64; combined with theological, 36–43; in infancy, 81–106; interactionist, 20–26; in later years, 317–326; limitations of, 26–27; at oedipal period, 153–163; at school-age period, 181–191; in toddler period, 131–145; in young adulthood, 251–264
Psychophysical unity, 55–60
Purgation stage of spiritual development, in counseling case study, 50–52, 66–67

Purposiveness, 162
Pythagoras, 188
Pythagorean theorem, 188–189

Q

Qualitative anxiety, 123–124
Quantum theory, 8, 13–14, 98
Quoheleth, 340

R

Radical Man (Hampden-Turner), 273
Rapaport, D., 22
Rational versus irrational numbers, 188
Rationality, 8
Reaction formation, 92, 184; of achievement, 181–182, 223
Reality principle, 21–22
Recapitulation theory, 271–272, 275–276
Reductionism, theological anthropology versus, 29–30
Reflexes, 100–101
Reformed tradition, 34
Regression, 183; and suicide, 85
Relational unity: *analogia spiritus* and, 110–111, 112–118; bipolar, above and below, 13–14, 33, 36, 39, 45*n*.29; Face of God and, 118–122; human spirit as *imago dei* and, 111–112; and interdisciplinary approach to human development, 36–38, 41, 54–55, 60; and koinonia, 194–199; neurological foundation of, 55–60, 73; psychological analysis of, in case study, 60–64. *See also* Divine Spirit-human spirit relationality
Relationality, 8–9, 16*n*.7; of girls versus boys, 181, 192–194, 221–223; between human spirit and Divine Spirit, 17–43; interactionist

Relationality, *(continued)*
psychological approaches and, 18,
20–26; and intimacy, 207; in marriage, 272–273; of opposites,
312–313; of school-age children,
185–186; in time, 41–42, 76–77
Release of energy, 88, 89, 105
Religion: critiques of Freud's view on,
165–167; Freud's view on, 149,
164–165; theological observations
on Freud's view of, 167–171
Repentance, 115–116
Repetition, 101
Repression: as intrapsychic functional
translation of "no," 93–94; and
role structures, 180; and school-age
children, 175, 183; of significance
of face, 95–96, 134–135
Resolution, 88
Resurrection, 340; as model of love,
270–271; Pannenberg's view of, 29
Revelation, 233, 307
Reversibility, 157–158
"Revitalization Moments" (Wallace),
248
Richard of St. Victor's, 313
Ricoeur, P., 145
Rigidity: of authoritarian personality,
216; of ideology, 214–215; of sex-
ual identity, 219; of work axis,
223–224
Ring, K., 328–329
Ritual practices, 296–297
Rizutto, A.-M., 154, 169
Role confusion, identity versus, 206,
207
Role structures: in school-age period,
179–181, 185; theological perspec-
tives on, 194–197
Rolling Stone, 204–205
Romans: 5:12, 271; 8:3, 271; 8:16,
34, 36; 5:1ff., 117
Russell, B., 11

S

Sabatier, A., 25
Same-sex peer groups, 206
Sanford, J., 302, 306
Sartre, J.-P., 124, 135, 143, 215, 218
Scanning, 88, 89, 105
Scheler, M., 5, 6
School-age childhood period: age of,
175; cognitive development of,
184–191; defense mechanisms of,
183–184; development of intelligence during, 186–188; epigenetic
task of, 176; girls versus boys in,
186, 192–194; inferiority and
achievement in, 181–183; inferiority and role taking in, 180–181;
moral judgment of, 191–194, 197;
motivation in work and, 177–178;
mythical and empirical worlds of,
176; narrative in, 190–191,
198–199; repression and, 175; role
structures/taking in, 179–181,
194–197; theological perspectives
on, 194–199; working in a social
context and, 178–179; work-worth
relationship and, 173–175
Scientific view: of human spirit, 5–10,
11–12; of miracles, 70–71; and theological anthropology, 26–36
Secret of the Golden Flower, 298
Segmentation of religion, 27–28
Self archetype, 293, 299–300, 304,
307, 308–309
Self-expression, in toddler period,
132–133
Self-objectification, in school-age
period, 185–186
Self objects, 161–162
Self-relatedness: in brain structure,
5–6; of human spirit, 14
Self-symbol mandala structure,
303–304

Self-theorists, 22

Self-transcendence: ego development and, 55; human spirit and, 12, 14; mathematics and, 11–12; neurology and, 5–6, 56–60, 73; and search for Face, 95–96; and transformation, 33–34

Semiotic function, 99, 153.103–104, 155

Senescence, 318

Senility, 318

Sensorimotor activity, 96

Sensorimotor intelligence stage, 98, 100–104

Sex roles, 170–171, 219–220

Sexual development: oedipal/Electra conflict and, 159–161; physical, 151; psychoanalytic view of, 159–171; sociocultural, 170–171; theological view of, 167–171

Sexual identity, 219–223; Jungian approach to, 303

Sexuality: and adolescent identity formation, 219–223; death and spirituality and, 150, 170–171, 220; Freud's view on, 163–164; and intimacy, 253–255; and oedipal stage, 149–150, 159–171; renegotiation of, in middle years, 285–286; and work, 252; in young adulthood, 252–255

Shakespeare, W., 14–15

Shame: autonomy versus, 131, 135–138, 143, 145–147; development of, in oedipal period, 162–163; development of, in toddler period, 137–138; guilt versus, 143, 148n.17, 162–163

Simon, 24

Simplification, 323–325

Sin: of Adam, 275–276, 279n.17; conviction of, and mortification, 114–116; origin of, 122–124; Pannenberg's view of, 29, 122–123. See also Original sin

Skinner, B. F., 19–20, 137, 177, 325

Social action theory, 39–40

Social approval, work and, 178–179

Social control: religious legalism and, 165–166; versus survival, in toilet training, 135–137

Socialization: in adolescence, 204, 231; and conversion, 231; of girls versus boys, 192–194; role structures/taking and, 179–181; work and, 178–179

Sophocles, 149

Space: adolescent identity and, 208–210; theological perspective on, 210, 333–334

Space bubble, 209

Sperry, R., 6

Spirit, logic of, 9–10. See also Divine Spirit-human spirit relationality; Human spirit

Spirit of God: human spirit and, 10–16; relational unity and, 13–14. See also Divine Spirit-human spirit relationality; Relational unity

Spiritual development: in counseling case study, 64–72; versus ego development, 72–73; hypotheses about, 72–77; stages of, 65–70. See also Human development

Spiritual drive, 170–171

Spiritus Creator, 17, 35–36; and conversion, 244–245, 246–247; in interdisciplinary method, 41. See also Creator Spirit

Spiritus Creator (Prenter), 244

Spitz, R., 83, 89–90, 92, 93, 107n.25

Stages of Faith (Fowler), 255, 258

Stagnation, in middle years, 286–288. See also Generativity versus stagnation

Stanard, R., 8

Staupitz, 227, 243
Stevens, A., 294, 315*n*.12
Story, C., 111
Structural Anthropology (Levi-
    Strauss), 248
Structuralist theories, 20, 23–26,
    191–192, 255–259. *See also* Cogni-
    tive development
Subjectivism, theological anthropology
    versus, 29–30
Sublimation, 183–184
Suicide, 85–86, 204, 224
Sullivan, H. S., 219
Superego, 161, 166, 178, 215–216
Swastika, 300
Swiss culture, 141
Synchronicity, 305–306
Synpractic speech, 152
Synthetic thinking, 326–327
Systematic Theology (Pannenberg), 30

                        T

Teleological concern, 290
Telesphoros, 297
Tennent, W., 328, 333
Teresa of Avila, 58, 68, 309, 312
Termination, 286
Territorial Imperative, The (Ardrey),
    209
Tertium quid, 37
Theological anthropology: applied to
    "Helen" case study, 54–55, 64–72;
    applied to infancy period,
    109–124; Barth's approach to,
    29–30, 31–33; defined, 27;
    Hendry's approach to, 34–35; and
    interdisciplinary approach to
    human development, 36–43; Pan-
    nenberg's approach to, 27–31;
    positions of, 27–36; Torrance's
    approach to, 31–33
Theological approach to human devel-
    opment, 17, 26–36; at adolescence,

228–229, 231–249; combined with
    psychological, 36–43; in infancy
    period, 109–124; to intimacy in
    young adulthood, 264–273; and
    moral judgment, 197; and motiva-
    tion of work, 177–178; in oedipal
    period, 163–171; and role struc-
    tures, 194–197; in school-age
    period, 194–199; in toddler period,
    145–147; and transformational
    narratives, 198–199
Theology and Social Theory (Mil-
    bank), 39–40
*Therapeutic Communication with
    Children* (Gardner), 191
Thomas, G., 107*n*.17
*Three Contributions to a Theory of
    Sex* (Freud), 83
Tibetan religions, 297
Tillich, P., 27, 37, 118, 198
Time: adolescent identity and, 208,
    210–212; cognitive development
    and understanding of, 190; eternal
    and "now," 232–233, 339–340;
    Jungian approach to, 305–306; in
    later years, 322, 325; mood and,
    211; pathologies of, 211; relation-
    ality and, 41–42, 76–77; theologi-
    cal, 211–212, 232–233, 333–334,
    339–341
1 Timothy 6:16, 34
Toddler period, 129–147; aggression
    in, 138–140; character disorders
    associated with, 140–142; con-
    structive alternatives in, 142–144,
    145–147; development of human
    freedom and, 130, 138, 144,
    145–147; developmental perspec-
    tive on, 130–131; negative side of,
    134–138, 139–142; normal resolu-
    tion of, 143–144; positive side of,
    131–132; theological significance
    of, 145–147; transitional dynamics
    of, 132–134

Toilet training, 133–138

Tolstoi, 309

Tomkins, S., 95

Tools, use of, in infancy, 102–103

Torrance, T. F., 7, 9, 10, 15, 26, 27, 30, 31–33, 34, 37–38, 194, 332

Transfiguration of the ego, 311–312

Transformation: in adolescence, 231–249; and autonomy, 145; and concept of "miracle," 70–72; and Creator Spirit-human spirit dynamics, 41, 59–60, 112–118; and ego, 55, 63, 72–74; five-step pattern of, 87–89, 105, 112–113; five-step pattern of, in oedipal period, 167–169; five-step pattern of, in scientific discovery, 189–190; five-step pattern of, in toddlerhood, 133–134; and life after death, 333–336; mediation of, 308; in multiple contexts, 247–249; neurological foundation of, 56–60, 73, 332; and Piagetian theory, 26; and self-transcendence, 33–34, 55; space-time dimensionality and, 212–213; in toddler period, 142–144

"Transformation and the Source of the Fundamentally New" (Halpern), 248

Transformational narratives, 198–199

Transitional objects, 133–134; "chum" or "best friend" as, in adolescence, 206; invisible playmates as, 154–155; "the dream" as, 259–260

Trauma, in infancy, 91–92

Travis, L., 289, 309

Trophotropic (TT) system, 57

Trust, basic: based on spirit-to-Spirit relationship, 215; and faith, 31; as justification for idea of God, 113

Trust-mistrust, 31; development of, in infancy, 87–88, 94–95; environment versus creative capacity for, 113–114

Turner, V., 180, 294

U

Ugandan child rearing, 87

Ulanov, A., 20, 303

Unamuno, M. de, 4

Unconscious, in Freudian theory, 20–22

Unification stage of spiritual development, in counseling case study, 53–54, 68–70

United States culture: achievement-oriented addiction in, 141; negative adolescent symptoms and, 204–205; space in, 210

Unity, neurological foundation of, 58–59, 73. *See also* Relational unity

Universe: parallels of, with human development and intelligence, 6–10, 24, 56, 188–190, 203; vastness of, 15

V

Van Deusen Hunsinger, D., 38

Van Gogh, V., 141

Van Leeuwenhoek, A., 19

Verbal realism, 156, 157

Vidal, F., 24–25

Virtual reality, 218

Visions: healing and, 62–63; intensification model explanation of, 56–60; life-after-death experiences and, 330–333; mandala archetype in, 309, 310

Von Kekule, F. A., 331

Von Weiszächer, C. F., 70

Vygotsky, L. S., 152

W

Wallace, A., 56, 63, 77n.4, 248, 330, 331

Watson, J. B., 19

Weber, M., 173

Wesley, J., 281, 309

Whatever Became of Sin (Menninger), 325

Whitehead, A. N., 11

Wholeness, in Jungian theory, 294, 301, 302–304, 307–308

Why Am I Afraid to Tell You Who I Am?, 254

Wigner, E., 63

Wiles, A., 188–190, 196, 247

Will, development of, in toddler period, 144

Williams, D. D., 267–268

Wink, W., 306

Wisdom 15:11, 111

Wolfe, T., 284

Women: empty nest syndrome and, 284–285; individuation of, 303; life expectancy of, 317; middle-aged, physical changes in, 282

Women Who Love Too Much (Norwood), 221

Women's Ways of Knowing (Belenky), 222

Word and Faith (Ebeling), 257

Work: in later years, 322, 324–325; motivation in, 177–178; and sexuality, 252; in social context, 178–179; theological view of, 177–178, 225–227; worth and, 173–175, 178–179

Work axis of identity, 223–227, 288

Work paralysis, 211, 224–225

Works of Love (Kierkegaard), 248–249, 276

World coherence, 176, 191

Worship, human development toward, 169–170

Worth: achievement and, 174–175, 181–183; work and, 173–175, 178–179, 223–225

Y

Young adulthood, 251–278; cognition in, 255–259; "the dream" in, 259–264, 262; intimacy and sexuality in, 252–255, 260–273; love of God in, 251–252; moral judgment in, 261–262; psychological approach to, 251–264; theological approach to, 264–273

Young Man Luther (Erikson), 115, 117, 234, 238–247

Younnis, J., 216

Z

Zaecheus story, 198–199

Zaleski, C., 329–331

Zimbardo, P., 211